The Legal Language of Scottish Burghs

OXFORD STUDIES IN LANGUAGE AND LAW

This series includes scholarly analyses and descriptions of language evidence in civil and criminal law cases, as well as language issues arising in the area of statutes, statutory interpretation, courtroom discourse, jury instructions, and historical changes in legal language.

The Legal Language of Scottish Burghs: Standardization and Lexical Bundles (1380–1560)
Joanna Kopaczyk

The Legal Language of Scottish Burghs

STANDARDIZATION AND LEXICAL BUNDLES (1380–1560)

Joanna Kopaczyk

OXFORD
UNIVERSITY PRESS

OXFORD
UNIVERSITY PRESS

Oxford University Press is a department of the University of Oxford.
It furthers the Universitys objective of excellence in research, scholarship,
and education by publishing worldwide.

Oxford New York
Auckland Cape Town Dar es Salaam Hong Kong Karachi
Kuala Lumpur Madrid Melbourne Mexico City Nairobi
New Delhi Shanghai Taipei Toronto

With offices in
Argentina Austria Brazil Chile Czech Republic France Greece
Guatemala Hungary Italy Japan Poland Portugal Singapore
South Korea Switzerland Thailand Turkey Ukraine Vietnam

Published in the United States of America by
Oxford University Press
198 Madison Avenue, New York, NY 10016

Library of Congress Cataloging-in-Publication Data
Kopaczyk, Joanna.
The legal language of Scottish burghs : standardization and lexical bundles
(1380–1560) / Joanna Kopaczyk.
pages cm
Includes bibliographical references and index.
ISBN 978-0-19-994515-3 (hardcover : alk. paper) 1. Law–Scotland—
Language–History. 2. Scots language—To 1700. 3. Scotland–Politics and
government–1371—1707. I. Title.
KDC296.K67 2013
340'.14—dc23
2013005304

9 8 7 6 5 4 3 2 1
Printed in the United States of America
on acid-free paper

To Józek and Dana

CONTENTS

PART TWO The Burghs

PART THREE The Legal Language of the Burghs

ACKNOWLEDGEMENTS

First and foremost, I wish to thank the Series Editor, Roger W. Shuy, for his encouragement and trust in this project. The writing process has benefited greatly from the comments on the initial publication proposal and from the feedback offered by anonymous reviewers.

I would like to take this opportunity to thank the Polish Ministry of Science and Higher Education for the individual grant (N N104 014337), as well as the Royal Society of Edinburgh, the Polish Academy of Sciences (PAN), and the Warsaw Scientific Society for their financial support.

I would like to thank Jacek Fisiak for first encouraging me to take up "a Scottish subject" and keeping a watchful eye over my academic progress at Adam Mickiewicz University in Poznań. This study relied on access to electronic repositories of early Scottish legal and administrative texts, most importantly, the *Edinburgh Corpus of Older Scots*. Its author Keith Williamson deserves my warmest thanks for letting me use his files and his time. Historical texts require special care when subjected to corpus tools. I was lucky to have met Dariusz Stróżyński, who wrote the customized software and patiently modified it according to my never-ending corrections. He also adjusted the spelling unification software to the requirements of the Scots language. Here I would also like to thank Alistair Baron, who developed the VARD 2.3 software for standardizing historical spelling and kindly shared it with me.

During the research phase, I was able to immerse myself in many excellent libraries. I would like to thank the helpful staff of Special Collections at the University of Edinburgh, the National Library of Scotland, the Ludwig-Maximilians-Universität library and Bayerische Staatsbibliothek in Munich, the Helsinki University library, and Staatsbibliothek in Berlin. I also chased up many colleagues whose work was yet forthcoming or who happened to have better access to some crucial resources. Here I would especially like to thank Hans Sauer, Claudia Claridge, Keith Williamson, Christiana Gregoriou, Agata Daleszyńska, Stanisław Goźdź-Roszkowski, Steve Murdoch, Christopher Williams, Matylda Włodarczyk, Radosław Dylewski, and Emilia Wróbel.

I wish to thank Barbara Kryk-Kastovsky for her feedback on Part One and Katarzyna Miechowicz-Mathiasen for casting her syntactic eye on Chapter 9. I owe a great debt to Hector L. C. MacQueen, who made me feel at home at the Law Library in Edinburgh, and to Scottish historians: David Worthington for comments on Part Two, and Edda Frankot and John Finlay for indispensable materials.

Words of thanks go to Jacek Głębocki for the maths, Agnieszka Frydrychewicz for the maps, and the OUP team, especially Hallie Stebbins, Emily Sacharin, Cammy Richelli, and Lynn Childress, for working towards a plausible calendar together.

Finally, I wish to thank Marcin Krygier for running the Reading Club at the Department of the History of English at AMU. Thanks to him and my fellow historical linguists, I have learned that even the most impressive piece of research is bound to have shortcomings, and I am acutely aware that any such faults in this book are solely mine.

I have been favoured with the friendship of three amazing academics who have been an unfailing source of stimulation, feedback, and support. I thank Joanna Maciulewicz for her wit, erudition, and common sense. Jane Grogan is an exemplary scholar and a friend who always finds the right words. I owe her a great debt for going through the whole manuscript with a fine stylistic comb and helping me since the moment I started putting the publication proposal together. Christiana Gregoriou always inspires me with her Mediterranean appetite for life and research opportunities.

My closest friends and family know that in terms of support, I appreciate both covert and overt. This is why Olga never stopped disturbing me and provided the laughs and distractions. Michał and Zosia were very good at hovering at a distance, and Nina and Majka monitored my progress with hope and pride. At home, I had constant and unlimited access to the best IT specialist and chocolate-cake baker, Darek, without whom many important things in my life, including this book, would simply not have happened.

This book is dedicated to the memory of my parents, Józef Kopaczyk and Danuta Sierpowska, who, I am sure, would have liked to join me on this academic journey.

J.K.

LIST OF MAPS

LIST OF FIGURES

LIST OF TABLES

ABBREVIATIONS

Adj	adjective
Adv	adverb
BNC	British National Corpus
C	clause
CED	Corpus of English Dialogues
Conj	conjunction
CSD	*Concise Scots Dictionary*
Det	determiner
DP	determiner phrase
DSL	*Dictionary of the Scots Language*
e15	early fifteenth century
ECOS	Edinburgh Corpus of Older Scots
EdHeW	Compilation of the Edinburgh Corpus of Older Scots, the Helsinki Corpus of Older Scots (relevant text types up to 1560), and the Wigtown Burgh Court Book
EFL	English as a foreign language
EModE	Early Modern English
FF	formulaicity factor
HCOS	Helsinki Corpus of Older Scots
intr	intransitive
L	Latin
la15	late fifteenth century
LAOS	Linguistic Atlas of Older Scots
LGSWE	*Longman Grammar of Spoken and Written English*
LSP	language for special purposes
med L	medieval Latin
Mod	modifier
MWU	multi-word unit
N	noun
NP	noun phrase
NUM	numeral
OE	Old English
OED	*Oxford English Dictionary*
OF	Old French
ON	Old Norse
P	preposition
PDE	present-day English
pl	plural

PoS	part of speech
PP	prepositional phrase
ppl	past participle
RCAHMS	Royal Commission on the Ancient and Historical Monuments of Scotland
Sc	Scots
sg	singular
s.v.	from Latin *sub voce*, literally 'under the word'
tr	transitive
V	verb
VARD	Variant Detector
vbl n	verbal noun, gerund
Wgt	Wigtown Burgh Court Book

The Legal Language of Scottish Burghs

1

Introduction: Scots as the Language of the Law

1.1. Language, Law, and History: The Scottish Dimension

People communicate through language and they organize the system of social rights and obligations through law. Both of these tools, linguistic and legal, tend towards standardization—a set of norms which reduces the range of options and variety, and whose aim is to construct a reliable and authoritative point of reference. This is the key juncture for language and law: legal texts constitute linguistic communicative events which have standardized in time into their modern, expected format. Delving into the historical stages of their development brings to life the conditions in which the texts were originally composed. This book shows how the extralinguistic reality, the relationships within the communicative community, as well as the intra-linguistic factors have shaped the discourse of the law.

Consider these two samples of legal texts from medieval Scotland:

Peebles Burgh Court Book, 15 November 1456

> Item y^{t} ilk day was mayd burg*is* joh*n* lyllay zongar & rob cady hys maych
> and of ye burges sylu*er* is at the balzeis wil ilk an of yam x Ss
> pleg*e* john lillay & tho*m* dekyson & ye sayd rob cady
> drauys hys land borch for yam bath scottyng lottyng wak & wardyng &
> for ye borou mall*is* payin

"Likewise, on the same day John Lily the younger and Rob Caddy his son-in-law [or brother-in-law, or even father-in-law] were made burgess. And of the burgess money, [which] is at the baillie's will, each of them [shall pay] ten schillings. Pledge: John Lily & Thom Deckison & the said Rob Caddy puts his land in surety for them both, scotting, lotting, waking and warding, and for paying the burgh maills."

Peebles Burgh Court Book, 26 November 1456

> jt is to rammem*m*er ye fryday ye xx^{ti} day and vj of the monath nowe*m*ber
> ye zer of god mccccl & vj zer yat wil mouat balze in yat tym
> has geyfyng sessyng w^{t} erd and stan to dic gybson of his land liand
> in ye cors gat and on ye north rau bethwen ye land of jamis thomson
> on ye est part on ye ta part & ye land of wil of ye ost on ye west part

> on ye toy*er* part and ya*n* i*n*contenent ye sayd dic gybson and jonot hys wyf an has bath & bath has an has ressyngit w^t erd & stan y^t said land

> "It is to remember that on Friday the twenty day and six of the month November the year of God MCCCCL & VI year that Will Mowat bailie at that time has given saisin with earth and stone to Dick Gibson of his land lying in the Cross Gate and on the North Row between the land of James Thomson on the east part on the one side and the land of Will of the Ost on the west part on the other side and then immediately the said Dick Gibson and Janet his wife one as both & both as one have resigned the said land with earth and stone."

> (Edinburgh, HM Register House, NAS B 58/8/1, $f1^r$–$f7^r$, transcribed by Keith Williamson for the *Linguistic Atlas of Older Scots*)

These are excerpts in Scots from the mid-fifteenth-century proceedings of the local court in Peebles in the Scottish Lowlands; the first records the acceptance of two new men into the ranks of the citizens—the burgesses—and the second gives details of land transfer. The texts clearly fall into the category of legal discourse. Their content and meaning was shaped by the contemporary legal reality in Scottish medieval towns, the burghs, where specific regulations governed how to become a burgess and how to sell and acquire land; hence the various fees, sureties, and witnesses. But what is most striking about these documents is the special nature of the language employed: beginning with specific vocabulary choices, such as *borch* or *scottyng* and *lottyng*, through the employment of characteristic syntactic patterns, to the overall structure of the court book entry. One notices a large degree of coordination (the ampersands and 'ands' in large quantities) and repetition, mostly structural—as in the repeated string of gerunds in the last line of the first text (all of them pertain to the obligation for every burgess to pay taxes and keep a nightly watch), or in the description of the land bearings in the second text. One can expect that other texts produced for the same reason within the same circumstances will share some characteristic features, and perhaps repeat the same lexical and syntactic choices. With several hundreds of similar texts, one can begin to build a picture of textual standardization in the legal discourse of the burghs, and such is the aim of the present investigation.

1.2. The Aims of the Book

The language in the British Isles is not homogeneous, and neither is law. Generally speaking, it is Standard English and the English common law, which have attracted attention as default objects of study, while another unique and independent tradition is to be found in the same island. Scots law has enjoyed continuous independent use on the territory of Scotland since medieval times, and its linguistic fabric stems directly from this separate history. The present book is based on Scottish material because it aims to shift the traditional optics; nevertheless, its methods are applicable to other languages and other contexts, and the findings may serve as a comparative base for similar studies from other legal and linguistic traditions.

The book has three main goals:

- to identify standardizing patterns by means of corpus-driven methods,
- to investigate textual standardization in relation to the structure and function of repetitive chunks of text,
- to explore how the language of the law responded to the external conditions in which it was produced.

To achieve these aims, I use a mixture of methodologies in an interdisciplinary manner. This research is anchored in the discourse approach to language, with a special emphasis on the language of the law. For the interpretation of linguistic data, I employ the functional approach, which links language use to its external conditions. To avoid an ad hoc commentary on a few selected aspects of the extra-linguistic context, this book uses descriptive historical tools to sketch a detailed social and historical background for legal discourse in medieval and early modern Scotland. I examine the importance of early urban centres, the burghs, for Scottish history, economy, and law, and pay attention to the social organization and the centre of legal power in the burghs. These aspects are all reflected in the language used in legal documents. The linguistic data is drawn from the most comprehensive electronic corpora of Scots available today for the earliest historical period. This research makes use of a new tool in historical corpus linguistics, lexical bundles, which promises a unique insight into the matter of textual standardization.

1.3. Interdisciplinary Investigation

1.3.1. LINGUISTIC FRAMEWORK

This work cuts across three disciplines: linguistics, law, and history, with a particular focus on a linguistic inquiry: the study of standardizing linguistic patterns. Part One of the book lays out the theoretical underpinnings of the whole project. The language under investigation comes from a specialized legal environment, which creates the interface with the law (Chapter 2). This legal environment, and the language produced within its context, comes from a specific moment in the past, the years 1380–1560, which creates the interface with history. Thus, the most suitable methodological framework for the investigation is historical pragmatics (the language in use in a historical context) and its subfield, historical discourse analysis.

While discourse is understood as a type of language use in a specific social setting, constructed to achieve specific communicative goals (Chapter 3), historical discourse takes these considerations into the past. This book is situated in historical discourse analysis, as defined by Brinton (2001: 139–140), and grows out of two related approaches within this framework. First of all, it is an example of *historical discourse analysis proper*, as it investigates a selected phenomenon within the scope of discourse analysis synchronically—at a given point in time. The phenomenon under study is the fixed and repetitive nature of text chunks in medieval and Renaissance Scottish legal texts.[1] On the other hand, it presents a *diachronically oriented discourse analysis*, as it observes changes in discourse structure and function in time, building an interdisciplinary bridge between discourse and diachrony.

Concerned with context and its influence on language, this discussion is rooted in a pragmaphilological approach to the language of the past. Here, I follow the original definition of pragmaphilology, as put forward by Jacobs and Jucker: it is a study which "goes one step further [than traditional historical linguistic studies] and describes the contextual aspects of historical texts, including the addressers and addressees, their social and personal relationship, the physical and social setting of text production and text reception, and the goal(s) of the text" (1995: 11). Pragmaphilological considerations are thus a necessary ingredient of historical discourse analysis. In this book, legal texts from medieval and Renaissance Scotland will be perceived through the prism of the communities which made them and used them.

More specifically, the patterns of usage in legal discourse will be interpreted in a functional framework (Halliday 1978; see also Chapter 3). This approach assumes three interrelated functions performed by elements of texts: the *ideational* function, related to the extra-textual conditions, the *interpersonal* function, related to the status of and relationships between discourse participants, and the *textual* function, related to the structural requirements of texts. As indicated above, the linguistic material to be fed into this functional interpretation has been taken from medieval and early Renaissance Scottish legal and administrative texts. In order to perform a comprehensive study of emerging patterns, I used the largest digitized collection of such texts—three combined electronic corpora: the *Edinburgh Corpus of Older Scots* (ECOS, Williamson 2008), the relevant part of the *Helsinki Corpus of Older Scots* (HCOS, Meurman-Solin 1993), and the Wigtown Burgh Court Book. Together, the three sources form the EdHeW collection (for details, see Chapter 8). The requirement of a rigorous and replicable study was met through the use of a corpus tool: an automatic extraction of repetitive chunks of language from the texts. The fact that sheer frequency renders chunks of language which are analysable according to both form and function was noticed by Biber, Conrad, and Cortes (2004: 399). The related method of extraction, known as the *lexical bundles* method (Biber et al. 1999; see also Chapter 4), has only recently started to be employed in historical linguistics (cf. Culpeper and Kytö 2002, 2010), so both its assets and drawbacks are still being discovered. This book is the first large-scale application of this method in the area and thus contributes to the ongoing research.

1.3.2. HISTORICAL FRAMEWORK

The historical sections in Part Two are primarily descriptive. A detailed grounding in social, legal, and, to some extent, political history of the Scottish burghs is an indispensable part of this investigation because it provides a comprehensive and systematic external context for the linguistic findings and interpretations. Britnell called for "a correct interpretation" of urban records and their use of formulaic language through "reconstructing the institutional and semantic contexts in which they were created" (1997: 4). I devote careful attention to the history of Scottish burghs (Chapter 5) as these were the places where medieval and early Renaissance discourse communities developed. These communities established the context for formal texts and were involved in the construction and preservation of the texts. Law as discourse is a historical phenomenon, a Foucauldian system of communication and power relations, embedded in a particular culture (Foucault 1972). The burghs used the records for "[t]he complex process of the textual construction of civic memory and identity, the defense and expression of power and authority, and the recording of adaptation and change" (Butcher 2004: 165). The discussion presents various aspects of living in a burgh (Chapter 6), with special attention paid to its government and economy, which underlie the legal context. The specific nature of Scots law, and its development in the context of early urban centres (Chapter 7), requires a more attentive treatment in view of the largely Anglocentric approaches to language and the law. Even when scholars appreciate the diversity of legal English (Tiersma 1999: 4; Solan and Tiersma 2012), the legal language of Scotland is left out of the discussion (cf. however, the recent analyses of modern Scottish legislation by Williams 2007, 2011).

It is important to include the Scottish legal tradition and its language into a wider perspective on legal heritage of the British Isles and Europe. In a recent three-volume guide to manuscripts of legal literature in Scotland, Professor Gero Dolezalek draws attention to "Scottish lawyers' capability to act as mediators and interpreters between English law and the continental European legal tradition" (2010: 1). The position of Scotland is special: it draws on the continental sources of law but at the same time remains in a constant dialogue with the southern neighbour. In Part Two, this book equips the reader with the necessary historical background of this situation in order to anchor the analysis of the language of the law in its idiosyncratic Scottish context. The reader thus gains a unique and profound insight into the specific nature of the earliest legal texts written in Scotland in the vernacular—into the recurrent topics and standardizing textual patterns, which become the focus of analysis in Part Three.

1.4. Scots: A Standardizing Vernacular

Scots is a sister-language to English, to employ the Neo-grammarian family-tree metaphor. Both languages stem from Germanic dialects which arrived on the British Isles in the fifth century, and reached as far as north of the river Tweed, into the Scottish Lowlands. Old Northumbrian, the Old English dialect extending into these northern settlement areas, came in contact with the Celtic languages of Scotland (Brythonic and Gaelic, also Pictish)[2] and with the dialects of the Viking invaders (Old Norse) (McClure 1994: 23–26).[3] It became the language of the Scottish court and early urban centres, the burghs, after the Norman Conquest of England, when large numbers of Anglo-Saxon speakers had fled to Scotland, including the English royal family. Influences from the south continued through a network of feudal relations and trade, ousting the earlier Celtic dialects from their privileged position. Murison (1974: 74–75) deems the early municipal law and administration the "vehicle of anglicization", writing about the Anglian—or Old Northumbrian—impact on burgh nomenclature and the place-names themselves. Chapter 5 provides more historical background for the early feudal influences on Scottish government and towns.

Paradoxically, the status of Scots today is more difficult to pinpoint than it was in the medieval and Renaissance times. For several decades, a debate has been advanced as to whether to treat present-day Scots as a dialect of English or as a separate language (McClure 1995a). On the wave of the revival in minority languages and the promotion of local languages as tokens of identity in twenty-first-century Europe, Scots has officially entered the public domain, for example, by being admitted as one of the languages of the Scottish Parliament (SPCB Language Policy 2011). Attempts to plan out and standardize the form of Modern Scots and to enhance its status and functions are ongoing (Corbett 2003; Scottish Government 2009).

The status of Scots in the medieval period was the same as that of any vernacular variety, including English, before standardization: it belonged to a dialectal continuum. Indeed, all Middle English texts can be placed on such a continuum, while the concept of "language" as we apply it today, with its ideological baggage, had not formed yet (cf. Costa 2009: 17). This fact has not caused any scholar to dismiss English as a fully fledged language at that time, it should be noted. The story of Scots is similar. From the late fourteenth century, Scots was gaining recognition as the official language of the Scottish kingdom and as a Scottish identity marker. Aitken (1979: 87) writes of "two nations [which] shared [the] island, each with its own distinct national tongue, King's Scots in Scotland and King's English in England". Nevertheless, the nomenclature still fluctuated—the Scots called this language *Inglis*, recognizing its roots and a degree of intelligibility with English dialects, while *Scottis* was reserved for Scottish Gaelic. The first extant usage of *Scottis* in the sense of 'the Lowland Germanic tongue of Scotland' dates back to Adam Loutfut's translation of a heraldry book "out of fraynche in scottis" in 1494 (McClure 1995b: 44), while a conscious application of this label to "our awin language", as opposed to *Inglis* or *Sudron* of England, was initiated by Gavin Douglas in 1513 (McClure 1994: 32–33). Although sixteenth-century perceptions of Scots and English range from an emphasis on contrast to an emphasis on resemblance (Bald 1928), the shift in nomenclature points to the recognition of Scots as a part of Scottish identity and an official emblem of the nation.[4] As Millar puts it, "[a]t the heart of nationalism, or, more correctly, a sense of large scale group identity, are

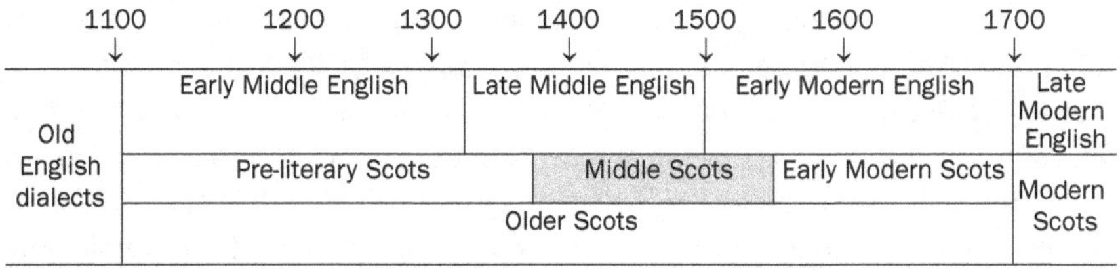

FIGURE 1.1 Periodization of Scots, based on Kopaczyk (2013), and English, based on Horobin and Smith (2002: 1) and Nevalainen (2006: 1-9)

often shared historical, cultural and... *linguistic* features" (2005: 9–10, emphasis in original). One should therefore treat Scots as one of the European vernaculars progressing towards full standardization, regardless of the fact that it never reached this stage (Agutter 1990; Bugaj 2004a). Scots was stopped on its way, due to anglicizing influences from the mid-sixteenth century onwards (Devitt 1989) and unfavourable, or at least ambiguous perceptions in the eighteenth century (Dossena 2005), when other European languages—English among them—were entering the final codification stage and becoming fully fledged standards (Burke 2004: 89–110). This is one of the reasons why the present investigation does not extend further than 1560—to capture Scots legal discourse when the language was still developing its own standard tools for formal situations. The starting point—1380—marks the appearance of substantial legal writings in Scots. Prior to this, the traditional periodization of Scots (Aitken 1985: xiii) notes a two-hundred-and-fifty-year gap in vernacular writings (Fig. 1.1), even though glosses in the Scots language had been appearing in various Latin documents before 1350 (Murison 1974: 80). I return to the relationship between Scots and Latin in early legal discourse in Chapter 7.

In this book, I will use the label *Middle Scots* to cover the period between the late fourteenth and mid-sixteenth century (see the shaded area in Fig. 1.1; the periodization of English is provided for comparative purposes), while the subsequent period will be referred to as *Early Modern Scots*. This is an unorthodox treatment of the periodization of Scots. I have altered the traditional timeline (see e.g. Aitken 1985: xiii) in view of language-internal developments in Scots, as well as extralinguistic criteria, such as the wide range of communicative functions characteristic of early modern vernaculars (see below). Bearing in mind the arbitrariness of any periodization, I discuss the revised version and its advantages in more detail in Kopaczyk (2013), and adopt the modified timeline in the present project.

Between 1380 and 1560, Scots was varied in terms of form, especially spelling (see Chapter 8 for the discussion of spelling uniformization undertaken for the purposes of this study). Relevant aspects of its grammar and lexicon will be addressed in the discussion of patterns emerging from lexical bundles in Chapters 9 to 12. Regardless of formal variety, Middle Scots was employed in a growing range of functional contexts. It was a medium for multiple literary genres in different styles, from the "low" verse of Dunbar and Kennedy's flyting, through instructive verse, to "courtly verse in the grand manner" practised with most flair by Dunbar (Aitken 1983, see also Corbett 1997: 214–238). Classic works of literature were translated into Scots, for example, *Eneados* [Aeneid] by Gavin Douglas in 1513 (McClure 1994: 32–33), while at the same time Scottish writings in translation found audiences abroad (Hubbard 2003: 37–38). Scientific discourse made its way into Scots through translation, as well as original work, for example, John Ireland's *Meroure of Wyssdome* (1490), although not without self-conscious comments on the part of the authors (Williamson 1982: 56). Williamson also found that Scots was taught in the so-called 'Inglis' or 'Lectour' schools even before the Reformation, which raises the question of vernacular literacy. Chapter 6 takes up the issue of education in the burghs and the establishment of early academic centres in Scotland.

Another area where Middle Scots was typically employed was in private and public correspondence, which has become the base of the recent *Corpus of Scottish Correspondence* (Meurman-Solin 2007a). Horsbroch (1999) draws attention to royal correspondence from England and other countries written in Scots to the Scottish court. He also enumerates Scots interpreters at various European courts and centres of trade (1999: 6, 9, 12), so it appears that the language was given recognition abroad as an autonomous means of international communication.

This book investigates features of Scots legal discourse, another area where the Lowland tongue was present very early on. Due to a different history of language contact, in Scotland, unlike in England, there was a direct shift from Latin to the vernacular in legal and administrative documents. Indeed, "the only vernacular which was sufficiently widespread, socially and geographically, to oust Latin save for solemn, ecclesiastical or academic purposes was Scots" (Barrow 1997: 138). MacQueen (2002a) suggests that "[b]y the second half of the fourteenth century... Scots had long been the regular language of the law outside certain matters of form, and the emergence of this language in legal documents and records simply reflected a well-entrenched fact." I return to this point in Chapter 7, where I also discuss further areas of difference between English and Scots law from a linguistic point of view. Scots showed much versatility as a means of expression and communication across the entire spectrum of language use, where legal and administrative texts occupy a special position. As noted for English legal discourse, such texts have the potential to create norms of usage, also in syntax and lexis, which can spread to other areas (Rissanen 1999). Meurman-Solin suggests two hubs of norm-formation in Scotland: "In the case of Scots, the norm considered prestigious may consist of practices followed by the local administration (in the royal burghs of Scotland) or those adopted by the regional central administration (in Edinburgh)" (1997: 4). The legal and administrative texts investigated here represent the whole Scots-speaking area of medieval and early Renaissance Scotland, so it will be possible to trace the sources of textual norms and to see if they correlate with centres of prestige.

1.5. Overview of the Chapters

As signalled above, the book is divided into three parts, which together compose an interdisciplinary investigation of standardization in the language of the law in a medieval and early Renaissance society.

Part One, 'The Language', comprises three chapters which outline the linguistic premises of the book. Chapter 2 discusses the relationship between law and language in view of the oral roots of communication, rituals, and rules. The outlook concentrates on the European West, where the Scots legal culture belongs. Legal discourse, as a specialized form of communication, is characterized by a set of specific features, which are described towards the end of the chapter. Chapter 3 addresses the concepts of context, discourse, and text. It offers ideas on how to reconstruct communicative events from the past, stemming from the discourse community perspective and from corpus methodologies. In relation to automatic extraction methods, Chapter 4 draws attention to the propensity of language to create fixed chunks which repeat in discourse, adding to its communicative force. Lexical bundles and their place within multi-word units are introduced, together with the phenomena of lexicalization and pragmaticalization as applicable to lexical bundles. I also attend to binomials, specific structures characteristic for the language of the law, retrievable in an objective manner by the lexical bundle method. A summary which follows brings together the main points of the theoretical part and provides a transition to the historical part of the investigation.

Part Two, 'The Burghs', provides the external background for the composition of legal texts in medieval and early modern Scotland. With an emphasis on the social and political ramifications of the Stewart rule, Chapter 5 sketches out the historical development of early urban centres which became the venue for legal discourse and legal text production. A specific Scottish perspective is sustained through the discussion of the relations between identity, language, and law. In Chapter 6, we visit a Scottish burgh and become familiar with its society and government, as well as its economy and place on the political map of medieval and early Renaissance Scotland. Chapter 7 concentrates on the specific nature of Scots law and its place in the burghs. The institutions and people responsible for the creation of legal discourse are discussed in detail, and so are the texts they produced. The second part of the book concludes with a summary of the main observations on the socio-historical conditions in which the corpus material under analysis was created.

Finally, Part Three, 'The Legal Language of the Burghs', examines the amount of repetition and fixedness in Scottish medieval and early modern legal discourse. Chapter 8 describes the EdHeW corpora and outlines the methodology of data extraction. Because the methods employed, especially the lexical bundles, are a novelty in historical linguistics, I explain the rationale for my methodological decisions, and what they mean for the analysis. Chapter 9 contains a detailed scrutiny of structural types of lexical bundles from EdHeW, to arrive at a summary of the most frequently repeated constructions from the point of view of form. Chapter 10 considers binomials and multinomials as ingredients of legal discourse, motivated by the "oral residue" (Ong [1982] 2002) in law, and by the requirement of semantic all-inclusiveness and clarity. Chapter 11 carries out a functional interpretation of bundle material, highlighting the most typical patterns emerging from the data counts. The findings again point to features of discourse flowing directly from the requirements of the medieval and early Renaissance legal context. Throughout the chapter, I provide links with the rich historical background introduced in Part Two, in order to show the context which inspired the repetition and fixedness of particular fragments of text. In getting to the heart of historical meanings, the *Dictionary of the Scots Language* (*DSL*), available online and comprising the twelve-volume *Dictionary of the Older Scottish Tongue* and its modern continuation, the *Scottish National Dictionary*, was invaluable. It was supplemented with the *Oxford English Dictionary* (*OED*) for a wider perspective on Scots legal vocabulary of the period. The analytic chapters finish with Chapter 12, which presents the symptoms of textual standardization in the form of the longest lexical bundles found in the corpus. This is the culminating point of the book, as the longest lexical bundles draw attention to the core functional elements of early legal discourse, and aptly illustrate the extent of fixedness in the corpus. Diachronic, as well as diatopic, trends emerge from data analysis, testifying to the mature character of Scots legal language at that time. Part Three is followed by overall conclusions which summarize the achievements of this study and point towards future research directions.

Each of the three parts may be read on their own by those with more theoretical, historical, or data-oriented interests. Together, the three parts form a comprehensive discussion of standardizing lexico-syntactic patterns, pointing to the specific nature of the language of the law in a historical Scottish setting, but also providing a point of reference for other legal cultures and traditions.

PART ONE

The Language

2

The Language of Legal Texts

2.1. Introduction

Part One sets out the linguistic framework of the study. Legal texts, which are at the root of this investigation, answer to the demands of the discourse situation: the historical and social setting, traditions and conventions, rituals, technical limitations, and communicative goals and functions. This chapter pays attention to the complex relationship between law and language, and the linguistic choices resulting from the requirements of the legal context, while the next chapter locates this specialized use of language in the discourse framework (Chapter 3). The two features of the language of the law, which are of major consequence in this discussion, are its repetitive nature and textual standardization. Hence, the last chapter in Part One looks at the phenomenon of repetition in language as a force for the fixing of crucial communicative elements (Chapter 4).

The language of specialized texts is shaped by the history of a given discipline and by its communicative requirements. Starting with an overview of terminology which tries to capture the relationship between language and law (section 2.2), the present chapter outlines the conditions in which the practice of legal documentation developed. To anchor legal discourse in its historical context, I pay attention to the oral and ritual roots of the law (section 2.3), as features of orality permeate written legal discourse and will emerge from the standardizing chunks of Scottish legal texts. The texts under scrutiny here come from manuscript material, so the question of stability and authority of written records is also considered. In order to illustrate how their linguistic form responded to external conditions, I move on to the specific features of legal texts from a specialized discourse perspective (section 2.4). This presentation of generic, lexical, and grammatical characteristics of legal texts will provide a point of reference for the corpus findings, discussed in Part Three.

2.2. The Terminological Maze

Language is a vehicle for law and, at the same time, its crucial element, the material and the tool for the creation, codification, transmission, and interpretation of law. The intricate connection between law and language has been a leading part of many inquiries into the nature of this specialized field of discourse. "Law is language," writes Walker, in the opening lines of his *The Scottish Legal System* (2001); "the law is a profession of words," says Mellinkoff (1963: vii) in his influential monograph; "[l]aw is language," again, for Gibbons (1999: 156) from his applied linguistic perspective; "[w]ith law expressed formally, in formal language, it is also natural to conclude that law is language" (Glenn 2007: 154); "[l]aw is the tower that language built" (Hutton 2009: 4); "[o]ur law is a law of words" (Tiersma 1999: 1). The relationship between law and language can be studied from many angles and it is often expressed in terms of *legal language* or *the language of the law* (for a detailed analysis of the application of these terms, see Kurzon 1989 and 1997). In this book, I follow Trosborg's understanding of these terms, whereby *legal language* is an overarching term for all uses of language connected with legal activity (legal drafting, verdicts, legal handbooks, lawyer's communication with laymen and within the profession, to name but a few), while the *language of the law* is one of the instances of legal language, connected with "constructing documents" and "laying down the law" (Trosborg 1997a: 19–20).

It should be remembered that law, as a social construct, answers to specific situational requirements and stems from a long tradition which has accumulated in the form of specific discourse patterns. According to Maley (1994), *legal discourse* is a multifaceted set of related discourses: judicial discourse, courtroom discourse, the language of legal documents and discourse of legal consultation; other scholars divide legal discourse into oral and written types (Conley and O'Barr 1990; Kurzon 1997). The recent *Oxford Handbook of Language and Law* (Solan and Tiersma 2012) provides a comprehensive overview of the multiple present-day contexts in which language and law intersect and interact. As this book concentrates on historical legal discourse, written records are the only resource available. I am not trying to overcome this limitation. Instead of seeking a methodology which would allow general conclusions about legal discourse to be drawn from writing alone, I acknowledge the special position of writing as a medium for the creation, preservation, and dissemination of law (section 2.3).[1] A disclaimer is also due at this stage. The present study does not concentrate on features of spoken discourse in legal settings, as retrievable from historical written records for a given period. Such studies, from reported speech investigations to speech acts, have been done previously by historical pragmaticians (Kryk-Kastovsky 2000, 2002, 2006b, 2009; Archer 2005; Włodarczyk 2007a; Doty and Hiltunen 2009; Culpeper and Kytö 2010), usually on the basis of trial proceedings and witness depositions.[2] I choose to concentrate on the language of written legal records and the processes which lead to the textual standardization of legal discourse in writing.

Legal discourse is the area of human communication *about* law, as well as the one which directly constructs law and provides context for its practice. It is to be expected that the language of the legal commentary and the language of the legal act will always depend on one another, for example, through the employment of the same terminology and formulae. It is true, for instance, that the syntax might vary in different legal genres and so will the rhetorical functions correlated with their specific task: persuasion, argumentation, declaration, obligation, and so on. But all in all, one may expect certain linguistic features characteristic of legal discourse in a given legal tradition, regardless of its individual incarnations (section 2.4 below).

2.3. Law and Language: Creation and Transmission

Through metaphor, legal discourse today preserves some direct references to the initial oral and ritualistic character of law and its subsequent evolution into the written domain. "[D]isputes are resolved in a court 'hearing'; lawyers advise their clients to 'put it in writing'; agreements must be 'signed and sealed'; judges follow 'the letter of the law', honor 'the binding force' of precedent, and rule 'by the book.'" This is how we conceptualize law and the legal domain of discourse—with constant reference to the "method by which it is communicated" (Collins and Skover 1992: 514). In order to fully explore the forms and functions of legal discourse, it is the medium—the spoken word, the handwriting or print—and the relevant tradition that first need attention.

The earliest communities which developed an organized social structure needed rules to sustain it.[3] Apart from symbols, artefacts, and physical rituals, speech was the primary medium for the preservation and transmission of their customs and rules. The spoken word, however, is volatile and beyond retrieval once it has been uttered, so even a memorized and repeated version may not be exactly the same as the initial output. Due to the changeable nature of human memory, oral traditions were constantly updated—what was irrelevant would be forgotten. The consequence for the legal context was that "[l]aw worth having and worth keeping was worth remembering", as Glenn (2007: 8) puts it. Oral traditions are dynamic in that they respond to pressures from outside and from within. The outside pressures might be connected to the changing circumstances in which a given community functions, for instance, the relations of power, social and cultural context, or rituals[4] and beliefs. The inner pressures might be caused by the constant risk of alterations and new interpretations in the oral transmission. This is why oral cultures valued formulaicity. "In an oral culture, knowledge, once acquired, had to be constantly repeated or it would be lost: fixed formulaic thought patterns were essential for wisdom and effective administration" (Ong 2002: 24). The constant recall was there to help not to forget and the formulaic patterns assured continuity (for specific linguistic features connected to formulaicity, see section 4.2). As Darwinists would have it, repetitive oral behaviour functioned as a series of tradition-forming memes (Drout 2006).

This initial relationship between social rules and orality has been present in the linguistic fabric of law in the Western European culture ever since (Glenn

2007). Law transmitted orally relied on special employment of language. That language could not be plain and ordinary because it was not put to plain and ordinary use. Oral communication in specialized contexts followed clearly delineated and traditionally transmitted patterns, which were seen as meaningful arrangements of meaningful elements. Language was also showing its performative side, which some scholars see as one of the reasons for the development of oral communication in general (Danet 1997: 20). In a legal context, the language created events of great significance and consequence, such as oaths or vows. It provided tools for changing the state of affairs, as in the case of wills, statutes, or verdicts. That the language was adjusted to the solemnity of the act had to be clear for the community. As Collins and Skover put it, "[v]isual and oral drama imbued the event with legal significance" (1992: 517). For example, an oath was typically set as a formulaic utterance, with poetic features often incorporating some degree of repetition, through alliteration, anaphora, invocations, and parallelisms. These characteristics enhanced the transmission of textual patterns down the generations of a preliterate culture. What is more, they were not simply adornments and mnemonic aids but they *contained* the law in the form of formulae, proverbs, and other repeated and expected elements (Ong 2002: 35). Literate societies continued these patterns of linguistic behaviour, as Kryk-Kastovsky (2009) has shown for illocutionary acts in early modern courtroom. Part Three of the present study contains lists of repetitive, formulaic strings, which are the token of the attention paid to the form of the legal text in writing.

When law relied only on the spoken word, it had to be supplied with various props, such as ritualized gestures and movements, the employment of objects with special significance, ceremonial dress, decoration (Danet 1997: 15–16) and other forms of visual drama. A direct continuation of these practices can be noticed in medieval and early modern Scottish burghs, which produced legal discourse under scrutiny in the present book. The court in a burgh could not be perceived as authoritative and valid until it was fenced (Walker 1990: 466–467)—literally protected from the outsiders by means of a fence, which functioned as an indication of the peace of the court and as a psychological barrier between the partakers and the watchers. This custom could be traced back to continental Germanic and Scandinavian tribal practices (Hamilton-Grierson 1924). Courts often took place outdoors, also in Scotland (section 7.3.4). During land transfer the ritual was enhanced by an obligatory prop, which was a clod of earth or a handful of stones from the actual plot of land under transaction. This symbolic parallel between transferring land and transferring a token (a clod of earth, a stone) in front of the community is part of the same tradition which requires modern lawyers to plead with wigs and robes on. Legal activity continues to be a spectacle with real effects. At the same time, language captures these important ingredients of the overall communicative situation—the binomial *erd and stan* 'earth and stone' emerges from the EdHeW corpus as one of the most formulaic strings (Chapter 10).

In Western European oral cultures, the experience of the law was immediate and contextualized. To be valid, a transaction required the presence of carefully selected, trustworthy witnesses, which was a guarantee of the authenticity and stability of a legal act. The invention and implementation of writing did not cause a revolution in legal procedure. People distrusted the new medium (Clanchy 1979: 231–257: Collins and Skover 1992: 528); an oral statement of a well-known witness counted for more. To the members of an oral community, writing was—at least initially—"mere graphic marks on parchment", devoid of significance or authority (Danet and Bogoch 1994: 103). Moreover, writing could be forged and was therefore less reliable than trustworthy witnesses, as common instances of forgery in the Middle Ages confirm (Stock 1983: 60–62). This early prejudice can be traced in fourteenth- to sixteenth-century Scots legal procedures where failure to appear in court to witness the case was punishable by law (Chapter 7). The fixed strings emerging in the EdHeW corpus capture the importance of witnesses, for example, *befor thir witnes* 'before these witnesses' (section 11.3.1, collective reference to people) or *in witnes of the quhilk thing* 'in witness of the which thing', one of the most formulaic strings in the early fifteenth-century documents (section 12.2.2).

Thus, at first, writing was only supplementary to oral procedures. The introduction of writing happened at different points in time and with different intensity, depending on the place.[5] From its inception in ancient Mesopotamia c. 3500 B.C. writing has been used in the context of urban communities. Ong (2002: 84–85) suggests that writing developed mostly as a practical tool for record keeping in the earliest Sumerian cities, long before it was employed for other purposes. As ancient cultures waxed and waned, the medieval Europeans "had to re-learn some of the lessons about institutionalization of writing which had been forgotten in the course of time" (Danet 1997: 21). Clanchy (1979: 175–201) suggests in his important monograph that the shift towards literacy (in Latin) happened around the twelfth century in the whole of Europe. He does not specifically mention Scotland but, as I have outlined in the introductory chapter, the northern dialects of Old English spoken in the Scottish Lowlands, which provided the base for the development of Scots as a separate language, enjoy the longest textual history, dating back to the seventh century and the carvings on the Ruthwell Cross. Since in pre-Conquest times Anglo-Saxon monks used writing as a memory aid in property transfers, the same was surely the case in Scotland. What should be borne in mind is that a written text was not yet treated as a legally binding act in itself. As MacQueen (2002a) points out, the significance we attach to the written record today conceals the intricate relationship between the written language of the document and the spoken language of the participant in legal discourse.

The success of writing was not unavoidable. At the turning point, large majorities were illiterate, including aristocrats and kings, while reading and writing were two separate skills and activities, practised by a handful of monks and scholars. The shift in the medium was to be promoted by institutionalized Christianity and feudalism. In the new feudal societies, the need of creating a stable reference point for social hierarchies, sanctioned by genealogies and land ownership, added to the popularity of writing. The trend became 'irreversible' (Stock 1983: 16–18) and there was no turning back to the purely oral mode. This is why imagining a pristine oral culture is difficult, if not impossible for people with the experience of literacy.[6] Ong summarized this detachment from orality by saying that "[m]ore than any other single invention, writing has transformed human consciousness" (2002: 77).

Writing was incorporated into legal culture not only because it provided a record and had a referential function. Equally important may have been the performative and symbolic aspects transmitted to written texts from earlier oral practice, as Danet (1997: 21) strongly suggests on the basis of early Anglo-Saxon wills. Of course, the transition to writing was not abrupt. At the beginning, the medieval attempts to create a document were quite self-conscious. There were meta-comments about the writing or about the oral ceremony it was supposed to represent. Danet and Bogoch postulated that early wills were written down "as supplementary evidence of what had occurred in the oral ceremony" (1994: 106). Other transitional aspects of orality in writing include signatures and crosses as an explicit reference to the witnesses (who often touched the cross with their sword or hand to indicate the personal connection) and ritualized religious and magical elements, such as curses.[7] From a textual point of view, standardized formulaic openings were present only in one-tenth of the wills, which indicated that the medium was a novelty (Danet 1997: 24–28) and standard textual patterns had not yet evolved. It must have taken time for the members of a community to realize that the new medium could be put to similar uses as the traditional one, speech—that it could be trusted, and could develop its own ways of establishing social relationships. One important consequence was the necessity to adjust the law too, and to incorporate this new medium into its discourse (section 2.4). These old and new characteristics of the law were aptly summarized by Collins and Skover (1992: 515–516): "Generally, 'law' in an oral culture tended toward the customary, the participatory, the ceremonial, the adaptable, and the contextual. When law became chirographic, it tended toward the present, the hierarchical, the informational, the spacial-temporal, and the artificial."

The introduction of writing gave more freedom to the authors, as their production did not now have to answer to mnemonic demands. At the same time, written records guaranteed the stability and durability of the law in a given culture. Writing meant fixing what used to be rather fluid (e.g. property exchanges were now formalized into wills and charters). Existing law-related procedures and activities were changed, as in the transition from oral summons by a town crier to written summons by an impersonal piece of parchment, the royal writ (Collins and Skover 1992: 526–527). Getting to know and trust this new medium, after centuries of oral custom, took time. In medieval Scottish burghs the position of the town crier was still kept (section 6.3.3), an intermediary between the oral and the written. "Charters were to be seen and heard…legislation…was to be read and proclaimed publicly in the king's courts and in other places where the people were accustomed to gather; brieves were to be read to the court before cases began" (MacQueen 2002a). The transition from the old medium to the new was not abrupt for one more reason: handwriting was still limited to a handful of skilled professionals who needed specialist equipment and time to produce their records. Moreover, "[w]ith only a few copies available for a widely dispersed population, chirographic writing alone could not reach many of the subjects of the realm" (Collins and Skover 1992: 525), especially when illiteracy was the norm. Therefore, the writings had to preserve some of the mnemonic aspects of written legal cultures, to help reproduce the laws orally when needed.

Although the material used in this book comes solely from handwritten records, it looks back on the oral traditions. At the same time, with the time-frame reaching 1560, it looks forward to the next revolutionary mode of communication: printing. As in the case of chirographic writing, the transition to print was not immediate and, in many aspects of legal culture, has not been completed even today. After all, to make a document legally binding, one must sign it by hand. It is not surprising that "[l]aw's scribal way continued long after the invention of moveable type, though print inevitably overtook script and assumed many of its characteristics without being hindered by many of its shortcomings" (Collins and Skover 1992: 529). Moveable type helped to overcome the time- and resource-consuming production of handwritten copies, the major obstacle to a wider and quicker circulation of texts.

By means of writing, and even more so by means of print, law could reach distant areas or call on distant times. Indeed, because the ancient Romans produced a culture of the written word, their ideas about the state, politics, society, and other crucial areas of human activity were preserved. Just as medieval Europeans rediscovered the culture of writing (Danet and Bogoch 1992: 133), medieval scholars rediscovered Roman legal traditions, mostly through the texts of the second/third-century *Digest*, which was a part of *Corpus Juris Civilis*, a collection of legal codes compiled for Emperor Justinian (Walker 1990: 13–14). In Scotland, it was the Roman law, together with the canon law, "that masterpiece of applied medieval logic" (MacQueen 1997: 69), that became the cornerstones of the budding Scots legal system and provided a source of reference and authority during its formative years (section 7.2.1).[8]

In time, the reverence for the original written word as the source of true meaning in the law was such that vernacular glossators and commentators were often criticized. Another reason was the fear of misinterpretation and corruption caused by the ambiguous nature of language. On the wave of opposition to the vernacularization of Latin in the Middle Ages, interpreters and especially legal language interpreters came under harsh attack from purists, who complained about "the legal commentators on the *Digest*, whose language they have adulterated with vernacular barbarisms" (Moss 2003: 36). Keeping to the proverbial 'letter of the law' remained a perennial concern. Renaissance commentators were anxious about linguistic ambiguity in law, which is why adherence to classical Ciceronian Latin, "on whose usage the educated will agree", was advocated (Moss 2003: 61–62).

Thanks to writing, texts could be standardized, regulated, and transmitted through time and space, and thus extend legal authority. Of course, before the introduction of print to Scotland, the dissemination of laws suffered from technical and organizational limitations. The royal statutes had to be copied and sent out to burgh officials and sheriffs to be read publicly. Under James II (1437–1460), whose rule is brought closer in section 5.4.3, "sheriffs and commissioners of burghs were to come to the clerk of the king's register to copy the statutes of the current parliament and cause them to be proclaimed throughout their sheriffdoms and burghs, . . . 'so that none be ignorant of them'" (Walker 1990: 254). The invention of the printing press enhanced regional dissemination of the law, resulting in its further detachment from individual and immediate contexts. The transition from script to print caused the law to lean towards "the depersonalized, the objectified and systematic, the controllable and inflexible, and the abstract" (Collins and Skover 1992: 515–516), epithets which encapsulate the features of printed legal culture.

In 1507–1510, Walter Chepman and Andro Myllar established the first Scottish printing press in Edinburgh on the basis of the royal charter granting them the right "for imprenting within our realme of the bukis of our lawis, actis of parliament, croniclis, mess [i.e. mass] bukis and portuus [i.e. portable breviaries] efter the use of our realme" (*First Scottish Books* 2006). This new tool gained special patronage from the burgh council there, as well as in Aberdeen and Glasgow in subsequent decades and centuries (Mann 2000: 7–33). Even if clearly advised in the founding charter, the printing of legal documents in Scotland began relatively late, with the printing of the Acts of Parliament in 1541 (Mann 2000: 236).[9] But soon the printing press provided the bulk of material for courts and parliament debates. The volume of production could be quite impressive, for example, "[t]he typical print run for a legal paper to be presented to the court was fifty to sixty copies" (Finlay 2007: 55). Nevertheless, the period of interest for this book reaches into this new technological world only by a fraction. Significantly, Dolezalek notices that "a medieval technique for copying, invented for legal literature in the late 12th century, remained alive in the circles of Scottish lawyers until the late 17th century" (2010: 11), so the chirographic culture of manuscript production, with its implications of close-knit professional communities, remains the best framework for our discussion.

2.4. Characteristics of Legal Discourse

2.4.1. PURPOSE, FUNCTION, AND FORM OF LEGAL TEXTS

"Law is bound by its form," note Collins and Skover in their opening line, commenting on the media through which law is transmitted (1992: 509). The texts under scrutiny in Part Three are handwritten and contain elements of earlier oral practice. The medium affects the form, therefore historical texts, composed in a different communicative environment and transmitted through different media, may exhibit their own characteristics even though they perform roughly the same function as their modern counterparts. The purpose of a text seems to be synonymous with its function; both relate to the reason why such a text has been created and what role it plays in a given area of social activity. The only shade of difference lies in the fact that purpose is static—it is the answer to the question why a text comes to life in a particular set of external circumstances. On the other hand, the function of a text is a dynamic concept—it answers the question of how a text fulfils its purpose and what effects it produces in the community. Legal discourse falls into the area of "language for specific/special purposes" (henceforth LSP; Bhatia 1993; Williams 2005). LSP areas are connected with pivotal planes of social activity, such as law, education, technology, or health care.[10] The language used in legal discourse has been interpreted by some "western and civilian theories of law...as a controlling element in individual and societal development" (Glenn 2007: 154). Indeed, legal discourse concerns both the community which creates rules of conduct and the individual who is obliged to obey, by choice or by default. Many current legal systems aspire to treat people equally, seeking to employ discourse which would "transcend human variation" (Conley and O'Barr 1990: 9). However, in historical times, law worked under different ideological convictions and was constructed by early practitioners according to both the prevailing social order and the traditions inherited from the past. Thus, the link between the linguistic form and function of the law was there from the very beginning.

The inextricable link between context, function, and form attracted the attention of linguists in the 1960s and 1970s, who followed in the footsteps of Jakobson and Firth[11] (e.g. Halliday 1978; see also Chapter 3). This methodological conviction underlies and inspires the discussion in the present book. Legal texts are expected to be authoritative and unambiguous; the way in which law is communicated should be clear and transparent, but at the same time solemn and formal. This requirement causes a certain paradox in the language of the law: "the aim of clarity and avoidance of ambiguity may also result in repetitiveness and verbosity" (Rissanen 1999: 192; see also Gotti 2012).[12] In order to cover all possibilities of interpretation, the language of the law engages in parallelisms and repetitions on the level of meaning and syntax. The beginnings of such choices of linguistic form can be traced back to the medieval period when vernacular languages were expanding their roles into the legal domain. As mentioned in the previous section, the departure from Latin in early modern legal discourse caused anxiety among contemporary commentators who feared that the language of common people would be too imprecise and mundane to cope with the law. Discussing the sixteenth-century French *Ordonnance*, which imposed the use of the vernacular instead of Latin in administrative acts and regulations, Charnock (2006: 66) calls this move "touchingly naïve". The introduction of the vernacular may not have improved the clarity of legal formulation, precisely because polysemy and ambiguity are inherent in any language, except one which is dead and therefore fixed in place, like Latin.

2.4.2. LEGAL GENRES AND SPECIALIZED DISCOURSE

In LSP the relationship between linguistic form and function becomes emphatically pronounced. The language answers to the requirements of a specific thematic, textual, or social domain, and becomes specialized—marked by specific terminology, phrases, characteristic syntactic structure, or discourse patterns.[13] The language of the law belongs to the area of specialized discourse because of its highly relational nature. Law never functions in a void; it always relates to specific social situations and does so through text. Bhatia (2008) has recently drawn attention to the need to consider external factors, and, most importantly, professional practices, in LSP analysis. On the basis of legal texts, one can investigate social issues permeating these official writings. As noticed by Conley and O'Barr (1998: 116–128), legal documents (e.g. remission letters) are instances of legal discourses of the past which can be used to reconstruct such social relationships as gender roles and power relations, similarly to trial records (Archer 2005; Kryk-Kastovsky 2010). In the present study, recurrent entries on burgh officials or men and women shed light on their position in burgh society and their typical formal activities. As the second excerpt in the introductory chapter has shown, husbands and wives may stand together in a Scottish medieval burgh court. Among repetitive strings in EdHeW there are those with female names, such as *ye said marion* 'the said Marion' (section 11.3.1), or with pronominal reference to females, for instance *for ye wrangus takin fra hir* 'for the wrongful taking from her' (section 12.2.4). Interpreted against the socio-historical background from Chapters 6 and 7, these recurrent chunks unravel the presence of women in a Scottish burgh.

The causal link between function and form in legal discourse has been commented on by Finegan (1982) in his study on testament language: "The language of a will must be clear enough to endure beyond a time when the will maker can clarify its intended meaning, and it must carry out tasks which the testator, perforce, will not be present to supervise; moreover, it must do these things for a world that may be quite different in crucial respects from the one existing at the time the will is drawn" (Finegan 1982: 114). This observation is very relevant in the context of the material used in the present study: burgh records and administrative documents. Professor H. L. MacQueen (personal communication) points out that with a shift from orality to literacy in legal matters, such writings were endowed with the special force of a repository—a resource for future reference. The community would resort to the records in matters of inheritance, in land dealings, in arguable cases, which is why the form of the records needed to be stable and interpretable regardless of how much time had already elapsed since their compilation (on communities and records, see section 3.6). This stability is achieved through standardization of text type working in legal genres (section 3.5). In a similar vein, Bhatia discusses style standardization in legal texts. He acknowledges the role of historical transmission and the long tradition in legislative writing, equipping legal draftsmen with "tried, tested and time-honoured linguistic expressions and style of writing" (1993: 117).

The nature of legal texts has often been described as conservative, detached from current neutral usage because of the adherence to tradition and standard models, obsolete as they may be in other domains. Interestingly, legal and administrative texts composed in specific locations before linguistic standardization of grammar and spelling reflect the local usage at a given point in time, as in specific Scottish burghs. Thus, the texts can be seen as exponents of a local dialect. For this reason they have been employed in the compilation of the *Edinburgh Corpus of Older Scots* (ECOS, Williamson 2008) and its incarnation as a dialectal search engine online—the *Linguistic Atlas of Older Scots* (LAOS) (on the authorship of legal texts, see section 7.4; on the corpora, see section 8.2; on the diatopic trends in textual standardization, see section 12.3). Meurman-Solin (2004a: 31) recognizes the usefulness of legal texts for localizing linguistic features, which can be applied in the study of written dialect representation in pre-print culture in Scotland. She also calls for the inclusion of research on formulaic language into specialized discourse studies from a historical perspective. "[I]t is necessary to consider the role of conventions and formulae which increase the general degree of conservatism in legalese" (Meurman-Solin 2004a: 31). In the present-day context, legal texts come across as standardized and therefore anonymous. There is little, if any, personal involvement and few visible idiolectal characteristics.[14] In historical data, however, due to the fact that linguistic standardization was either still in progress or, in some cases, had not even started, individual authorial features do stand out; moreover, they are crucial for understanding how legal genres developed. The standardization of legal text types was also in progress (for standardization in discourse, see section 3.5), and writers had to yet achieve a full consensus on the formal features of drafting official documents. It is interesting to consider whether the notaries or clerks were really perceived as 'authors'. The survival of protocol books attributed to particular notaries, known by name (Cairns 2000: 86–101), is perhaps a testimony to the esteem in which these official writers were held: their work was to be kept in one piece and preserved under their name (more on legal practitioners follows in section 7.4).

In the corpus used for this study, the following legal genres have been identified by corpus compilers: court books and court records, letters (e.g. signet letters), judgements, charters (e.g. quitclaims, resignations), contracts (e.g. marriage, sales), indentures (lease, grant, tack, wadset), assizes, protocol books, cartularies, bonds, obligations, and leases (section 8.2). This list illustrates generic diversity within legal discourse; as Finegan observes of historical wills, "the language of the law is not uniform" (1982: 119). Of course, there will be different degrees of fixedness in various legal texts. Janigová notices that statutes have formal character but "not as formulaic or frozen as that of legal instruments such as deeds, contracts, wills, etc." (2008: 82). Trosborg (1991) suggests that legal discourse should be divided into sub-domains and only then can one turn to individual legal sub-languages. In this study, the material does not claim to be representative of all possible legal contexts. It is limited to administrative records and documents compiled in order to aid legal procedures in Scottish medieval and early modern burghs; as such, it constitutes a coherent, single-register compilation. What is more, non-a priori corpus methods have been used to extract fixed fragments of legal discourse therefrom, so that whatever is uniform in the material, will surface in the search. Chapter 8 explains this procedure in detail. Studies carried out on present-day data with the use of the same corpus tools have already exposed the "repetitiveness and... fixed macrostructure" of legal texts in an objective manner (Goźdź-Roszkowski 2006a: 148). This methodology has not yet been used to explore historical legal discourse, so the discussion in the present book opens new ground for diachronic comparisons.

2.4.3. LINGUISTIC FEATURES OF THE LANGUAGE OF THE LAW

The language of the law stems from oral and ritualistic traditions, but at the same time it is carefully crafted to enhance clarity and comprehensiveness. These seemingly contradictory facets of law are married through linguistic formulaicity. On the one hand, formulaic language continues the mnemonic patterns of oral legal codes by using various kinds of repetitive devices (e.g. alliteration, anaphora, syntactic parallelism) or by employing a standard, unaltered phrase for specific textual functions (e.g. openings, appeal to authority, enumeration, closing statements). On the other hand, formulaicity provides textual stability and goes hand in hand with the requirements of written language, such as the elimination of ambiguity (Britnell 1997: 4). Formulae are related to practices and procedures at court. It was common in Scotland that a witness was absent from court proceedings (Walker 1990: 472–474), so the formula *oft times callit* and *not operit* frequently appeared in the records, most often in exactly the same form, as the longest repetitive strings testify (section 1). When formulaic reference was made, for instance, to burgh authorities, it could be expected to include all members of the burgh council, always repeated in the same manner in subsequent documents of the same kind, so that none of the meaning was lost. This is an idealized picture, of course, because formulae vary in their susceptibility to alterations. Some may, indeed, remain unaltered, while some will exhibit more freedom in their formulation. In general, though, writing gives the opportunity to compare previous records, draw on earlier practices of wording and aim at precision and continuity. To evoke a present-day parallel, the recent international proposal of Model Law claims to overcome lexical indeterminacy but at the same time keeps selected customary archaic legal expressions for greater precision (Gotti 2008: 89–108).

The features separating ordinary language and the language of the law were listed in the seminal monograph by Mellinkoff (1963), who, from a lawyer's perspective, aimed to present a comprehensive description of English language of the law, tracing the historical roots of its peculiar features. Admittedly, the features identified by the author belonged solely to the layer of lexicon. His other aim was to stigmatize the eccentricities and mannerisms of legal discourse: its wordiness, dullness, pompousness, and lack of clarity. But the breadth of Mellinkoff's inquiry is hampered by the inadequacy of his linguistic tools. Since Mellinkoff's times, legal language has been changing, albeit at its own pace, so the old criticisms may have less power, as Tiersma (2006) proves in his recent critique of legal language 'myths'. Be that as it may, subsequent scholarship has always situated itself in relation to Mellinkoff's research, as Biber and Finegan (1994: 4) also point out, and the present book will do the same.[15]

Mattila (2012) takes "ordinary language" as his point of departure in the most recent discussion of legal vocabulary. Whether legal discourse differs from ordinary usage was first tested empirically by Finegan (1982) on the basis of wills compared against a control sample from the Standard Corpus of Present-Day Edited American English.[16] He noticed that the peculiarity of the language of the law stems not only from the lexical usage, as stressed by Mellinkoff, but also from specific grammatical patterns (for instance, frequent conditional structures, exceptional length of sentences, or heavy reliance on declaratives; see also Hiltunen 2012). I share Finegan's methodological conviction about "the role of function in determining linguistic form" (1982: 113), which found its confirmation in his empirical research. The language of specific legal text types is linked to the functions they perform, while the written mode helps to achieve the stability of record or legal act. Burgh records, as texts which were to serve as a source of future reference in land dealings and other transactions, preserved oral formulae and tokens of ritualistic behaviour—a testimony to their legality.

Charrow, Crandall, and Charrow (1982: 178–182) notice that the distinct nature of legal discourse lies, among other things, in the separate diachronic development of this specialized type of language. They list four factors responsible for the departure of legal discourse from ordinary usage: historical, social, political, and jurisprudential. When it comes to the historical reasons, it is true that language change works at a slower pace in legal discourse. The stability and formulaicity of form guarantee the force of a document, which is why such discourse evades updates. An interesting parallel can be drawn with any type of discourse where the message attracts attention to itself. In his linguistic analysis of poetic language, Leech noticed the important function of "extra regularities" (1969: 64), whose motivation lies in the aesthetic effect, possibly also mnemonic. It is apparent that in legal language these extra regularities—formulaicity and repetitiveness—are used as tools of transmission and institutionalization at the same time (see sections 4.4.4 and 4.5 on repetitive elements in legal discourse). A good parallel for ritualized and formulaic expression is also the language of religion (for an overview of religious discourse and genres, see Kohnen 2010), which tends to be archaic and to resist change because of the authoritative fixedness and elements of oral mnemonic devices such as repetitions (such as in the lengthy lists of genealogies in the Bible). From a semiotic point of view, Danet (1997: 17–18) notices that formulaic sequences are characterized by indexicality (explicit reference is missing in oral formulae but often obligatory in written ones), intolerance of structural variation, and high and formal register.

Among the formulaic expressions most often identified with the language of the law one finds binomials, such as *heed and care*, *will and testament*, *peace and quiet* (Mellinkoff 1963: 121–122; see also Danet 1984; Hiltunen 1990; Danet and Bogoch 1992; Jackson 1995; Beveridge 2002; Witczak-Plisiecka 2007; Mattila 2012). Their frequency in legal texts is higher than elsewhere, making them "clearly a style marker in law language" (Gustafsson 1984: 125). I introduce binomials in more detail in section 4.5 and devote the whole Chapter 10 to the binomials found in the Scottish corpus. Binomials are repetitive from a syntactic point of view (as they are built of two coordinated constituents from the same grammatical category) but also from a semantic angle. In the language of the law one comes across binomials in all grammatical categories. In fact, their employment may not be a conscious attempt to intensify meaning but rather represent the stylistic requirements of legal discourse. The alliterative character of these phrases and their semantic repetition may indicate that the purpose of doubling is ornamental and embedded in the oral tradition. Because of the apparent lack of functional justification, this practice attracts criticism in modern times, when the clarity of the message has become more important than stylistic traditions. Calling for reform in the language of the law, Charrow, Crandall, and Charrow (1982: 182) argued that there are few legitimate reasons for retaining the binomial pairs. The last thirty years have not brought about much change in this respect, and more recent studies in legal linguistics still list binomials as redundant (Galdia 2009: 102, 107). Research into other areas of specialized discourse has shown, however, that the seemingly unnecessary and redundant coordinated pairs in fact constitute the marker of a specific discourse situation. In their research into the language of health reports, Crawford et al. (1999: 338) talk about "cohesive philosophy of care" based upon "tight generic rules" which are signalled through binomials, reported speech patterns, and lexical density. The same connection between binomials and legal language was frequently exploited by writers who wanted to introduce legal motifs into their literary work.[17] Repetitive constructions and formulaic phrases like *seen, heard, and understood*, were also employed in poetry as a reference to legal language but then interpreted metaphorically to suit the purpose of the literary text. A good fifteenth-century Scottish example is Henryson's employment of phrases such as *reull and steir* in his *Testament of Crisseyde* (Mathews 2002: 51, 53) (for more on the definitions and motivations for binomials, see section 4.5).

Law is constructed out of words, and words carry the possibility of different interpretations and manipulations of meaning. Political reasons for the linguistic fixedness of law have therefore been recognized: "vagueness and ambiguity in legal language is intentional," say Charrow, Crandall, and Charrow (1982: 182). In a way, a hermetic language suited to the purposes of a select group of influential and powerful people can be perceived a token of elitism which these people would want to keep to themselves. They desire the sole authority for the interpretation of legal writings. As studies of courtroom discourse indicate, lay people are "the vulnerable party" because of their "usual ignorance of legal regulations and the legal jargon" (Kryk-Kastovsky 2006a: 165). Lawyers use language as their instrument of trade, as well as the source of knowledge about it, and may therefore be resistant to change their practice and their jargon, which constitutes an in-group marker (cf. the discussion of discourse communities in section 3.6). Some may suspect that this is why the language of the law is impermeable to a non-specialist user and that it is a hard task to implement simplifications. While some of that may be true, more objective, jurisprudential reasons for keeping legal discourse separate from ordinary use should also be borne in mind. These reasons are connected with the practical employment of vocabulary and expressions in their specific legal meaning, distant from a common understanding of a term, for example, *heir, income, adultery* (Mellinkoff 1963; Danet 1980; Jackson 1995; Witczak-Plisiecka 2007), cf. the meaning of *entre* 'entry' in *ische and entre*, extracted from the EdHeW corpus (for more binomials, see section 10.2.3).

There is no denying that an interpretation of a legal text and its application to the social context relies on the meaning of individual lexical items, phrases, and collocations, as well as larger formulae. Walker insists that "an important part of both the study and the application of law consists of the correct appreciation and understanding of the uses and meanings of words, the accurate formulation of thought in words so as to convey precisely the meaning intended, and the careful analysis of language used so as to extract from its precise connotations and implications. Attention to word-meaning and usage is of practical importance in legal study" (2001: 101–102). The elusive nature of meaning, its adaptability to context and ambiguity of interpretation are of no help in legal discourse. The problem is that language used in legal contexts is not constructed exclusively out of specialized terminology. In legal discourse, "what one person considers to be a specialized term, the other one admits it as a part of general vocabulary. The higher degree of text comprehension, the lower degree of specialization" (Grabarczyk 1989: 188–189). A strict division between general lexicon and professional terms is therefore rarely possible. Unlike medicine or engineering, law often utilizes everyday vocabulary, for example, *negligence* or *charity* (for 'legal homonyms', see Tiersma 1999: 111–112), which Walker (2001: 102–103) sees as a problem in legal language's capacity for precision (on polysemy and synonymy in legal vocabulary, see Mattila 2012). Such items undergo specialization of meaning but at the same time they open more possibilities of interpretation. "As common words occur more frequently, they can be expected to occur in more different discourse situations than technical terms; the risk of ambiguity is therefore greater" (Charnock 2006: 65).[18] Interestingly, Scots law preserves the distinction between the specialized vocabulary of the law and neutral vocabulary better than the English common law. In his preface to the glossary of Scots law terms, Gibb states clearly:

> The separation of lawyer's and layman's language in Scotland is the more acute because a Scots lawyer may have a technical term for the expression of some idea which the layman usually expresses by an English word that is at once a lawyer's and a layman's word. [To give an example], few Scots laymen would use "sequestration" which, however, is the correct legal expression for bankruptcy in Scotland. (Gibb 1992: ix)

I take up this point again in Chapter 7 (section 7.2.2), discussing the differences in the respective histories of Scots law and English law. To continue the lexical reflections, there is also a reverse trend where legal phraseology penetrates regular casual discourse (Simon 1960, 1962, 1965; Walker 2001: 2) and literature (e.g. Sokol and Sokol 2000). This intriguing enrichment of non-professional lexicon falls, nevertheless, outside our current interests.

Still concentrating on lexicon and phraseology, it has been suggested that genres and discourses can be predicted from their lexical make-up (Dudley-Evans and StJohn 1998: 86–87; Stubbs and Barth 2003). Surely the lexical fabric distinguishes law from any other field. The selection of lexicon in the specialized discourse of law is governed by the purpose of the communicative act, as well as by its functional background, in turn related to the social, historical, political, and cultural environment. Similarly, language contact situations also create different outcomes in legal texts than they do in other areas of language use. The older linguistic tools of the law, especially Latin, serve as a source of borrowings and calques, and provide a link to authority and tradition. Due to its presence at English courts of law and in legal writings, the French language left its footprint on the English legal lexicon (Mellinkoff 1963; Hiltunen 1990; Tiersma 1999; for French influence on other European legal languages, see Mattila 2012). This is where the Scots law differs from the southern neighbour (section 7.2.2). However, to blame different results of language contact for all the lexical intricacies of Scots law is far-fetched.

Turning to grammatical constructions favoured by legal texts, several studies and overviews have concentrated on considerable sentence length and complexity (Gustafsson 1975; Jackson 1995; Williams 2005; Witczak-Plisiecka 2007; Hiltunen 2012). Galdia (2009: 98) points out that simple sentences are rarely found, which will have its consequence in frequent clausal coordination. Many scholars have observed unusual cohesive devices in the language of the law, e.g. *said* or *such* in a premodifying function, and specific patterns of coordination and subordination (Mellinkoff 1963, Danet 1980, Hiltunen 1990, Jackson 1995). The present research shows that especially *said* and a range of other cohesive premodifiers formed fixed strings in early legal Scottish documents, too (sections 11.3.2.1–11.3.2.2). Finegan (1982: 115) singles out the absence of second person pronoun and the ubiquity of passive voice, which "arise from the discourse situation, or are necessitated by it".[19]

Williams (2005: 35) estimates that about a quarter of all verbal constructions in Present-Day legal English are passives. Passives in participial phrases have also been singled out by Charrow, Crandall, and Charrow (1982: 176) as the structures "responsible for most of the jurors' comprehension problems". Other complex structures appearing in legal texts include truncated phrases, phrases with "as to", nominalizations (Crystal and Davy 1969; Jackson 1995), as well as discourse features "such as the repetition of an entire paragraph, with slightly different wording and organization" (Charrow, Crandall, and Charrow 1982: 177). In her study of statutes, Janigová observes that "repetition rather than pronominal reference [works] as cohesive device" (2008: 83). The repetitive nature of legal discourse, be it on the structural or the semantic level, comes to the fore in the analytic chapters of the present study (Part Three).

Jackson (1988: 37) noticed that the language of the law is non-referential; in other words, it makes reference to its own reality rather than to the extra-textual world. This is why the use of deictic terms, which anchor the text in time and space, will be different than in regular language use. Mellinkoff (1963: 12–13) criticized the abundance of the expressions performing a deictic role in the language of the law, such as the 'where', 'there', and 'here' words: *hereby*, *whereas*, *theretofore*, etc. In my analysis in Chapters 11 and 12, I treat such expressions in legal Scots as tokens of textual cohesion. The non-referentiality issue will also be re-examined in view of the lexical bundles extracted from the corpus.

As for the social reasons detaching legal discourse from other uses of language, the performative role of the law should also be considered. For Charrow, Crandall, and Charrow, the performative character of legal language lies in the fact that "[l]egal language carries the force of the law: the statement is the act" (1982: 181). Legal texts are inherently performative, which stems from their function and the institutional authority of the legal system. Important parts of legal texts will have the form of direct or indirect speech acts and will thus create and change extralinguistic reality (Kurzon 1986; Trosborg 1995; Kryk-Kastovsky 2002, 2009).[20] Directives come across as the most conspicuous legal speech acts (Maley 1994; Tiersma 1999; Schane 2006; Witczak-Plisiecka 2007). Prohibition, permission, and obligation are carried in legal texts by specific linguistic constructions (Trosborg 1997b). Performativity is enhanced with what Danet (1997: 28) called "linguistic stylization", which is universal for oral, often ritualized communication. This conspicuous element of legal discourse was taken up by authors of other genres, who would employ legal linguistic tools to draw attention, for example, in performative eighteenth-century newspaper headlines, such as "This is to give notice" (Studer 2008: 125). As illustrated above, performativity and ritualization can be found at the base of legal discourse.

Of course, one should remember that legal discourse includes diverse communicative situations, and there will always be differences in use. Still, legal discourse can be perceived as a separate, specialized area of human communication, governed by its own rules and, most importantly, behaving differently than regular usage with respect to diachronic pressures. Gotti (2012) stresses that in legal discourse, "[o]ld formulae are preferred to newly-coined words because of their centuries-old history and highly codified, universally accepted interpretations." The discussion above has shown that the roots of fixedness and codification in legal language should be sought for in its social function and channels of transmission. One should remember, though, that interpretations of legal meanings, phraseology, and syntactic choices may depend on specific cultural and historical conditions. As the final illustration, let me use the famous juxtaposition devised by Symonds in 1835, where an ordinary proposition, "I give you an orange", turns in the language of the law into: "I give you all and singular, my estate and interest, right, title, claim and advantage of and in that orange, with all its rind, skin, juice, pulp and pips, and all right and advantage therein, with full power to bite, cut, suck and otherwise eat the same" (quoted in Trosborg 1997a: 30). If a jargon or a type of discourse can be thus ridiculed, it means that it possesses easily identifiable, characteristic features. Legal drafting nowadays may strive for plainness in language but it will have difficulty in shunning the historical legacy which is much more than a simple accumulation of unnecessary residue. Rather, it is a product of the sources and functions of law since its historical inception.

3

Exploring Language of the Past

CONTEXT, DISCOURSE, AND TEXT

3.1. Introduction

The study of textual standardization in legal discourse requires a reflection on how the form of texts responded to the circumstances of their creation. This chapter provides linguistic methodology behind the exploration of historical discourse. One of the main methodological premises of this project is the influence of context on text, discussed in the first part of the chapter (section 3.2). It is followed by an outline of the functional approach, stemming from the works of Halliday (section 3.3), which provides the analytical framework for the qualitative analysis carried out in Part Three. Earlier studies of various features of text show the versatility of this approach and its applicability to diachronic studies of linguistic patterns. I also draw attention to the importance of genre and register in shaping the texts in the expected manner (section 3.4). It becomes necessary to separate the notion of language standardization, observed from the outside, from linguistic standardization, observed language-internally, also on the level of text (section 3.5).

Human communication takes place within a specific social context, which becomes more tangible and well-defined in specialized communication. With this in mind, I introduce the concepts of a discourse community and a community of practice (section 3.6) to account for the coherent nature of Scottish legal documents produced in medieval and early modern burghs. The external conditions in which the texts were produced are sketched out in detail in Part Two of the book, with Chapter 7 concentrating on the law in the burghs and on the authors of legal documents. The present chapter finishes with a survey of corpus approaches to historical questions in linguistics (section 3.7), where I argue for the use of corpus tools for the extraction of formulaic and standardizing elements of legal documents. As standardization is linked with repeated use of selected structures, the next chapter looks at repetition, fixedness, and formulaicity, as well as at lexical bundles as a specific corpus tool to extract such patterns.

3.2. Language Use and Context

The approach to communication adopted in this book takes into account not only the purely abstract linguistic structures available for communication but also the actual decisions of the user to employ a specific type of construction. Such decisions, conscious or not, are motivated by the context of the communicative event. The answers to the questions of the 'who, how, why, what for, and when' of language use will explain the selection of specific structures. Therefore, in order to understand why communication takes place in a given manner, one needs to look beyond form and combine its descriptive study with the analysis of function in context, which is the essence of a discourse approach to language.

One of the key theorists in the evolution of the notion of *context*, as in the "context of situation", was Bronisław Malinowski who identified it as a major factor governing human behaviour and its interpretation (Malinowski [1923] 1966). It is context that gives a linguistic exchange its meaning, and as such it should be distinguished from *co-text*, the immediately surrounding lexical neighbourhood in a text (Tognini-Bonelli 2001: 87–88). Jakobson included context in his list of six necessary ingredients of a communicative act, together with addresser, addressee, message, channel, and code, which correspond to the six basic functions of language. Context would thus enable and bring forward the referential function, which often is "the leading task of numerous messages" (Jakobson 1960: 353). It follows from data analysis in the present book that reference to language-external context indeed leads the way in early legal discourse (Chapter 11).

The discussion of context has continued in the works of functionalists (Firth [1957] 1968; Halliday 1978; Sinclair 1991, 2003), ethnolinguists (Hymes 1974a, b), and pragmaticians (Mey 1993, 2011).[1] Sperber and Wilson (1995: 15–16) extend the notion of context from the physical surroundings to the abstract mental states of the speaker. Widdowson (2004: 43) prefers to capture context as a certain "configuration of knowledge", a central cognitive concept of the schema theory. While every language user will have his or her own individual assumptions about the world, those which are shared will constitute the basis for a community (cf. the discussion of discourse community in section 3.6). For van Dijk (1997), context can be approached locally (the setting, participants, their roles, goals, etc.) and globally (organizational or institutional actions, social groups, institutions). In this understanding, context is a combination of external situational, cultural, and social parameters. Among the approaches to context identified by Fetzer (2007: 5), context is also understood as a relational construct, creating a complex network of mutual relations between actions, their surroundings, and the participants.

The realization that language should not be studied in isolation from function and context stems from the disillusionment with purely formal approaches to language. Abstracted linguistic structures, as in generative-transformational theories, lie at the heart of theoretical models of language but come across as artificial when confronted with real recorded linguistic data. Purely structural descriptions of patterns may indeed provide information about preferred forms at a given point in time, and they are useful as a summary of possible variants. However, unless one looks at the distribution of such variants with regard to context, there will be little to explain the employment of those described patterns. As Halliday (1978) suggested in his influential monograph, language is a social semiotic where variation is provoked by social context. "The more specifically we can characterize the context of the situation, the more specifically we can predict the properties of a text in this situation" (Halliday and Hasan 1976: 22). To turn this around, each text exhibits a specific selection of features which answer to given communicative demands and functions.

Van Dijk (1997: 1) defined *discourse* as "a form of language use", realized and dependent on three interrelated dimensions: language use, social interaction, and communication of beliefs. These are the levels of higher-order operations of language (McCarthy and Carter 1994: 38),[2] which cause lower-order forms of language to convey meaning in a required manner. Grammar, in its widest sense, therefore, emerges from use, and use, in turn, is related to linguistic function. The discourse-functional approach to language puts forward that "grammar originates in recurrent patterns in discourse, and these patterns continually shape it" (Cumming and Ono 1997: 112). It is therefore advisable to step outside the traditional Aristotelian concept of a grammatical category, to which a given element either belongs or does not. Otherwise it will not be possible to account for the existence of functional elements which do not constitute complete phrasal units (as in the case of material studied in this book) and which cannot be easily classified into grammatical categories (Chapter 9). In the discourse-functional approach, the system of language "does not have or need *one underlying theoretical order* because it is *constantly creating multiple modes of practical order wherever discourse takes place*" (de Beaugrande 1997: 40, emphasis in original). The constant need for more and more complicated rules for recovering structures and meaning in purely formal analyses of language arises because of this theoretical disconnection. Instead of theorizing on the basis of abstract models, discourse analysts and functional linguists favour corpora searches, in addition to other sources of data. Properly designed corpora searches enable the researcher to observe language in actual use. Complemented with a scrutiny of external context, they allow the study of emerging patterns in relation to non-linguistic parameters (section 3.7).

3.3. Discourse and Text in a Functional Perspective

3.3.1. DEFINING DISCOURSE AND TEXT

As an interdisciplinary concept, *discourse* has been defined in various ways, depending on a particular focus: structural, functional, anthropological, or social. Bhatia perceives discourse as "*language use* in institutional, professional or more general social contexts" (2004: 3, emphasis in original) and identifies four strands in discourse analysis: discourse as text, discourse as genre, discourse as professional practice, and discourse as social practice. Thus, some scholars equate *discourse* and *text* (Stubbs 1996; Trosborg 1997b: 4), considering them to be two rather blurry and often overlapping categories which, in a structural hierarchy, are placed above the level of sentence (Trudgill 2003; Chafe 2003; Crystal 2003). I support Widdowson's criticism (2004: 1–16) of this simplification, however. A text is a linguistic communicative event, regardless of its size or formal complexity, while discourse provides a contextual framework for its analysis.[3] When we accept this understanding of discourse, the perspectives of genre, professional practice, and social practice become three interrelated facets of a contextual framework, which shape the emerging texts. In this vein, Tomlin et al. signal the "relationship between discourse and text structure" (1997: 67). In the previous chapter, I discussed legal discourse and the situational context in which legal texts are produced. The term *text* may refer both to written and spoken communication; this investigation focuses on the features of written texts, without disregarding the mutual influences of both modes, as signalled in Chapter 2.

Text is best defined in relation to use and context. Halliday and Hasan (1976) treat text as the ultimate level of linguistic analysis but not in a structural sense. "A text is a unit of language in use [...] A text is best regarded as a SEMANTIC unit: a unit not of form but of meaning" (Halliday and Hasan 1976: 1–2, emphasis in original). Meaning is in the use—the choices made by the user depend on the situation and are meaningful. What follows from this approach is the recognition of different functions of text and its dependence on the extralinguistic conditions. A more radical view has been proposed by Hoey (1991), who rejects the structuralist approach to text altogether. He claims that just as the notion of a "sentence" is a kind of metaphor, the notion of a text is one too, and it is "overused".[4] He proposes to see text as "organized rather than structured", while patterns of text organization are "provided, not obligatory" (Hoey 1991: 29). Thus, the inventory of patterns is never complete and is subject to the creativity of the users—of the speaker or writer who creates the text and the listener or reader who perceives and understands it.

Coherence, the organization of the text stemming from its extra-textual function, and cohesion, the semantic and syntactic connectivity of linguistic elements within a text, hold the text together and make it meaningful. The terms originated in the functionalist approach. Halliday and Hasan maintain that "[c]ohesion is expressed partly through the grammar and partly through the vocabulary" (1976: 5), whereas Hoey goes one step further to suggest that "to a great extent, cohesion is the product of lexical relations (rather than grammatical ones)" (1991: 26), whereby parallelisms and lexical repetitions serve a connective function in the text (for a further development of his ideas on lexical relationships in text, see Hoey 2006). This is why the lexical bundles method becomes an apt tool for revealing the internal structure of texts (see Chapters 4 and 8 for the methodology employed in this book).

The functionalist school provides a general framework which can serve to interpret and understand the form of text with regard to its function in discourse, or, in other words, in a multifaceted contextual setting. Among text functions one finds narration, argumentation, explanation, and instruction (Kohnen 2001: 198), which, on the one hand, emerge from the way a text is structured and, on the other, determine the selection and patterning of elements within a text. This is where we can talk about *texture*, the quality of 'being a text', relying on cohesive relations, anaphoric reference, pronoun use, and establishing relations within a text. Exponents of text linguistics (Dressler 1972; de Beaugrande 1997, 2000) refer to this property as *textuality*, and apart from purely linguistic features, they mention intentionality, acceptability, informativity, and situationality (de Beaugrande 2000: 171), as well as intertextuality, which implies relations with other texts (de Beaugrande 1997: 53). The meaning and function of a text will thus be dependent on multiple extralinguistic factors, which de Beaugrande saw, perhaps pessimistically, as the source of "complicated and impenetrable formulas" (1997: 52–53) governing the creation and form of a text.

According to Halliday (1978: 31), features of text can be derived from a situational-semantic configuration on three well-defined semiotic planes of *field*, *tenor*, and *mode*: the role of a given communicative situation in context, the status of the participants in conversation, and the role of language in the exchange.[5] These three factors will influence the choice of meanings and forms to render a specific communicative function, and the dimension of such choices is referred to as *register*. The features of register can be directly linked to specific functions of a text. The *ideational* function will relate to field, the *interactional* function—to tenor, and the *textual* function—to mode (Halliday 1978: 116–120, 123). It is important to note that in this framework the ideational function covers both the direct reference to the world outside language (the *experiential* function) and the logical relations between linguistic structures, which Halliday also sees as stemming ultimately from the experience of the external world (the *logical* function) (1978: 48–49). An interesting interpretation of Halliday's model can be found in Martin (2010: 12), who talks about ideational, interactional, and textual meanings "building" field, tenor, and mode. So the relationship between register and the functional elements seems to be working both ways: the features of text depend on the situational characteristics, as much as they create, or "build", the communicative context.

3.3.2. APPLICATIONS OF HALLIDAY'S FUNCTIONS

Halliday's functional approach to linguistic patterns has had a major influence on subsequent scholarship and has lately inspired corpus-based generalizations about language use. The framework of field, tenor, and mode, translating into the ideational, interactional, and textual functions, has been applied to the study of fixed elements of discourse, also in relation to genre differences and diachronic developments in genres. Scholars have been bending this framework to suit their research questions and their specific linguistic material (see e.g. Moon 1994; Biber et al. 1999: 41–43; Biber, Conrad, and Cortes 2003, 2004; Culpeper and Kytö 2002, 2010). These adaptations have not always been successful and may point to the most important problematic issues in using this framework.[6] The remainder of this section will provide background for the categories adopted in the present study, engaging with the problems and discrepancies visible in other adaptations of Hallidayan functional categorizations.

The classification used in this book follows from the Hallidayan framework and divides the extracted recurrent strings into three basic functional groups. External circumstances in which a text is produced will be at the centre of *referential* bundles. Thus, the first functional category relates to various aspects of field but, contrary to Halliday's ideational function (1978), it does not contain the so-called logical component embedded in language structures.[7] In its interpretation of the original framework, my study is closer to Biber, Conrad, and Cortes (2003, 2004) who in this context talk about the referential function, especially regarding identification and focus, as well as time and place reference. As they put it, "[r]eferential bundles make direct reference to elements in the physical world or the textual context" (Biber, Conrad, and Cortes 2003: 79). Still, the latter aspect—the textual context—has been assigned to a separate category in the present study, in accordance with the original Hallidayan *textual* function. This second functional group includes the repetitive strings which become part of discourse in order to hold the text together, to give it cohesion and linear progression. In other words, these fragments of text relate to mode and incorporate features such as coordination, parataxis, anaphoric reference, and the like. In this regard, my study is similar to Culpeper and Kytö's (2010), who classify discoursal, narrative-related, and organizational elements of text under the textual function. Finally, the last functional category in the present study includes *interpersonal* fragments, stemming from the focus on the participants of the communicative situation, which means that the relevant repetitive strings are centred on tenor. This category corresponds to Biber, Conrad, and Cortes's (2003) interactional and stance bundles, and their subsequent reformulation as conversational and stance categories (Biber, Conrad, and Cortes 2004). The present research uses material which is not interactive in nature: it lacks question-and-answer sequences and it does not contain the context for personalized expression. However, it does contain speech-act related as well as modalizing chunks of text. The label *interpersonal* was therefore chosen to represent this category, following Culpeper and Kytö (2010) and the original delineation of this function by Halliday (1978).

It is clear that labels and categories may vary in the post-Hallidayan studies. The apparent lack of consensus in categorizing discourse functions is not only a product of scholarly progress and constant revisions of the paradigm. In fact, much of this classification is directly related to the type of texts under consideration and their purpose. As pointed out early on by Jakobson, one can "hardly find verbal messages that would fulfill only one function", while the structure of a text "depends primarily on the predominant function" (1960: 353). Some functions will be prominent in a study of dialogues and textual features of spoken discourse (Culpeper and Kytö 2010), and different ones in academic discourse (Biber, Conrad, and Cortes 2004). Moreover, the same fragment of text may often be multifunctional depending on the context, or even perform more than one function at once (Chapter 11). Different studies may then see the primary function in a subjective way.[8] Conscious of this fact, Biber, Conrad, and Cortes delimit primary functions on the basis of "the most common use" (2004: 384), in other words, the frequency of a given function. The present study also recognizes the decisive role of frequency in the extraction and classification of standardizing elements of text.

3.3.3. REGISTER IN CONTEXT

Language users have a range of formal and functional choices (the question of choice is explored, for instance, by Zwicky and Zwicky 1982: 213–214) and, consequently, a range of available registers. The question put forward by Halliday was that of what situational factors determine which linguistic features. Following on that, Conrad and Biber see register as "a cover term for any language variety defined in terms of a particular constellation of situational characteristics" (2001: 3), so it is defined extralinguistically but carries linguistic differences depending on these very situations. This is where register differs from discourse. Discourse provides an extralinguistic framework for text analysis, while register is a property of the text in use; it is its linguistic fabric which answers to particular situational demands.

In a recent textbook, Biber and Conrad (2009) present analytic tools for the study of register, genre, and style, the "fundamental varieties of language". Their account is based on a substantial body of research, completed in the last three decades, which has sought to provide a framework for the analysis and classification of registers and related phenomena. There are specialized registers (with little linguistic variation) and general ones (with more linguistic variation). They can be classified situationally (or contextually, Hymes 1974b), and linguistically (Biber 1988, 1989, 1994; for register variation, see the summary in Biber 1995). A member of a linguistic community has access to various registers, depending on the circumstances. Many scholars would thus see register as "an open-ended set of varieties (or styles) of language typical of occupational fields, such as the language of religion, the language of legal documents, the language of newspaper reporting, medical language, technical language, etc." (Trosborg 1997b: 5), stressing its reliance on extralinguistic situational characteristics. Ure (1971) was one of the first linguists to focus on lexical density in different registers, mostly for didactic purposes.[9] The sheer realization that registers may differ with regard to the number of content words, grammatical words, fillers, and so on, was a step towards correlating register features with situational requirements and pressures (such as time in spoken communication). The present work follows this tradition of associating specific lexical and structural features with different registers, concentrating on one of the most formal types of register and discourse: the language of legal documents.

What should be remembered in the discussion on register is that language users learn how to adjust their linguistic behaviour to situation. There are conventions for forming discourse and every language user varies in their textual competence. Proficiency in register differentiation varies among speakers and writers, and will depend on their background, education, familiarity with a specific linguistic situation, and possibly other personal factors. As Biber and Conrad point out, some registers are simply acquired, while others require explicit instruction (2009: 2–3). Therefore, the study of register acquisition should illuminate our understanding of register variation. In this book, register transmission is equally important. The analysis of repetitive chunks of text shows that the clerks and notaries were keeping up certain procedures, thus standardizing the formal register of legal discourse. They were also copying previous patterns and creating a specific way of phrasing their documents. Every subsequent generation of legal writers must have become familiar with the peculiarities of phraseology and text structure in order to become proficient in their work (on clerks and notaries as a discourse community, see section 7.4). The knowledge was passed on—deliberately to some extent—and our modern legal register very much stems from those earlier choices, as explorers of legal language always underline (Mellinkoff 1963; Maley 1994; Tiersma 1999; Gibbons 2003).

3.4. Genre and Text Type

Genre is perhaps the least clear of the discourse-related categories. Devitt (2004: 4) warns that "[a]t its worst, [it] is a trivial and dangerous concept" so one needs to approach it with caution. The term is newer in linguistics than in literature, where its application can be traced back to the classical Aristotelian and Socratic generic distinctions in verbal art (Frow 2006: 55–71). Its literary connotations sometimes make it difficult for the term 'genre' to be used as a clear notion in language studies. Some scholars use both *genre* and *text type* interchangeably.[10] Others (e.g. Görlach) prefer to employ the term *text type* when analysing language use and looking for a valid categorization of texts with any communicative function, be it aesthetic, informative, didactic, instructional, or argumentative (Görlach 2001, 2002, 2004). Meurman-Solin perceives *genre* as a categorization tool allowing one to "group texts... by topic... or by function... or a combination of the two" (2001: 241). Many linguists treat genre as a socio-cultural construct, which makes it dynamic and changeable, according to the communicative needs of the users (Bex 1996; Taavitsainen 2001a). Some others see genre as "a group of texts that share specific discursive features" (Gill and Whedbee 1997: 163), while for McCarthy and Carter, "genres are... staged, goal-directed language events" (1994: 26), which highlights the question of purpose, so relevant in specialized discourse texts.

In one of his earliest paper on this topic, Biber (1989) proposed to treat genre as an extralinguistic category, governed by purely non-linguistic factors. According to this approach, genres are distinguished and recognized by mature language users on the basis of cultural functions, situational employment, or literary connotations. In discourse typology, genres of various types will be "known and used as such by language users, [for instance] conversations, ads, poems", differentiated by some "common agreement" (van Dijk 1997: 7). This invokes the concept of *Erwartungshorizont*, the 'horizon of expectations' postulated by Jauss (1970) in literary criticism. The users have an idea what to expect from a given text, what a particular cultural and linguistic convention will look like, and how a specific communicative purpose will be achieved by means of this text. What follows from the 'horizon of expectations' is a certain degree of standardization and model procedures (Conklin 1998). This knowledge of and about genre models is accumulated through acculturation: we learn about the surrounding social and cultural conditions through texts, spoken and written, and develop a recognition of linguistic conventions, as well as an ability to produce them. The proficiency of doing so is governed by individual predispositions, and also by the need and access to particular communicative contexts. In every community, there are certain social events and situations which require specific linguistic usage. Such situations may be recurrent, enhancing the process of fossilizing those linguistic choices which go hand in hand with a given situation. In this context, Sandig and Seltig talk about "conventionalized or standardized solutions, that is text conventions" (1997: 145) with a particular social meaning.

Genres are conventional also for another reason: users attach labels to the models of expression for a given situation and purpose. Texts which have a specific function and have been composed according to expected patterns in a particular situation may be labelled as a recipe, a sonnet, a manual, and so forth. Such an approach agrees with Görlach (2001, 2002, 2004) who treats the existence of metalinguistic labels for individual genres (which in his nomenclature are called *text types*) as the first token of their separate character.[11] In historical linguistic studies, genre labels are needed to delineate entities which contain tokens of language change, or which undergo change. Rissanen (1996) recognized the problem of the lack of an adequate categorization system for text written in the past. He also added that "it seems impossible to create a valid all-purpose classification of texts for diachronic studies" (1996: 230–231).

Even though the same label may be applied, individual "[t]exts within particular genres can differ greatly in their linguistic characteristics.... [At the same time] different genres can be quite similar linguistically" (Biber 1989: 6). The distinction between genre and text type becomes clearer: genre is defined extralinguistically while text type is defined intralinguistically. Biber (1989) also shows why text typology is needed: by getting down to the typical features of particular text types we ensure comparability. It becomes possible to situate a text against other texts, and thus the need for more precise methodology than observation and scholarly introversion is satisfied. This approach works for synchronic studies but if text types could, indeed, be based purely on linguistic features, it would seem impossible to capture the diachronic dimension within a text type. Given the ever-changing nature of language, it is to be expected that the range of text-type features will be different for every period. Would that, in turn, suggest the existence of incompatible, diachronically unconnected text types? For the study of language change viewed diachronically at a higher level of complexity (text and discourse) the definition of text types needs revising.

Kohnen (2001) points out that text types cannot be viewed solely as a bundle of linguistic features and cannot be defined without reference to functional and situational aspects. He suggests a definition which highlights the dynamic nature of text types, viewed as a pattern of communication characterized by a specific function, context, and form. Hence, language change may operate on various levels within a text type, for instance, in syntactic patterns or lexical choices.[12] The discourse structure may change, rendering a shorter or a longer text, or a more or less formulaic one, with an alternating range of stylistic or pragmatic devices. The function and context will also be subject to change, which reflects the connection between language and its users, language and society. Kohnen's text types, while more comprehensive than Biber's and useful for accommodating the concept of language change, become too similar to the notion of genre presented above. Taavitsainen (2001a) follows with a helpful clarification of the two labels. She employs the term "genre" with reference to "inherently dynamic cultural schemata used to organize knowledge and experience through language" (2001a: 139–140), and follows Biber in defining text types according to linguistic features of texts. Thus, genres can be perceived as a certain cognitive frame which inspires the production of a specific text for a specific purpose in a given context. Genres may also possess secondary features which may not be required at a given point. What is also relevant is that genres may overlap, merge, and blend, as Taavitsainen's (2001b) discussion of medieval medical recipes clearly shows. Thus, "genres are dynamic" (Gill and Whedbee 1997: 164; Taavitsainen 2001a: 139) and changeable in nature; genres respond to the developments in the external social context and depend on its demands.

Conventions are subject to change due to social and cultural developments. Hence, genres have a diachronic dimension: some genres come and go, others change their linguistic profiles. This is where the concept of text types returns. In Taavitsainen's approach (2001a), as in Biber's, text types are defined by the (co-)occurrence of linguistic patterns in texts, which may, however, be present in different degrees. Biber moved away from the traditional division into preconceived genres and wanted to see how specific linguistic patterns, identified on the basis of statistical counts, were distributed across a multi-genre corpus, to reveal affinities between traditional divisions, as well as new text-type categories (Biber 1989 and later). The category of official documents, to which the texts analysed in the present book belong, spreads across three different text types in Biber's analysis: scientific exposition (text type 3), learned exposition (text type 4), and general narrative exposition (text type 6). Both text types 3 and 4 are "markedly non-narrative (dimension 2) and nonpersuasive (dimension 4), and both are extremely informational in production (dimension 1) and explicit in reference (dimension 3). On dimension 5, both clusters are characterized by an abstract style" (Biber 1989: 27). The documents studied in this book follow the same tendencies.

It is necessary to recognize the link between the repetitive nature of a given social task or situation and a textual, linguistic pattern which becomes associated with it. I will call this text-type standardization (section 3.5) and will be looking for symptoms of such a process in Part Three of this book. How to establish what is linguistically typical? Corpus methodology provides answers to this question (section 3.7). From a genre point of view, text-type standardization will happen within a particular constellation of extralinguistic conditions, so one can also speak about genre standardization. Devitt devotes a whole chapter to the normative character of genres and insists that genres at the same time "act as standards and permit variation" (2004: 89). She also reminds the reader about the changeable, diachronic nature of genres. In the same vein, Meurman-Solin (2001: 244) advises that especially when working with historical corpora, a given genre has to be redefined from a functional, social, and cultural perspective. Sub-variables, some of them participant-related (such as age, sex, occupation), some of them text-related (such as handwriting versus print, register, text transmission, and cultural background) will be important in the redefining process (see section 8.2 on the generic classification of the database used in this study).

Genre is a factor "conditioning processes of linguistic convergence and divergence in an environment of various coexisting norms, whether local, regional or national" (Meurman-Solin 2001: 241). What follows is that, in view of standardization as a process of extracting prestigious and efficient variants from an array of existing and competing forms, genre influences the choice of such forms for standardization purposes. This links to Devitt's idea that "[b]oth genres and language standards...regularize and standardize discourse" (2004: 142). Legal genres will be of special importance here, as they enjoy high social prestige and are often perceived as a product of a rational, educated, and principled mind. They evoke certain reverence because of their underlying tradition and power to establish and control patterns of social behaviour. As noticed by Rissanen, legal genres exhibit invariance, lack of affect, generality, and prestige, all of which are important in linguistic standardization (1999: 191). This is why it can be postulated that legal genres may play a role in language standardization in a more general sense.

3.5. Standardization in Discourse

At the end of the previous section, I hinted at two different, but related, phenomena. In terms of standardization, on the one hand, the focus may be placed on extralinguistic conditions, connected to such notions as prestige, authority, degree of intelligibility, or usefulness, thanks to which a group of language users begins to promote a type of usage characterized by these factors and slowly converges on some kind of a selected model (Milroy and Milroy [1985] 1991: 22–23). Thus, out of a variety of dialects, one is chosen and accepted as a supra-regional norm. I will call this process *language standardization*. On the other hand, standardization is an intralinguistic process of form selection, a diachronic emergence of patterns operating on all levels and in all functions of language, not necessarily at the same pace. I suggest that this should be called *linguistic standardization*. Locher and Strässler are on a similar track when they say that "Standard English is independent of pronunciation, register and style, which may have been standardized independently" (2008: 3). They do not, unfortunately, draw a conceptual distinction between the two aspects of standardization. In a way, this distinction has been reflected in a separate discussion of standardization of English from "an institutional perspective" by Nevalainen and Tieken-Boon van Ostade (2006), who then move on to "focussed language" on different levels of analysis.

By separating these two related phenomena more clearly, we avoid the problem which Milroy and Milroy faced: how to talk about standard language when it is only orthography that seems to be standardized in Present-Day English ([1985] 1991: 22). To use an example from the history of English, we may observe relatively slow standardization of spelling in the Middle English period as opposed to a much quicker standardization of morphological markers for the plural, which for some time was dialectally conditioned. Even when the same plural marker {S} was already levelled out across nominal paradigms and became the standard regular inflection, it was still spelled in a multitude of ways, reflecting the dialectal pronunciation and/or spelling conventions (McIntosh, Samuels, and Benskin 1986: 465, 521). It was only after the introduction of printing that the spelling conventions associated with the most prestigious dialect spread across England. This is where the two aspects of standardization meet: extralinguistic conditions promote the south-east Midlands dialect, which, in turn, develops standardizing patterns of spelling, pronunciation, and grammar.

The need for a thorough discussion of standardization of the English language is becoming more and more pronounced. In the two-volume handbook of *English Historical Linguistics* (Bergs and Brinton 2012), there are separate chapters on standardization in invididual periods, and there is a seven-chapter section on the socio-historical aspects of the emergence of Standard English. Language standardization in Scotland has also been addressed by several studies (e.g. Leith 1997; Dossena 2003; Görlach 2004; Bugaj 2004a; Millar 2005); however, linguistic standardization in Scotland has not been so thoroughly reviewed. The pioneering study by Devitt (1989) provides a very informative account of the chronological and textual patterns of convergence on a common morphological and syntactic norm, but the argument concentrates on the period when "to standardize" meant "to anglicize" (1560–1630). For earlier periods, an in-depth, comprehensive study of linguistic standardization in Scots has not been attempted so far. Middle Scots has been a rich resource for the study of dialectal variation on various linguistic levels (Aitken 1971; McIntosh 1978; Romaine 1982; Johnston 1997; Meurman-Solin 1997; Williamson 2000, 2002a). Uniformization of patterns, however, has attracted little interest and this book aims to follow one of the potential threads of investigation.

Linguistic standardization, whereby convergence on a norm happens on a particular level of analysis, is diachronic in nature. In fact, any discussion of standardization will have to incorporate diachronic considerations because standardization is a process: it has a duration in time and its effects can therefore be observed gradually. The levels which usually constitute the focus of standardization studies, such as spelling, morphology, or syntactic structures, will not be discussed here. Instead, standardization will be observed on a more general level of linguistic functional complexity—on the level of text (section 3.3.1).

Arguably, writing is a more powerful medium of standardization than speech. Ong (2002: 104ff.) discusses the written culture of *grapholects*,[14] which allows the elevation of a selected written dialect to a supra-regional position. In the earliest history of writing in Scots, it would be difficult to look for centres of prestige rooted in the production of texts. The court was peripatetic and not one but four burghs enjoyed a status higher than the others (Chapter 5). In time, the balance of power shifted to Edinburgh, which became the Lowland centre of regional and national administration, the largest and most prosperous burgh, the seat of the court and the home of the printing press in Scotland. It was Edinburgh which became the hub of linguistic standardization through the dissemination of texts. As pointed out by Millar (2005: 89), the Edinburgh variety was associated with a standardizing spelling system and "prescriptive norms for the language". By the same token, the grapholects of Edinburgh scribes and clerks may well have been copied in the process of transmission of textual conventions. The diatopic patterns emerging from the EdHeW data confirm these observations and are discussed in detail in Chapter 12.

The form of the text depends on its contents, purpose, and external context. Extralinguistic circumstances often require the replicability of communicative patterns; in other words, they force linguistic communities to form their discourse according to rules and conventions. The latter are a part of tradition, as they emerge in time on the basis of frequent and repeated usage. Text standardization can be seen as a consequence of these communicative demands. Standard patterns are recognizable, replicable, and predictable, and they ensure that the same communicative task will always be carried out with equal effect and force. Specialized discourse displays standardization on the level of text to a great degree. Gotti (2012) notes that "[t]extual standardization occurs in all disciplinary fields but it is stronger in legal genres, particularly when a text is not free-standing but is an adaptation of an earlier text." Legal texts standardize because of this cumulative effect, which is related to textual transmission in a professional community of practice. When the language involved in text production is the carrier of action, also the appropriate formulation of the text will determine its force. This leads to the well-formedness (or not) of a given text, and wherever there is an issue of well-formedness or correctness, standardization is implied. Bazerman draws attention to "regularized genres and features of language as part of the rise of regularized social systems of practice" (1990: 81) in the context of scientific discourse. Taavitsainen (2001b) considers the levels of textual standardization in remedy books and surgical treatises, where the first genre is more standardized in format and language choices because it had a more utilitarian nature. Frade aptly summarizes the role of standardization in legal discourse, on the basis of contracts: "most of the operative clauses in contracts are the same irrespective of their labels. In fact, most forms of contract being used nowadays are remarkably similar. The standardization of contracts seems to follow the current attempts of states and organizations to unify and harmonize legal rules" (2007: 49–50). Even though in the medieval and early modern period states and organizations did not overtly intervene in the creation of standardized forms of legal discourse, some degree of institutionalization of textual practice was certainly present. Part Two of the book sheds light onto the external context for the creation of legal and administrative texts in medieval Scotland. In these texts, standardizing patterns were emerging very clearly, as the analysis of texts in Part Three will demonstrate in more detail.

3.6. Networks and Communities

Historical linguists have been working with the concept of *social networks*, adapted from Milroy's present-day sociolinguistic study (1980) of Belfast English. Social networks are based on individual contacts between language users; they are "personal communities which provide... a framework for solving the problems of... day-to-day existence" (Milroy 2000: 218). Social networks are built by means of personal ties, varied in quantity, kind, and strength as they may be. It transpires that the strength of social networks is conducive to different kind of changes in language use; strong ties in social networks allow less variation and innovation than loose ties which create better conditions for language change (Milroy and Milroy 1985, Milroy 2000: 218). In order to match it to historical data, the applicability of networks should be extended to the medium of writing, not necessarily speech, which encapsulates the social dynamics in a different way (see the recent volume on the written word as linguistic evidence, Hickey 2010). Indeed, Nevalainen (2000), Fitzmaurice (2000), and Bergs (2000) tested this model on historical written data, stressing the importance of meticulous investigations into the nature of society and extralinguistic conditions at a given point in time.

In this book, the extralinguistic conditions for text production and the profiles of the potential authors are given adequate space in Part Two, which works as a background for the linguistic analyses of emerging patterns in Part Three. Nevertheless, caution is needed with regard to the conditions of text compilation and the genre under scrutiny: the same person may write letters choosing different verbiage and syntax than when writing a petition or pamphlet. One should not forget about the role of manuals, formularies, and genre traditions which provide the language user, the writer, with a toolkit of linguistic choices (see Bergs's comments on the formulaic use of the relative pronoun *whom* by the Pastons, 2000: 245–246). Social factors are therefore not the sole cause of linguistic choices. In the context of Scottish legal and administrative records, it would be difficult to extract individual linguistic characteristics of the text authors and correlate them with social factors. Perhaps on a smaller scale, one could attempt a social network analysis of the Edinburgh court scriptoria, which seem to emerge as a source of norms in the Middle Scots period (Chapter 12). However, to explain the textual standardization in formal discourse, one must take the pragmatic and functional aspects into account.

So far, the discussion in this section has concentrated on *a* user of language who is ready to fulfil communicative goals by adjusting the linguistic production to the functional requirements of the context. In specialized language use, this anonymous general user becomes more defined—he or she belongs to a discourse community. To complement the established concept of *speech community* (Labov 1972b), Swales proposed *discourse community* for three reasons: first, communication does not only happen through the spoken medium;[15] second, the linguistic behaviour of a community may be dictated by discoursal reasons, and not only by social variables; and third, the membership in both types of community relies on different criteria (1990: 24).[16] The relationship between the community and discourse is a two-way traffic. The community is specified by the kind of discourse in which it engages. As Bazerman put it in his discussion of scientific discourse communities, "a community constitutes itself in developing its modes of regular discourse" (1988: 79). So, on the one hand, a community is built because certain discourse goals are to be fulfilled, and at the same time this community constructs texts which will fulfil these goals. Stygall (1991: 235) argued that modern lawyers constitute a discourse community because they "continue to write what ordinary readers consider unreadable texts".

Swales proposed six defining characteristics of a discourse community: "there are common goals, participatory mechanisms, information exchange, community specific genres, a highly specialized terminology and a high general level of expertise" (1990: 29). I conceive of the medieval and early modern Scottish burgh as a discourse community in itself, while the legal professionals constructing texts will constitute a community of practice within it. Relatively compact in terms of population (section 6.3.1), the burghs had clear common goals—financial, representational, or organizational. Individual exchanges within a burgh happened on a daily basis between the inhabitants representing various social groups (Sanderson 2002: 178). Collective communications were carried out in a specially designed manner, with the help of a special official, the town-crier, whose job had its sources in the earlier oral practices (Chapters 2 and 6). The burgh community had its own participatory mechanisms and a strong sense of identity, enhanced through formal political and social representation and activity. From an economic point of view, it acted as a corporate entity (Chapters 5 and 6). Members of the community would engage in the exchange and transmission of information, becoming active participants of legal affairs, transactions, agreements, as well as taking part in burgh court and burgh council sessions. The textual outcome of this engagement would be shaped by specific linguistic patterns within specific genre conventions, fulfilling at the same time the requirement for discourse-specific lexis. The final criterion put forward by Swales (1990) has to do with expert knowledge and community membership. Here, I would contend that burgesses must have been well aware of their roles and obligations within the burgh. The most specialized sub-community would be the professionals composing legal and administrative texts—notaries and burgh scribes (section 7.4; also Williamson 2002b). They can be seen as a separate *community of practice*, joined by mutual engagement and joint enterprise, and sharing a repertoire of lingustic resources (see Wenger 1998 for the concept of a community of practice; and Jucker and Kopaczyk, forthcoming, for the application of this framework to highlight the social loci of language change). Early legal professionals worked in an organized and hierarchical community towards a common public goal: to witness and record legal proceedings. Not only did notaries and scribes shape, preserve, and transmit legal and administrative records, but they were also marked out by such external tokens of appearance as a black robe, a round *biretta*, and a clean shave (Symms 1993: xiii; see also section 7.4, and Kopaczyk, forthcoming).[17]

In the early urban context, the important factor which brought the burgesses together was their involvement in formal discourse through specific written genres. As argued above, notaries and scribes in particular can be perceived as being linked through the medium of writing and through legal discourse: "inherited, borrowed or recontextualized" (Meurman-Solin 2004a: 28). They also provided such links for the community. Other burgesses were not only actors in formal dealings on the local legal stage (Chapters 6 and 7). At the same time, they constituted an audience for the official communication through texts, and as such can be described as an *interpretive community*, or *text community*. The idea of interpretive community, advanced by Stanley E. Fish (1976) within critical literary studies, implies that a group of readers construct the text in a shared manner. It could be extended to the burgh context: formal affairs were carried out through text and interpreted by the community and this is how the texts composed by notaries and clerks had an impact on everyone's lives. As a consequence, the community of the burgh used legal and administrative texts in the creation of a collective memory and in identity formation, which constituted the necessary framework for what Butcher describes as "processes of self-replication and transformation" (2004: 157).[18]

Within the functional paradigm, the background of the community's dealings will constitute the field, but it is the tenor which constitutes the plane where the relationships between the community members come to the fore in a communicative situation. Tenor will depend on the social characteristics of the participants, their power relations, status, and social function. These characteristics, in turn, will influence the realization of a given participant relationship, for instance, the author–addressee relationship. The discourse community paradigm suits the present investigation better than a purely socio-historical approach, as the specialized character of communication imposes specific requirements on language users. Of course, discourse features depend on the social and historical factors, too (as discussed further in Part Two), but the functional dimension of text production should be treated as another necessary drive behind linguistic choices.

3.7. Discourse of the Past: Corpus Approaches

Modern corpus linguistics provides tools to establish what typifies a given type of text (for a recent discussion of how corpus studies inform discourse studies, and vice versa, see Virtanen 2009). Before vast electronic corpora, some inquiries could not be conducted for technical reasons. Halliday and Hasan have captured that situation aptly: "it still seems as if linguistics has all this time been at about that point in its development where physics was in the sixteenth century, before technology made it possible to carry out systematic experiments" (2000: 201). Today such systematic experiments, or rather systematic inquiries, are conducted on large repositories of searchable text with the help of automatized queries. Halliday and Hasan (2000) point out, however, that the searches alone will be just the first step in the discovery of how texts work. "The new freedom that comes with access to large quantities of data will become a truly democratic force only to the extent that the data are matched by a socially accountable theory of semiotic systems and processes" (2000: 209). This is why the interpretation of counts should be firmly set in a wider functional framework, making connections between the form of language and its employment for a specific purpose or effect.

Corpus methodology is constantly evolving. First of all, corpus linguists focus either on a selected linguistic feature and search for its distribution in the material, or they can concentrate on a specific variety or text type and study the association patterns and co-occurrence of various features (see e.g. Biber, Conrad, and Reppen 1998: 5). Some such queries are purely quantitative and descriptive and provide valuable summary or a reference point for other studies. They situate the feature or text under scrutiny against the rest of linguistic production. However, in order to answer the question why a specific text is structured the way it is, one should embark on a qualitative analysis. In this book, the functional framework is treated as a source of potential explanations for the quantitative findings (Part Three). For many, this is the way to marry formalism and functionalism in search of satisfactory results (e.g. Biber et al. 1999; Cortes 2002; Biber, Conrad, and Cortes 2003; Biber 2004; Cortes 2004; Biber, Conrad, and Cortes 2004; Wang 2005; Goźdź-Roszkowski 2006a, 2006b, 2011; Biber and Barbieri 2007; Tracy-Ventura, Biber, and Cortes 2007; Culpeper and Kytö 2010).

Historical linguistic investigations should recognize the "bad data problem", formulated by Labov, who drew attention to the fact that historical textual material is "produced by a series of historical accidents" (1972a: 100), which, in his view, means that the researcher is not able to control the data. What is more, Labov insists that "given the imperfect character of historical records, it seems inevitable that we must rely on present data to interpret them" (1972a: 101) and offers the uniformitarian principle as a methodological link between past and present linguistic processes. I agree with Romaine's critique of this standpoint (1982: 121–126), where she defends the validity of written records for a historical investigation not only into possible spoken linguistic patterns but also into written language features in their own right. The question of corpus design, be it in an electronic or any other format, is as valid for historical texts as it is for modern corpus research. It is also important to steer away from the trap of circularity, as Sinclair (2004) and Butler (2004) point out. The choice of texts for a corpus should not rely on their linguistic features—there would be little surprise if a study found a particular feature in a collection of texts which, indeed, contains this feature—but rather on extralinguistic factors.

Rissanen (2000) and, more recently, Rissanen (2008), Claridge (2008), Curzan 2009, and Kytö (2010, 2012) offer a comprehensive introduction into how corpus research has enabled historical linguists to build robust searches and answer complex questions, and provide a description of all major historical corpora, their scope and methodology of compilation. Some attention is also paid to non-English historical corpora, especially by Claridge (2008: 243ff.). Historical Scots corpora are given space, too, notably in the multi-genre *Helsinki Corpus of Older Scots* (c. 1450–1700, c. 1 million words, Meurman-Solin 1993) and the regionally varied *Edinburgh Corpus of Older Scots* (ECOS), created by Keith Williamson at the University of Edinburgh (2008). As Rissanen observed, thanks to this resource, "[o]ur knowledge of the early Scots language can be further improved" (2000: 11). With ECOS finished recently, these are the earliest available historical corpora Scots, and both have been employed in the present study. A detailed presentation of the database follows in Chapter 8.

In a historical corpus, time becomes yet another parameter of change, which thus makes it possible to trace diachronic developments of specific linguistic features. Rissanen contends that historical corpus studies should look at genre (or text type, see section 3.4) as another variable in the interpretation of data. He sketches a vivid parallel: "[i]gnoring this dynamism [the relationship between language and its users] would seem to make just as much sense as an attempt to describe a galloping horse by analysing the tissue of its muscles and measuring the distances between its hoof prints" (1996: 227). Importantly, the compiler of a diachronic corpus must answer the question whether "the same" register or genre continues to exist throughout the periods included in the corpus (Biber, Conrad, and Reppen 1998: 252), and whether the modern eye overlooks other texts which for the contemporaries would have had similar properties. One way of dealing with this problem is to employ a broad definition of a genre (or register), as is done in the Helsinki corpus family. The inclusion of a wider range of texts enables the scholar to trace intra- and inter-register developments.

Another solution is to rely on the extralinguistic parameters of production and reception of texts, and on their general theme. Scholars have thus arrived at corpora of medical texts (e.g. Taavitsainen and Pahta 2010), correspondence (e.g. Meurman-Solin 2007a), or indeed, official documents such as those used in the present study (Williamson 2008). Working on a specialized corpus is a way of dealing with the problem of genre representativeness in general corpora, as the extent of the available material may be limited by various external factors and "sample sizes tend to be small" (Hinneburg et al. 2007: 138). A specialized corpus tends to be larger than an individual sample in a balanced, representative corpus, which is a way to overcome the "bad data" limitations discussed above. When a corpus is centred on a specific area of communication and social activity, it is easier to pinpoint the core characteristics of genres within this area, and to trace their diachronic development.

Moving on to research methods, corpus studies are usage-based and text-based (Gries 2006). The most common tools are frequency lists, concordance lines (word in context), and collocations, to which lexical bundles have recently been added (for their place among other fixed elements of language, see Chapter 4). The methodology used here breaks out of the typical search for lemmas, words, or constructions which have been selected by the researcher a priori. Lexical bundles are a typical example of corpus-driven rather than corpus-based research methodology (Lewandowska-Tomaszczyk 2005: 133; Biber 2009). Corpus-driven methods have been advocated for linguistic research into discourse to avoid under- and overinterpretation (O'Halloran and Coffin 2004). The researcher does not select a structure to be looked for in the corpus, but rather draws data from the corpus by means of rationalized and automatized queries; he or she does not know exactly what the query is going to submit. Lexical bundles also serve as a particularly suitable tool for research into specialized discourse, which tends to be standardized and repetitive both in specific expressions on the level of a phrase and in the overall discourse structure. Goźdź-Roszkowski (2006a: 148) draws attention to the fact that so far fixed repetitive expressions have been given little attention in the context of the language of the law. Culpeper and Kytö recommend the lexical bundles method for historical study to avoid a certain "atomistic" bias and not to "miss much of what is going on" (2010: 141). The present study is an answer to these calls, looking at the results of automated extraction from the generically coherent corpus of historical Scots legal and administrative documents.

4

Repetition, Fixedness, and Lexical Bundles

4.1. Introduction

One of the main aims of the present project is to identify repetitive and fixed lexico-syntactic patterns in historical corpus material. Therefore, this chapter is devoted to fixedness and prefabrication in language use, with emphasis on specialized discourse settings. I explore the relationship between repetition, frequency, and fixedness in communication (section 4.2), showing how different linguistic disciplines and schools of thought can contribute to its understanding. The discussion then proceeds to specialized discourse and its requirements, reflected in the function of repetitive, formulaic strings in competent production of specialized texts. The second part of the chapter (section 4.3) will delve into the question of prefabrication, in search of a convenient conceptualization of lexical fixedness processes and products. I suggest that prefabrication should be considered an umbrella term for lexicalization and pragmaticalization. The latter term has to be redefined and extended in its scope, to include longer strings, for instance, such as those retrieved by the lexical bundle methodology. Lexical bundles, the main research tool in the present analysis, are a novelty in historical linguistics, which is why their structure and function are given a careful scrutiny (section 4.4). Finally, in section 4.5, expressions characteristic for legal discourse—binomials and multinomials—will be thoroughly examined: from motivations, through structural considerations, to their semantic interpretation. Such constructions extracted from the Scottish corpus are given full attention in Chapter 10.

4.2. Repetition and Fixedness in Language

4.2.1. GENERAL REMARKS ON REPETITION AND FIXEDNESS

One of the properties, or 'design features', of human language (Hockett 1958: 137–144) is its communicative creativity. At the base of creativity lie invariants, and the selection and combination of these (Jakobson 1971: 223–224, 243–244). This traditional Saussurian outlook, summarized and extended in Lyons (1977: 70–85), suggests that humans have the capacity to produce an infinite number of meaningful structures (productivity) thanks to an unlimited inventory of arbitrary linguistic units (arbitrariness). Chomsky would add that these infinitely diverse units are arranged in accordance with a limited number of linguistic rules (Lyons 1981: 228–235). Nevertheless, the thought that human communication may, in fact, be at least partly built out of fixed units frequently repeated in an appropriate context, has been vexing linguists for quite some time (for a useful overview of corpus-linguistic and psycholinguistic approaches to fixedness, see Butler 2005). One of the first scholars to challenge the traditional view of rule-governed assembly of items from an infinite pool was Bolinger in the 1960s, recently paraphrased by Erman and Warren (2000: 30): "we store a large number of complex items which we manipulate with comparatively simple operations." What followed from that assertion was that the complex items would often be used repetitively in an unchanged form. The observation that linguistic behaviour may be (and often is) repetitive in nature, prompted Hymes to come up with the concept of *routines*: structured in time, having "a beginning and an end, and a pattern to what comes between" (Hymes 1974a: 442).

During the 1980s, linguists identified the need to redefine the scope of creativity in language more and more sharply. Language started to be perceived as a universal encoder and a cultural encoder (Tannen 1987). The cultural encoder view is concerned with "ideas that are familiar to the language community, with how things are *commonly said* in that community" (emphasis added). Thus, the members of a cultural community are equipped with conceptual schemata, constructed linguistically out of readily recognized patterns. There came a realization that a lot of language and communication is "relatively prepatterned, repetitious and imitative" (Tannen 1987: 216), which does not mean, however, that language lacks creativity. Indeed, apt users build creatively out of prepatterned elements which they deem appropriate for a given context. The most influential input in this discussion came from Sinclair, who formulated the *idiom principle* stating that "a user has available to him a large number of semi-preconstructed phrases that constitute single choices, even though they might appear to be analysable into segments" (1991: 110). A large part of communication is produced in fixed (semi-) prefabricated chunks. The connection with repetition lies in the fact that some of these chunks are more frequent than others—they are repeated for some reason, often in exactly the same form. This observation inspired research into fixedness and formulaicity, and the realization that applied linguistic perspectives and generative theories account for idiomaticity in an inadequate manner (Hudson 1998: 68; see also Sinclair 1994, 2003; Biber, Conrad, and Cortes 2003). The recent years have also brought about an increased interest in the role of repetitive—or repeated—structures in storing, retrieving, and understanding language.[1]

Patterning and fixing occurs both in speech and in writing; however, these two modes may exhibit preference for different kinds of fixed units. Psycholinguistic research proves that fixed repetitive items are stored as single entries in mental lexicons (e.g. Wray and Perkins 2000; Wray 2002: 15–18), which makes them easier to retrieve quickly, as is often needed in oral communication under processing pressures. It is easier to retrieve at least partially fixed linguistic strategies to form a message effectively and quickly, which goes hand in hand with Sinclair's idiom principle. Culpeper and Kytö (2010: 17–18) explore this issue using speech-like, speech-based, and speech-purposed historical texts, trying to pinpoint the characteristics of dialogues of the past. They have shown that "some word combinations (e.g. I DON'T KNOW) play a special role with regard to the on-line planning pressures of *speech*, and are thus presumed to be characteristic of the spoken medium" (Culpeper and Kytö 2010: 103, emphasis added). Indeed, studies based on different methodologies have independently shown that speech is richer in fixed expressions (McCarthy 1998; Hudson 1998: 49 n. 3; Biber et al. 1999: 993–1024; Erman and Warren 2000: 50–51; Culpeper and Kytö 2010: 88–98, 402). One should remember, though, that specific communicative situations will choose specific types of fixed expressions. The frequency of multi-word fixed expressions depends on the medium, as well as genre and register. Biber, Conrad, and Cortes have noticed, for instance, that academic prose has more text organizers but conversation has more interactional fixed chunks. Similarly, idioms would rather occur more frequently in fiction than in an actual conversation (2003: 74). The language of the law can be expected to contain its own characteristic choice of fixed expressions (section 4.2.4).

The "enormity of the freezing phenomenon" has been recognized by Cooper and Ross (1975: 63). This observation concerns a multitude of fixed elements in the language: starting from reduplicative word pairs (*knock knock*, *hear hear*), through collocations and fixed phrases, to idioms and formulaic sequences (Hudson 1998; Wray 2002). Because the field can be approached from so many angles, it is necessary to narrow down the scope. In this project, the objective is to single out lexical strings—lexical bundles—which are repeated often enough to start creating a pattern in the corpus material (section 4.4). In this manner, they contribute to standardization on the level of text, delineated in section 3.5. My second focus will be on fixed and repetitive units typical for legal discourse retrieved by the lexical bundle methodology such as binomials and multinomials (section 4.5).

4.2.2. LEXICAL FIXEDNESS AND FORMULAICITY

Research into lexical fixedness has been inspired by Firth's observation that studying language from the point of view of single lexemes is inadequate as it ignores the fact that words combine to form larger structures (Culpeper and Kytö 2010: 103). In the same vein, Makkai (1978) put forward that idiomaticity is a universal property of human languages. Sinclair's idiom principle (1991) is very much a product of this approach towards language structure and function (see also Sinclair 1994, 2003). In connection with lexical fixedness, Weinert (1995: 182) proposed two basic research issues: "the best way to define and identify fixed word combinations, and analysis of the discourse functions that these word combinations perform" (Biber,

Conrad, and Cortes 2003: 71–72). These questions are still topical in modern language studies, and especially in language teaching,[2] but equally so in historical linguistics. Culpeper and Kytö admit that "[m]uch less work has been done on linguistic fixedness in early English" (2010: 103). The present book aims to fill this gap for medieval and early modern legal discourse, on the basis of records in Scots.

Problems in defining fixedness arose early. Malkiel (1959: 117) drew attention to the fact that some fixed phrases (in his case—irreversible binomials, see section 4.5.2) may, paradoxically, be coined on a one-off basis, which can be taken to mean that frequency is an arbitrary measure of fixedness (see also Wray 2002: 25–31). Hudson (1998: 26–27) agreed that recurrence and repetition are factors in fixing chunks of language but not necessarily. Some potential prefabricated expressions are hapax legomena—they occur in texts only once. Had there been some repetition, they would clearly qualify as fixed elements but since there is none, they may be suspected of being just a one-off spontaneous formation. Even with the help of corpora, no matter how vast, some formulaic sequences may not surface in adequate numbers due to the selective nature of corpora (Giammarresi 2010: 265). The issue of hapaxes in fixed phrases should thus be addressed with respect to frequency and medium, but at the same time it should be sensitive to different discourse situations. For instance, specialized discourse may create more opportunities for fixed expressions to surface (see Kopaczyk 2009 on binomial hapaxes in legal discourse).

Coming back to the definition of fixedness, Hudson suggests the following: "fixedness [is a] process whereby orthographic words group together and congeal into fixed expressions that become units in their own right" (1998: 1). There are two problems to be addressed here: the interpretation of the word *become* and the semantic scope of the word *unit*. When it comes to the first issue, one should consider the forces which fix chunks of language. The discussion below will therefore concentrate on repetition, lexicalization, and pragmaticalization. Talking about the second problem—the units of language—Hudson's criteria for fixedness were solely attributable to complete phrasal structures, hence her proposal of a word-class typology of fixed expressions (1998: 34ff.). However, the traditional Saussurian paradigmatic conceptualization of a linguistic unit needs to be refined in the context of fixed chunks of language. As shown by means of the lexical bundle methodology (Chapter 8), fixed strings of language are not always phrasal in structure and are not a product of morphological and syntactic rules. Rather, they stretch across phrase boundaries, or constitute fixed parts within a phrase, and the reasons for that should be sought in pragmatics and discourse structure, as well as in language processing.

Other criteria of fixedness, at least for phrasal units, include syntactic and morphological constraints, collocational constraints, non-salient, opaque, or figurative meaning, as well as the impossibility of analysing the parts separately (Hudson 1998: 5–10, 35). Such symptoms of fixedness may be exhibited to various degrees. In Hudson's view (1998: 35), semantic opacity is a major underlying cause of fixedness, which, however, will not explain fixedness, for instance, in the legal context. In legal texts, transparency of meaning—even exaggerated, as in the example with the orange in the closing paragraph of Chapter 2—is one of the required features. In the search for a reliable indicator of fixedness, frequency of occurrence or, in other words, the degree of discoursal repetition, proves to be the best candidate. Biber maintains that frequency alone suffices to extract multi-word formulaic sequences which can be treated as "discourse frames" (2009: 290). Indeed, earlier research (e.g. Biber et al. 1999: 38–40) provided confirmation for the key role of frequency in fixedness and formulaicity. Therefore, in this study the major focus will be placed on frequency and the immutability of form,[3] which is reflected in the employment of the lexical bundle methodology.

4.2.3. REPETITION AS A FORCE FOR FIXING: THE ROLE OF FREQUENCY

In corpus linguistics, frequency is a tool for the identification of repetitive patterns in language. As Biber, Conrad, and Cortes put it, "it identifies patterns of use that otherwise often go unnoticed by researchers" (2004: 376). Individual word frequency need not concern us here,[4] but rather the frequency of appearance of larger language chunks in an unchanged form. Stubbs (2002: 215) notices that measuring frequency in phrases is more challenging than doing the same in individual lexical items. He suggests two methods of analysing phrasal frequency: the strength of mutual attraction of pairs of content words and identification of most frequent uninterrupted word-forms. The latter method is, in fact, largely synonymous with the lexical bundle approach (section 4.4), which consists in extracting repeated uninterrupted strings of words. In order for a sequence to make it to the top of frequency counts, it must be repeated to a substantial degree and will be more prone to fixing in the same form. Although the interpretation of frequency measurements usually differs from study to study (Wray 2002: 28–31), there is no doubt that in every corpus some strings will be more frequent than others. It is true, however, that the decision as to what numeric count should be treated as indication of formulaicity is taken post hoc in an arbitrary manner (see the discussion in Chapter 8).

Frequency of use indicates the requirement for a given string to appear in a given context, as well as its appropriateness in that context. This assertion is in keeping with what Biber, Conrad, and Cortes write about lexical bundles: "Given that lexical bundles are extremely common multi-word combinations, used widely across the texts within a register, it stands to reason that they serve fundamentally important discourse functions" (2003: 73). The most frequent bundles will therefore point towards textual standardization (section 3.5; Chapters 11 and 12). If something appears frequently, it is apparently necessary in a given context. Since it is necessary, it constitutes a fundamental feature of discourse in that context.

4.2.4. REPETITION IN SPECIFIC TYPES OF DISCOURSE

Repetition happens for many a reason. On the one hand, to repeat means to lack a more exciting, genuine replacement for a structure already used, which may evoke the impression of monotony and lack of skill. On the other hand, repetition may be used on purpose for a rhetorical effect, like emphasis or drawing attention, as well as for building connections within the text. So, paradoxically, in this capacity it is a welcome attribute of literary texts. There are a number of literary tropes involving repetition, listed and commented on both by historical (Puttenham 1589: Book III) and modern criticism (Persson 1974; Cuddon and Preston [1977] 1998). One of the most efficient poetic strategies involving repetition is alliteration, widely employed in the Anglo-Saxon period (Minkova 2003). Ogura makes a connection between alliterative poetry and a synonymic disposition of Old English: "Owing to the alliterative verse style and the frequent rendering for Latin vocabulary, Old English has abundant supplies of synonyms for alliteration, variation, and repetitive word pairs" (e.g. *come and go*) (2002: 11). Alliteration and repetition are still effectively used today, for instance, in advertising (Cook 2001: 145–147). Generally speaking, repetition allows the message to attract attention to itself, which is a prime example of Jakobsonian poetic function (Jakobson 1960: 356).

Repetition has a stylistic function on three levels: lexical,[5] syntactic, and semantic[6] (Persson 1974). Lexical repetition was explored by Hoey (1991: 83) and interpreted as a means of providing cohesive links between lexical items. Admittedly, legal texts are very dense in such links (Hoey 1991: 92), partly because they ultimately stem from oral ritual performances (section 2.3). I agree with Leech (1969) and Danet (1997) that performativity is enhanced, or even achieved, by means of linguistic stylization and poeticization, where, as pointed out above, repetition plays an important part. Leech (1969: 62–72) discusses the powerful nature of parallelism in poetry and language in general, noticing the connection to rhetorical emphasis and memorability in linguistic parallelism. This "introduction of extra regularities not called for by the basic rules of language" has also been detected by Danet (1997: 28) in ritual genres based on oral interaction. Repetition of specific lexical strings may not be obligatory in other types of discourse, or it may concern a different selection of items. In genres based on oral rituals, repeated lexical strings play the role of a stylistic and functional device.

It is not only the type of discourse but also its structure which has a bearing on the employment of repetitive structures. Some parts of structure are more fixed in their form and require specific constructions to occur at a particular juncture, for example, *I grete you well* repeats in the openings of Margaret Paston's letters (Wood 2009: 199–201, 206–207), in line with the conventions of *ars dictaminis* of the period (Nevalainen 2001: 205). In court proceedings, certain formulae would be expected to open and close the interrogation, as Archer (2006) summarizes for both modern and historical courtroom; the participants would have little choice but to repeat the same lines every time they take part in this type of discourse, if they want to achieve a communicative success. In sum, it is the overall structure that repeats from one text to the next, because of the expectations of a given genre; at the same time, some parts of that structure might promote the repetition of very specific textual elements.

The applications, as well as results, of repetition will thus vary depending on the genre (Wang 2005: 508). By that token, the proficient and appropriate use of patterns expected of a genre points to the *generic competence* of the writer or speaker (Bhatia 2004: 142–152). The ability to recognize the communicative load of these patterns indicates such competence on the part of the audience. Just like the scribes who followed the rules of *ars dictaminis* in medieval correspondence, and the recipients who understood the meaning of formulaic elements in these texts, users with a high degree of generic knowledge and competence belong to a discourse community (Swales 1990) and are able to construct the text according to rules and expectations. It is a community of language users who engage in some kind of a socially and linguistically defined discourse. Among them we find members who not only construct this discourse and cooperate towards a shared communicative goal, but who are also more proficient in this role than non-members. With mechanisms of mutual engagement and learning, such groups can be perceived as communities of practice (Jucker and Kopaczyk, forthcoming; see also section 3.6).

Specialized discourse is performed in the context of social institutions, such as courts of law, banks, hospitals, or schools. Some set expressions, appearing repeatedly in this discourse in the same form, and within the same structural parts, will be connected to the institutional settings, while some will not. Pawley noticed that "it is important to separate those form-meaning pairings that have institutional status in the culture from those that do not, as well as to denote particular kinds and degrees of institutionalization" (1986: 116). Therefore, in research into repetitive constructions in specialized discourse, it is necessary to explore which of them are there because of the institutional context and which are there because communication as such often utilizes multi-word chunks, according to Sinclair's idiom principle discussed above. This distinction in data interpretation can be achieved by means of a functional analysis of the most frequently repeated strings, in which the analytic part of this book will engage.

4.3. Multi-Word Units and Prefabs

One of the outcomes of lexicalization is units of meaning composed out of more than one lexical element (cf. Brinton and Traugott 2005); in other words, lexicalization produces *multi-word units* (henceforth MWUs). They are defined by Biber et al. (1999: 58) as "a sequence of word forms which functions as a single grammatical unit". MWUs are a tangible example of what has been pointed out at the beginning of this chapter: that language is largely made up of fixed repetitive chunks. This phenomenon has been studied by lexicographers and language acquisition specialists, who have tried to categorize such chunks and account for their production and retention. There is a common recognition of the fixing forces operating in the lexicon but the actual multi-word material seems too diverse to be easily pigeonholed. Studies into lexical fixedness have concentrated on idioms, binomials and multinomials, collocations and formulae, to name a few, each group with its own distinct structural characteristics and reasons for fixing.[7]

Due to the vagueness of the term, many types of lexical combinations have entered the discussion under the label of MWUs. Erman and Warren's perspective on MWUs (2000) seems more satisfactory, as they avoid the notion of a "unit", let alone "grammatical unit". They use the term *prefab* and stress the fact that the chunks are retrieved simply as some kind of a whole, and not necessarily as sentential, clausal, or phrasal constructs. According to their definition, a prefab is "a combination of at least two words favoured by native speakers in preference to an alternative combination which could have been equivalent had there been no conventionalization" (Erman and Warren 2000: 31).[8] I would also add, had there been no standardization on the level of text (section 3.5). A competent user, able to recognize and having a preference for certain types of fixed expressions, need not only be the native speaker, but simply anybody who is competent (also through relevant education and community membership) to construct texts of a specific genre. An important observation is that identifying prefabs is intuitive to some extent and as such may vary among language users. "[W]hat is a prefab to some members of a language community need not be a prefab to all members...They are probabilistic, some more than others" (Erman and Warren 2000: 33). In this way, prefabs are unlike the traditional structural units of language—unlike phonemes or noun phrases. Between the lines another issue is signalled, namely that research into prefabs (e.g. when compiling a list of such expressions) should not be driven solely by intuition. Corpus methodology solves this problem by relying on frequency as an objective measure of formulaicity, and this is the approach taken in this book. Of course, other factors may be helpful in further delimitation of the findings. Erman and Warren (2000: 32) point towards *restricted exchangeability*, whereby "at least one member of the prefab cannot be replaced by a synonymous item without causing a change of meaning and loss of idiomaticity" (e.g. *I can't see a thing* vs. **I can't see an object*).

It is clear that the notion of prefabs is larger in scope than the notion of MWUs produced by the forces of lexicalization. Prefabrication includes lexicalization as a sub-process whose main outcome is the production of structurally complete and semantically opaque units (Lehmann 1995; Brinton and Traugott 2005).[9] In addition, I would suggest that prefabrication can be considered an umbrella term for various processes producing MWUs and other fixed chunks of language whose role in communication does not stem from their purely lexical semantics but is a product of a given context. Such chunks will be responsible for the production of a specific text-type or for conveying a particular discourse function. The process behind the formation of those fixed multi-word chunks, closely linked to discourse and context, can be called *pragmaticalization*.[10] It is another process of lexical fixing, steered by the requirements on the level of text, within specific discourse conditions. Even though they do not explicitly use the term 'pragmaticalization', Erman and Warren (2000: 36) talk about pragmatic prefabs, which typically serve as discourse markers, feedback signals, performative routines, or hedges.

In the most recent summary of scholarship on pragmaticalization, Claridge and Arnovick (2010) accept that this phenomenon is quite diverse in nature and discuss almost the same categories as Erman and Warren (2000). Their illustrative examples include *well* as a discourse marker, *pray (you)/prithee* as a politeness marker, *Jesus!* and *Gee!* as two related single-word interjections or swear words, *as it were* as a hedge, and two conversational formulae: *good-bye* and *bless you*. This list includes several pragmaticalized items made of more than one word. It may be argued that the expressions which start as more than one lexical item can be classified as prefabs. These pragmatic uses of prefabs are found in addition to purely lexical and grammatical functions. Such an understanding of pragmaticalization already expands its earliest application, which is to describe "one of two paths in the change from lexical item to function word", the other path being grammaticalization (Claridge and Arnovick 2010: 165).

By introducing MWUs and other prefabs into this discussion, the scope of pragmaticalization widens from single-word expressions and short phrases to chunks of any length whose appearance is driven by the context. The way we understand pragmaticalization depends on how we understand *context*. As argued in Chapter 3, context is a combination of extralinguistic factors which stem from a given communicative situation, the institutional and cultural setting, as well as from the social characteristics of the participants. So context will provoke and demand the implementation of specific linguistic tools, often in the form of fixed chunks of language, regardless of their length. This understanding of the mutual relationship between fixedness in language and the context-driven functions of prefabricated items makes it possible to analyse longer fixed strings from a functional perspective in specialized discourse. Figure 4.1 summarizes the mutual relationships between the three processes of interest: prefabrication, lexicalization, and pragmaticalization.

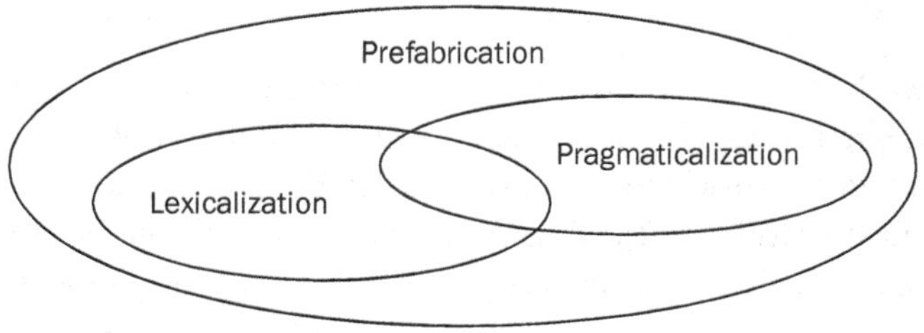

FIGURE 4.1 The processes of lexical fixedness

In the figure, I picture lexicalization and pragmaticalization as partly overlapping, which requires some explanation. The process of pragmaticalization allows for structures which also answer to the criteria of lexicalization specified above (e.g. syntactic restrictions, substitution with a single lexical unit) but at the same time their appearance in communication is regulated by discourse and context requirements. Such semi-lexical, semi-pragmatic fixed elements of discourse will be characteristic of specialized domains. An example of such a construction would be a binomial pair in legal discourse or some of the lexical bundles extracted from legal texts (section 4.4.1, Fig. 4.2).

The last point to make is that the products of lexical prefabrication can combine with each other and with other elements of language to make longer prefabs, to become part of one another or to appear in a sequence (Erman and Warren 2000: 51). Their length and syntactic structure will vary, according to specific contextual conditions, which may allow for element insertion, substitution, or deletion. Before the advent of corpus linguistics, it was virtually impossible to retrieve such constructions in a systematic manner, even from written texts, and to look at their frequency and degree of fixedness. The methodology which now allows us to retrieve such prefabricated strings from a corpus is the lexical bundles method.

One could speculate that in writing there is more time and space for linguistic creativity, so that pre-patterning and fixing of lexical strings in memory is not necessary. However, the written medium has its own pressures, from prescriptive grammar rules to genre conventions, and prefabs play an important role in creating valid written texts. Fixed expressions constitute an indispensable part of specialized discourse, such as religious texts, academic writing, scientific treatises, or, indeed, legal texts. The authors of such written texts follow rules and conventions characteristic for a given tradition, brought about—or, rather, developed—during the standardizing process operating on the level of text. Not only are prefabs simply present in written texts but they also answer to specific conditions stemming from the required textual function. In this context, let us concentrate on lexical bundles which will be extracted from Scottish medieval and early modern legal writing to investigate their role in textual standardization.

4.4. Lexical Bundles

4.4.1. DEFINING LEXICAL BUNDLES

Since the work of Douglas Biber in the 1990s, there has been a growing realization among linguists that attention should also be paid to lexical sequences which are fixed but do not answer to phrasal criteria. In the centre of this new approach is the so-called *lexical bundle*, which, according to the definition in Biber et al. (1999: 990), is a recurrent string of words in a text, regardless of its semantic or phrasal structure, repeated frequently enough in exactly the same form.[11] The lexical bundles are extracted automatically by a computer program which moves through the text using an $n + 1$ algorithm (where n is the number of words in a bundle): it starts at each word boundary, and delivers strings of words of the length n. The material thus extracted is very diverse, and in fact the majority of such strings will not be interesting to a linguist at all (see Part Three for the bundle counts in Scots data).[12] The sifting out of the 'uninteresting' strings relies on the frequency of repetition of a given bundle in the corpus. It is crucial to remember that frequency is not used to explain the patterns but to identify them. Consequently, previous studies on lexical bundles accepted frequency as the sole criterion for the identification of the repetitive strings (Biber et al. 1999; Biber, Conrad, and Cortes 2003, 2004; Goźdź-Roszkowski 2006a; Culpeper and Kytö 2010, and others). Every time, the researcher sets a cut-off point, a threshold, which would eliminate the unimportant data and bring the emergent repetitive bundles into focus (for a review of different cut-off points in selected studies, see section 8.5.3). Thus, the methodology of lexical bundles is frequency-driven and corpus-driven (rather than corpus-based; see the distinction explained in section 3.7). The reasoning behind such methods is inductive—the researcher does not set any prior expectations as to what will be found in the corpus; the data extraction is purely automatic and its objective results are then subject to interpretation. Culpeper and Kytö conclude that "[l]exical bundles, though defined and retrieved purely on the basis of frequency, clearly have non-arbitrary structural and functional characteristics" (2010: 140). These structural and functional properties constitute the main focus of the analytic chapters in this book.

Lexical bundles answer to the definition of prefabs presented above. They are used in discourse in an unchanged form, they may become available either from memory—activated while creating discourse on the spot, or—in the case of written material—ready to be copied from earlier instances of the same type of text.[13] Lexical bundles, however, are unlike idioms; idioms are formulaic, fixed in word-order, in the selection of constituents, and syntactic properties, and are relatively rare (Biber, Conrad, and Cortes 2003: 73–74). Lexical bundles appear above a strict cut-off point, adjusted to the length of the corpus and its thematic characteristics, and they are very, or substantially frequent. Because they are, by definition, built of more than one lexical item, the question arises as to whether to treat them as a subgroup of fixed expressions. Biber et al. disagree and argue that lexical bundles "[u]sually... are not fixed expressions, and it is not possible to substitute a single word for the sequence" (1999: 989). If we accept that, indeed, a fixed expression should be replaceable by a single lexical unit, than lexical bundles truly cannot be placed within this group. This, however, is a narrow understanding of fixed expressions, which requires them to be phrasal constituents with specific semantic qualities. In the wider sense adopted in this book (see the previous section), lexical bundles are also fixed because they repeat in an unchanged form with substantial frequency. It is true that they do not typically function as single units of lexical meaning, ready to be substituted with a different expression available

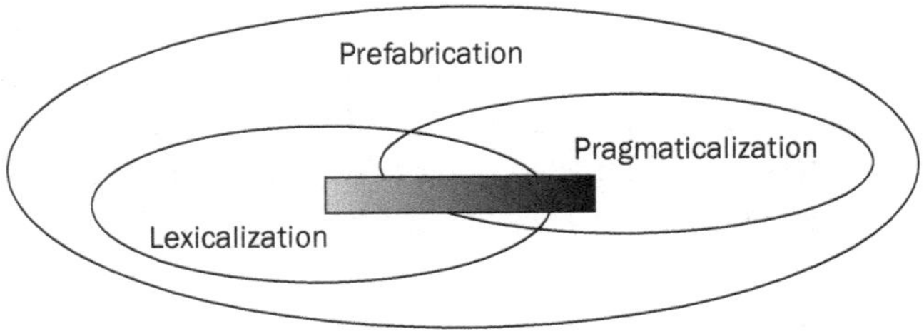

FIGURE 4.2 Lexical bundles and the processes of lexical fixedness

in the lexicon. They do, however, fulfil pragmatic roles in discourse. In specialized discourse, standardized textual practices, which are visible in lexical bundles, can often be explicitly presented in metalinguistic collections of appropriate expressions or phrases, in various "guides to style" and practical handbooks. Such prefabricated lexical strings may weigh either towards lexicalization or pragmaticalization (Fig. 4.2).

The horizontal stripe represents the place of lexical bundles on the 'map' of lexical fixedness (cf. Fig. 4.1). As the bundles come in different lengths, their semantic and structural properties will also be different. This is indicated in the figure by the gradient colour of the stripe, which means that some bundles may be more lexical and phrasal in nature (especially the shorter ones, like binomials), whereas other fixed repetitive chunks of language, extracted by the lexical bundle method, will weigh more towards creating discourse patterns and marking the text type.

In this book, lexical bundles are used in two senses: on the one hand, the term refers to a particular kind of prefabs, on the other, to the method of their extraction. Within the data pool created by means of the lexical bundle methodology, one can search for other prefabs or MWUs, for example, binomials and multinomials. This procedure has been used by Bastow (2010), who noticed recurrent binomials in the top 3- and 4-grams in US Department of Defence speeches and found out that they most often refer to people (cf. the findings in Chapter 10). Adopting this approach, researchers can carry out corpora searches without making a priori assumptions about which binomials or multinomials should appear in their material. In this way, greater precision and a more comprehensive coverage of this phenomenon may be achieved.

4.4.2. THE STRUCTURE OF LEXICAL BUNDLES

Lexical bundles are built of more than one lexical element, ordered in a fixed manner, and they perform a specific function. The lexical bundles methodology typically renders lexical strings whose structure is not complete grammatically (cf. the definition of lexical bundles above). The proportion of structurally complete bundles varies depending on the medium and genre. Biber, Conrad, and Cortes discovered that "only 15% of the lexical bundles in conversation can be regarded as complete structural units, while less than 5% of the lexical bundles in academic prose represent complete structural units" (2003: 77). On the one hand, the extracted bundles may be shorter than a phrase, indicating a grammatical frame into which the string can be expanded or which can be filled in with various items, saving the part which turns out to be a lexical bundle. Consider *of ye said*, the most formulaic 3-gram in EdHeW (section 9.3), a prepositional phrase fragment which can be followed by diverse nominal complements. In fact, some extended versions of this bundle emerge among formulaic 4-grams, for example, *of ye said landis*, *of ye said burgh*, *of ye said ser*. I address the question of bundle overlaps in more detail in Chapter 8. On the other hand, lexical bundles may spread beyond phrase boundaries, pointing towards typical complementation patterns of a given phrase, or the most typical contexts in which the phrase appears. Previous studies have shown that a bundle may begin at a phrase boundary and provide a bridge to the next structural unit, with the last words of a bundle belonging, in fact, to the next phrase or clause (Biber, Conrad, and Cortes 2003: 77). The present investigation identified multiple examples of non-phrasal bundles, such as *three estatis of*, *in that tyme and*, *sal pay for his*, which posed a challenge for a structural classification. Chapter 9 offers a solution to this problem, using the idea of *phrase fragments*. It is clear that lexical bundles reveal fixed elements of text structure which are not necessarily phrasal in nature. Had a different method been employed, a distorted picture of textual standardization would have emerged.

Attempts have been made to categorize lexical bundles grammatically, in spite of their elusive structure. Altenberg (1998) makes the following division:

(1) full clauses (independent, e.g. *thanks very much*; dependent, e.g. *as you know*),
(2) clause constituents (multiple, e.g. *that you know*; single, e.g. *sort of thing*)[14]
(3) incomplete phrases (e.g. *out of the*).

Biber, Conrad, and Cortes (2003) notice that in spoken discourse distinction should be made between question fragments and declarative clause fragments. They pay attention to the most prominent structural unit and what surrounds it in a lexical bundle, for example, a verb phrase introduced with a pronoun (e.g. *I don't know why*). Sometimes a bundle is, in fact, a frame whose elements might be exchanged but the structure stays the same, for example, preposition + determiner + sg noun + of + determiner (*at the end of the*, *as a result of the*, *in the middle of the*). Such frames may be extracted from a corpus tagged for parts of speech (PoS frames, see Stubbs 2007; Fletcher 2003/2004). This is an interesting thread to pursue, as it points to structural rather than lexical fixedness in language. At present, though, this inquiry falls beyond the scope of my research.

Grammatical characteristics are briefly discussed in what is thus far the only historical discourse study which uses the bundle methodology (Culpeper and Kytö 2010). In it, bundles from the historical corpus of dialogues are set against PDE trials and plays. The patterns emerging from the PDE material include full or partial prepositional phrases and noun phrases (*in relation to*, *a matter of*, *yes my Lord*, etc.) and full or partial verb phrases (*would have been*, *there was a*, *I don't know*[15]), which are fewer in number. In the historical corpus, however, verb phrases or their parts are more numerous and the nominal and prepositional fragments are rarer (Culpeper and Kytö 2010: 118–119). The authors interpret these differences as a shift from more interactive verbal style in dialogue representation and in oral practices to a more informational nominal style (which corroborates Biber and Finegan's findings 1989, 1992, 1997).

4.4.3. THE FUNCTION OF LEXICAL BUNDLES

The employment of repetitive, fixed lexical chunks in discourse can be best explained within the functional framework (section 3.3). The earliest attempt to categorize repetitive lexical strings functionally is that of Altenberg (1998), who correlates his functional categorization with the initially established structural types (section 4.4.2). Thus, full independent clauses could have the function of responses, epistemic tags, and metaquestions; dependent clauses—of comment clauses, indirect questions, and apposition markers. Clause elements would be employed as frames, onsets, stems, and so on, while incomplete phrases would simply be interpreted as part of collocational frameworks.

However, the most influential take on the matter of communicative functions in discourse, adopted since the late 1990s for the functional interpretation of lexical bundles, stems from the work of Halliday (1978). As discussed in Chapter 3, he distinguished the ideational, textual, and interpersonal functions, played by various elements in discourse. Since then, his framework has been modified and adapted to bring out the most characteristic features of particular communicative situations. The functional categorization out of necessity should rely on the most prominent function of a bundle. In Halliday's words, "[i]n general... we shall not find whole sentences or even smaller structures having just one function" (1973: 108). Lexical bundles may also be multifunctional, which is why their categorization may be arbitrary to a certain extent. Biber, Conrad, and Cortes admit that there is still plenty of work to do to achieve "a comprehensive analysis of discourse functions associated with recurrent word combinations, and a comparison of registers in the use of those expressions" (2003: 83). The functional interpretation adopted in this book does not claim to be exhaustive, but it attempts to be relatively simple and straightforward (section 3.3.2) to enable future comparative studies.

4.4.4. LEXICAL BUNDLES IN SPECIALIZED DISCOURSE

Research into the frequency and function of repetitive constructions has prompted Culpeper and Kytö to observe that "particular word-combinations characterize particular text-types (e.g. IN ORDER TO is particularly characteristic of Academic writing)" (2010: 103). Following the assertion made about the language of the law and, generally, about specialized discourse in the previous two chapters, the patterns of lexical combinations in specialized texts will be subject to particular communicative demands. As research into MWUs has a very strong Second Language Acquisition background and a pedagogical bent, the method of lexical bundle extraction has been used to study academic discourse (Biber, Conrad, and Cortes 2004), and more generally understood spoken and written university registers (Stubbs and Barth 2003; Biber 2006; Biber and Barbieri 2007). Other types of specialized discourse where lexical bundles (or a similar automated extraction method) have been employed include religious discourse (Youmans 1990; Shrefler 2011), fiction and *belles lettres* (Stubbs and Barth 2003), political discourse (Partington and Morley 2004), medical language in doctor–patient interactions (Crawford et al. 1999), and the present-day language of the law (Goźdź-Roszkowski 2004, 2006a, 2006b, 2011).

Certainly, practitioners of a given discipline who find themselves immersed in its discourse and who have experience of how to communicate effectively within it, will have intuitions about what is appropriate, what is frequent, and what is expected and characteristic. Experience and intuition served researchers before the advent of corpus technologies. In such seminal works as Mellinkoff's *Language of the law* (1963), one finds intuitive compilations of expressions typical of legal discourse in the eyes of the author, professor of law and an authority on the subject. Nevertheless, it would be futile to search there for comments on frequency or for exhaustive lists of examples. The expressions are a subjective selection and only some of them are given qualitative treatment and a contextual analysis (Mellinkoff 1963: 345–366). Newer works on legal discourse (Tiersma 1999; Gibbons 2003) also rely to a large extent on previous, qualitative scholarship. Goźdź-Roszkowski's studies (2004, 2006a, 2006b, 2011) are paving the way for more inductive research into legal genres. No one has yet used lexical bundles to see word by word what exactly happens in a historical legal text.

4.4.5. LEXICAL BUNDLES AND STANDARDIZATION

If one can talk about the lexical core (Lee 2001: 251), there should also be space for a core made up of longer fixed expressions recurring most frequently in a given register. Repetition of unchanged discourse elements is key on both the level of contents, as well as on the level of constructing larger textual patterns and cohesive links, which form particular register characteristics. Biber, Conrad, and Cortes notice that "local repetitions reflect the immediate topical concerns of the discourse. In contrast, lexical bundles can be regarded as the more general lexical building blocks that tend to be *used frequently by many different speakers/writers within a register*" (2003: 75, emphasis added). This is one of the symptoms of textual standardization—the acceptance, maintenance, and spread of specific patterns for a given communicative situation.

In modern grammars, especially of English, the search for a model—a linguistic standard—is no longer solely based on prescription and tradition. Thanks to the availability of vast electronic corpora of spoken and written language, scholars can extract standardized patterns—those most common, most useful, and most appropriate in a given context, genre, or medium (cf. Biber et al. 1999).[16] This enables a revolutionary shift in thinking about correctness and appropriateness in linguistic usage. The collective user of language becomes the source of norm through repetitive employment of the same, standardized patterns, changing the prescriptive mould into which standard language had always been pressed.

4.5. Binomials and Multinomials: A Feature of Legal Language

4.5.1. MOTIVATIONS FOR BINOMIALS AND MULTINOMIALS

The other group of fixed expressions built of more than one lexical item relevant in the context of legal discourse are binomials and their extended versions: multinomials. The definition of (irreversible) binomials was first offered by Malkiel: "the sequence of two words pertaining to the same form-class, placed on an identical level of syntactic hierarchy, and ordinarily connected by some kind of lexical link" (1959: 113). Norrick (1988: 73–74) pointed out the discrepancy between this definition and the examples given. A more recent understanding of the term says more about the relationship between the constituents of a binomial (or multinomial). Bhatia defines binomials and multinomials in the following manner: "a sequence of two or more words or phrases belonging to the same grammatical category having some semantic relationship and joined by some syntactic device such as 'and' or 'or'" (1993: 108). He cites some typical examples, mostly from legal language, of single-word binomials, such as *signed and delivered, act and omission, sold or transferred*, and phrasal coordination: *consists of or includes, in whole and in part, the freehold conveyed or long lease granted*. In binomials, two elements from the same grammatical category are coordinated, whereas in multinomials one or more coordinated elements will be added (for a focus on multinomials, see section 4.5.4 below).[17]

Gustafsson remarked on the ubiquity of binomials in prose texts and, more generally, in modern language (1976: 623). She considered them a frequent type of construction, but noticed that the same combination rarely gets repeated. In fact, the vast majority were hapaxes and those repeated "were due to the subject matter of that particular text" (Gustafsson 1976: 625). Corpus inquiries into binomials confirmed this observation (Benor and Levy 2006). In the *LGSWE* corpus, binomials turned out to be a rather rare construction (Biber et al. 1999: 1030–1036): the highest frequency threshold was 40 items per million words. However, the same corpus showed discrepancies in the frequency of binomials with regard to the medium: speech versus writing. In view of these contradictory findings, it is necessary to explore the motivations for binomials and multinomials in different communicative settings.

The stylistic value of repetitive structures was recognized and exploited by literary traditions. As signalled in section 4.2.4, in the poetic function of language alliteration comes to the fore. Malkiel (1959: 122) observed that alliteration has "a powerful welding effect" on the lexical coordinated pair, thus increasing its "strength and appeal". It seems that Germanic languages make use of this feature to a larger extent than other languages, and that consonants are most productive in such patterns (Malkiel 1959: 123–124; see also Lambrecht (1984) for binomials in German). In Old English poetry, which initially was only oral, the repetition of the same sound at the beginning of words within a line often resulted in alliterative coordinated pairs, for example, *wanode ond wyrde* 'diminished and injured' in *Beowulf* (Kendall 1991: 110). The production of such pairs may thus be seen as a result of the stylistic pressures of alliteration, as well as the mnemonic aid for the oral transmission of text. The ritualistic aspect is present here, too. In Anglo-Saxon curses, binomials feature as a mnemonic device but at the same time they added solemnity to the utterance (Danet and Bogoch 1992: 152–154; see also Hiltunen 1990: 25–26). Minkova (2003: 41) has observed that many verses in Old English alliterative poetry are in fact complete structural units with a formulaic status, while their formulaicity is most likely to stem from matching onsets, a tradition which continued throughout the Middle English period in literature and in everyday language (2003: 80–81). An interesting cultural phenomenon can be observed in early Germanic societies, whereby the names of siblings often produced alliterative pairs, formulaic and multinomial in nature, for example, *Ohthere* and *Onela*, *Heorogar*, *Hrothgar*, or *Halga*, *Eanmund* and *Eadgils* (Minkova 2003: 81). To the question of why alliterative phrases stayed in language, Minkova answers that the decisive factors were the continuity of verse tradition, lexical heritage, linguistic naturalness, and psycholinguistic appeal. The last two reasons are supported by other studies concentrating on phonological motivations in binomials, which also point towards the general perceptual preference for alliterative coordination (Wang 2005). Interestingly, Kendall (1991: 112–115) noticed several examples of word pairs in *Beowulf* which did not answer to the alliterative pattern. The driving force behind these pairs is rhyme, for example, *sæla ond mæla* 'seals and meals', or semantic reasons, for example, *dæges ond nihtes* 'days and nights'. The discussion below, and in Chapter 10, pays attention to these motivations, too.

In rhetoric, the figure of speech which emphasizes a single concept by means of relexicalized repetition is known as *hendiadys*, or "two for one". Employed for a rhetorical effect, for instance, by Shakespeare's plays, such expressions open up multiple interpretations, making comprehension more challenging. Hamlet speaks of "the book and volume of my brain", which may be understood as 'the expanse of my brain', or as 'the book-like volume', or as 'the big book of my mind' (Shapiro 2005: 287–288). It is no surprise that binomials and multinomials were noticed quite early by scholars looking into the properties of speech. Having originated in the oral, ritualistic practices of early communities, the language of the law immediately found its way into binomial studies. Koskenniemi noticed the contrast between the stylistic, rhetorical use of binomials in literature and their more utilitarian character in specialized legal discourse. "In legal language a double expression is generally employed for the sake of precision and not merely for rhetorical emphasis" (1968: 78). She was of the opinion that one of the core features of legal language was clarity and comprehensive reference, so that seemingly superfluous synonyms actually added to the comprehension of a given text. Gustafsson estimated that binomials are over five times more frequent in legal texts than in other prose genres (1984: 125) and also suggested that in legal contexts binomials offer true semantic complementation (1984: 133–134). Binomials may also be perceived as an icon and index of the authoritative character of legal language, and they may enhance its performative force.[18] Scholars typically consider them to be an important ingredient of the language of the law (cf. Bhatia 1993: 108; Hiltunen 1990: 55; Tiersma 1999: 31–32, 61–65).

Mellinkoff was the first to study coordinated structures in the context of legal vocabulary enrichment, especially from French and Latin sources (1963: 60–135). He was rather dismissive of these constructions, classifying them as mannerisms, and called the employment of multinomial strings "a worthless doubling" of synonyms (1963: 349). At the same time, Mellinkoff admitted that this usage "may have been once rationalized as necessary translation" (1963: 120). Thus, it seems that the foremost reason why such coordinated phrases appeared at all was linked to the need to translate a legal concept from the language of the conqueror and administrator (French) into the native Anglo-Saxon tongue (or the other way around). Charrow, Crandall, and Charrow (1982: 179–180) notice, for instance, that in the case of *give, devise, and bequeath* the native *give* would suffice because it covers all the meanings present in the phrase. Mattila (2012) uses binomials such as *acknowledge and confess* or *will and testament* to illustrate the translational motivations for what he calls "synonymy in legal terminology".

Similarly, the 'translation' hypothesis is employed to account for Latin/vernacular pairs, bringing the sophisticated Latin legal jargon closer to its inadequately educated user,[19] as in *legal and lawful*, *giver and donor*, *peace and quiet*. Even though Mellinkoff advocated keeping some of these combinations in legal language for clarity's sake (1963: 345–349), he was generally in favour of their elimination, for "the language of the law as customarily written uses too many words" (1963: 25). Textual fixedness enhanced by printing was to blame, too. For Craies, lawyers "were encouraged to prolixity by the invention of printing, and *diluted their native language* by that cautious use of synonyms which is the most common characteristics of deeds and statutes" (Craies 1971: 22, cited in Janigová 2008: 82, emphasis added). Regardless of the alleged translation value of the pairs, they were (and still are)[20] condemned as an unnecessary burden in utilitarian texts.

In the vein of the 'translation' hypothesis, Jumpertz-Schwab (2000) checked sixteenth-century translations of Latin prose texts into Scots for phrases and expressions motivated or unmotivated by Latin originals. The collected examples show that the Latin source may not contain a binomial where in the translation such a construction does appear. The vernacular version consists of a direct importation of the Latin word, followed by a coordinated native element (which may, in fact, be an earlier borrowing), for example, Sc *þe cosmography & Tabellis of Ptolemy* vs. L *Cosmographia*, Sc *in allegories & dark sentences* vs. L *tanta allegoriarum*, Sc *mechanical or handy craftis* vs. L *mechanicas artes* (Jumpertz-Schwab 2000: 84–107). This would support the 'translation' hypothesis, where a binomial is created to facilitate the understanding of an unfamiliar term. More importantly, however, in the majority of cases binomials were used in the Scots translations without any underlying Latin prompt or pattern, which would indicate that binomials are motivated by other factors than the purely etymological.

When it comes to legal texts in Scots, inspired by Latin originals, one notices a close linguistic interplay in the multi-word coordinated strings. In medieval burgh laws, first available only in Latin as *Leges Quatuor Burgorum* (section 7.3.1), and then, successively, in more and more numerous Scots versions, around 20% of all calques (the literal word-by-word translations of Latin) are in fact binomials or multinomials (Kopaczyk, 2011b: 7–8). Examples of calqued binomials include:

	Latin	Scots
(1)	*sustentari et vestiri*	*sustenyt and cled*
(2)	*prepositus ballivus vel bedellus*	*aldirman bailye na beddel*
(3)	*lapidem et pondus*	*stane and punde*
(4)	*fideles et bone fame*	*lele and of gud fame*

In the EdHeW corpus, these specific pairs have not been found, however some of their lexical ingredients do form other binomials, for example, *aldirman and balzeis*, *erd and stan*, or *lele and trew* (section 10.2). Interestingly, the word order in the coordinated pairs may be swapped, as in the following examples from the *Leges*: L *capere nec attachiare*—Sc *chace na tak*, L *ponderando vel mesurando*—Sc *mesurande or weyande*, L *dare vel vendere*—Sc *sell or geyff* (for more discussion of word order in binomials, see section 4.5.2 below).

On closer inspection, though, the relationship of Scots vernacular legal texts with their Latin predecessors becomes less straightforward. There are two ways in which binomial and multinomial constructions could have differed in both language versions. First, Latin coordinated phrases need not have been rendered in the same manner in Scots, for example, L *utlagus domini regis... vel proditor regis*—Sc *the kyngis traytour*. The second, more pronounced trend was to expand Latin with a native formula[21] as in:

(5) L *capitali domo*
Sc *the hevyd hous of law and resoune*

(6) L *nec posset nec vellet*
Sc *walde nocht or for poverte is nocht of power*

(7) L *vendent*
Sc *byis and sellis*

The most unexpected influence, however, seems to have been captured in the Latin version of the laws, which clearly contain latinized vernacular binomials from earlier oral patterns. Examples in the *Leges* include (Kopaczyk 2011b: 12):

	Latin	Scots
(8)	*blaa et blodi*	*blaa and blodi*
(9)	*loth et cavyl*	*lot and cavyll*
(10)	*wrang et unlaw*	*wrang and unlàuch*

The presence of Scots binomials in the Latin text of the *Leges* affirms the original oral character of vernacular laws in Scotland. The transactions and rituals must have been carried out initially in the language of the people,[22] only to be captured in the elevated medium of Latin when medieval Europe began institutionalizing the law. The borrowing of the Scots concept of *wrang* 'wrongful doing' into the Latin text confirms the typically Scottish perspective on breaking the law; as explained in section 7.2.3, the concept of *wrang* was central to medieval Scots law, while linguistic evidence suggests its lack in contemporary legal Latin.

The above findings help to see binomials and multinomials as a special linguistic feature which adds effectiveness to oral ritual language, captured subsequently in writing. These are not superfluous synonyms, although in regular, non-ritualistic discourse they would not be required for successful communication. The language of the law, however, needs ritualization and formulae to work as an effective tool to shape reality. Danet (1997) encountered over 100 different binomials in her work on the language of Anglo-Saxon wills, four per will on average.[23] Salmi-Tolonen found examples of binomials in the textual function: *if and in so far as* (1994: 23), as did Heffer (2003: 237), in "You do not convict *unless and until* you are sure of guilt", in the summing-up of a case by the judge. Studying Early Modern English statutes and similar Scots material for comparative purposes, Dossena (2001) concludes that coordinated adverbs, such as *really and truly*, *wittingly, willinglie and of purpose*, *deceytfullye or unlaufullye*, have an intensifying modal power because of the repetition. Therefore, they "contribute to the definition of the illocutionary and perlocutionary force of individual propositions" (Dossena 2001: 126). It follows that the synonyms are not redundant. The effect is enhanced even further by stacking coordinated adverbs and verbs in close proximity, as in *wittingly and willingly aiding and assisting thereunto* (Dossena 2001: 121). The same tendency to produce strings of multiple synonymous expressions will emerge in EdHeW (section 10.3.2).[24]

Earlier research into binomials opened intriguing directions of inquiry: from psycholinguistic motivations, connected with the presence of repetition and parallelism in language in general (section 4.2), through aiding comprehension, sustaining original Latin patterns, and preserving accuracy, to stylistic word play and phonological motivations (see section 4.5.2 below). Due to methodological discrepancies—small text samples, little support in numerical evidence, intuitive claims—these paths need to be explored again with the use of modern tools. In this book, binomials and multinomials have been collected from Scots legal and administrative texts in a systematic manner—using the lexical bundle methodology. It has been observed by Biber et al. that "[m]ost binomial phrases occur too infrequently to be considered part of recurrent lexical bundles" (1999: 1031); however, research into specialized discourse, such as the legal texts examined in Part Three, brings evidence to the contrary. Binomials and multinomials can be retrieved from among lexical bundles because they function as a genre marker. They constitute a text-type feature in those genres which, on the one hand, rely on parallelism and emphasis stemming from the mnemonic devices in oral rituals, and, on the other hand, tend to clarity and comprehensiveness. Both aspects are married in legal discourse, whose institutional setting may promote additional functional interpretations, for example, marking the boundary between the lay people and the experts.

4.5.2. THE STRUCTURE OF BINOMIALS AND CONSTITUENT ORDER

Biber et al. (1999: 1030–1036) stress coordination as the defining factor in binomials and notice that nouns feature in such constructions most often (for Scots material, see Kopaczyk 2009: 91). However, other major grammatical categories can also build a binomial (verbs, adjectives, and adverbs; for adverbs, see Dossena 2001). It is relatively easy to extract binomials on the basis of their syntactic properties alone (Hudson 1998: 16), but there are two issues which raise problems: first, the order and fixedness of constituents in a binomial pair, and secondly, the distinction between a coordinated pair which is or is not a binomial on semantic grounds. This last aspect constitutes the core of discussion in section 4.5.3 below.

When it comes to the link between the constituents of a binomial pair, I am interested only in coordinating conjunctions. It is true that Malkiel (1959: 129–130) also saw prepositions as a valid link in his definition of binomials, whereby the expressions *little by little* or *time after time* would qualify here, but since then research into binomials has taken a narrower view. The most common coordinating conjunction in a binomial or multinomial is *and*, which suggests addition, expansion of meaning, or a creation of a cohesive whole. On the other hand, there are also constructions with *or* and *nor*, which introduce contrast (an alternative) and excluding options (disjunction).[25]

The question of the stability of constituents, on the one hand, and their reversibility, on the other, was asked from the very beginning (Malkiel 1959). Diachronically speaking, there seem to have been more reversible binomials in Old English and Middle English than today (13.1% in Koskenniemi's study (1968); also noticed by Gustafsson 1976). This issue remains to be researched with modern corpus methods, as traditional scholarship often relied on too small samples and mainly on literary texts. The forms and lexical choices in those texts could not really be compared with each other, let alone with modern language data (cf. Mollin's (2012) study based on the British National Corpus), which displays much more variety in generic and regional terms (against what 'language' of today can we compare Old English poetry?).

The order of elements in a binomial pair was first addressed in Malkiel's seminal paper (1959) on irreversible and reversible word pairs. His answers to the "primordial question" about the order of A and B include (1959: 142–155):

- the chronological priority of A (e.g. *divide and conquer, hit and run*)
- cultural ranking (e.g. *fish and chips, cups and saucers*)
- precedence of the stronger of two polarized traits (e.g. *to buy and sell, yes or no*)
- patterns of formal preferences (e.g. *fast and furious, law and order, part and parcel*)
- precedence of A due to internal diffusion (e.g. *head and shoulders, hot and spicy*)
- transmission of sequences through loan translation (e.g. *Father, Son and Holy Ghost, divide and rule*)[26]
- the interplay of the above.

The potential order of importance and interplay between formal and semantic factors has resounded in many subsequent investigations. In their paper on the "world order", Cooper and Ross (1975) argued that if a parameter accounting for freezing constituents in a particular order is established correctly, it should predict any potentially frozen combinations and account for freezes at past stages of language development, too. In Darwinistic terms, such parameters would explain the retention of "good" freezes and the abandonment of those which are less stable in a language. A "good" freeze is supposed to include a common semantic feature, "a certain degree of similarity" (Cooper and Ross 1975: 71). By that token, *love and hate* or other polarity items will be more stable combinations than *love and swim*.

The first three of Malkiel's arrangement parameters are continued in the Me-First criterion put forward by Cooper and Ross (1975). The Me-First constraint aims to explain the order of elements on semantic grounds, placing lexical items which are more relevant to the prototypical experience in a given culture in the first slot. The prototypical American 1970s sitcom character, Archie Bunker, provided the authors with a reference point for the semantic ordering in *man and boy, husband and wife, sooner or later, here and there, friend or foe, mom and dad, life and death*, and so on (1975: 64–71). This is where the universality of the semantic parameters collapses, unless one looks for a prototypical experiencer for every set of discoursal circumstances under investigation, and takes into consideration the rules of discourse in a specific situation.[27]

A similar factor in establishing the order of constituents in a fixed phrase is psycholinguistic in nature. Scholars agree that the first place in a multi-word unit is "more potent" (Cooper and Ross 1975: 85), where potency is seen as "the ability of a referent to participate in a number of semantic relations in addition to its fundamental meaning". Some rules observable in ordering elements in freezes confirm the general processing schemata of human brains, reflected also in metaphors and other uses of language, for example, UP precedes DOWN, RIGHT precedes LEFT, VERTICAL precedes HORIZONTAL, and so on (Cooper and Ross 1975: 82–92; see also Lakoff and Johnson [1980] 2003: 126–138). Markedness as a formal and perception-based criterion for constituent order does carry some explanatory power (Włodarczyk 2007b) but not in all cases.

Cooper and Ross's study (1975) also included phonological constraints controlling the specific order of elements in binomial pairs. They considered the sonority sequence, vocalic sequence, increasing obstruency, or syllable structure, going back to Pāṇini's 'short-long' model of preference (Cooper and Ross 1975: 58ff.). It turned out that in fixed phrases a different selection of phonological factors will be valid depending on the language. Gustafsson (1974) confirms the "from shorter to longer" theory, stemming from earlier intuitive statements (Behaghel 1909), research into other languages (Sanskrit, Avestani, Linthuanian, and Old Norse in Krause 1922) and Bolinger's study (1962) of response preferences with binomial pair varying order. Her findings suggest that regardless of the syllabic or phonemic length of the pair members, the speaker has a tendency to prolong the B element.[28] Additionally, sentence-final binomials are longer, and the tendency is stronger in formulaic expressions. Oden and Lopes (1982) bring back the points made about phonetic constraints, noticing that the rules themselves require a hierarchy, an order in which their application will explain the position of constituents in a coordinated fixed phrase. On the side of semantics, they add that there are conjoined phrases "whose meaning does not determine their frozen order (e.g. *this and that*, *wear and tear*)" (Oden and Lopes 1982: 673). On the other hand, as noticed by Gustafsson (1976), some frozen binomials—if reversed—lose their idiomaticity or institutionalization, for example, *heads or tails*, *law and order*. In legal discourse, the order of binomial constituents may tend towards fixing because of the historical context and social requirements. Fixed patterns continue a tradition, establish authenticity, and reinforce the authority of the text.

A different argument about frozenness of constituent order comes from frequency studies, which have shown that the more frequent word precedes the less frequent one in a binomial (Fenk-Oczlon 1989: 517). Moreover, it seems that the frequency of occurrence of the whole expression might be another reason for the irreversibility within a binomial pair (Gustafsson 1976: 629). The users remember the order because the expression is used frequently enough to be stored in a specific form. This observation might be taken further towards the lexicalization process, whereby the binomial would lose its semantic transparency and be retrieved as a single unit from the mental lexicon. Not all binomials are like that, though. As mentioned previously, some coordinated pairs have a very specific semantic relationship whose presence and transparency is crucial for a communicative task, for example, clarity in legal discourse. Some binomials and multinomials are too infrequent to consider their fossilization in structure to be a result of common everyday employment.

4.5.3. MEANING IN BINOMIALS

Non-compositionality of meaning has been stressed as a defining feature of prefabs, especially idioms (Fernando and Flavell 1981: 17). Since binomials have been listed here under the overarching category of prefabs (section 4.3), this could imply that the individual meaning of their constituents does not play a role in the overall interpretation of the expression. This is far from the actual usage. Moon's study (1998: 120) has shown that at least 40% of fixed expressions exhibit some lexical variation, which has obvious repercussions for the overall meaning of the construction. When it comes to binomials, the semantic criterion has been employed to argue for the order of constituents in a pair (section 4.5.2), but in fact little attention has been paid to the relationships of meaning between the coordinated elements or to the meaning born out of this coordination.[29]

Gustafsson (1976: 633) suggests semantic markedness as one criterion whose presence makes a binomial prone to lexicalization. In other words, if a binomial is used in a specific context, with a highly specified meaning and function (perhaps also pragmatic), it will be a better candidate for fixing and lexicalization. Part of speech seems to play a role here, too. Numeric counts of binomials suggest a general primacy of nouns, followed by verbs and other constructions (see Chapter 10). However, in specific functions other parts of speech may serve the role better, as in modalizing and adding emphasis by means of coordinated adverbs (e.g. *deceytfullye or unlaufullye added*, *really and truly my Prisoner*, Dossena 2001: 116–117).

There are three options for constructing meaning in a binomial pair. It may be a compositional sum of individual meanings of element A and element B (A + B), or a non-compositional extended or modified new meaning AB (cf. Malkiel 1959: 138), or even C, if the transparency is gone altogether and a new complete unit of meaning is produced. A good example of the first kind would be *black and white*, where the meaning of the whole retains the separate identity of its components, the second kind could be *fish and chips* or *husband and wife*, where the binomial stands for something more than the individual meanings of A and B in separation,[30] and the third possibility could be *rock'n'roll*, where neither rocking nor rolling is actually present in this kind of music (at least not in its current understanding).

Research into binomials in specialized discourse, however, points to a more complex picture. Following an investigation into sixteenth-century Scots legal texts (Kopaczyk 2009), the most prominent group of binomials proves to be those which exhibit semantic repetition, so that A equals B. Of course, this is not just crude reiteration, although such cases also happen, but rather creating a single unit of meaning where the second element does not introduce any new information.

The second element is there for other reasons than semantic ones. I suggested a label *binomials proper* (cf. 'iterative' binomials in Norrick 1988) to refer to pairs with semantic repetition, which are lexically transparent but which pragmatically and stylistically function as one unit, for example, *brother and fraternite, escheit and tak, clenȝe and make clean*, or *assent and consent*. In such binomials the selection of elements and their arrangement will depend on the phonological shape, etymological background, translation from earlier traditions,[31] as well as stylistic and rhetorical conventions, handed down by the members of the discourse community. Binomials proper were also employed by the clerks in EdHeW, for example, *art and part* or *giffin and grantit*, and will be discussed in detail in section 10.2.4.

There are other possibilities of semantic relations between constituents in a binomial pair. Earlier research established the following relationships: complementation, cause and effect, metonymy, hyponymy, contrast, and metaphor (Kopaczyk 2009: 92; cf. Malkiel 1959; Koskenniemi 1968; Cooper and Ross 1975). It seems that the intricacies of meaning, highlighted and honed in binomial pairs, help to fulfil the objectives of legal language: the precision of reference and inclusion of all relevant options (see Chapter 2). The semantic motivations behind binomial pairs will be discussed in Chapter 10. But for now, what is perhaps surprising is that these semantically motivated pairs are accompanied by large numbers of binomials proper—those not driven by the need to clarify meaning. In my opinion, this observation brings the oral and ritualistic character of law back into focus and shows that repetition typically serves an aesthetic, stylistic, and institutional purpose rather than comprehension needs.

4.5.4. MULTINOMIALS—EXTENDED VERSIONS OF BINOMIALS

There has been little research concentrating primarily on tri- and longer multinomials, even though the phenomenon of stacking roughly synonymous words into longer sequences has a long tradition, at least in English, and a wide generic presence. Multinomials, especially trinomials, are touched upon by Malkiel (1959: 114, 120–121) who gives examples from several languages of trinomials with a fixed obligatory order of elements. On the basis of *Protestant, Catholic, and Jewish*—where the last element due to its clearly contrasting cultural tone will always come in the final slot, and juxtaposing it with *Christians, Jews, and Muslims*—which may be rearranged depending on who is talking, he points to the arbitrary arrangement of elements according to the speaker's viewpoint. Sauer (2011, 2013) has explored the employment of such strings as *wretchedness, sin, and cursedness*, or *leave, forsake, and retreat* in Late Middle English literary texts. Pharr (1945: 147) draws attention to a trinomial used in the excommunication formula, *by bell, book, and candle*, modelled on an original Latin anathema whose content was motivated by the props of the ritual. In fact, the same wording was used in Scotland during the Reformation, as Dawson (2007: 112) illustrates. Tiersma (1999: 61–65) lists several trinomials typical of English legal discourse in the medieval period, for example, *presents, gives, and exhibits the subscribed petition*, and those surviving until today, for example *give, devise, and bequeath*.

Interestingly, Malkiel suggests that "increasing complexity" in extralinguistic reality may inspire a binomial to be extended to a multinomial sequence; simply, more referential elements are needed and are therefore added, for example, *on land and on sea* expanded to *on land, on sea, and in the air* (1959: 121). This extendable nature of multinomials was later noticed by Gustafsson, who defined a multinomial as "an enumerative sequence [which] may contain several members, according to the varying situation in the topic we are talking about" (1975: 17). I would suggest that these structures tend to be situational extensions of binomials; they start as a binomial and are extended by adding more coordinated elements when the context requires (see section 10.3 for the multinomials found in EdHeW). The selection of lexical items used in the expansion will depend on similar factors as obtained in the case of binomials: semantic and phonological. It seems that the length of a multinomial may be conditioned by the referential function, as well as the discourse characteristics, especially when the communication is taking place in a specialized domain. It would be worthwhile to address the preference for groupings into threes[32] as a part of the cultural heritage and the persistence of triads in various institutionalized and ritualized contexts (histories, chronicles, legends, or myths).

PART ONE

Summary and Conclusions

Studying the language of the law in a historical setting reveals the intricacies of the original relationship between the role and the function of law, and the language employed to achieve its goals. As I have shown in Chapter 2, the forms of language in the legal context were initially stimulated by the oral medium. This channel gave priority to constructions which would answer to the mnemonic demands and at the same time enhance the importance of a legal event. Repetitive structures and stable formulae were easier to remember; they formed a part of a given legal tradition handed down from one generation to the next and, because they were different than everyday common use, they created the impression of situational significance. Regardless of the shift to the handwritten medium, which happened in the Western European culture around the twelfth century (Clanchy 1979: 175–201), the law retained these conspicuous features of orality. It is an important observation in the context of the earliest Scottish legal and administrative texts and the stable, frequently repeated chunks which surface in the analysis in Part Three. The written mode of preserving and transmitting law also found its own use for repetitive constructions, whereby the requirements of clarity, all-inclusiveness, and authority could be satisfied. Towards the end, Chapter 2 listed the linguistic features of the language of the law in view of the two mediums available for legal discourse at inceptive stages.

Two issues remained to be addressed: the form and identification of repetitive constructions, and their role in legal discourse. In order to address the role of fixedness and repetitiveness in legal texts, I paid attention to the question of context and the relationship between context and text in Chapter 3. I presented the functional framework for the interpretation of discourse functions embedded in repetitive elements of texts, to be employed in the analytic chapters in Part Three. The three functional categories which will serve as the frame of the analysis stem from Halliday's semiotic planes of field, tenor, and mode, and consist of the referential, interactional, and textual function, which are sensitive to the demands of the register. What is important for the present work is that the features of language—frequently repeated stable text chunks among them—perform these functions to fulfil register demands. A skilled creator of a legal text makes use of such standardized textual patterns and shares his goals, practices and results with the rest of the discourse community, responsible for the production of similar texts or involved in their reception. In medieval and early renaissance Scotland, legal activities converged in burghs: the hubs of administration and commerce, and this is where we find the communities creating legal discourse. This thread will be followed shortly in Part Two, where the historical and social background of the EdHeW corpus is explored.

In order to set a frame of reference for the repetitive chunks of discourse to be drawn from the corpus, I looked at how repetition and fixedness manifest themselves in language in Chapter 4. The realization that a substantial part of linguistic behaviour follows repetitive patterns underlies the idiom principle (Sinclair 1991) and provides background for the present discussion of formulaicity, its forms and its functions in discourse. Drawing on Erman and Warren (2000), I proposed a wider understanding of prefabrication: a process which gives rise to fixed multi-word strings, prefabs, regardless of their structural or semantic features. Such prefabs can play different functions in context and become loaded with pragmatic and discoursal meaning. In Part Three of this book, a very specific type of prefab, the lexical bundles, undergo a detailed formal and functional analysis to reveal the most stable elements of early legal texts. As characterized above, the lexical bundle methodology provides an opportunity to extract such fixed and repetitive structures from a corpus in a non-a priori manner, without presupposing what the texts have to offer in this respect. Interestingly, the bundles help to identify discourse-specific lexical patterns, such as binomials and multinomials, typical of legal discourse.

It would be possible to start discussing the extracted bundles without further ado. This book, however, takes a different stand towards analysing language in context, namely that the actual context has to be brought forward with enough precision to enable informed engagement with the data. The reader need not be an expert in medieval Scots law to find the data interesting. Neither can I assume the knowledge of social relations in a Scottish burgh, which surface with clarity in standardizing chunks of early legal discourse. I have resolved to give the reader the possibility to recognize the meaning of the corpus material, available as it was to the compilers and original users, at least to a substantial degree of approximation. Part Two has been written with this thought in mind and will help to situate early Scots legal discourse in its full socio-historical and legal context.

PART TWO

The Burghs

5

Burghs in Scottish History

5.1. Introduction

Part Two of this book serves to contextualize the production of legal documentation in medieval and early modern Scotland. The historical documents which provide the linguistic data for analysis were composed in a characteristic urban environment and within a specific institutional and social framework. This chapter pictures the burghs as an intrinsic element of the political, social, and geographical landscape in Scotland. Each burgh played multiple roles: it was a commercial centre, an administrative centre, a refuge, a cradle of industry, a military outpost, and a landmark with the high kirk tower and the tolbooth. Today the burghs are also the key to the linguistic map of historical Scotland because they provide us with easily localizable texts: burgh records, charters, and court proceedings. More accessible in the electronic corpus format, these legal and administrative texts remain the source of information about the language itself, as well as about the reality that it describes and represents.

To understand the circumstances in which the texts took their shape, I examine the beginnings and development of early urban centres in Scotland (sections 5.2 and 5.3). In the next chapter (Chapter 6), I concentrate in more detail on the inhabitants of the burghs and the institutions they created, as well as on burgh economy—a central issue emerging from the linguistic analysis in Part Three. The short pen-portraits of Scottish rulers, with a special emphasis on their relations with the burghs (section 5.4), serve to illustrate the changing conditions in which urban societies functioned and to bring out the external context for the development of the law in Scotland, which is the core topic of Chapter 7. The remainder of the present chapter discusses the discrepancies between living in the Highlands and in the Lowlands (section 5.5), and the emergent Scottish identity in which the burghs had an important part to play (section 5.6). This common identity feeds into, and draws from, the separate tradition of Scots law and also the initial stages of standardization of the Scots language.

5.2. Before the Burghs

The notion of urban settlements has undertones of self-sufficiency and internal social organization. Although without formal documentary recognition, some forms of such human groupings existed in Scotland since the Bronze Age in the form of hillforts (Duncan 1975: 7–10), which had a palisade and a strategic vantage point over the surrounding area. Making short-term military visits in the Scottish Lowlands, the Romans used these traditional posts as signal stations (e.g. Eildon Hill North, RCAHMS, n.d.) and forts. Archaeological findings suggest that these places were inhabited by relatively large groups, not just soldiers but also craftsmen and other people of use. Indeed, fortresses which gathered a substantial population in an organized manner and provided conditions for craftsmanship and trade "were described as *civitas* or *urbs* by Bede and Eddius" (Lynch, Spearman, and Stell 1988: 2). A Roman fort at Traprain Law, an earlier tribal capital, was still occupied by the locals after the garrison had left, until in the fifth century the fort's inhabitants moved north to another important site, Din Eidyn, which was later to become Edinburgh (Duncan 1975: 29–31, 35).

5.3. The Development of Urban Centres in Scotland

How should we define a burgh in its early stages? Historians trace the term *burgh* back to the concept of 'burgage'—a form of land ownership in a town (Hall 2002: 10), whereby property was held from the king. Linguistically speaking however, the etymology brings us ultimately to a Germanic source,[1] and it is likely that medieval charters have popularized the Latin term among historians. "A *burgus* is literally a fortified enclosure.... In the feudal context a burgh can be described as a protected and privileged commercial centre whose administration is in the hands of the burgesses" (McWilliam 1975: 28). A burgh can also be defined by what sustains it; "[a]n agglomeration of houses... outside and dependant upon castle or monastery, and growing up around a market", the last feature being a crucial indicator of urban development in Europe (Duncan 1975: 465). A medieval burgh, however, was not just any town. Mair stresses the special position of an early burgh in the feudal network, as well as its visual and architectural features: "It was a place with privileges, mostly for trade, and a particular form of government granted by the king. It was a place with the right to have gates and walls, and in the High Street, a mercat cross and tolbooth. It was often small, often with a population of less than a thousand, but it was a special place, and proud of it" (1988: 5).

The origins of medieval burghs were for a long time shrouded in mystery. Nineteenth-century historians, ploughing through archival texts, had to surrender and admit that "the origin of the oldest burghs of Scotland is unknown, and their early history is obscure" (Marwick 1897: v). Tentatively, the beginnings of Scottish burghs were placed in the twelfth century (Renwick 1910: ix). Today we have more theories about the origins of urban centres in Scotland. Some modern approaches suggested the 'free village' theory, whereby the burghs could stem from continuous rural settlements (section 5.2). Their establishment could also be prompted by a change of circumstance, for instance, the creation of a castle around which urban life could develop. Other scholars suggested abbeys and religious centres as possible magnets for urbanization (Symms 1986: 6), but opponents claim that the presence of monasteries did not have to provoke lay settlement—quite the contrary, in fact, it may have discouraged it (Mair 1988: 8). There is also the 'romanist' theory, which links medieval towns directly with earlier Roman settlements. This, however, is not valid for Scotland. Scottish burghs are quite unique in this respect, closer in nature to urban centres in northern continental Europe (Lynch, Spearman, and Stell 1988: 1). The Roman Empire never really extended into Scotland,[2] so what may be a substantial source of urban development in the south of Great Britain does not present a satisfactory answer for urban growth north of Hadrian's Wall. Celtic and pre-Celtic hillforts were abandoned at some point and did not constitute a base for further urbanization. But it may have been the Vikings who stimulated the growth of trading posts in Scotland. Such early trade bases could well have continued over time, provided that the demand and supply of goods were sustained.

In any case, towns thrived because of favourable conditions, when there was "a good cause to grow" (Burke 1971: 53). Such good causes may simply have been geographical, for example, a favourable trading location (Symms 1986: 7), a natural harbour, or busy crossroads (Fox 1983: 74), or could have been created on purpose, for example, by designing and building a town from scratch or granting privileges to specific settlements, such as the right to hold markets and fairs, pursue special trade, or protect and confirm the interests of the Crown in an area. This was the case with royal burghs, the first of them dated by historians back to David I's reign (1124–1153)[3] (Bingham 1974: 7; Duncan 1975: 470–477; Stringer 2005: 60). King David I was an innovator and a keen observer of technological progress in Europe. He invited skilled foreigners, especially from Normandy and the Low Countries, to plan and build his towns. For instance, the records mention Mainard the Fleming "as marking out the earliest streets in St Andrews in the twelfth century" (Hall 2002: 11). It should not come as a surprise that certain "similarities in law and custom" emerged, if we compare Scottish burghs with "urban communities in the Low Countries and in parts of France" (Symms 1986: 39). Innes also illustrates parallel developments in urban growth in Europe: in Italy, Spain, the Netherlands, France, and England (1868: xxi–xxxv).

What brought Scotland even closer to continental Europe was trade. Overseas trade was rising on an unprecedented scale in the eleventh and twelfth centuries due to progress in Flemish cloth-making technology. Now there were opportunities for Scottish wool to be transported over the sea and sold with profit, which gave rise to the demand for trading and shipping facilities. Another important factor in the development of trading centres was the availability of silver coinage, "an essential means for the growth of specialized production and marketing, and, therefore, of towns" (Duncan 1975: 464).[4]

Unfortunately, there is no direct or documentary evidence for the existence of burghs in Scotland in the eleventh century.[5] Fox suggests that "it is possible that the first granting of burghal rights was, in any case, verbal and undertaken before witnesses" (1983: 76). As pointed out in Chapter 2, before the appearance of written tokens of legal events, law relied on the oral medium, which makes Fox's suggestion very plausible. Indirectly, Berwick and Roxburgh are described as burghs before 1124, to be followed by Edinburgh, Dunfermline, Perth, and Stirling between 1124 and 1130 (Duncan 1975: 465).[6] Astill suggests, nonetheless, that by the eleventh century several settlements in Scotland had gained economic independence and became distinct enough from the rest of the rural countryside to merit the label of an early urban settlement. The subsequent formal recognition of their status was a token of feudal 'promotion' to the level of a royal burgh (Astill 2008: 44–45).

When it comes to documents directly linked with the existence of burghs, "[a]n early use of the term *burgus* is found in the famous charter of 1159 to Kelso Abbey", containing a number of earlier grants confirmed by Malcolm IV (1153–1165) (McWilliam 1975: 28). The oldest extant charters and granted privileges for Scottish burghs date back to the 1160s[7] and the reign of King William the Lion (1165–1214), the oldest surviving one confirming the erection of Ayr. It was William who implemented and fully exploited the idea of feudalism in Scotland. In a feudal system, all the lands belongs to the king who then grants it to his tenants, asking for various favours in return, for instance, an annual rent paid by the burghs to the king's chest (Renwick 1910: ix; sections 6.3 and 6.4). William's numerous grants of land were extended to newcomers from south of the border, as well as the Continent, especially Flanders (Duncan 1975: 175–182, 476–479; Fox 1983: 76–77). Hence, the multilingual and multicultural character of early medieval burghs in Scotland had a profound effect on the linguistic situation. In a multilingual context, it was beneficial to have a *lingua franca* for everyday communication. The burghs were centres of the budding Scots language, a process enhanced by Anglian presence in the Lowlands since the first Germanic invasions (section 1.4) and a continuous wave of newcomers from the south, especially after the Norman Conquest. McClure (1994: 29) draws attention to the fact that the vocabulary connected with burghs is almost entirely Old English. The discussion in the analytic chapters in Part Three sheds further light on this observation in the context of legal and administrative writings. Among frequent binomial pairs, for instance, one finds those built out of Latinate loanwords (*executouris and assignais*), those which mix earlier and later borrowings (*airis and assignais* 'heirs and assignees'), and those which are etymological hybrids (*bind and obliss* 'bind and oblige', for more examples, see Chapter 10). It seems that the official language of the burghs reflected the continental feudal influences and the impact of Latin in the realm of law, which I discuss further in Chapter 7.

In turbulent times of constant warfare and looting, safety was of utmost importance. The burghs had "the right to be protected by a wall or palisade, with gates which could be guarded and closed at night" (Mair 1988: 11). When it came to safeguarding their economic interests, in David I's charter of 1364 all the burgesses were granted "free leave to buy and sell everywhere within the liberties of their own burgh" (Donaldson 1970: 67), which effectively meant that all goods made elsewhere needed a licence to be sold in the town and were priced with duty tax (king's customs) added on top (for more economic context, see section 6.4). The king also forbade foreign merchants to sell their goods to anybody but the merchants of Scottish burghs. Another important source of income for the burgh was an annual fair or a weekly market. The burghs had a monopoly on trade and the king decided in his charter how many fairs and markets would be allowed, and how often a burgh could hold them. Royal burghs had a great advantage in the form of foreign trade monopolies: no other burgh could export their own produce overseas or sell imported goods at a local market. In such hubs of commerce and various human affairs, the issue of government and control comes to the fore. The burghs had the right to govern themselves through commonly elected town councils which had the power to pass laws pertaining to local matters (Ewan 1988: 231–233). Even though such an arrangement may sound surprisingly democratic, in fact power was kept in the hands of few (sections 6.3.2 and 6.3.3).

Thus, the most important urban centres in medieval Scotland, constituting the natural focus of this book as venues of legal and administrative text production, were royal burghs. These burghs were simply created by royal charter, possibly based on an earlier oral proclamation, which could explain the use of a formula "know ye that I have given", indicating an earlier action on the part of the monarch, where one could expect an utterance along the lines of "I hereby give…", which would stress the immediacy of the speech act and the event itself.[8] The king gave an oral permission to his landowners to erect a place for trade and crafts, sometimes close to a castle (Mair 1988: 10). Royal charters were subject to annulment or reconfirmation, since they could perish in wars or fires. There were also old charters in need of amendments or extensions, and most surviving charters are of this secondary kind (Mair 1988: 11).

Apart from privileges, the charter specified the burgh's obligations. The burgesses, in their capacity as royal tenants, were obliged to keep law and order, and perform "the (nominal) service of watching and warding; or, as it is commonly termed, 'service of burgh, used and wont'" (*OED*, s.v. *burgage*, n.1a). To control the place and ensure the flow of income, the king would establish his financial and judicial representative in the burgh, the bailie (*ballivus regis*). The bailie supervised "the collection of the king's rent and administered the royal jurisdiction", and even though later he was elected from among the burgesses, he "must have been at first appointed by the crown" (Innes 1868: xl–xli). The kings required military service, revenue or 'cess', decided proportionally by the Convention of Royal Burghs (section 6.5) on the basis of income. It seems that the money for the large part stayed in the burghs and could be invested, since "the Scottish merchants were in the extraordinarily favourable position of being the main producers of money for the crown at a time when the crown had no particular reason to demand it" (Wormald 1981: 46). Such a picture emerges from a comparison with Europe and England, where sweeping wars were being waged[9] during the times when Scotland was mostly busy with domestic affairs (sections 5.4.1–5.4.7). The burghs were also supposed to sponsor special events like royal weddings and provide supplies and accommodation for the peripatetic Scottish court (Mair 1988: 13–14). In 1296, the seals of Aberdeen, Perth, Stirling, Edinburgh, Roxburgh, and Berwick were attached to the Auld Alliance treaty between Scotland and France (Walker 1990: 425–426, 443, n.77; Donaldson 1970: 45; on the Alliance, see also section 5.4.6), testifying to the importance of burghs for internal, as well as external, politics of the time.

Initially, when everybody knew their place, the feudal system of royal grants and privileges was efficient and peaceful. A degree of imbalance was introduced by the expansion of baronial burghs and burghs of royalty (or regality, as they were also called). The king could give permission to set up a burgh of barony on land previously granted, which was seen as a privilege for a particular lord or a sign that the king was not exceedingly powerful in that area (McWilliam 1975: 32). The church was also a great landowner and fostered ecclesiastical burghs whose inhabitants, however, had "a position lower in the social scale than that enjoyed by burgesses of royal burghs" (Marwick 1897: vii). Burghs could change their owners or be granted by the king to his vassals. For instance, the royal burghs of Nairn and Kirkcudbright became burghs of barony[10] and regality, respectively. Glasgow, set up in 1170s as a royal burgh, was then granted to the Bishop of Glasgow, enjoying "all the freedoms and customs" of a royal burgh (Marwick 1897: v). Sometimes the status of a burgh was even more complicated, as in the case of Dunfermline, which was "an ecclesiastical burgh of barony or burgh of regality (or *both* of these) under the abbey" (Beveridge 1917: viii, emphasis in original). In any case, burghs competed with each other for profit and privileges, and were seen as a source of income for their owners.

At the end of the twelfth century, "there were 38 burghs in Scotland" (Fox 1983: 76). By the end of the thirteenth century, there were around forty royal burghs and twenty-three baronial or ecclesiastical burghs (Map 1; cf. Pryde 1965: 3–25, 42–48). Until the seventeenth century, as many as 197 burghs of different types were founded (Hall 2002: 7), some of them disappearing from the pages of history as time went by.

Map 1 illustrates the geographical distribution of royal burghs and the approximate dates of their formal recognition through royal charters. The urbanization of Scotland is uneven due to the Highland–Lowland divide, discussed further in section 5.5. The most important place-names, which will surface later in the discussion, have been included in the map, together with the locations where the

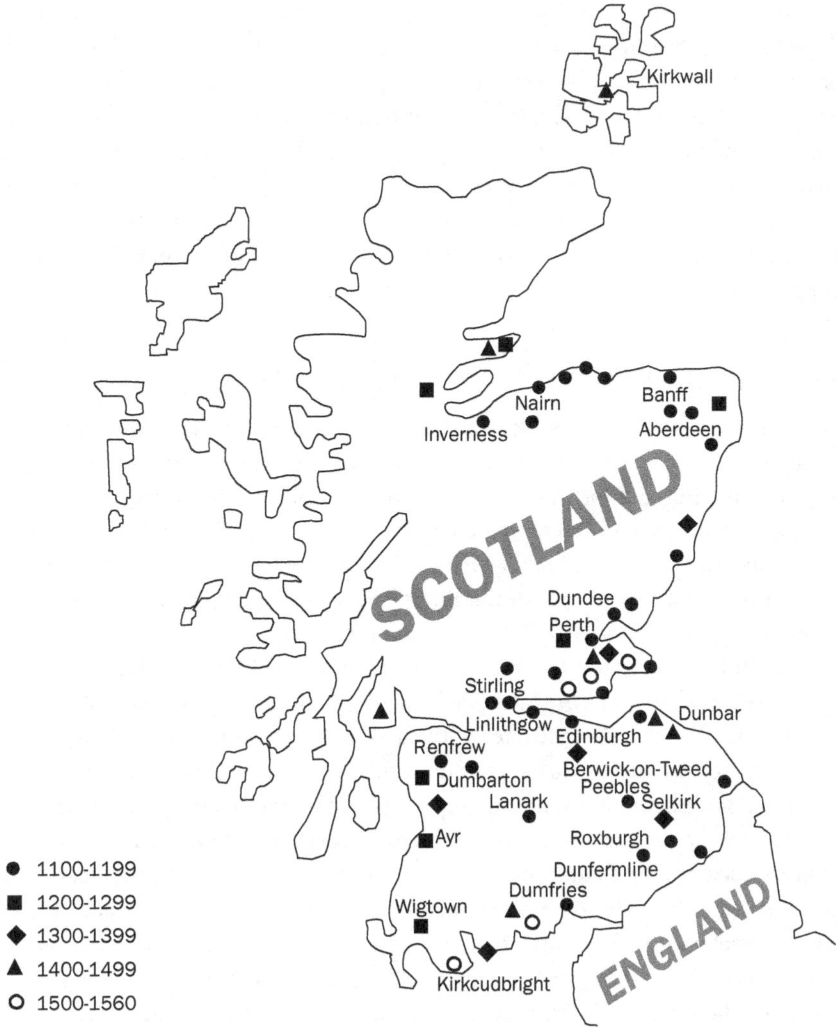

MAP 1 Royal burghs of Scotland (1100–1560) based on Mair (1988: 218–219)

EdHeW texts were composed. Thanks to localizable texts, it will be possible to comment on regional patterns of standardizing use at the end of Chapter 12.

5.4. Scotland and the Burghs (1380–1560)

In the period of most interest to the present study, the burghs flourished and prospered. During the fourteenth and fifteenth centuries, thirteen more royal burghs were erected to control the domestic and foreign markets. Another crucial characteristic was that royal burghs governed themselves (section 6.3.3) and could pass legislation protecting their interests. They also took part in creating legislation for the whole country in parliament. The royal burghs were "later considered to be the only free burghs, and baron's burghs [were] considered to be unfree" (Walker 1990: 419), thus unable to decide what was best for the community rather than the lord. It seems that burghs could have a very individual character and population make-up, so even though parliamentary legislation may have concerned them all, it would not be realized in the same manner, nor would it offer the same privileges everywhere (see e.g. the discussion of merchants versus craftsmen, their definition and privileges, Symms 1986: 54–55).

5.4.1. EARLY STEWARTS (1371–1406) AND THE BURGHS

The period on which this book is centred, 1380–1560, coincides with the rule of the Stewart dynasty (1371–1603), the kings who ruled for almost 350 years; who, in spite of the initial difficulties and frequent cases of royal minority, consolidated Scotland internally and strengthened its position externally. Five Jameses sat on the Scottish throne in that time, which is why the bundle *james be ye grace of* [*god*] makes a frequent appearance in the EdHeW corpus (section 11.3.1). During their reign the country witnessed "further development of central administrative and legal institutions" (Barrell 2000: 137), in which the burghs also had a part to play. They were represented in the Scottish Parliament[11] alongside nobility and clergy—forming together the Three Estates of the assembly. It is important for the present discussion because several lexical bundles with reference to the parliament and the *thre estatis* have been found among repetitive constructions (see section 9.2–9.3). The firm position of the burghs in the country's government (section 7.2.4) was not a coincidence. As Bingham puts it, "[i]t was the prosperity of the burgesses which had won them the right to be consulted in Parliament; their presence and consent were especially necessary in the business of arranging taxation" (1974: 25)[12] and in deciding how the money was to be spent. When King David II (1329–1371) was held captive by the English, during which time the future founder of the royal dynasty, Robert the Stewart, acted as Regent, the Parliament had a difficult financial choice to make. Either they could agree to the weakened king's proposal of English succession and no ransom to pay, or they could refuse to accept English rule and pay a ransom for their monarch. The Parliament, in which the burgesses had a say, chose to pay, giving a good example of financial politics producing independence, and ultimately the establishment of a new indigenous dynasty after David II died without a male heir.

Robert the Stewart[13] was crowned Robert II in 1371. At the beginning of his rule, the country was in poor condition after two outbreaks of plague,[14] costly ransoms, and depreciation of the currency implemented by David II (Bingham 1974: 27). Even the financial echoes of the Wars of Independence were still heard, while the country was torn by internal conflicts between powerful Highland chiefs[15] and a struggle for power between royal sons. Towards the end of the fourteenth century, constant warfare with England, especially over the Borders, was a bottomless sack. Thus, due to their economic privileges, the burghs could do much more than simply contribute to the taxation chest. Soon the most prominent royal burghs—in this case Edinburgh, Perth, Aberdeen, and Dundee—were powerful enough financially to act in 1424 as guarantors for the release of King James I, who had been kept hostage by the English,[16] and to act as bankers for the king's debts incurred in England (Walker 1990: 426; Donaldson 1970: 73–75).

5.4.2. JAMES I (1406–1437) AND THE BURGHS

On James's return, a new era for Scotland began. "[T]hough not the founder of the Royal House of Stewart, [he] was the founder of the greatness of that House" (Bingham 1974: 36). During his years as a prisoner at the English court, the energetic prince had the opportunity to learn horsemanship, sword-wielding and archery, as well as practice wrestling and hammer-throwing. He kept a keen eye on all diplomatic affairs concerning Scotland and made occasional gestures to remind everyone about his imminent return.[17] Showing his gentler, more refined side, he broadened his knowledge of French, still the language of the court in contemporary England, and mastered Latin, although in personal and literary writings he preferred Inglis.[18] He is often recognized as the first Scottish Makar (Scott 1967: 9–11), composing original poetry in his vernacular, drawing inspiration from Chaucer and other classic authors (Mapstone 2007: 274–275), even if his authorship of *The King's Quair* has been questioned (Kinghorn 1970: 11–13).

Although James's reign did not see the recovery of Berwick and Roxburgh from English hands, into which they had fallen before together with several minor Border towns, it had a beneficial effect for other Scottish burghs. Like his predecessors, the king encouraged craftsmen from Flanders and England to settle in Scotland and teach their trade. Not only did it strengthen existing commercial connections and created new opportunities for townspeople, but it also added to the multicultural and multilingual character of the burghs.

The king aimed at further consolidation of power in the country, threatened by the mighty position of local magnates and lairds,[19] especially in the Highlands (section 5.5). There was little respect for law among men who were supposed to be its keepers. The king faced an ambitious task, to which he allegedly reacted thus: "If God grant me life, though it be but the life of a dog, there shall be no place in my realm where the key shall not keep the castle and the bracken-bush the cow" (Bingham 1974: 48). Soon, he followed with calling up the Parliament and passing laws on the enforcement of order and protection of private rights and property (see the excerpts in Donaldson 1970: 75–81). He was also eager to establish universal laws throughout the kingdom, so that nobody could be placed above this law on the basis of particular privileges. This legislation was also supposed to ban adherence to local laws, as was still the case in the traditionally Celtic cultural areas: Galloway in the south-west or in the Highlands (on the development of Scots law, see section 7.2). James's efforts had a financial motivation, too. The authority of the monarch could not be strengthened when the chest was empty. An efficient apparatus for tax collection was indispensable and every effort had to be made to restore lands to the Crown wherever possible. The king, however, resolved to "gently strain milk, and not wring blood, from the breast of his country" (Bingham 1974: 50). A major rise in taxation would wait till the times of James V (Lynch, Spearman, and Stell 1988: 9; section 5.4.6).

James I's legislation obviously concerned the burghs when it came to taxation, as well as other public matters. The king explicitly disfavoured one of the most popular pastimes: "Item it is statut and the king forbiddis that na man play at the *fut ball* under the payne of iiii d." (Donaldson 1970: 78, emphasis mine), the reason being that other sports could be more useful in terms of safety and combat, as it was with archery, which the king ordered everybody to practice from the age of twelve. Begging in burghs was regulated, so that nobody between the age of fourteen and seventy should beg in a burgh or on land, but "thai be sene be the consall of the toun or the commonis of the cuntre that thai may nocht wyn thar leffing otherwayis", for instance, "pass to craftis for wynning of thar leving and that under payn of birninge on the cheyk and bannyssing of the cuntre" (Donaldson 1970: 79). This shows how important it was to engage in regular work for the benefit of the community, and that the community was expected to support entrepreneurial spirit. The laws even concerned themselves with daily dress. The amount of pearls worn as burgess's attire was regulated by law, possibly to reserve the pearls, abundant in Scottish waters, for export (Bingham 1974: 85). However, it seems plausible to suggest that such a law was most of all a means of safeguarding the visual tokens of status. Even though current scholarship shifts the perspective on James I's reign to highlight the ruthless methods of controlling the kingdom (Brown and Boardman 2005: 85–86), in light of the king's wide-reaching reforms, or at least intentions to reform, his contemporaries allegedly appreciated him as *noster legifer Rex*—"our law-giver King" (Bingham 1974: 47, 55).[20]

5.4.3. JAMES II (1437–1460) AND THE BURGHS

After the assassination of his father by intimidated nobles, James II became king in his minority. The country underwent another decade or so of domestic disorder and conflict between powerful lords (Bingham 1974: 66–74). On his coming of age and a political marriage to the Duke of Burgundy's niece, Scotland gained new trading opportunities with Burgundy, Holland, Brabant, Zeeland, and Flanders (Bingham 1974: 74). Still, some burghs suffered from the savage outbreaks of border warfare with England in the 1440s and 1450s, especially Dunbar and Dumfries. Seeking to strengthen his position as a legitimate ruler of Scotland, the young king held his Parliament. The assembly, burgesses present, passed legislation confirming the intentions of the late King James I to provide the people all over Scotland with legal protection (e.g. against sudden eviction from land) and to ensure the implementation of justice. There was also new law passed regulating quarantine in case of the plague. Until then, the ill were to be evicted by force. Now they could remain in the isolation of their homesteads, which was a step towards a more humane treatment of the ailing (on social issues in the burghs, see section 6.3.4).

The burghs under James II gained a new source of military protection—the gunnery, with the most famous bombard Mons Meg manufactured in the Low Countries (Bingham 1974: 82), currently held at the Edinburgh castle.[21] Archery was still very much encouraged for reasons of safety,[22] though the invention of artillery began changing the art of warfare. The new sumptuary laws further specified lawful outfits of burgesses—commoners were not to wear "silk, scarlet or marten fur, unless they held municipal office" (Bingham 1974: 85, see James I's laws discussed above). We can thus infer that the burgesses were already wealthy enough to dress like nobles, which was an unwelcome practice as it would blur visual social distinctions and had therefore to be regulated. To stop the expansion of overambitious nobility, it was decided that no regalities[23] would be given without Parliament's consent. James II's Parliament also distributed more judicial power to the burghs and established local debt courts, which could handle debts of £5 and under (Bingham 1974: 84). The formulaic binomial *fraud or gile* 'fraud or deceit', emerging in large numbers from the corpus (section 10.2.2), also recalls the money matters settled in burgh courts.

James II met his untimely death at Roxburgh during yet another border struggle with the English. As hinted above, the king was a gunnery enthusiast and received a blast standing too close to a gun overcharged with gunpowder. He was mournfully lamented by his grateful subjects, who praised him for bringing peace to the land but at the same time feared possible turmoil due to the heir's minority.

5.4.4. JAMES III (1460–1488) AND THE BURGHS

Thanks to the diplomatic efforts of the Queen Mother who granted refuge to the Lancastrians during the War of the Roses in England, Scotland regained the burghs of Roxburgh and Berwick. After his mother's untimely death, however, the fourteen-year-old king had to face a coup d'état by yet another clan of conspirators, the Boyd family, who had managed to establish themselves as sheriffs and stewards of several Lowland burghs. Thanks to a number of mutually favourable political marriages, the lords were pacified. Marriage also worked favourably towards strengthening Scotland's position in the international context, as James III gained a Norwegian bride with the Orkneys and Shetlands as her dowry. Thus, the country took its final geographical shape.

James III's reign was not without its economic difficulties, especially inflation, which the king wanted to withhold by introducing copper farthings for smaller transactions and charity. These blackish small coins proved unpopular with the people and the king's monetary reform failed (Bingham 1974: 106). We cannot be sure whether the bundle *of ye vsuale mone of scotland*, emerging as a frequent string in the late-fifteenth-century part of EdHeW, refers specifically to James III's currency. The king was also reluctant to assert the rule of law, which the Parliament urged him to do no less than six times over the period of fourteen years. He did pass a special act regulating the registration of legal acts in books in 1466, but little could be done to salvage the growing unpopularity of the king, already aggravated by unmanly pastimes and interests, dubious relations with his male companions,[24] as well as deaths of his two popular brothers in unclear circumstances.

To make things worse, a full-scale war with England was looming in the 1480s, avoided only due to papal intervention. This did not stop another ambitious royal brother, the Duke of Albany, from conspiring with the English against James III.[25] To make matters worse, the king confined himself in the Edinburgh castle, after his outraged nobles reversed the army from its route to meet Albany at Berwick. An impasse followed, the public growing more and more favourable towards the king in view of the English threat, and finally the burgesses of Edinburgh demanded the king's release. This attitude was rewarded by the king by his raising the Provost of Edinburgh to the rank of sheriff, and granting the citizens the privilege to rise to arms under their own banner (Bingham 1974: 110–111). The citizens of Berwick had less luck, for their status remained anomalous, the town in English hands, within a Scottish county.

5.4.5. JAMES IV (1488–1513) AND THE BURGHS

In the late fifteenth century, in spite of the decline in trade, the royal burghs looked for commercial opportunities as far as the Baltic and Austria but the major trade contacts were still based in the Low Countries (Walker 1995: 321, 349–353). James IV strove to stabilize the country internally and to strengthen its position on the European scene. The Spanish ambassador, Pedro de Ayala, met the king in mid-1490s.[26] The ambassador commented on the king's remarkable knowledge of foreign languages:

> He speaks the following foreign languages: Latin, very well, French, German, Flemish, Italian and Spanish. . . . His own Scottish language is as different from English as Aragonese is from Castilian. The King speaks, besides, the language of the savages who live in some parts of Scotland and of the Islands. (Bingham 1974: 122)[27]

The knowledge of Gaelic and Celtic customs may have helped James IV in extending royal control over the Lordship of the Isles, though the process was not free of difficulties. Several rebellions had to be quashed and the king recognized the need for personal involvement. Even though his achievements were not to prove permanent, he managed to win the Highlanders' loyalty and approval, which may have been aided by James's knowledge of Gaelic. Much less smooth was the task of establishing peaceful relations with England. But after a period of mutual distrust and hostility, peace was brought about by the long-negotiated political marriage of

James IV with Margaret Tudor, Henry VII's daughter, third in line to the English throne (Dawson 2007: 59–65).[28]

Law and order in the country were among the king's priorities. The Court of Session, set up by James I and continued by James II, was revived and sat regularly in Edinburgh, which paved the way for this town to act fully as the country's capital.[29] James IV's legislation was concerned with improving the conditions of life: with an economy based largely on agriculture, Scotland needed a boost of favourable laws for trade and early industry. It was decided that coastal towns should build large fishing ships (20 tons) and staff them with *stark idill* "strong idle" local men. A lot of investment, and allegedly all the oaks of Fife,[30] went into building a proper navy for the country, including the largest warship of the time in Europe, the *Great Michael*, "the likely model for Henry VIII's *Great Harry*" (Dawson 2007: 76). Agriculture was also improved by encouraging the lease of land by *feu*—a fixed rent, instead of military service or other type of manual labour offered in return. The land feu was to be heritable, which aimed at instilling in tenants the feeling of security and the will to invest in their family's future: taking greater care of the land, establishing orchards and gardens, erecting stronger farm buildings and generally cultivating the property with greater responsibility (Bingham 1974: 139).

James IV brought his country into a new era in terms of education (Dawson 2007: 53–55; see also his involvement in the foundation of the University of Aberdeen, section 5.5), passing the first law establishing compulsory education in 1496:

> It is statute and ordanit throw all the realme that all barronis and frehaldaris that ar of substance put thair eldest sonnis and airis to the sculis fra thai be aucht or nyne yeiris of age and till remane at the grammer sculis quhill thai be competentlie foundit and have perfite latyne and thereftir to remane thre yeris at the sculis of art and jure sua that thai may have knawledge and understanding of the lawis.[31] (Donaldson 1970: 92–93)

Any landholder who disobeyed and did not send his heirs to school was subject to a fine of twenty pounds, a substantial sum at that time (one fourth of a yearly salary of William Dunbar, the favourite court poet). The intention behind this act was to place the administration of justice in local competent hands, especially because the royal apparatus of justice had so far been distant and hard to reach, and had to deal with all crimes and allegations, even the minutest ones.

The greatest invention of the time, the printing press, did not go unnoticed by the versatile king. He licensed Chepman, a wealthy Edinburgh merchant, and Myllar, a printer educated in France, to set up the first such press in Scotland in 1507 (Dawson 2007: 81). The king's grant allowed 'for imprenting within our realme of the bukis of our lawis, actis of parliament,[32] croniclis, mess [i.e. mass] bukis and portuus [i.e. portable breviaries] efter the use of our realme, with additiouns and legendis of Scottis sanctis...and al utheris bukis' (*First Scottish Books* 2006).

To Chepman and Myllar we also owe beautifully printed collections of poetry by Dunbar and Henryson, as well as Scottish editions of Chaucer.[33]

James IV met his end at one of the most disastrous battles with England, at Flodden in 1513. The truce between the two kingdoms had been broken by the ambitions of the new English king, Henry VIII, who continually provoked James both on the international scene and at home, and refused to recognize the independence of Scotland. James IV led his army against the English and, like a medieval warrior-king, threw himself headlong into battle at its early stages. He was killed and his body was never properly identified nor was he given a burial worthy of such a charismatic and efficient leader.

5.4.6. JAMES V (1513–1542) AND THE BURGHS

Yet again, the kingdom entered a period of royal minority—the king was only seventeen months old—and the citizens were afraid of the domestic unrest such a situation typically brought about. In 1520, for instance, a proper battle was fought in the streets of Edinburgh, an outlet for the power struggle between the pro-English House of Douglas,[34] now that Margaret Tudor, Queen Mother, was related to them through her second marriage (Dawson 2007: 94–95), and the powerful pro-French Lord of Arran (Bingham 1974: 157). In the end, the king freed himself from his custody or, indeed, captivity, in the hands of the Douglases, and regained power, determined to bring back law and order to the country. During his reign, the College of Justice was formally established (Dawson 2007: 125–127; see the attempts of his predecessors above, and section 7.3.2); however, "Scotland did not experience, during the reigns of James IV and V, the same degree of centralisation of government that took place across its southern border" (Robinson 2008: 26).

New legislation was also needed to control the spread of religious heresy in the country, as Lutheran ideas were becoming increasingly popular. This was a time when the smell of the heretics' bodies burning on stakes lingered in burgh streets, causing distress and distrust in the traditional religion, and alienating the burgesses' clerical sympathies. It is possible that the king's marriage to Marie de Guise, a member of an influential French Catholic family, was intended to enhance the position of Catholicism, as well as to strengthen the Auld Alliance with France (on the involvement of burghs in the Auld Alliance, see section 5.3). Little, however, could be done in view of the loose conduct of the bishops, openly breaking celibacy, amassing riches, and giving a demoralizing example for the parish clergy, who were already hated for, among other things, their unscrupulous execution of mortuary dues[35] (Bingham 1974: 177–178).

James V's rule culminated in a deepening conflict with England, fuelled by Henry VIII's imperial ambitions, his lack of respect for the weaker neighbour, as well as Scotland's obligations to the Auld Alliance and her involvement in continental plots against Henry under the Pope's banner. The country was on the brink of internal turmoil again. There was increasing social unrest related to religious issues, and opportunities for a new wave of aristocratic ambitions, since the two male royal heirs died prematurely. Not only was Scotland left with yet one more infant heir, an inopportune routine in the Stewart dynasty, but this time the heir was a six-day-old female.

5.4.7. MARY, QUEEN OF SCOTS (1542–1567) AND THE BURGHS

During Mary's reign, the position of the burghs in parliament became firmly established. Neither war nor peace could be proclaimed without the agreement of at least five major burghs and their councils (Walker 1995: 322). In the sixteenth-century records, references to *ye quenis grace* and *oure souerain lady* (section 11.3.1) had frequent occasions to surface. At the start of Mary's minority rule, the burghs in the Borders and Lowlands suffered substantial damage when the English army was confident enough to march as far as Edinburgh in 1544 and 1545, burning and looting the capital, as well as burghs and abbeys on the way (Bingham 1974: 191).

In the 1550s, religious dissent culminated in the Calvinist teachings of John Knox, who was supported by a number of Scottish nobles sympathetic to Protestant ideas and opposed to the incommodious and costly connection with Catholic France. As a result of Knox's zealous preaching, "outbreaks of iconoclasm" followed in Perth, St Andrews, Stirling, Linlithgow, and Edinburgh (Bingham 1974: 198), and the country faced religious rebellion. This development was to the liking of the new English monarch, Elizabeth I, who had yet to firmly establish her rights to the throne and was looking for a Protestant ally. If the Scots would turn their backs on the Catholic heiress Mary and her French supporters,[36] Elizabeth would have sought to finish the perennial struggle between the two countries. Indeed, the Treaty of Edinburgh in 1560 brought about some new stability and the route to religious revolution lay open (Dawson 2007: 212–215). The Reformation Parliament was summoned later that year, attended by unprecedented numbers of minor nobility and burgesses. The jurisdiction of the Pope was abolished, the celebration of Mass was banned and the *Confession of Faith* by Calvin was accepted as the defining writ of the new state religion (Bingham 1974: 199–200). Mary went back to Scotland, but in the face of the successful Reformation her position in the realm was weakened, especially as she continued to practise openly as a Catholic.

Historians draw attention to the parallels between Scotland and England: "the close proximity of the two British realms and the analogous positions of their young unmarried queens" (Carpenter 2003: 194–195). From Mary's unfortunate marriage with Lord Darnley, the heir of Scotland was born. As James VI's godparents were the King of France and the Queen of England, his person held the promise of peaceful future relations between the long-term enemies. Nevertheless, Mary's situation at home was becoming more and more unstable, due to her alleged involvement in her husband's murder and an injudicious marriage to one of the conspirers. She was imprisoned by the nobles, and made to relinquish her crown to her thirteen-month-old son. Mary fled to England where she sought refuge and a base for her ambitions to reinstate herself as a ruler in Scotland, even, if necessary, through a Catholic coup d'état. Quietly, she also continued to pursue her aim to be recognized as the legitimate heiress to the English throne, should Elizabeth die childless (Bingham 1974: 218–219). This ambition, as well as her continued adherence to Catholicism in the years of imprisonment, led her to execution in 1587, twenty years after she had left Scotland in the hands of her minor son.

5.5. The Country Divided: Highlands and Lowlands

Part of the difficulty in ruling the country and providing equal care and supervision for the people rested in the fact that since its beginnings under Kenneth MacAlpin in 843 A.D., Scotland had effectively been made up of two very different areas: the Highlands, which comprise the west, the north-west, as well as the Inner and Outer Hebrides, and the Lowlands, spreading in the south and south-east. In the period central to the present book, the differences between the two areas were multiple: starting with social organization, through forms of agriculture, patterns of settlement, to linguistic issues and culture. The mountainous west was less urbanized than the Lowland east: "It was the east coast that maintained trading links with the continent and the Baltic, and there burghs grew up" (Wormald 1981: 41; see Map 1). It is crucial to remember that Lowland burghs were also affected by the difficulties the Crown experienced with Highland lairds. Their largely disruptive influence on Scottish domestic politics has pervaded the previous sections in this chapter. On the international scene, urban centres on the west and east coasts had their defining differences, too. "The west coast burghs engaged in trade with France, Germany, Spain, Italy and the west coast of England, the east coast burghs with the Low Countries and northern England" (Hall 2002: 37), as archaeological excavations have shown.

For Stewart rulers, the Highlands were more often than not a matter of serious concern and a source of trouble. James I prudently decided to base his court at Perth, at a more or less equal distance between the Lowlands and the Highlands, as the lairds could not be ruled from afar. The Lords of the Isles, as well as other Highland nobles, frequently conspired against the Kings of Scots behind their backs.[37] It was difficult for the Scottish Crown to control the Highlands, as their rulers enjoyed a great degree of independence. They habitually did not answer the calls to Parliament and had to be threatened with fire and sword to obey. For their mutual benefit, during the reign of James III (section 5.4.4), the Lord of the Isles was created Lord of Parliament (Bingham 1974: 99). James IV's reign (section 5.4.5) also witnessed Highland rebellions under Lord Lyle and Earl of Lennox in the west and Lord Forbes in the north, which had to be crushed in an exemplary manner. Afterwards, the king could show his grace and restore the Lords to their previous possessions, thus establishing his authority in the area (Bingham 1974: 124).

The Highlands and the Lowlands differed in mentality, culture, and in the level of education and refinement. Gaelic bardic tradition read alongside Scots courtly poetry illustrates "the profound difference between the Highland and

Lowland cultures" (Bingham 1974: 126). Education in the Highlands was actively promoted by James IV (section 5.4.5), who saw to the establishment of Scotland's third university in Aberdeen (1495), boasting the first faculty of medicine in the British Isles (Bingham 1974: 140).[38] It was much easier to get to Aberdeen from the outskirts of the kingdom than to St Andrews, and the islanders also had the University of Glasgow within easy reach, so a sound educational future was secured for the more remote and poorer areas. Latin was the *lingua franca* of education, but it is plausible that students from the Celtic-speaking Highland areas learned Scots in order to communicate in Lowland burghs. The Lowlands, especially the mid-eastern area, described as the centre of power in Chapter 6 and identified in Chapter 12 as the centre of textual standardization, could provide attractive opportunities for those who knew Scots and could participate in the urban culture and business.

5.6. History and Identity through Language and Law

Divided into two parts as the Scottish kingdom may have been, it was in the Lowlands that the awareness of national identity developed. In medieval Scotland, the heroic past was a unifying factor; it underlay political discourse and became a theme of literary works where the kings and knights became heroes of the 'nation' and the whole knighthood. Hoppenbrouwers sees the Declaration of Arbroath, a plea to restrain English hostilities extended by the Scots to Pope John XXII, as a "prototypical document in which a nobility, provided with chivalric ideals, acted on behalf of an entire nation" (2006: 216–217). The opening passage, translated from the Latin original, clearly illustrates how the *origo*-to-destiny myth (Hoppenbrouwers 2006) grounds a medieval portrayal of a people:

> Most Holy Father and Lord, we know and from the chronicles and books of the ancients we find that among other famous nations [Lat. *naciones*] our own, the Scots, has been graced with widespread renown. They journeyed from Greater Scythia by way of the Tyrhenian Sea and the Pillars of Hercules, and dwelt for a long course of time in Spain... but nowhere could they be subdued by any race, however barbarous. Thence they came... to their home in the west where they still live today. The Britons they first drove out, the Picts they destroyed, and, even though very often assailed by the Norwegians, the Danes and the English, they took possession of that home with many victories and untold efforts; and, as the historians of old time bear witness, they have held it free of all bondage ever since. (Fergusson 1970: 7)

Set against this colourful picture, how would a medieval burgess define himself in terms of group identity? The knighthood and the higher clergy had affinities and relations reaching beyond the frames of one locality, if not one dynastic monarchy. "The cosmopolitan and in-crowd character of aristocratic culture, [meant that]

Scottish knights would always in a sense feel solidarity with knights from other nations, even hostile ones, such as England" (Hoppenbrouwers 2006: 216). For a burgess, the most immediate source of identity would naturally be the relationship with his family, next with the town and the position one occupied in the local community (the linguistic importance of interrelated communities has been addressed in section 3.6). An important unifying factor would be the relationship towards the superior—the king, in the case of royal burghs. Would a burgess feel part of the Scottish nation? "The community was perfectly conscious of the concept of nationhood, insofar as it was centred on the person and role of the king, but for much of its daily life the burgh looked inward," claims Symms (1986: 340).

The merits of this theory lie in its appreciation of the burgesses' need to look inward but also outward for a sense of identity. On the one hand, burghs were more introverted, focused on the matters of community, even despite their wide trade relations (section 6.4.3). On the other hand, they were actively engaged in the kingdom's internal and external politics through their representation in the Scottish Parliament (sections 5.4.1 and 5.4.2; section 7.2.4). Therefore, when it comes to the situation in Scotland, it is difficult to agree with Edington who claims that "initially the idea of representation of the nation was almost uniquely attached to the nobility, and in particular to the nobility in its chivalric aspect. This is most evident in nations that had to wage war constantly, such as the Scots" (1998: 69). Clearly, Scottish nobility waged many a war in the medieval times but the money for the military pursuits came from taxes levied by the Three Estates, not just the knighthood, acting as the Parliament of Scotland. What is more, there was a difference between small-scale wars in the name of a local lord, which probably added little to the feeling of national identity for those who were called up in arms, as opposed to wars with England, a long-term enemy of the whole nation. Indeed, as Hoppenbrouwers puts it, "[t]he idea of a nation as a political community in which all (male, well-to-do) members counted was beginning to make itself felt by the end of the Middle Ages" through the emergence of representatives of estates in early parliaments (2006: 215). The parenthesis in the quotation—"male, well-to-do" people—is justified; after all, Scottish burghs were also hierarchically arranged in terms of social structure, which meant that power was beyond the reach of women, the non-burgesses or even the less wealthy or less influential rightful burgesses (section 6.3).

As signalled in the introductory chapter, common Scottish identity was manifested through elevating the Scots language to the emblem of nationhood (section 1.4). Legal regulations, increasingly recorded in the vernacular, concerned people's daily lives, giving them common background and common experience. The premises of the law were changing together with the times: from feudal legal codes to reformulated classical tradition in the early modern period (section 7.2). "The result of... adhering of people to modern, rational law, was the creation of new identities in Europe, those of nation-states, the people of which could be identified by their citizenship. The people became neither local, nor European, but somewhere in between" (Glenn 2007: 157). I would argue that in Scotland legal tradition played, and still plays, a visible role in Scottish identity creation. Not only was it a product of historical continuity and a significant token of self-rule and independence, but it also distanced Scotland from its powerful southern neighbour. Scottish tradition, including its laws, was transparent for a Scot, for a member of the Scottish nation. Even the laws of the burghs, the *Leges Burgorum*, were translated from the original Latin into the vernacular, disseminated in several manuscript copies, and eventually printed, so the people could access them, understand them, and follow them. The material collected for the analysis in this book—administrative and legal records from Scottish burghs—testifies to the versatile character of Scots and its progression towards a language standard.

6

Living in a Burgh

6.1. Introduction

The lifestyles and activities of burgh inhabitants were varied. This chapter concentrates on the conditions of living in a burgh (section 6.2), who the inhabitants were, how society was structured, how the burgh was governed, and how the people of the burgh earned their daily bread (section 6.3). This external context must be explored in detail because its many facets manifest themselves, directly and indirectly, in burgh records and other legal and administrative documents. One of the most frequent topics is land, its inheritance and the financial implications thereof. I also aim to reconsider the customary view on Scottish poverty during the late medieval and early modern period. As a result of royal privileges referred to in the previous chapter, the burghs became thriving centres of crafts and trade, bringing financial profit for their citizens and the Crown. In section 6.4, I examine the position of the burgess class in the financial and social context, and sketch the experiences of other inhabitants of the burghs in their daily pursuits. As Chapters 9 to 12 will show, the formulaic reference encountered in texts has a clear link to the themes examined in the present chapter: the government of the burgh, the land and other commodities, trade and markets, and so on. The final section (6.5) will sketch out the position of the burghs as crown dependencies, as well as the mutual relations between early urban centres, which provides context for the potential geographical spread of textual preferences.

6.2. A General Outlook

A traveller approaching a burgh would see a typical vista: one- or two-storey buildings, made primarily of timber,[1] erected to face the main communication routes; the high street and—in some burghs—the vennels[2] sprouting from it in a perpendicular fashion (Fox 1983: 77–78). The two most prominent buildings in a burgh, the kirk and the tolbooth, the seats of (respectively) the godly and the earthly government, were typically made of a longer-lasting stone, whose colour depended on the region and the type of material in the nearest quarry. Much of the ecclesiastical architecture of the burghs was torn to pieces on the wave of religious upheavals, the Reformation leaving few medieval urban churches in Scotland. Similarly, practically all medieval tolbooths fell in time into disrepair and slowly vanished from the landscape.[3]

The markets in Scottish burghs were held along the High Streets, which were at that time two to three meters wider than the modern street layout would suggest (Hall 2002: 19). Another typical feature of burgh design were backlands, which emerge in the binomial *bakland and forland* in the EdHeW corpus (section 10.2.3), where the owners of a plot of burghal land would conduct their trade (Hall 2002: 13). Not all industries were based in the burgh. Pottery kilns were set up well beyond town boundaries due to their hazardous nature (Hall 2002: 21)—after all, one spark would be enough to reduce a timber-built settlement to ashes.

Even though life in burghs was by no means bucolic, in many respects it was better to live in a burgh than outside it. Both free and unfree people (section 6.3.2) could, for instance, count on its common protections. It is true that few burghs were fortified enough to withstand a stronger military attack—usually just a stretch of backland marked the town boundaries—but some had ditches and a local castle (Hall 2002: 19). Some burghs also had a properly fortified wall. Often the collective nature of a human settlement was a protection in itself, as in the case when the treacherous Duke of Albany invaded Scotland in 1484 (section 5.4.4; also the repetitive reference to Albany in the corpus material, section 11.3.1) and the burgh of Lochmaben was the first on his way. Luckily, the annual fair was on and the town was crowded with men ready to stand up to the attackers, which they did with success (Bingham 1974: 112).

6.3. People of the Burgh

6.3.1. SOURCES OF INFORMATION AND DEMOGRAPHICS

The inhabitants of the burghs become familiar to us through a number of sources. Burghs are mentioned in historical accounts and documents. The inhabitants also left behind texts composed for their own administrative use, where the characters come to life as we read about their daily matters and which can be used to explore formal discourse of the day, as I do in Part Three. Through the texts, the burgh community shapes itself into a discourse community, bound by the production and reception of public genres (section 3.6). From the extra-textual perspective, the last thirty years of urban archaeology[4] have brought a substantial body of knowledge about life in medieval and renaissance burghs in the form of street layouts, remnants of buildings, artefacts, and various objects of everyday use.

Establishing the size of a typical burgh and its population numbers is not a straightforward task. Urban historians warn about the impossibility of setting any "precise lower limit to the size of a town" (Clark and Slack 1976: 5); however, one might engage in informed speculation. Around the year 1200, Scotland had about 500,000 inhabitants. Later the numbers shrank because of the Black Death,[5] but then began a steady increase in population numbers, which reached 800,000 by 1560. About one-fifth of the then population lived in the burghs, so there were about 160,000 people in more than forty royal burghs (see Map 1, section 5.3) and numerous burghs of barony (Mair 1988: 23), while Edinburgh alone numbered between ten and fifteen thousand inhabitants (Walker 1995: 321). Rarely did other burghs boast thousands of inhabitants;[6] usually their population was counted in hundreds. Fox suggests a population of around 600 people for an average Scottish burgh in the fifteenth century (1983: 85). What follows is that the social networks in early Scottish urban centres must have been tight, making the idea of a discourse community (section 3.6) a highly relevant framework for analysing of texts circulating within and among the burghs.

6.3.2. SOCIAL HIERARCHY

People knew each other well and lived in a world of clearly defined roles. Each person in a burgh had a specific function to fulfil. These functions were linked to one's social status, skills, and personal wealth. The burgesses were the free inhabitants of the burgh. To enter this city elite, one had to fulfil certain conditions. A prospective burgess needed money to purchase a plot of land and to manage it. It was not an option but an obligation. A burgess was bound to have a rood of land (also known as a toft) and to swear allegiance to the king, the community of the burgh, and the king's bailies (*ballivus regis*), who early on were responsible for transferring the yearly rent directly to the king. Initially, the monarch nominated the bailie himself (section 5.3), but from the thirteenth century onwards, bailies were elected according to specific burgh regulations and had to swear fealty both to the king and to the 'good town'. In the analytic part of the book, burgesses and bailies surface in numerous lexical bundles, for example, *aldirman and balzies*, *balzies and consail*, *was maid burges* (Chapters 10 and 11), and in longer formulaic fragments of legal and administrative texts, for example, *item that ilk day was maid burges* (Chapter 12).

A prospective burgess could come from any level of society, as long as he was able to prove that he had spent at least one year and a day in a given burgh, in accordance with a law dating back to the earliest urban legal codes of Scotland, the *Leges Quatuor Burgorum* (section 7.3.1); a similar custom can also be found in England. This prospect often encouraged serfs and bondmen to try their luck, hiding away in a burgh for a year and a day, and, if unchallenged by their lord, becoming free. This prompted the lords to establish measures promoting loyalty, for instance, the possibility of acquiring freedom for the serf and his descendants through actual payment for labour. "Otherwise he might have sought escape by flight, and [achieve] ultimate emancipation by obtaining burgess-ship in a burgh, or receiving orders in the church. That the ranks of the burgesses of important towns were so recruited is well established", Marwick concludes (1897: xiii–xiv, n. 2).

Burghs operated as magnets for people from all over the country and even from beyond its borders. At the earliest stages of urbanization in Scotland, foreigners invited by Scottish monarchs helped to build and organize towns. Contacts between Scottish and foreign merchants were encouraged and people from continental Europe came to settle in the burghs (section 5.3). At any given time there were also large numbers of non-burgesses living within town limits. In fact, one can picture the un-free population as "the submerged part of the iceberg" (Symms 1986: 52). Thus, apart from addressing the burgesses, burgh charters did refer directly to the lower sector of the population, employing the expression "men, natives and serfs", found for instance in Glasgow charters.[7] The unfree seem to have lived in poorer quality buildings in the backlands. However, excavations suggest that the conditions of living for non-burgesses were not squalid, as one might suspect (Hall 2002: 14). Among the second-rate group of burgh inhabitants Symms lists stallangers, apprentices, servants, journeymen, craftsmen, most widows, and large numbers of the poor (section 6.3.4). "In the larger burghs the poor made up the major part of the population, and the only influence that they could bring to bear on burgh government was through mob activity" (Symms 1986: 53). This last point serves to indicate the undemocratic character of burgh government, which is the focus of the next section. It seems likely that non-burgesses formed an important and accepted part of the community, going about their daily business and leaving its government to the wealthier and the more influential. The lexical bundle material supports this final conclusion, as only one 3-gram, *crafftismen of ye* 'craftsmen of the' appeared nine times in seven texts in the corpus. Otherwise, references to the less powerful inhabitants of the burghs did not appear frequently enough to qualify to the discussion of formulaic patterns in the records.

6.3.3. BURGH GOVERNMENT

The earliest royal burghs were set up first and foremost as sources of royal revenue. It should not come as a surprise, then, that power in early burghs was placed in the hands of the *bailies*, the rent collectors. They were also in charge of various customs and fines and "answered the Chamberlain as to all matters of local import" (Pryde 1937: xxii). The bailies made their payments on a more or less yearly basis and were subject to exchequer audits (*Stirling records* 1884: vi). New burgesses swore loyalty to the bailies, alongside the king and the burgh community, which highlights the importance of that office. In some burghs there was an individual chief magistrate, called the *alderman*,[8] the *provost* or, the *burgh-grieve*. Some sources suggest that he functioned in "law-codes rather than as an actual official in being" (Pryde 1937: xxii), but burgh records clearly indicate the active presence of such an official in many areas (the binomial *aldirman and balzeis* is to be found among the top formulaicity range, see section 10.2.2). In the earliest collection of burgh laws, *Leges Burgorum*, one comes across a Latin phrase *prepositi et ballivi*, also used in Latin versions of burgh charters and rendered in the vernacular as *provost and baillies*.[9] At first, the terms seem to vary in meaning depending on the context.

> Applied to an officer of a town, [the term 'provost'] indicated a position corresponding to that of a *praetor* or *praefect*, or *quaestor* or *burgh greve*. Sometimes this title was given to a petty judge, and sometimes to a subordinate officer under a steward or bailiff who had charge of the interests of the lord of a town, village, or rural district, –in which last case the duties of the *prepositus* had reference to the looking after matters connected with the cultivation of the soil, or cattle, or pasture [...] But there is nothing to indicate a gradation of rank between the *prepositi* and the *ballivi*. (Marwick 1897: xvii)

This, however, is the situation in the thirteenth century. In later periods a hierarchy of power emerged, with the chief officer in town called a provost or an alderman, and the bailies treated as second in rank. The order of reference to these offices in binomial pairs found in the corpus may be a reflection of this hierarchy—*balzeis* always come second when coupled with *aldirman* or *provost* (section 10.2.3). Nevertheless, Walker (1995: 320) points out that in spite of legal regulations, in various burghs the office of a provost or even a burgh council may not have been present at all.

In any case, power in a burgh was held in the hands of a few. The most influential group among the burgesses were merchants who were the first to capitalize on trade privileges (section 5.3) and organized themselves into associations for the protection of their working environment and trading conditions, the so-called guilds. In some burghs, the office of the dean of guild, the leader of the merchants, was established but the practice was not uniform either chronologically or geographically (e.g. in Dundee in 1515 or in Glasgow in 1605, Pryde 1937: xxvi). The lexical bundles *dene of guild* and *ye said dene* were too infrequent to qualify to the final discussion here, but they did emerge in the corpus. A colourful nineteenth-century depiction of the merchant class is offered by Innes, who saw the guild as "by far the highest of the public bodies or confederations, [which] sometimes almost swallowed up the power and management, and even the funds and property, of the burgh. Its members stood aloof from the crafts, and shrunk from mixing with men who worked with their own hands" (1868: xlvi–xlvii). Burgesses who "worked with their own hands" were craftsmen, who, in turn, saw themselves as no lesser than the merchants. The members of the most important crafts, such as shoemakers or smiths, started organizing themselves into guilds no later than the merchants—the Guilds of Glovers and Hammermen in Perth trace their beginnings to William the Lion and the twelfth-thirteenth centuries (Hall 2002: 20).

The collective governing body of the burgh was a burgh council, mentioned in the most stable lexical combinations in the EdHeW corpus (*consail and comonite* or *ye lordis of consail*, see sections 10.2.3 and 11.3.1). The council was elected by all free men of the burgh (Smith 1955: 607). This practice may evoke elections in a democratic society, but the merchants seem to have established themselves gradually as a sort of oligarchy, keeping the power to themselves. There was no equality among the burgesses and larger burghs developed "a fairly high degree of sophistication" (Symms 1986: 5) when it came to the hierarchy of political and social control. Burgh councils, "the consale of the communite of the burgh", are mentioned as early as the twelfth century in *Leges Quatuor Burgorum*, as bodies comprising of "gud men of the toune the quhilk aw to be lele and of gud fame".[10] One may only speculate who the good men were and what, indeed, "community" means in this context. Elections to the burgh council were held every four years and, until the mid-fifteenth century, the whole community took part. It is conceivable that such occasions did not always proceed peacefully or could not always be contained easily: in 1469 the parliament passed an act that "the old council should choose the new, and both together elect the magistrates and officers; one member of each craft should have voice in the elections" (Pryde 1937: xxv). This procedure, also known as *co-option*, was supposed to make things smoother and, perhaps, more objective. But some scholars see it as a pathway to an unlimited power for the town elite who, acting as an oligarchy, would back each other up in the elections in order to be the first ones to cut the financial cake (see section 6.4 on burgh economy).

The administration of justice lay in the hands of an assize, a type of jury, consisting of "xij of the lelest burges and of the wysast" (*Leges*, cxii). Only the less frequent lexical bundles in EdHeW contain direct reference to the assize, for example, *be ane assise* (20 tokens in 17 texts) or *assise has ordanit* (17 tokens in 13 texts). In larger towns, a burgh court had a lockman or a hangman at its disposal, for immediate implementation of the verdict (on burgh courts, see section 7.3). Loyalty and honesty was also expected of the four *lyneris* 'liners' (L *lineatores*), chosen by the alderman at the advice of the burgh council, whose task was to provide correct and detailed measurements of the burgh lands (*Leges*, cv; Pryde 1937: xxiv). Their work was accompanied by various formalities and town celebrations—after all, this was the way to settle land disputes between burgh inhabitants, maintain the commons and other lands for public use (e.g. roads or paths), and ensure that weaker landowners were not bullied by stronger neighbours. The lexical bundle material from EdHeW shows recurrent references to land measurements and location, for example, *on ye west*, *on ye est*, *lyand in ye* 'situated in the', or *betuix ye landis of* (section 11.3.1). Of other important offices, the treasury is an invention dating back to the fifteenth century. The official responsible for burgh finances comes in records under various names: *pursemaster* (Peebles), *treasurer*, *rentmaister* (Lanark) (Pryde 1937: xxvi) (on burgh profits and financial responsibilities, see section 6.4 below).

In different burghs, the establishment of the local kernel of power proceeded at a different pace and gave rise to a variety of specialized official posts. Much care was taken to ensure the comparability of production standards across the country, as well as the quality of goods on sale in a burgh. The *Leges* mention a number of jobs connected with what we might term today 'quality assessment': flesh and fish prisers, wine and ale tasters, as well as visitors of markets who passed judgement on the produce on offer (on the specific legal regulations concerning the sale of food, see the discussion of *Leges* in section 7.3.1). Other vital jobs included timber-masters, "masters of common work, hospital-masters, kirk-masters, pier-masters, brig-masters, and so on.... Water-bailies are found at the larger burghs, such as Edinburgh, Aberdeen, Glasgow, Ayr and Irvine: their duties were to attend at the harbour, see that all goods were duly entered for payment of customs, punish fraudulent sales, maintain perches, and prevent the casting of stones or ballast into the channel" (Pryde 1937: xxvii–xxviii). The burgh also required daily services to be performed for the community, hence the employment of paid servants such as a crier (also called a *seriand* or *serjeant*, responsible for issuing writs), a drummer, a piper (or fifer), a knock-keeper (the person supervising the town clock) or a bell-man. Town rubbish (a rich source of information for an urban archaeologist), containing shreds of various textiles, leather, and wood, was removed by *pynnouris*, piners or shore porters, whose dealings and wages were noted in burgh records.[11] All these people worked towards the common good and safety, and helped run the urban settlement effectively. Unfortunately, the names of their professions surface rarely in the form of lexical bundles in administrative records; it is only *seriand* that forms stable lexical patterns, probably because it is connected with the legal context, for example, *be ye seriand* (14 tokens in 9 texts).

6.3.4. SOCIAL ISSUES

The basic unit of social organization was the family. Extant journals and letter collections bring burgh families closer to the modern eye, but some of that information may also be drawn from official documents and laws.[12] From these texts it transpires that the burgh privileges for a male citizen extended to women and children in the family (Hall 2002: 14). Many of the earliest laws concern children heirs, as well as widows, seeking to provide them with comparable living conditions to those they had enjoyed during their fathers' and husbands' lifetime. Both sons and daughters could inherit land and buildings after their father's death (Booton (1987: 52) established that heiresses constituted between 2.5 and 8.5% of the inheriting parties in the fifteenth–early sixteenth-century Aberdeen), on condition that the widow kept half of the house if she had not been assigned separate accommodation before (*Leges*, xxiii). Moreover, the phrase *to ye langar lefar* 'to the one living longer', recurrent in burgh records (sections 11.3.1 and 12.2.3), indicates that both the husband and the wife had property and both could inherit (for an analysis of marital economy in medieval Scotland, see Ewan 2005). As Dawson puts it, "marriage was treated more as an alliance between kin groups than a choice by individuals" (2007: 62), which meant that an eligible adult rarely remained unmarried. Widows and widowers usually remarried, and there even was a legal provision for a situation when a burgess had had more than one wife and children from many marriages: the children of the first wife would inherit the possessions acquired during that marriage, and subsequent children the goods gathered during subsequent marriages (*Leges*, xxiv).

The burgh was the hub of social life—a centre of learning, worship, various social connections, relationships, and norms. It has been noticed that burghs were also the "focal points" out of which "literacy was beginning to spread" (Symms 1986: 8). This favourable attitude towards education and cultural growth was possible because royal burghs could capitalize on trade privileges and set aside some of their revenues to support schools. Education was legally regulated by the burgh council. Special laws were even passed to introduce instruction in foreign languages, such as the teaching of French in Edinburgh, established in 1574 and conducted by a native speaker from France, on a burgh salary (*Edinburgh records* 1882: lxxv).

When it comes to health issues, the burgh offered better conditions than elsewhere. On the basis of an archaeological survey from several monastic houses around Perth, which also served as hospitals, researchers estimated "the average lifespan in medieval times... to be 35 years for males and 31 years for females" in Scotland (Hall 2002: 30). In burghs, this age must have been higher. Nourishment and eating habits depended on wealth and social status, but generally speaking, people in burghs ate better. The main source of meat was cattle, alternating with sheep, and it seems that pig-rearing did not play much of a role in burgh economy (section 6.4). The diet was based on cereals and meat, supplemented with forest fruit or even imported delicacies, such as figs.[13]

There were burgh provisions for treating the ill and maintaining the poor. Coastal burghs, which were developing fast because of trade, by the fifteenth century boasted leper hospitals, and within the next hundred years such institutions could be found in all major Scottish burghs (Hall 2002: 30). Poverty was seen as a normal state for the lower social ranks. Even though taking care of the poor was the duty of the local parish, the burgh also provided three conventional methods of poor relief: special licenses for beggars,[14] alms-giving, and poor-houses, which could work as hospitals and were often referred to as such. Begging was first regulated by law by James I's parliament, which said that nobody between the age of fourteen and seventy, capable of working, could beg (Donaldson 1970: 79; for James's legal reforms, see section 5.4.2). In his introduction to the burgh records of Ayr, Pryde paints a persuasive picture of the poorest society sector, with multicultural overtones: "the burghs did a good deal towards relieving the misfortunes and miseries of what must have been a large drifting mass of cripples, defectives, homeless vagrants and unemployable strangers [...] Among those assisted were many Irishmen and Englishmen, a Norwegian and a Frenchman, two Dutchmen, some shipwrecked Bretons, a Hungarian and some wandering Greek scholars" (Pryde 1937: lxxxii), which gives an idea about the truly international character of medieval Ayr (see section 5.3 on the foreigners in early burghs).

The spiritual needs of burgh inhabitants were catered for by the parish kirk, as well as friaries perched at the gates, where land was cheaper or where they actually continued a pre-burghal place of worship (Hall 2002: 26, 29). The burghs were also centres of legal activity for the community, as well as the rural neighbourhood (for a more detailed discussion of justice and courts in the burghs, see section 7.3). All of this—a high degree of social organization, education, health provision, legal and religious services—allow us "to see the burghs as oases of relative sophistication surrounded by the very basic simplicities of sixteenth-century rural life" (Symms 1986: 8).

6.4. Burgh Economy

6.4.1. EXPENSES AND PROFITS OF THE BURGH AND ITS INHABITANTS

In this book, a burgh often comes across as an animated, if not personified entity. The burgh is born, grows, has interests, takes care of itself, and earns money for itself. This approach follows an observation made by Symms (1986) that a burgh acted as a "corporate entity", ensuring best conditions for its own growth. How was this end achieved? Since the main resource for the burgh was its own inhabitants, it was crucial to have control over the population numbers and to maintain a sufficient number of burgesses, replacing them or creating new ones (through inheritance or purchase of rights), if need be (Symms 1986: 41–42). Burgh councils did so cleverly by increasing the number of new burgesses, even to forty plus new people, when the town was in a financial nadir.[15]

Perhaps it would be more conventional to start with sources of income, but a more prominent, unifying feature for all free citizens of the burgh was having the same expenses—the financial responsibilities to the Crown. Each royal burgess was a crown vassal and was obliged to pay a yearly rent to the king, the so-called *scot and lot*, an expression with prominent presence among the binomials and multinomials (sections 10.2.4 and 10.3), as well as in other lexical bundles, see *for scottyn lottyn* in section 11.3.1. Scot and lot was collected by the bailies and passed to the treasury (section 6.4.1; see also Symms 1986: 313–318).[16] In time, more of this money tended to stay within the burgh. In the fourteenth and fifteenth centuries, two principles of financial management established themselves. First of all, the grant of the so-called *feu-ferme* tenure provided greater financial autonomy for the burgh, which gradually allowed it to keep more and more money to itself. Initially, the Crown had the right to all the revenues of its urban vassals: the rents, court fines, customs, and tolls. After feu-ferme was introduced, more of this money could be invested in the burgh.[17] Still, the burgesses had to pay an annual rent to the Crown. The percentage to be paid may have depended on the burgesses' negotiation skills to establish the most favourable conditions of payment for the town.[18] This is why burgh officials, such as the alderman or bailies, often travelled to Edinburgh not only to pay their rents but also to discuss possible alleviation of taxes, exemption from military duty, or other obligations to the Crown. Of course, the town had to set some budget aside for these trips, too.

The other development concerned the burgh government and the question of who had the power to take decisions in common financial matters. At the beginning, the burgh council and magistrates were elected by the whole community but once this practice gave the floor to co-option (see section 6.3.3 on burgh government), the burgh money, as well as municipal authority, fell into the hands of "a narrow oligarchy of 'the better sort'" (Pryde 1937: xv–xvi). The income could be divided according to its three major sources: burgh court fines (section 7.3.4), petty customs and fees (*parva custuma*), and land rents, naturally with a degree of variation from place to place.

The money earned by the community and exempt from royal appropriation was referred to as the common good (Pryde 1937: xx). All kinds of taxes, rents, and fines, known collectively as *maills*,[19] were gathered in a burgh. The inhabitants paid *watir-maills* for using a source of water. They paid *sellar maill* if they wanted to store goods in burgh storage space, for example, in various cellars and vaults under the tolbooth. Also "market-stances in the streets, were let to various craftsmen and vendors of produce" for a relatively small price, not much of an income for the burgh (Pryde 1937: xxxiv). Still, if anybody wanted to sell from a stall, they were expected either to become a burgess (and meet the necessary costs, as explained above), or if it was not feasible for reasons of financial status, they had to pay an annual stallage.[20] If a burgess had cattle or sheep, he would often pay *girse-maill* for pasturage. Among other interesting payments one finds *buttock-maill* (the earliest DOST quotation from 1528, s.v. *offerand* 2a; cf. s.v. *buttok* n.), a fine for immoral conduct.

6.4.2. LAND AND PROPERTY

Land was a commodity of great importance for the burgh community, as we see in the ubiquity of reference to land in legal discourse. Many lexical bundles analysed in Part Three bear connection to land measurements (e.g. *on that ta part*, section 9.3, Type P2 of prepositional phrase fragments), to rituals of land transfer (e.g. *erd and stan*, section 10.2.3), or to specific lands as part of inheritance (e.g. *ye said landis*, section 11.3.1). Land was a passport to burgess-ship, and it could be sold, as well as bought, within specific legal regulations. For instance, as outlined in *Leges Burgorum*, if a burgess was in good health, he could choose whichever buyer he pleased for his landed property, on condition that it had previously been bought off somebody else. However, "serious restrictions were imposed upon his alienating his heritable property, even under pressure or necessity" (Marwick 1897: xv). If a burgess faced penury or debt, he could not simply sell his heritable land to the best bidder. The right to buy first belonged to the next heir (*Leges*, xlii). The seller had to wait for the heir, even if he was out of the country; forty days if he sojourned in "the next kingdom"; twice forty days if still further, and so on. If there was no heir, the buyer had to be another burgess. If land within a burgh was not enough, the burgesses could come into the possession of outlying lands, a common practice (Renwick 1910: x) which testifies to the prosperity of the inhabitants.

Communal burgh land was divided into arable strips, cultivated according to the open-field system characteristic for the medieval period in Europe, with three-field crop rotation to sustain better harvest. The field strips were also supposed to "rotate among the burgesses, pasture being used for their cattle, and muirs and waste land for their free disposal, to be put to the best and most profitable use" (Pryde 1937: xxxiii). Such practices survived well into the eighteenth and nineteenth centuries. Because land was such an important source of income and sustenance for the community, it was crucial to protect burgh land from neighbouring landowners, who were often eager to encroach on burgh property (Renwick 1910: xiii). This is why medieval burgh laws devote much attention to the issue of heritable land, eager to keep it lawfully in the hands of the burgesses. Common lands were not only profitable for the community in monetary terms. The inhabitants of the burgh were in a privileged position because they had access and rights to pasturage, quarrying stone if available, "gathering peats, heather, moss and rush from the muirs, and even... drying clothes on greens and commonties" (Pryde 1937: xxxiii).

The burgh also made money on common property. A substantial source of income was the town's mill, as all burgh inhabitants were obliged by *thirlage*[21] to grind their corn in the burgh mill (Symms 1986: 88–94)—and to pay the so-called *multure* for the service. Renwick (1910: xv) deems multure "one of the principal sources of revenue". Some of the profits from milling went to the local parish kirk but the bulk became part of the common good and was spent for the benefit of the town, mostly on bridgework and strengthening the town wall for better protection. Walls and bridges were there for safety but they also meant that getting into town, with produce to sell, for instance, could be controlled—hence another income opportunity for the burgh. It was customary that "all strangers and unfree chapmen paid duties on loads, whether of man or beast, passing through the ports or over the bridges" (Pryde 1937: xliv). Other common buildings and structures, either earning money for the burgh or drawing on the common good for maintenance, included the tolbooth, which was a council chamber. Lexical bundles in the EdHeW material contain a recurrent string *haldin in ye tolbuth of ye samyn* (section 12.2.4), which indicates the typical venue of local administrative and legal proceedings. In most burghs, the tolbooth also served as a prison, admittedly in need of repair all the time, together with common forges or smitheries (like in Selkirk), and the tron—the public weigh-beam, "carefully controlled" (Symms 1986: 95–102; see also the discussion of measurement standards in section 6.5).

6.4.3. INDUSTRY AND TRADE

Burghs were the hubs of early industries. Local raw materials, organic (from animal husbandry, crop cultivation, and fishing) and mineral (from metalworking and stone quarrying), were turned into goods for sale on the local market and abroad. By royal privilege, burgesses enjoyed freedom of trade, which really meant "[a] monopoly of trade and manufacture against the outer world" (Innes 1868: xlvi). In such favourable conditions, the inhabitants busied themselves with a variety of professions and occupations. The towns were largely self-sufficient when it came to food, drink and basic goods. It seems that bakeries and slaughterhouses were run by men, while "[b]rewing ale was a female occupation" (Dawson 2007: 22). Local craftsmen produced clothing, shoes, basic furniture and utensils, various tools, and also weapons. In household inventories one also comes across products aimed at a more refined customer, although "these were not produced locally, but were from larger burghs or from abroad" (Symms 1986: 14), which points to trade connections in and out of Scotland. Access to a harbour was crucial to a burgh's economic success, as the examples of Perth, Dundee, and Dumbarton show (Hall 2002: 19). Street names preserve some evidence for medieval and post-medieval town crafts and early industries (cf. the Candlemakers Row in Edinburgh or Baker Street in Stirling). As noted in section 6.3.3, representatives of the most important trades, such as clothworkers and shoemakers, leather workers, bakers, or smiths, began to form guilds and aimed for more influence and power within the burgh social structure. Specialized trades were based at some selected burghs, for example, in Ayr the excavations revealed facilities for bell casting and glazing (Hall 2002: 40).

Another important source of income was trade. The Parliament of James III passed legislation which ordered that "na man of craft use merchandise be himself, his factouris or servandis" (Donaldson 1970: 84), which meant that craftsmen could not sell their products on their own but had to distribute the goods through merchants, giving the latter a chance to make profit. Perhaps this is also why merchants saw themselves as a group standing one level higher than craftsmen in the burgh social pyramid—after all, they were the ones who enabled the manufacturers to earn their money, the ones on whom craftsmen were dependant (on the competition between merchants and craftsmen, see section 6.3.3). By royal prerogative, in Scottish burghs markets occurred at a specified time and place. The goods to be sold there were taxed and the money went to the common burghal pocket. The earliest burgh laws specified that goods brought by ship should be purchased in port in the presence of selected burgesses, for example, salt and herring were to be sold on the ship (*Leges*, ix; see also Marwick 1897: viii).

Royal burghs made good use of their right to engage in trade overseas. As far as export is concerned, major commodities shipped from Scotland to Europe included "[a]nimal skins, hides, cheap cloth and salt" (Hall 2002: 23). Among major imports in the fifteenth and sixteenth centuries was timber from the Baltic region. Other everyday objects found by urban archaeologists include cooking pots from the Low Countries and Scandinavia, high-quality tableware from Germany and France, olive jars from Seville and stove tiles from the Baltic, and bear testimony to extensive Scottish trading relations (Hall 2002: 21–23). Trading vessels needed protection on the unstable waters dividing Scotland from the rest of Europe. English privateers, often acting on their king's incentive, if not outward encouragement,[22] often attempted to appropriate the cargo and antagonize Scotland, which at times led to serious sea battles.

6.5. Contacts between Burghs

The earliest urban legal codes in Scotland, to be discussed in more detail in section 7.3.1, were the *Leges et consuetudines quatuor burgorum, Edinburg, Rokisburg, Berewic et Strivelin, constitute edite ac confirmate per regem David* (Innes 1896), dating back to the twelfth century and the beginnings of urbanization in Scotland (section 5.3). There is thirteenth-century evidence that these four burghs, Edinburgh, Roxburgh, Berwick, and Stirling, acted collectively through a common council in establishing laws, in the interpretation, as well as the application of justice (Walker 1990: 439). This council became known as the Court of the Four Burghs (*Curia Quatuor Burgorum*) and can be treated as an early parliamentary body, with its seat in Edinburgh since James II's rule (section 5.4.3; see also section 7.2.4 on the development of Scottish parliament). Due to the fact that Berwick was a border town constantly falling from Scottish into English hands and vice versa, and Roxburgh was taken over by the English in mid-fourteenth century, they were replaced in the Court of the Four Burghs with Lanark and Linlithgow (Map 1).

Common areas of interest and potential concern among all burghs meant that, sooner or later, other burghs would want to engage in mutual formal contacts. "[I]t was inevitable that machinery for formal cooperation should be developed" (Symms 1986: 337–338). So at the beginning of the fifteenth century, the original Court of the Four Burghs transformed into the annual Convention of Royal Burghs, led by the Chamberlain (*Lanark records* 1893: xx; Walker 1990: 441), and including representatives from all over the country. This convention may have also had roots in other annual meetings of Scottish burgesses, for example, in those which were typically devoted to merchants' concerns, or in the burgess faction of the Scottish parliament. A unifying factor was that royal burghs stood in natural opposition to the construction of baronial burghs in the vicinity (section 5.3). It proved beneficial to act together and secure one's own interests. Undoubtedly, there must have been a degree of "rivalry and jealousy" between the royal burghs; the Convention must also have served as an outlet for mutual charges and challenges. Sir James Marwick, editor of the Records of the Convention, gives an account of its capacities and concerns:

> It defined the rights, privileges and duties of the Burghs;...it sent commissioners to foreign powers, and to great commercial communities, entered into treaties with them, and established the staple trade of Scotland wherever this could be most advantageously done...; it allocated among the whole Burghs of the Kingdom their proportion of all extents and taxes granted by the three Estates of the realm; it adjudicated on the claims of Burghs to be admitted to

the privileges of free Burghs, and to be added to its roll; it took cognisance of weights and measures'. (Smith 1955: 662)

It seems that burghs stayed in constant contact on various levels. There was, of course, trade, which motivated burgh merchants and other inhabitants to travel and keep up contacts all over the country and abroad. People from neighbouring burghs could frequent each other's markets, especially when these were held on complementary dates (see section 7.3.2 for the link between markets and local court sessions).

Besides regular shopping, bumping into acquaintances and common entertainment, there was a very practical reason for visiting other town's markets—one would have been tempted to check whether the vendors were cheating on the measurements. Did a pint of ale hold the same amount of ale there as it did here? Very early on, the four major burghs, acting as the Convention of Royal Burghs, agreed on establishing the four standard measurements, *the just mesouris*, something along the lines of the modern standard metric measurement units, kept at the Parisian suburb of Sèvres. Edinburgh held the standard of the ell for measuring fabric length, the ell-wand, Stirling had the pint as a typical measurement of liquid volume, Linlithgow had the firlot for measuring the volume of solids (e.g. grain or flour), and Lanark held the stone weight (Pryde 1937: xliii; *Lanark records* 1893: xx–xxi).[23] All the other burghs, in whose vital interest it was to run their markets smoothly, copied the standard weights and measures for their own use. The copies had to be stamped with the seal of the burgh and compliance with the official standards was required by law (*Leges*, xlvii). Once such a model stick or pint or stone was worn out, it was necessary to go to one of the Four Burghs and have a new one copied from the standard.

Even in later times, the burghs kept in contact with each other and regulated the necessary formalities among themselves. "[I]n 1595 they agreed that no burgh commissioner might present an article to Parliament without getting prior consent from the other burghs, on a pain of a fine of £100" (MacDonald 2002: 30), which clearly shows that the burghs had learned by then to keep a uniform policy line in the national arena, or at least to keep each other informed about individual initiatives. Such close contacts in the official sphere between burghs and their officials helped create a favourable environment for the spread of textual practices among the clerks and notaries. This issue remains to be explored in Part Three.

7

Law and the Burgh

7.1. Introduction

The previous chapter concentrated on life in the Scottish burghs and on its inhabitants. These aspects create the social milieu for formal discourse and the language of the law. It now remains to consider the institutional context in which legal and administrative texts were produced in medieval and early modern Scotland, to achieve the full contextualization of the corpus material examined in the analytical Part Three. It is necessary to recognize the significance and uniqueness of Scots law: its sources, procedures, and institutions, before I proceed to the analysis of its standardizing language. In this chapter, I identify the distinctive traits of the legal situation in Scotland at its inception and earliest stages of development, as it drew on continental sources of the law and mixed them with local customs (section 7.2). In Scottish burghs, law and order was regulated by burgh laws, exercised and supervised by selected officials in burgh courts. These institutions are given attention in section 7.3. Burgh courts were venues where the daily concerns of the burgesses could find an outlet, the wrongdoers were called to account, and property changed hands lawfully. Legal and administrative records in medieval and early Renaissance Scotland were written in specific socio-historical conditions and by a specific group of people. The characteristics of the text compilers—the medieval and early modern men of law in section 7.4—as well as descriptions of the legal genres that they produced (section 7.5) conclude the chapter, leading on to the analytical part of the book.

7.2. A Historical Overview of Law in Scotland

A legal system incorporates "legislative organs, executive agencies, an establishment of courts and tribunals, of individuals who act as judges, clerks, prosecutors, gaolers, legal representatives and advisers . . . a coherent body of particular principles, doctrines and rules of law, with techniques of handling them" (Walker 2001: 23). Scottish legal system is unique in several respects. In this section, I will trace its origins and examine how its characteristic features developed, what they were (and still are). It is important to remember that Scots law did not develop in a remote and distant place, without external influence. Even though the individual character of the law in Scotland should be recognized without question, a wider appreciation of the neighbouring legal systems and traditions, both in England and on the Continent, provides the necessary external context.

What sets the Scottish legal system apart is the fact that it is indigenous. In many places, legal codes from elsewhere have been imposed on the local population but in Scotland the law grew naturally within the country and out of its own institutions. Of course, there were influences from the outside but not impositions as such. Scottish legal system drew, to varying extents, on two strong legal traditions: civil law, whose principles and tools go back to the Roman law, and common law, which grew out of feudal practices in the south of the island. Therefore, it is often seen as a "mixed legal system" (Dieckmann 2004: 329; see MacQueen 2000 for a detailed list of its civil law and common law features). There is nothing derogatory in this term, however, and no suggestion of inferiority to an "unmixed" system, such as the English one. As Walker puts it, the Scottish legal system "is not narrowly parochial, having shared in drawing something from the legal systems of antiquity, nor yet insular, having strong historical connections and logical affinities with legal systems of and derived from continental Europe" (2001: 23). In fact, Scots law has been regarded a potential model for the *ius commune* of modern Europe in the private law sector (MacQueen 2000). It has recently regained its independent voice after the devolution and is leading the way in Plain Language drafting (Williams 2011: 141–142).

The history of Scots law before the late seventeenth century—in the times before Stair and his law codification (e.g. Ford 2007)—tends to be divided into three phases: medieval, feudal (pre-Roman), and Roman (e.g. Smith 1955). The remainder of this chapter will make reference to these periods to show how the law in Scotland gained its unique nature. From a linguistic point of view, it is to be expected that the waves of different external traditions shape its discourse and characteristic features, providing lexical, as well as structural, influences on the local texts. It is also necessary to remember that Latin was the first written language of law in Scotland. Vernacular writings began appearing in the twelfth century, and the first large collection of vernacular writings is the Scots version of *Leges Burgorum*, dated back to 1455 (section 7.3.1). Parliamentary records in roll form, "semi-official and non-continuous" (Walker 1990: 1), can be traced back to 1292 and are scattered among various manuscript collections. In 1466, James III passed a special act, which required that "þe kingis rollis and regesteris be put in bukkis" (Reeves 1893: 6), and from then on a collection of statutes and other legally binding decisions was produced in the form of official and continuous Acts of Scottish Parliament (for more on James III's reign in connection with the burghs, see section 5.4.4). On the wave of technological advancement and governmental propaganda, the records of the Scottish Parliament were printed by Robert Lekpreuik in 1565 (Mann 2000: 155, 237).[1]

7.2.1. SOURCES OF THE LAW

The earliest law codes of medieval Scotland were of Celtic origin. These developed from the oldest chthonic laws,[2] whose "chain of *traditio* is as long as the history of humanity" and which "simply emerged, as experience grew and orality and memory did their work" (Glenn 2007: 60). As I argued in Chapter 2, orality was an important feature of early law and its imprints can be clearly seen at later stages of its development, up to the modern times. Admittedly, the records of Celtic laws survive in substantial numbers (Brundage 2008: 70–72), but the codes do not seem to have had substantial influence on law in post-Celtic Scotland (Walker 2001: 41). A few residual items of Gaelic legal terminology are used in eleventh- to thirteenth-century texts, or even as late as the Statutes of Iona (1609), but one should at the same time remember that the Hebrides were for a much longer time under a kin-based lordship system, stemming from Celtic traditions. Interestingly, the Statues, among other things, mention the Celtic custom of handfasting,[3] which may have been evoked in succession disputes. Some attention was paid to the Celtic echoes in Scots laws by Sir George Mackenzie even in the eighteenth century (Smith 1955: 604). Even though Celtic laws were not officially codified nor followed, it is plausible to suggest that the early Scots did resort to Celtic rules of succession when the hereditary line was not secured. In general, one could conclude that the Scots followed the laws of the dominant group, socially and politically; this approach promoted the laws developed in the Lowlands (see section 5.5 for the status of the Lowlands as compared to the Highlands).

Civil law, the law of ancient Rome, or what was considered to be the law of Rome, filtered through medieval translations and interpretations, had a major impact on the formation of the Scottish legal system, as it did on the Continent.[4] Smith argues that "[i]t had inculcated a respect for principle rather than for precedent; it had encouraged the profession to look to the learning of Europe for solutions to new problems, and it may well have saved Scots law from absorption by English law" (1955: 621). Law historians suggest that the Roman law may have been introduced in Scotland in connection with canon law influences (MacQueen 1986, 2002b; Walker 2001; Sellar 2000: 16). In any case, the eleventh-century revival of Roman law was not as important for Scotland as the second wave of its impact, that of the fifteenth century and later. It was a time of new conceptual stirrings in Europe and "[t]he fifteenth-century revival of Roman law was one aspect only of an intellectual force which swept through every channel of intellectual, aesthetic and ethical activity" (Smith 1955: 618). James IV's parliament passed the Education Act (1496), requiring the eldest sons of all barons and freeholders to learn Latin and study law for three years (Donaldson 1970: 92–93, see the original quote in section 5.4.5), and the curriculum was geared to acquaint the students with ancient Roman legal thought. By the sixteenth century, Roman law was sometimes employed to fill in gaps in native Scottish customs and the common law (Walker 2001: 38). Contemporary lawyers make a note of such practice: "In

Scotland there is the greatest scarcity of written laws and therefore, naturally, in most matters we follow the Civil Law", wrote Thomas Craig around the year 1600 (Watson 1987: 561), signalling also the fact that law in Scotland was not yet codified at that stage.

Feudal laws dominated medieval Scotland's attitude towards inheritance and land ownership, as well as the social hierarchy. Feudal society was organized on a contractual basis. It meant that the overlord was the ultimate owner of land and would grant it to his tenants in return for homage and military service. The system itself originated in Lombardy around the eleventh and twelfth centuries and was codified in the *Libri Feudorum*, which was apparently used in Scotland and the Continent but not in England (Watson 1987: 564–565; see section 7.2.2 on the differences of the legal systems within the two kingdoms). It is important not to attribute feudalism to English influence on Scots law; Smith reminds us that "feudalism was [a] European, not an English political and economic system" (Smith 1955: 608). Still, England acted as an intermediary in the introduction of feudalism in Scotland, as this was where King Malcolm III Canmore's sons (especially David I, 1124–1153) became acquainted with these new ideas and brought them home (see section 5.3 on David's role in the establishment of Scottish burghs).

Feudalism entailed two essential legal implications: laws of succession and laws of land ownership. Succession was based on primogeniture, whereby the eldest son inherited from the *caput*; then property and rights could go to a single daughter and her husband, or could be split among many daughters, with the eldest one as a successor (Dickinson 1937). These laws obtained at every feudal level, starting with the king. Both *Regiam Majestatem*, the earliest and most important text in medieval Scots law, and *Leges Burgorum* (section 7.3.1) distinguish between heritage (land and non-movables) and movable property (Walker 1990: 628). Scholars cannot agree as to the actual sources of the Scots laws in this respect and suggest Roman, Anglo-Saxon, or Norman French sources (Smith 1955: 608).

Scottish land law, however, has been deemed "one of the areas of undisturbed indigenous growth over centuries" (Meston, Sellar, and Lord Cooper 1991: 23). The pre-feudal concept of *seisin* (Scottish *sasine*, also known as *gewehr* in the Germanic world), central to property law, rested on the recognition of the right of a free man to hold a stretch of land (Williams 1876). It may have been "joint or collective in nature" (Glenn 2007: 131) and did not require formal acknowledgement of ownership as long as it was confirmed by communal memory. Interestingly, one of the recurrent binomials in the EdHeW corpus is, indeed, *charter and sesing* 'charter and sasine' (section 10.2.3). Early feudal law was based more on custom than on written codes (Walker 1990: 16). In time, with the transition from an oral to chirographic culture discussed in Chapter 2, a principle of 'faith in records' developed in Scotland. It carried regard for registers of sasines and grants, as well as charters and other documentary material to do with land ownership (Hector L. MacQueen, personal communication).

The feudal machinery of justice relied on local courts which were given jurisdiction over a neighbouring area, and only in a selective range of powers, the most crucial of which was the right to try cases involving land ownership (for burgh courts, see sections 7.3.2–7.3.4). Any extension of these powers had to be granted and confirmed by the king. In time, the execution of law became centralized in higher courts, not in local feudal courts, which may be seen as the end of the 'medieval' (in the sense of 'feudal') period in Scots law. At first, centralization became embodied in the central Court of Session, which slowly took over the jurisdiction over heritage from local feudal courts. With the establishment of the College of Justice (1532), judicial powers were transferred from the parliament to this newly created institution, another step "along the road to a permanent central civil court" (Walker 1995: 510). Pleading in Scottish central courts was based on the "Romano-canonical model... [which] should be seen as less of a novelty and more as a continuation of an established, native tradition" (MacQueen 1986: 405).

When it comes to canon law, scholars emphasize its formative influence on the Scottish legal system and on the legal culture in Scotland. "[T]he Church can be seen to have provided an impetus for change quite apart from the breadth of its jurisdictional claims. As the guardian of the spiritual and moral health of Christendom, it brought a wholly different kind of pressure to bear upon secular law and custom, a pressure which seems to have borne fruit in Scotland" (MacQueen 2002b: 290). Godfrey (2002) also points to the importance of canon law in the nomenclature and formation of early legal institutions and traces thereto the sources of laws encoded in *Regiam Majestatem*. Of course, the Reformation changed the scope of ecclesiastical interference in secular matters. It excluded such areas as marriage, legitimacy, and succession from canon law and subjected them to secular jurisdiction. It should be noted that prior to these revolutionary changes, the canon law in Scotland followed continental practices—its applications resembled those in France, rather than in England (Walker 2001: 45–46).

Straightforward continental connections can also be seen in maritime laws. Even though the administration of these laws lay in the hands of officials characteristic of Scotland (e.g. the Dean of Guild and the Water Bailie), the codices themselves bore witness to international relations and cooperation. A Scottish translation of the twelfth-century French admiralty laws, *Roles d'Oleron*, was compiled around the second or third quarter of the fourteenth century,[5] the Scots were familiar with Scandinavian sea laws from Visby[6] (cited in Balfour's *Practicks, or A System of the More Ancient Laws of Scotland* in the sixteenth century), and they adopted the standardized international form of the major maritime legal documents, for example, the charterparty[7] (Walker 2001: 49–50). In other areas of legal action, the Scots looked for foreign examples if they did not have their own practice or if the issue was not regulated by the Roman law; then, for example, comparisons were sought with the practice of the Low Countries (Watson 1987: 567–568).

7.2.2. SCOTS LAW AND ENGLISH LAW

In view of these intense foreign contacts, it is necessary to reconsider the relationship between Scots law and its closest neighbour. The legal systems of today provide a testimony to the different histories of the two countries and traditions, and give rise to glossaries, dictionaries, comparative analyses, and other helpful tools for lawyers in the United Kingdom and the European Union.[8] This situation suggests that English and Scots law grew independently and each drew on different resources or used the same source with varying outcomes (e.g. Norman feudal laws). Today, English law relies on precedents and common courts (*ius commune*, common law),[9] whereas Scots law draws mostly on the principles of Roman law, even though there is an admixture of *ius commune*, too. In Scotland, the value of precedent is "rather lower" (Watson 1987: 562), so applying legal measures consists in consulting an authoritative codex or act, rather than in scanning a multitude of case reports.[10]

The beginnings, nevertheless, could have followed parallel lines in both kingdoms. In his influential legal history of Scotland, Walker admits that by the end of the thirteenth century, "English law had been a major, indeed the major, external influence on the law of Scotland" (1990: 12). However, he offers two scenarios: either the bodies of early laws, as represented in the Scottish *Regiam Majestatem* and in *Glanvill*, the most important English treatise on the form and procedures of the king's court (*curia regis*), dating back to the twelfth-century (Ramsay 2008: 270–272), were simply similar, or the Scots copied from the English. In any case, English law tended immediately towards institutionalization and centralization, while in Scotland these developments came considerably later. Scots law was largely oral as opposed to English law which was based on the records of precedent; Reid and Zimmerman (2000: 44) suggest that this is why the need for special legal training and institutionalization developed earlier in England (see section 7.4 on Scottish men of law).

With growing hostility between the two kingdoms, especially during the times of Edward I and the Wars of Independence, the legal systems grew more and more distant, even though they functioned within the same feudal social and political setting. Watson (1987: 564–565) maintains that *Libri Feudorum*, the outline of feudal laws, was used in Scotland and the Continent but not in England. This is the period in which Scotland turned away from its southern neighbour and looked for legal guidance to the Continent (Robinson, Fergus, and Gordon 2000: 164). This is also the period when *Quoniam Attachiamenta* was written, a fourteenth-century text on the procedure in a feudal court, pertaining only to Scottish legal customs and considered by many the "earliest purely Scottish legal work" (Walker 2001: 129; see also Smith 1955: 613; Reid and Zimmerman 2000: 44). Within the next two hundred years, the two systems started polarizing quite clearly in the eyes of contemporary legal commentators: "the learned say that the English use municipal law when the Scots are governed by the Civil Law", said Thomas Craig in his *Jus Feudale* around 1600 (Watson 1987: 557–558).

Historical differences between Scottish and English law systems are reflected in legal nomenclature. The trilingualism of law in medieval England (Anglo-Norman, French, Latin) was never the case in Scotland to such a great extent. In England, statutes and town records were put down in "law French" (Steiner and Barrington 2002: 9) and law was exercised through the medium of French in local courts up to the fifteenth century (Thomson and Morgan 2008: 26–27). On the contrary, in Scotland the texts pertaining to law were composed either in Latin, the medieval European legal *lingua franca*, in Scots, or on occasion translated from Latin into Scots.[11] For instance, the *Leges Quatuor Burgorum* were first compiled in Latin and then translated directly into the vernacular (section 7.3.1). Careful scrutiny of both versions reveals mutual influences between the two languages of medieval Scots law (Kopaczyk 2011b). Because of this close relationship between Latin and Scots, as well as Roman law serving as a resource for the legal system in Scotland, Scots legal terminology often stems directly from Latin (for Latin calques in Scottish legal texts, see MacQueen 2002a). Despite the fact that Latin borrowings are present in English as well, the differences may lie in the morphology of the borrowed items, or in the meaning and scope of a given term (on special requirements for legal lexicon, see section 2.4.3). A few illustrations of this discrepancy may be found in comparative legal studies and dictionaries. For instance, where Scots law may use a direct Latin term *beneficim cedendarum actionum* (or simply 'benefit of assignation' or 'right to assignation'), in the English nomenclature one finds *assignment* or *subrogation* for the same concept (Dieckmann 2004: 340–341). In Scotland, *aliment* means both 'alimony' and 'maintenance' (Dodds 1927: 44). Other legal terms (e.g. *negligence* or *bankruptcy*) are used in English law even though one may find them outside the legal context. In Scotland legal terminology is more hermetic, rarely admitting everyday words and giving preference to specialized vocabulary, be it from Latin or from the native tongue. MacQueen gives the example of *borgh*,[12] originally Old English but Scotticized by the fifteenth century, as belonging to Scottish "own terminology" (1986: 405). Lexical bundles in the EdHeW corpus reveal the employment of this word in several stable combinations such as *fand a borch*, *follow a borch*, *a borch that*, with *strekit a borch* belonging to the most formulaic 3-grams in the texts (section 11.3.3). The material also confirms the position of Latin as a source of loanwords (see section 10.2.4 on etymologically motivated binomials), and, possibly, calques, as in *Anno Domini* rendered as *ye yhere of oure lord*, or *hac presentes literas* becoming *thir present letteris* (cf. MacQueen 2002a), especially in the early fifteenth century (Fig. 11.1).

7.2.3. THE 'DARK AGE'

Traditional historiographers of Scots law created what MacQueen has termed a "depressing consensus" (1986: 403), talking about the so-called 'Dark Age' between the fourteenth and early seventeenth centuries (Lord Cooper 1952; Smith 1955; see also Carswell's (1967) discussion of the legal profession in Scotland). The investigation in this book falls exactly within this time span. Why would that period provoke a label suggesting a backward, provincial nature of Scots law? Lord Cooper draws attention to the flaws in the system of courts: "there was plenty of law in Scotland and plenty of lawyers to apply it; but unfortunately an absence of tribunals adequately manned and equipped, in which the law effectively applied in contested litigation" (1952: 24). Smith backs him up, suggesting that it is only with the introduction of "new judicial machinery", the Court of Session in 1532, that justice became more efficiently executed (1955: 610). More recently, Godfrey adds to this view citing "the absence of a treatise on Scots law between the fourteenth and early seventeenth centuries" (2002: 118).

But remembering that "[t]he period from 1329 to about 1600 is a period of political strife and economic troubles, of weak kings and frequent royal minorities, which was an unkindly background for the development of law" (section 5.4), Walker (2001: 127) refrains from calling this period a 'Dark Age'. The apparent shortcomings of the Scottish legal system of that period should rather be put down to the patchy character of the surviving textual material and to the general transitory nature of the law at that time, I contend. It is true that the kings did not possess stable authority or could not delegate power to lower level officials, that they were bombarded with petitions and appeals from various courts. MacQueen (1986: 411), however, puts Scotland in the European context and notices that Scots law of pleading of the time followed practices which generally stemmed from the rediscovered Roman law after the twelfth-century medieval renaissance. Another alleged fault of the Scots law between the fourteenth and seventeenth century seems to have been "a tendency to oversimplify all problems with the question whether the defender had done 'wrang'—thus leaving the law vague, formless, delictal in outlook, and without clear principles to develop" (Smith 1955: 616). This, however, was a doctrine upon which law was to be built in the future, in a more fine-tuned and mature version. Moreover, *wrang and unlauch* is an indigenous Scottish invention, "a well-established legal concept" during the period in question (MacQueen 2002a). Interestingly, in Scottish laws written in Latin, this term is often code-switched (see the discussion of binomials in section 4.5.1). At the time of compiling the documents in the EdHeW collection, *wrangus* deeds are a major concern: the most formulaic lexical bundles refer to *ye wrangus haldin* (sections 11.3.1 and 12.2.4), *ye wrangus takin*, or *ye wrangus occuping*. It is worth noting, though, that the gerunds in these phrases actually narrow down the scope to the actual type of legal transgression (see also the discussion of other potential extensions of this phrase fragment in section 9.3). We should perhaps look at this 'dark' period in the history of Scots law as a stirring moment, laying the foundations for what was to come next.

7.2.4. SCOTTISH MEDIEVAL AND EARLY MODERN LEGISLATURE

By the end of the thirteenth century, the Scottish Parliament had been established as the acting force of the king's law. "The Scottish Parliament was a unicameral institution, normally consisting of three, but sometimes four, estates [...] The key elements of Parliament—the estates of clergy, nobles, burgesses and (after 1587) lairds or 'barons'—were, to varying degrees, separate and self-conscious components of society" (MacDonald 2002: 23). Because of that self-conscious nature and self-interest, tensions between the estates must have arisen, as they had to work on Scottish jurisdiction and legislature as one chamber, sitting and voting in one room, with a simple majority of votes needed to approve a proposition under debate. According to MacDonald, this fact brings the Scottish Parliament closer to its counterparts on the Continent, while Wormald (1981: 20–21) points out that the representation of the burgess class in parliament constitutes further contrast with the parliament in contemporary England.

The burghs were an important and experienced player in the parliamentary machinery. The first mention of the third estate, the burgh commissioners, can be found in an indenture from 1326 (Walker 1990: 221, 224). It was not only in the parliament where the burghs could negotiate their interests or shape common policies. Their general annual assembly, the Convention of Royal Burghs (section 6.5), started in 1405, initially as a meeting of two or three representatives from each royal burgh (Walker 1990: 441). This was a venue for discussing matters that touched upon the well-being of the burghs, such as taxation, internal administration, or settling disputes. Acting as a corporate body even outside the parliament, the burghs of the time may be described as "the most self-conscious, organized estate" (MacDonald 2002: 29), even causing some envy because of their structured and unified actions.[13] "The burghs felt impelled to protest against excessive custom-dues.... They sought exemption from, or commutation of, military obligations, they met to discuss grievances" and other matters of legal nature (Pryde 1937: lxx). One of the keenest areas of interest for the burghs was trade, especially foreign trade. As I have shown in Chapter 6, this was a major source of income for the most powerful burgh elite, the merchants. Those merchants who operated in royal burghs were the only traders given permission by the king to conduct foreign trade, so they were vitally interested in foreign politics and wanted to have a say in various economic, as well as diplomatic and political affairs. Perhaps this is also why, in the long run, the burghs may have been the instigator of multicameral tendencies in parliament, to gain more independence and more say in central decision-making.

In spite of the large degree of self-government and autonomy, in the sixteenth century the Crown interfered in the nominations of burgh officials and handed out privileges which undermined the liberties and monopolies of royal burghs (Walker 1995: 322–324). Taxes steadily grew and the burgesses watched the decision-making closely. As parliaments were usually held in Edinburgh, it meant travel and longer sojourns for burgh representatives. It is not certain whether the Crown influenced the choice of the parliament's members in any way. "The fact that the burgh commissioners came largely from the same burghs year after year, even though most of those burghs rarely sent the same commissioners, indicated that status among the burghs, rather than royal choice, dictated the burghs' representatives" (MacDonald 2002: 44–45). Many could not afford the trip (or did not want to spend money from their own pocket) so they relied on the burgh money, similarly to other burgh officials travelling to Edinburgh in connection with legal matters or to pay the yearly rents. When legislation was being produced, the representatives of the estates were supposed to, or even commanded to stay on. It seems valid to suspect that there must have been unofficial meetings of the three estates during that time, beyond the formal context of a parliamentary sitting (MacDonald 2002: 25).

7.3. Law and Order in the Burghs

7.3.1. LAWS OF THE BURGHS

The earliest municipal laws in Scotland are known as *Leges Quatuor Burgorum*, the laws of Four Burghs—initially the most influential urban centres in Scotland: Edinburgh, Stirling, Roxburgh, and Berwick (Map 1).[14] The laws established by the representatives of these four burghs were supposed to alleviate the need for separate charters concerning legal regulations in other individual burghs and were accepted by all urban centres in Scotland (Lanark records: xi–xii). This solution can also be seen as the way to strengthen the feudal network of royal burghs, with streamlined policies and uniform regulations.

The Latin text of the laws was compiled in the twelfth century, during the feudal reforms of King David I (1124–1153), and is said to have been influenced by the laws of Newcastle (Smith 1955: 606). The compilers of the recent volume with Scottish historical documents agree that *Leges Burgorum* "drew heavily on English borough practice" (Erskine, MacDonald, and Penman 2007: 58). However, Newcastle at that time was changing hands to and fro between England and Scotland. David I, who is credited with early urbanization of Scotland (section 5.3), carried out several campaigns into Northumberland, which Stringer called "extensive conquests" (2005: 45). In fact, Newcastle hosted David I's court from 1141 onwards, and it seems that the laws of the burghs were designed there through deliberations and negotiations involving both English and Scottish burgesses. In the text of the laws we find a direct reference to "the assise of the New Castell" (in the Latin version—*assisa tenta apud Novum Castrum*), dealing with the recovery of land by a previously replaced proprietor, which the editor describes as the "result of a conference between the Burghs of England and Scotland". Another law, this time about selling lands on one's deathbed, is equipped with the editor's comment that "this…part of the matter [was] consulted upon at Newcastle", suggesting that representatives of English and Scottish burghs conferred and devised the legal codes together (Innes 1868: 48–49). Similarly, an important law on the division of hereditary possessions among the heirs of a deceased burgess was "[o]ne of the matters consulted at Newcastle" (Innes 1868: 55). These hints indicate that the compilation of Scottish burgh laws may not have been simply an imitation of English laws but an active dialogue with a more extensively urbanized neighbour by the assembly of representatives of the Four Burghs.

Later copies of the laws, rendered in the vernacular, may be found in many medieval burghs, which shows the growing prestige of Scots as a medium of formal discourse. The first extant vernacular copies date back to 1455 (MS W.4 ult. in the Advocates' Library, Innes 1868: xx), even though the assumption that earlier versions must have existed remains plausible. The laws were printed in the early seventeenth century by Skene, and later critically revised in accordance with manuscript versions. One of the best-known editions (Innes 1868), referred to above and in the remainder of this section, included parallel Latin and Scots versions of the laws in one hundred and nineteen chapters.[15]

The law which appears as the first one in Innes's edition, and seems to be "[o]ne of the older burgh laws" (Renwick 1910: x), specifies the annual rent, the so-called *burgh maills*, payable to the feudal sovereign by the burgesses for holding each "rud of land" (*pro perticata terre*). In medieval Scotland, the king was the owner of all land, so he was the one to grant land to the burgesses in return for the money which the Crown always needed. When it comes to land inheritance, appropriate regulations were outlined in the *Leges*, stressing the rights of the male heir, as well as other children. There were provisions for keeping the lands within the burgh, and potential points of contention between children and widows were addressed (*Leges*, xxi–xxiv), as well as inheritance issues within the so-called "fre mariage" (*Leges*, xli). With the development of feudalism new solutions were introduced, for example, that the land could be sold or let in the presence of witnesses. Recurrent fragments in the EdHeW material often contain reference to witnesses, for example, *befor thir witnes* (section 11.3.1), *and beris witnes*, or *in ye witnes*. In fact, the long bundle *in witnes of ye quhilk thing* 'in witness of the which thing' emerges as one of the most stable combinations in the early fifteenth century (section 12.2.2). The role of a witness was an important one and there needed to be provisions for the unavailability of the witnesses, who may have died or left the area before they had been called upon to prove somebody's right to hold the land. "If at any time there was a dispute as to ownership, the right to the land was decided (if the witnesses were dead) by twelve men who could speak to the narration of their fathers, or of those to whom they would give as much credence as to themselves" (Smith 1955: 607). Such trustworthy "gud men of the town" appeared frequently in the laws as the advisory-cum-judicial body. In the EdHeW records, there is talk about *xii wordy men* and *gud men of* (the town), but these expressions do not repeat in the form of lexical bundles too often. However, among the binomials extracted from the present corpus, *lele and trew* 'loyal and true' shows a large degree of formulaicity (for the method of gauging formulaicity, see section 8.5.4). This expression was also used to describe the witnesses in a burgh court.

Leges Burgorum regulated the burgh government, as discussed in section 6.3.3. The laws also specified who could become a burgess and outlined the fealty pledge taken by each new burgess: "to oure lorde the kyng and to the bailyeis and to the communyte of that burgh" (Innes 1868: 4), stressing the relationship of an individual with the sovereign, his representatives, and the whole community. As the analytic chapters will show, the EdHeW material is filled with references to *balzeis and comonite* (for the binomial, see section 10.2.3; for other lexical bundles, see section 11.3.1). The inhabitants of royal burghs had special privileges and answered to no other superior but the king. Attractive a prospect as it was, it must have inspired many people to seek freedom and safety within the town walls. In fact, one of the laws stated that a serf (*thirl*) may become burgess if he had managed to dwell in a burgh for a "tuelfmoneth and a day" without being challenged by his lawful lord (*Leges*, xv, section 6.3.2).

We learn from the *Leges* how trade, the crucial economic activity centred in burghs, was regulated and organized. For instance, there was a law which forbade salt and herring to be sold at the market, even though other merchandise from ships could well be "brocht to land" (*Leges*, ix), as well as regulations concerning the conditions for slaying animals and the subsequent sale of meat (*Leges*, lxiv–lxv). If anybody was caught selling "rotten pork and salmon" (*porci et salmones corrupti*), the meat was confiscated and given to the lepers "without ony manere of question" (*Fragmenta Collecta*, xlv; Innes 1868: 183). The laws took care of the production and sales standards, establishing penalties for fraudulent trade, as well as unscrupulous competition; for instance, no town official was allowed to make a living from baking or brewing while in office (*Leges*, lix). On top of that, burgh councils were expected by James I's law to elect a warden of the crafts whose task was to monitor the quality of workmanship and set prices. This legislation concerned "masonis, wrychtis, smythis, talyeouris, webstaris and all uthiris elik" (Donaldson 1970: 81).[16] Fees for holding a stall at the market were specified, as were standards of measure and weight (*Leges*, lxviii, see section 6.5 on which burgh held which standard). Other regulations concerned the location and management of mills and ovens.[17] Additional safety features in the burgh included special laws in case of leprosy (*Leges*, lviii).

Individual burghs may have had their own additional regulations, for example, the burghs with access to water tracts had separate shipping laws (see Frankot (2010) for maritime laws in late medieval Aberdeen). Peebles burgh records talk about regulations on gambling and games, using burgh money to build dykes and walls, and employing a hangman (*Peebles records* 1910: xvi). Interestingly, the laws contain several passages (*Leges*, iii, xii, xxvi, xxix, xxxii, xxxiv) on how to handle various situations involving "ane uplandis man"—a non-burgess, a rural dweller: what to do if such a person is attacked at the market or challenged with theft, or who solves a conflict between an "uplandis" debtor and a burgess who had lent him cattle. Instances of conflict between burgesses and merchants are also regulated in the laws, as are conflicts between the inhabitants of royal burghs and ecclesiastical burghs, or burghs of barony (*Leges*, xiii; see also section 5.3 on different types of burghs), and violent behaviour in general, including bloodshed (*blodewit*) and an assault with a stick (*stokisdynt*). There are also guidelines on how to reclaim one's possessions or money from a debtor, with a provision that no burgess may distrain another (*Leges*, xliv).

There are a few Scandinavian legal terms in the *Leges Quatuor Burgorum* (Kopaczyk 2011b), which again evinces the multicultural character of Scottish burghs from the very beginning. The Scandinavian influences on Scottish legal practices included the rules of *burlaw* (ON *býjar-lög* 'law community'), which in Scotland meant "the local law governing small townships or villages" (Dickinson 1937: cxiii). These laws mostly concerned living in good and peaceful neighbourhood, so beneficial for the growth and prosperity of burghs (Symms 1986: 18).

7.3.2. THE CAPACITY OF BURGH COURTS

The highest legal authority in medieval Scotland was *curia regis*, the king's court (Robinson, Fergus, and Gordon 2000: 157), but the pyramid of justice had a wide base in all kinds of local courts. "[A]t strategic centres the King had established his castles and his sheriffs to represent him as judge and administrator" (Smith 1955: 610), while the burghs exercised their own jurisdiction through a separate burgh court (*curia burgi*). The beginnings of burgh courts can be traced back to early councils of officials, "appointed as *prepositi* or *ballivi* to administer the burghs on king's behalf" (Dickinson 1957: lxxx, n. 4). In general, burgh courts could deal with both civil and criminal offences. The distinction relied on the type of punishment involved, as specified in *Regiam Majestatem* (Walker 1990: 523; see also section 7.2.1): criminal actions were punished by death or chopping off limbs, while civil pleas incurred penalty in money. The primary civil concerns of burgh courts were matters of land tenure and ownership, inheritance issues and the financial implications thereof (Smith 1955: 610; on the importance of land in burgh economy, see section 6.4.2). Other matters were linked with the fields outlined by *Leges Burgorum*: the admission of burgesses,[18] monitoring the markets, producers, and sellers, problems with settling debts, and reacting to the 'strublans of the town'.[19] While *strublans* or even *wrangus trublance of ye* (town) appears in the EdHeW material only occasionally, the reference to new burgesses creates one of the long standardizing strings: *item that ilk day was maid burges* (section 12.2.3).

Every burgh's history was different when it came to the most common offences. Burgesses accused one another of petty thefts, unpaid debts, trespassing, unscrupulous trade, or breaking the rules of good neighbourhood. Other cases were more serious, bordering on criminal actions, for example, *bludewite*[20] or *deforcement*[21] (see also Sanderson 2002: 187–189). Deforcement was most common in the burgh of Carnwath (Dickinson 1937: civ). In Stirling burgh court book, there were 326 entries regarding debt and "[e]ven more striking [was] the total number of 337 non-appearances, leading to amercements" (Symms 1986: 25). As EdHeW includes entries from that court book, no wonder that the word *amersyment* often appears in formulaic strings (section 11.3.1). Sometimes local courts would be given special permission from the king to deal with higher offences.[22] These special powers could depend, for instance, on whether a burgh had a provost, who was also a sheriff with a far wider jurisdiction than a regular alderman. The effectiveness of the system was monitored by a network of royal officials: the burgh courts were supervised by the chamberlain (Smith 1955: 611; Godfrey 2002: 112–113, n. 19). He could appeal to the Convention, also referred to as the 'Parliament' of the Burghs.

The most important court in the whole year was the head court whose dates were correlated with important religious celebrations: Michaelmas, Yule, and Pasch (Walker 1990: 433–434). The head courts were responsible for guarding the privileges, confirming existing laws in a burgh, and passing new ones. The administration of the burgh (section 6.3.3) was elected during the Michaelmas court (Symms 1986: 21). In fact, explicit reference to that holiday emerges in lexical bundles, too, for example, *day efter michelmess*, but not in the most formulaic ones (section 9.2). Throughout the year, "intermediate courts, *curiae legales*, were held at fortnightly intervals" (Walker 1990: 433). There were also minor temporary courts for the duration of fairs and for handling minor offences, for example, *pies-poudrees* or dusty-feet courts for pedlars (Marwick 1897: ix). A pedlar, selling goods from his portable stall, was treated on equal terms with burgesses while the market lasted, and had the right (and, if summoned, the obligation) to come before the court.

Burgh courts supplied an opportunity to hear others and to be heard. They were a venue for voicing personal objections and demanding that law and order be kept. "The use of a public forum as a sounding board for aspects of inter-personal relationships took advantage of the public nature of private life in a small, crowded and socially interdependent burgh. Personal characteristics were public knowledge, and it was, therefore, safer for business transactions to be publicly aired rather than to be wholly private matters, and as such likely to attract gossip and innuendo" (Symms 1986: 354–355). Symms brings back into focus the idea of a close-knit community, people who live and work together, who know each other and are aware of each other's interests and personal characteristics. In this milieu, the burgesses in court participated in creating a discourse community (section 3.6), fulfilling at the same time the role of audience and creators of discourse.

The end of the medieval period in Scots law and jurisdiction came with the establishment of the College of Justice (1532), during the reign of James V (section 5.3.6). The supreme civil court sanctioned the dealings of various men of law in early modern Scotland (section 7.4), who until then had put the accounts of their dealings in the *acta* of their councils (Finlay 2000: 1). In the 1520s there operated an embryonic central court, the Court of Session, staffed by semi-professional judges (Donaldson 1970: 105). These new forms of public administration and courts point to a gradual strengthening of the legal system in sixteenth-century Scotland (Godfrey 2002: 111).

7.3.3. SOCIAL MAKE-UP OF BURGH COURTS

An exemplary list of persons engaged in court proceedings, together with the details of their office, is given in the preface to the burgh records of Dunfermline:

> So early as 1488 the burgh affairs of Dunfermline were managed by a prepositus (or alderman), two bailies, and an 'assize' of burgesses, together with a 'common clerk' (often a priest), a 'dempstar' (who pronounced the sentence of court), and two sergeants. The municipal year ran from Michaelmas with three head courts, viz. those next after Michaelmas, Christmas and Easter, while ordinary courts were sometimes held fortnightly, though often recorded at much longer intervals. The prepositus or alderman (these titles being convertible) was chosen each year at the head court after Michaelmas, and the bailies at the same time. Bailies other than those chosen at the Michaelmas court are occasionally found acting during the year; and possibly these may have held office by interim appointment, though no election of that kind is recorded. The term council (consall) does not occur until 1515, and indeed the customary 'assize' would appear to have been a more or less arbitrary selection from among the burgesses, who sat upon one court and might or might not be called for the next. (Beveridge 1917: xv–xvi)

The names of these offices surface clearly in the referential bundles, discussed in section 11.3.1. They also form frequent binomials, for example, *aldirman and balzeis* or *balzeis and consail* (section 10.2.3). Indeed, the core participants in administering justice were the bailies. Initially, they were royal tax officers, appointed by the crown, who in time became members of the burgh council (section 6.3.3). The earliest legal provisions stated that the burgesses should choose their representatives collectively and directly (*Leges*, lxx). *Statuta Gilde* specified that the whole community should choose their council. This close connection between the people and their representatives has surfaced in the binomials in EdHeW: *consail and comonite* 'council and community' is the most frequent binomial motivated by hyponymy (section 10.2.3). Election procedures were further regulated by the parliament, which issued a statement protecting the local administration centres from "multitud and clamor of commonis sympil personis" (*Lanark records* 1893: xxviii). Clearly, the meetings of all the burgesses must have been difficult to contain. In fact, due to "gret truble and contensione" at yearly elections, the parliaments of James III (section 5.4.4) decided that the old council should choose the new council and that "thair salbe of the aulde consale of the yer befor foure worthy personis" continuing their work in the newly elected governing body (Donaldson 1970: 84–85).[23] It was also ordered that the members of each craft of should choose their representatives who would then have the right to vote in the council elections.

In this way, burgh councils reflected the composition of the medieval society and were not created by means of a statute or similar legislation.

The highest official in the town council, the alderman or provost (the Scots versions of the *Leges* do not translate the Latin *prepositus* consistently, Kopaczyk 2011b: 12), was, in turn, elected by the council. His task was to select people for important functions in town, for example, liners (*lyneris*), who were responsible for measuring out the plots of burgh lands. Such appointments were made only "at the sicht and be the consale" of the burgh community (*Leges*, cv) and the alderman and the bailies had to make sure that no complaints were filed to the chamberlain who could order financial penalties, had this been the case. A special function in a burgh court was performed by an inquest, an approved group of witnesses, usually fifteen in number, who performed the role of a jury. References to the inquest do not form the most formulaic bundles, but they do recur in EdHeW, for example, *inquest abone wryttyn*, *ye said inquest*, or *inquest has ordanit*. The role of inquest was significant in inheritance matters (*Lanark records* 1893: xxviii), as well as in penalizing merchants for false weights and measurements (*Fragmenta Collecta*, xlviii; Innes 1868: 184). Other persons could also appear at the head court as advisors and specialists, for example, tasters of ale (*gustatores cevisie*). When it comes to the roles played by individual burgesses, a good example is an early sixteenth-century burgess of Selkirk, John of Bellenden, who appeared before the burgh court some forty times in nineteen years, in various capacities: as a witness, a pursuer, but most often as a defendant (Symms 1986: 31–32).

7.3.4. PROCEDURE AND PUNISHMENT

Burgh courts were required by law to meet every fifteen days throughout the year to punish "lawe-brakers" (*Fragmenta Collecta*, xxxiii; Innes 1868: 177). Apparently, even this frequency of meetings was not sufficient. Symms noticed that "[b]y 1544 the court seems to have been meeting every week to deal with small pleas" (1986: 19). Before the court could open its proceedings, it had to be formally constituted through the so-called *fencing*[24] (see section 2.3 on legal rituals). The procedure probably stemmed from a Scandinavian custom of "symbolically delineating the area of a court" (Cairns 2000: 18), described in Latin as *curia firmata* (Hamilton-Grierson 1924: 54). The recurrent event was mirrored in repetitive formulae in burgh records, such as *ye curt effermit* (section 11.3.3), which becomes the core of a longer standardizing chunk (section 12.2.4). After the ceremony was completed, the list of suitors and witnesses was called out before the court. A person could lawfully be summoned to court only by a "bedal" or sergeant in front of witnesses, confirmed by a written proof (*Fragmenta Collecta*, xxx; Innes 1868: 176). If a burgess wanted to file in a private lawsuit, he or she could do it by a "bill of complaint" (Dickinson 1937: xcix).

All participants were called in three times before being pronounced as absent. Numerous recurrent references to *ye first*, *ye sycund*, and *ye tyrd curt* in EdHeW (section 9.5) create a picture of long-lasting court hearings. Non-appearance was recorded and subject to amerciament,[25] and could result in even harsher punishment for notorious absentees (Dickinson 1937: xcix–c). In the fourth court, eight shillings were paid for non-appearance, while ultimately a burgess may have been deprived of burgh freedoms, a last resort threat for bringing people before justice (Symms 1986: 26). Standing before the court, one had to take an oath; the bailies, as well as the provost and other burgesses, had to confirm their burgess status before they could be heard at court (*Fragmenta Collecta*, xxxiv; Innes 1868: 177). They did not have to speak in person. A procurator could be hired to plead his or her case (Dickinson 1937: cii; on men of law, see section 7.4). The court sitting began with reading out the minutes of the last meeting and before proceeding to new matters, any unfinished ones were given attention (Symms 1986: 20 n. 12). Verdicts were decided by the jury. After hearing the statements of both parties involved, the jury would retire to deliberate, and on return presented their 'deliverance' as the decision of the whole court.

For lesser crimes, sanctions imposed by burgh courts included fining, as well as confiscation (*poynt and distrenȝe*), both providing a steady source of income for the burgh (see section 6.4 on burgh economy). Another type of penalty was imprisonment in a tolbooth or by warding (a sort of self-imprisonment) (Symms 1986: 27–28). In Dunfermline records, among various instruments of punishment, we find the *sentens of cursing*, an excommunication for non-payment of debt (Beveridge 1917: xix).

In the case of a serious crime, criminals had to be caught red-handed and the punishment was the gallows. In contrast to extensive accounts of civil lawsuits, criminal actions do not receive much space. Dickinson comments that "the entries are so brief that they afford no clue as to the procedure which was followed". He presents two reasons for this state of affairs. First, the court ordered capital punishment if the accused was found guilty of murder or serious theft; "he was hanged and that was the end of it". Secondly, "the procedure itself was so summary that no fuller entry could be given. Suspicious characters received but short shrift" (Dickinson 1937: ciii). I would suggest that civil cases were much more common at burgh courts than grave offences, which gives another reason why criminal action rarely featured in the records.

Courts were not only a place where culprits were doomed and victims met justice. A crucial activity of this official body of burgh administration was also the supervision, recognition, and verification of various dealings connected with land transfer. In his meticulous edition of early municipal laws, Innes praises "the judicial care with which, in Scotland, all the procedure connected with the transfer of heritable right to burgage property was conducted" (1868: xxxvii). The procedure had the form of a special ceremony, the *livery of seisin*, which in a symbolic way enhanced and underlined the character of the deed. It was carried out outdoors, on the land under transfer: the granter took *erd and stane*—earth and stone—and passed it to the bailie representing the burgh court together with an *outpenny*.

The bailie would then perform the same activity and give the *erd and stane* to the grantee, together with an *inpenny*.[26] Similarly, even if a burgess had to forfeit his tenement to the Crown for non-payment of the yearly burgh maills, there was a way of recovering this land, involving the symbolic elements of "earth and stone". First, a piece of earth and a stone from the tenement in question were displayed in front of the bailies at three consecutive courts. Subsequently, the tokens were put in a bag, confirmed with the bailies' seal and, at the fourth court, produced in front of the bailies by the pursuer. Thus, the symbolic repossession of land was completed (Innes 1868: xxxvii–xxxviii). The binomial *erd and stan* is one of the most formulaic expressions in the EdHeW corpus (section 10.2.3), which goes hand in hand with the historical records. Rodger and Newman observe that the custom of "earth and stone" was a default procedure in land transfer in the early fourteenth century, whereas towards the end of the Middle Ages "the notarial instrument of Sasine [became] the sole permissible proof of transfer" (1988: 49). The notary public confirmed the deed in writing, by means of producing a special document—*breve testatum*. In time, this became the only lawful way of transferring land.[27]

To conclude, in burgh courts daily matters in the lives of burgh inhabitants found their public forum. Burgh courts were not simply a part of the royal machinery for imposing justice and law but, maybe even more importantly, they "promoted a sense of community and a degree of independence" (Symms 1986: 29). Moreover, one can imagine that such meetings, bringing people of all walks of life together, could have been an occasion not only for solemnity but also for merriment. In Viking sagas, "the meetings of the local courts were occasions for festivity as well as for the execution of the law. There were jugglers and drinking booths, and the people 'came in great numbers . . . palavering and merry-making' [quoting *Grettir* c. 72]'" (Dickinson 1937: cxi–cxii). In free royal burghs, administering justice could be seen as an occasion for strengthening the ties within the community, so common entertainment would have served the same practical function.

7.4. Men of Law

The legal profession developed rather slowly in Scotland. In the earliest times, lawyers did not have to have a proper educational background; the most important factor was their intention and willingness to serve society, and an oath before the college of justice.[28] "[T]he only legal professionals we can identify with certainty before 1500 are the church lawyers [who, by this token, also had influence in secular jurisdiction] and notaries" (MacQueen 1986: 420). Finlay (2000), however, prefers to assert "with reasonable confidence" that no legal profession, defined along the same lines as contemporary legal profession in England, existed in Scotland before 1500. English law was quick to require specialized, institutionalized learning because very early on it became entrenched in a particular reality, with the history of precedents and common law (section 7.2.2). Legal education was thus centred on the courts of justice and the chancery (Finlay 2000: 2–3; cf. Brand 1992). The majority of early men of law were in holy orders (Symms 1993: xi), which equipped them with literacy skills, Latin, and rudiments of canon and civil law. Early lawyers in Scotland were a heterogeneous bunch, referred to by various names: notaries, procurators, advocates, assessors, or forespeakers—terms which by no means represented clear-cut distinctions between the dealings of respective people. On the contrary, these terms were often used interchangeably (Finlay 2000: 3, 9–10; cf. Carswell's (1967) attempt to determine some division of prerogatives among early Scottish lawyers). This confusion in nomenclature seems to lessen with time. As Finlay puts it, "there was certainly a progression from 'forespeaker' and 'procurator' to 'advocate'" (2000: 11), which indicates semantic standardization and a decision to groom terminological chaos. In the EdHeW corpus, only the term *forspekar* emerges in a few repetitive lexical strings, mostly between 1410 and 1440.

Legal education definitely had impact on these developments as it grew in importance in the fifteenth century. Scottish universities (St Andrews 1411, Glasgow 1451, Aberdeen 1494) mostly taught canon law, with only St Andrews teaching civil law for a short period in the sixteenth century. Therefore Scottish students of law very often trained for their profession on the Continent, in universities such as Wittenberg, Bourges, Poitiers, or Paris, as well as in the Netherlands, in Louvain, Leiden, or Utrecht (Smith 1955: 619; Finlay 2000: 6; Walker 2001: 133; MacQueen 2002a).[29] This is one more reason for continental legal practices (Roman and feudal laws) permeating those in Scotland.

In this book, two legal professionals are of special consequence, those who created the textual material under scrutiny here: the notary and the scribe. The function of the notary was not only the keeping of records but, more importantly, their authentication (see also section 10.2.3 for the binomial *notar and witnes*). This is a consequence of the transition from the oral character of legal transactions, authenticated by seals, oaths, and witnesses (Finlay 2009: 394), to the era of written documentation (section 2.3). The notary public, an occupation which followed from the practice in Roman Law and was introduced in Scotland around the thirteenth century (Durkan 1983: 22; Finlay 2009: 393), was of vital importance for the paperwork of the increasingly bureaucratized legal machinery.[30] How awkward it must have been for the Dunfermline burgesses, when in 1498 an entry in the records was cancelled because the notary's fee was not paid (Beveridge 1917: xviii). The notary public was granted legal authority by the highest powers: at the very beginning—by the Holy Roman Emperor (as his powers extended then throughout the Continent), or by the Pope (Symms 1993: xii), which is why initially there were very few notaries and they had to travel extensively to authorize documents all around the country (Durkan 1983). Consequently, there was much concern about authenticity of the notaries (Murray 1910: 9–14; Carswell 1967: 51), to which fifteenth-century parliamentary legislation in Scotland testifies. After 1469, notaries had to be authorized by the Scottish monarch, and after the Reformation by the lords of council, to guard against unqualified or false notaries, even under death penalty (Finlay 2009: 395, 398).

The second group of writers responsible for keeping legal and administrative records were the scribes and clerks of council. This job, rather mechanical in nature, was one of the crucial public offices in medieval and early modern towns. Admittedly, in many places the town clerk was the only public officer "qualified to write out compts with the customary formalities" up to the nineteenth century (Pryde 1937: cxiv). "The customary formalities" also applied when clerks of council put down the burgh council's proceedings. The writers had to be familiar with the expected generic features, as well as the necessary terminology, and be able to construct legally binding documents. By 1540 legislation, their skill and trustworthiness was subject to examination before the lords of council in Edinburgh.

The rise of notaries and scribes went hand in hand with the growth of legal machinery across medieval Europe. Acts of Scottish Parliament list them in one breath in related statutes: "writaris notaris and scribes in our soverane lordis courtis of Justice" (Finlay 2009: 396). In the EdHeW corpus, the extraction of lexical bundles rendered several cases of *public notar and common writar*, especially in Peebles. Robert Scott, a clerk of session between 1539 and 1592, was referred to as 'clerk', 'writer', or 'scribe', even though his areas of responsibility and expertise were clearly greater (Sanderson 2002: 195). As Brundage (2008: 394–395, 400) points out, the two professions are not easily distinguishable because of the gradation of skill and knowledge among the notaries. Some of them simply acted as legal secretaries, some as more skilled and independent craftsmen, and some could have been properly schooled in law, not to mention eminent high officials who practiced as notaries and used their authority as notary public to confirm documents. One may thus assume that the texts included in the EdHeW corpus were written by notaries and scribes from various walks of life—from humble town clerks to professionals with wide repute. The textual patterns which emerge from the records, as well as a high degree of lexical and structural formulaicity to be explored in Chapters 9 to 12, point to linguistic standardization of legal documents, regardless of who wrote them. The necessary prerequisite, however, would be access to tradition and the existing body of texts, either through formalized education or through imitation of earlier records, protocol books of former notaries,[31] and formularies (Gouldesbrough 1985). It has been argued in section 3.6 that notaries and legal scribes can be perceived as a community of practice, as they "produce similar kinds of texts with similar objectives" (Williamson 2002b).[32] In order to do that in an officially binding, authoritative and stable manner, notaries and writers had to share a repertoire of linguistic tools, so the expectation of similar or even identical lexico-syntactic patterns is well-founded.

7.5. Legal Records

Notaries and clerks at burgh courts composed documents which today open a window on the life and customs of medieval and early renaissance Scots. Of course, the writings do not paint a full and comprehensive picture of the society, nor do they survive in large quantities. Nevertheless, they constitute a unique source of historical, social, and linguistic information[33] about the burghs and their inhabitants. Butcher argues for a reassessment of urban legal and administrative records in terms of "a social and communal literature" (2004: 161), which can provide new tools for looking at the medieval society. As Symms put it, "the deliberations of the burgh court often contained many of the strands that went to make up the total network of urban life" (1986: 1). When it comes to content, documents written in burghal institutions abound in descriptions of misconduct and law-breaking. As Renwick rightly observes, "[b]urgh court records illustrate the saying that men's evil manners live in brass, their virtues we write in water.... Thefts, assaults, and abusive language provide the bulk of the cases brought into court" (1910: xxii). In all probability, though, the life outside burgh courts had a peaceful side to it, too.

Historians notice the fragmentary nature of the data for the earliest periods of vernacular writing (Symms 1986: 17). The earliest surviving burgh records date back to the fourteenth century, although in some places (e.g. Lanark), the earliest municipal proceedings come from the mid-fifteenth century (*Lanark records* 1893: xxi). The records expand in volume and coverage as the time progresses, hence the discrepancies in word count for different sub-periods in the EdHeW collection (section 8.2, Fig. 8.1). They also contain more and more formulaic responses and utterances, for example, for the "falsing of doom", which translates as questioning the verdict (*Fragmenta Collecta*, lii; Innes 1868: 185). I argued in Chapter 2 that formulaic expressions, unchanged and stable in their form, added authority and force to the legal documents. As notarial protocol books show, the documents produced by notaries were rigidly structured. Donaldson notices that there was "little variation from the first recorded instance in Scotland in 1287 until the year 1847" (1952: vi). The instrument, as the final version of the document was called, began with the invocation "In Dei Nomine", followed by a narrative of what happened ("was acted, spoken and done") in presence of witnesses.[34] To prove the authority of the notary, the *docquet* included the notary's name and scope of power, as well as a statement that he wrote everything in his own hand. Finally, the document was finished with a *signum* unique to every notary. Initially, the documents were compiled *post factum* from notes which the notary would take in his protocol book but "when the notary was clerk of a local or burgh court, almost the whole entry in the protocol book was in instrument form" (Donaldson 1952: vi).

Keeping records of the court proceedings and rulings became important for several reasons. First, the document was an official account of what the burgh court ruled and how it was done, and as such it could be used in appeals to a higher court. Secondly, it provided a reference point for other legal actions, especially with regard to land transfer and inheritance issues. The records constituted a repository of decisions and events for future reference and helped to establish and maintain burghal traditions and historical continuity.

Various other documents also survive as supplementary material written and used in Scottish burgh courts. One early Scottish legal instrument was a *brieve*, similar to an English writ. Smith (1955: 613) notices that sometimes brieves were copies of English writs but with time the typically Scottish style of brieves became increasingly standardized. In courts, bills were submitted, most often with a view to lodge a complaint, and the answers were written on the back (Symms 1986: 19). Early wills contained references to property and persons, heavily contextualized in the earliest examples, such as 'I'm leaving my best field to my favourite son' (Danet 1997: 28–29; see also the discussion of orality features in early law in section 2.3). In time, such documents became more and more uniform in style and universal in the applicability of patterns. In section 2.4.2 on legal genres, I have summarized the range of Middle Scots documents included in the EdHeW corpus; these are primarily charters of all kinds (bonds of manrent and obligation, grants, quitclaims, leases, arbitrations, etc.), burgh court records, and notarial protocol books. Together, they belong to the same register and the same unique legal culture of Scottish burghs, which was the focus of the present chapter. The structure and content of these texts will therefore reflect not only the general characteristics of legal discourse but also the typically Scottish legal concerns.

With the shift from orality to written records in the realm of law, there came the need to guarantee the force of the documents through their format and stability. It was the skilled, professional text compilers who were able to record the decisions and proceedings in writing in an authoritative manner, with the expected features of formulaicity and immutability. In the next, analytic part of this book, corpus methods will be used to bring out the formulaic nature of early Scottish legal texts. Throughout Part Two, I have supplemented the discussion with references to the fixed strings emerging from the corpus and corresponding with the crucial aspects of Scottish legal practice in medieval and early renaissance burghs. It remains to be explored in detail which linguistic constituents—specific syntactic strings and patterns of lexical choices—and in what quantities recur in the texts, and how they contribute to textual standardization of early Scottish legal texts.

PART TWO

Summary and Conclusions

Research into discourse patterns in historical texts would not be complete without careful attention to the circumstances in which the texts were conceived. Without this knowledge, our interpretation of linguistic choices in the texts would suffer from the lack of proper contextualization, which could result in superficial analyses, misunderstandings, and unwarranted conclusions. Historical discourse analysis requires true interdisciplinarity. In order to understand how discourse was formed at a given point in time, and why it was formed in a specific way, one needs to engage in a detailed study of the period in question.

The present project faced a manifold challenge at the start: not only are the texts under scrutiny historical, but they also come from the area of law, a specialized field of discourse. Moreover, they were written in Scotland, a country whose legal traditions are indigenous and unique, as well as unfamiliar to wider audiences. The third complication stemmed from the fact that the linguistic fabric of the texts was woven from the threads of life in the burghs, medieval and early renaissance Scottish towns. Burgh inhabitants and their daily concerns come to the fore in formulaic legal discourse, as signalled through the numerous links between the historical Part Two and the analytical Part Three.

These difficulties were addressed one by one in the preceding chapters. At the beginning of Part Two, the burghs were situated in the historical and political developments of the period. Chapter 5 traced the beginnings of urbanization in Scotland, which went hand in hand with the fluctuating consolidation of the Scottish kingdom and its position on the international scene. The burghs played an active role in domestic politics, shaping their own common policies in burgh assemblies and sending representatives to the Scottish Parliament. As the short pen-portraits of Scottish rulers have shown, the monarchs had a connection with the burghs going beyond a simple grant of the royal charter. The burghs backed them up against domestic and foreign enemies, supplied their treasuries, paid their ransoms, hosted their courts and kept the king's peace. Simultaneously, these early urban centres provided context for the compilation and execution of burgh laws, surveyed in Chapter 7. They were also the venue of social interaction, captured in legal and administrative texts comprising the EdHeW corpus.

To follow up this theme, Part Two has given space to various aspects of living in the burghs and the social hierarchy there. The labels for government offices and administrative functions which recur in the lexical bundles, such as *bailie*, *alderman*, or *council*, have been described and placed in situational context. Chapter 6 outlined the social relationships within a burgh, bringing out specific roles played by various members of the population, while Chapter 7 expounded the legal background for the rights and obligations of the officials and burgesses, as reflected in the legal texts. The socio-historical inquiry has also revealed why reference to land transactions and inheritance is so frequent in the EdHeW corpus. Land ownership was the prerequisite for burgess-ship and a source of income both for individuals and the community, and as such occupies a prominent place in the recurrent fragments of legal and administrative texts.

The documents also reflect the indigenous character of Scots legal regulations and legal language. The final section of Chapter 5 has shown how Scottish identity could pertain to burgh dwellers and how it was manifested through language and law.

In Chapter 7, I explained why Scots law, drawing on continental civil codes, is different from the common law of its southern neighbour. At the same time I highlighted the common feudal grounds from which medieval legal practice arose. Ample space was also devoted to law and order in the burghs—most specifically to burgh courts, their members and procedures. It is remarkable how closely the standardizing fragments of early legal discourse reflect the most conspicuous aspects of burgh court dealings, for instance, the ritual fencing of the court or the penalties for notorious non-appearance.

Finally, Part Two closed with a focus on the compilers of legal texts and on the fruit of their work. In the period of limited literacy, the very skill of drafting documents was possessed by a narrow and rather homogeneous group of people. As explained in the theoretical part (section 3.6), the burgh itself can be treated as a discourse community, but within it, a more pronounced community of notaries and scribes can be discerned. Due to the common communicative competence and goals, they can be perceived as a community of practice, a community which may become, and which did become, as the subsequent chapters will show, the locus of language change—the textual standardization in progress.

Equipped with the knowledge of the extralinguistic conditions, we may now proceed to extract the most frequent and stable lexico-syntactic patterns from the EdHeW corpus. At the start of Part Three, this collection of texts, as well as the method of lexical bundle extraction, is presented; in the remaining part of the book, the discussion moves on to engage in the interpretation of forms and functions of lexical bundles, informed by the extensive socio-historical background surveyed in the preceding chapters.

PART THREE

The Legal Language of the Burghs

8

EdHeW Corpus Material and Lexical Bundles

8.1. Introduction

The present chapter begins the analytic and data-oriented part of this study. Legal language produced in the medieval and early modern Scottish burghs has been segmented into lexical bundles. The lexical bundles have been assessed in terms of frequency and fixedness and the most frequent ones have been examined from structural and functional angles, to highlight which areas of early legal discourse displayed textual standardization. The interpretation of the observed patterns is anchored in the historical background of Scottish burgh life and early Scots law, presented in detail in Part Two. As the discussion in the next chapters will show, without the in-depth contextualization, the presentation of lexical bundles would be little more than a list of frequently repeated chunks of text. It is the extralinguistic context that gives us the chance to discover the reasons behind textual standardization and the areas of discourse which rely on stable communicative patterns.

In section 8.2 below, I introduce the legal texts which lay at the base of this study: the EdHeW corpus. It consists of the earliest extant vernacular legal documents in Scotland, transcribed and digitized in the major part from the original manuscripts. This unique and complex material has not yet been explored in this format, which is why it should be approached with meticulous care. When it comes to research tools, as noted in Chapter 3, historical discourse analysis draws increasingly on corpus methodology. By extracting repetitive chunks of text, the lexical bundles, it was possible to investigate the formulaic nature of early legal discourse in Scotland, as well as pinpoint the structural and functional elements undergoing standardization. Due to the specific nature of the linguistic material in EdHeW, however, corpus tools needed to be applied with extra caution and with appropriate settings. Sections 8.3–8.5 explain in detail how the lexical bundle extraction proceeded and suggest solutions for the problems any historical corpus analysis may encounter (e.g. the issue of word divisions, punctuation, or spelling variants). As this study is the first one to apply lexical bundles to historical texts on such a scale, the transparency of procedure is of great importance. In this chapter, the reader will have a chance to assess the challenges and appreciate the benefits brought about by the new methodology. I address the specific nature of lexical bundles in terms of their length, frequency thresholds, and bundle overlaps. I also develop a special formulaicity measure to gauge the degree of formulaicity in particular extracted sequences which are analysed qualitatively in the remainder of Part Three.

The present chapter is a technical introduction to what constitutes the analytic part of the book. Having established the database of lexical bundles, according to the adopted procedures and rationale, I begin the analytical part with a formal analysis in Chapter 9, to get to the core of which grammatical patterns were fixed to the largest extent in early legal discourse in Scotland. The structure of lexical bundles, however, is elusive due to the method of their extraction. The bundles extracted here ranged from three to eight consecutive elements, which meant that at their shortest they could either be a phrase or constitute a part of a phrase, while at their longest they could contain parts of two or more grammatical units (section 4.4). To find a way of presenting this heterogeneous material, the shorter bundles (3- to 5-grams) were separated from 6- to 8-grams. The choice of this division is not as arbitrary as it may seem. The bundles above six consecutive elements tend to overlap to a large extent, so they are best analysed together (see the discussion of overlaps in section 8.5.5); they are also fewer in number (compare the word percentages in Table 8.5).

Thus, Chapter 9 sets out the grammatical properties of short lexical bundles, using the concept of phrase fragments and categorizing the chunks by the grammatical category of the most prominent element into noun phrase fragments, prepositional phrase fragments, verb phrase fragments, and clause fragments. We thus gain a unique insight into the structural features of fixedness in early legal texts. Lexical bundles have also turned out to be a ready pool of other multi-word units, characteristic for legal discourse; from the phrasally complete bundles, I have selected binomials and multinomials to be given separate space in Chapter 10, as they are often recalled as one of the typical lexical features of legal discourse (section 4.5). These coordinated structures, such as *erd and stan* or *aldirman and balzeis*, have already surfaced in the socio-historical discussion of legal procedures in Scottish burghs in Part Two. Here, they are discussed in terms of their grammatical properties, and also, more importantly perhaps, in terms of the factors which motivate their employment and the selection of particular lexical items in the coordinated string.

After these mostly structural considerations, the discussion returns to lexical bundles and their functions in early legal texts composed by Scottish notaries and clerks. The functions of short bundles are discussed in line with the Hallidayan framework (section 3.3) in Chapter 11, in order to assess which of the functions (referential, textual, or interactional) was most often carried by these repetitive fragments of text. Chapter 12 concentrates on long bundles—their form, function, and the emergence of standardizing textual patterns in a diachronic, as well as regional, dimension. The lexico-syntactic choices in the legal language of Scottish burghs reveal the ways in which they matched the communicative requirements, as well as the conventions, of the discourse situation.

8.2. Corpora Characteristics

The material used in this study provides the most comprehensive coverage of medieval and early modern legal Scots available in electronic format today. The majority of the digital transcriptions of manuscripts are the work of Dr Keith Williamson (University of Edinburgh) who prepared a corpus of localizable Scots texts, tagged grammatically and, to some extent, lexically, to use it as the base for the *Linguistic Atlas of Older Scots* (LAOS) online. With the completion of LAOS, its underlying files have been gathered into the *Edinburgh Corpus of Older Scots* (ECOS), providing c. 390,000 words of manuscript text in a diplomatic annotated electronic transcription. The date coverage of this material extends between 1380 and 1500 (for a summary of corpus information, see Table 8.1). The texts included in the LAOS/ECOS material are official in nature and comprise a variety of legal text types (see also section 7.5 on legal records in Scotland), mostly charters of various kinds (indentures, marriage certificates, grants, etc.), through parliamentary legislation to burgh court proceedings and rulings.

The other available resource, the first and last resort for any historical linguist dealing with Scots before the completion of ECOS, is the *Helsinki Corpus of Older Scots* (HCOS, Meurman-Solin 1993), compiled on the basis of text samples from various text types and genres. I have selected the files linked with legal discourse: parliamentary records, burgh court proceedings,[1] and burgh records. The excerpts are based on printed editions of manuscript material, localized on the basis of extralinguistic data, and checked against the originals by the corpus compiler. The HCOS samples comprise about 107,000 words of text, dated back to the period between 1450 and 1560. The inclusion of the HCOS in my data expands its chronological coverage to 1560, a date customarily accepted as the end of the Middle Scots period (compare the discussion of periodization in section 1.4) and the onset of anglicizing trends in Scotland (Devitt 1989). To complement the sixteenth-century data and expand regional coverage, I added the transcript from Wigtown Burgh Court Book (henceforth Wgt, 1512–1534), which is a south-western text (Maps 1 and 2) and amounts to c. 77,000 words (for an analysis of its grammatical features, see Bugaj 2004b). Thus, the whole material for the present study, the EdHeW compilation, extends between 1380 and 1560 and comprises 0.57 million words of medieval Scots, which today constitutes the largest electronically searchable database of that period in the history of Scots.

Historical corpora are necessarily limited to the materials that have survived till present. No one can estimate how much textual material was lost on the way due to mould, fire, rodents, human neglect, purposeful destruction, and other factors beyond our control. Another limitation is connected to the extent of digitization

TABLE 8.1
Corpus counts

	Corpus length (words)	Corpus dates
ECOS	389,514	c. 1380–1500
HCOS	107,533	1450–1560
Wgt	77,640	1512–1534
EdHeW = total	574,687	c. 1380–1560

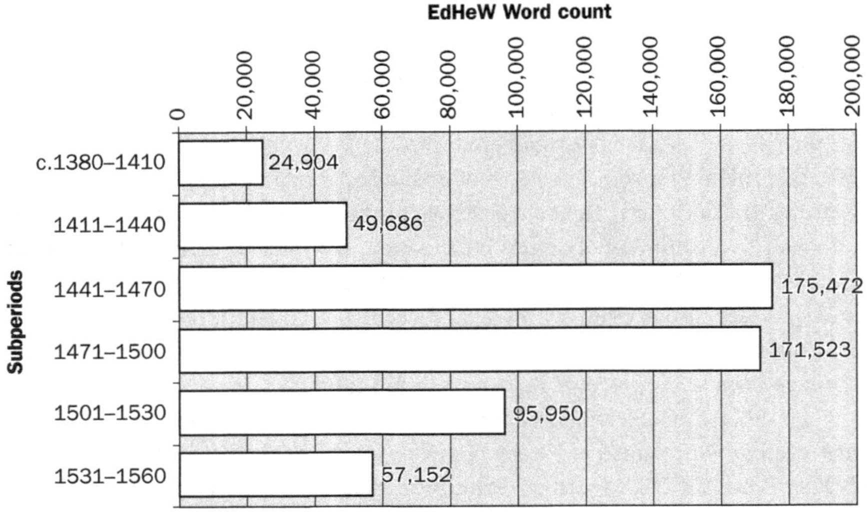

FIGURE 8.1 Word counts in EdHeW by sub-periods

of existing historical material, either involving the originals (as was the case with ECOS), previously edited and printed material (as was the case with HCOS), or unpublished transcripts (as was the case with Wgt). There is more in the archives to digitize. One can only hope that sufficient funding and support will be available in the future to expand our linguistic knowledge of historical Scottish texts. Figure 8.1 summarizes the uneven chronological spread of the corpus word counts.

The collective corpus has been divided into six 30-year periods. This is more or less the length of time required for another generation to grow up and, potentially, introduce change. The least represented period is the initial one, simply because of the scarcity of texts.[2] The best represented period covers the last sixty years of the fifteenth century due to the chronological overlap of ECOS and HCOS[3] and generally due to the more extensive production of texts and the rate of their survival. By combining the corpora, it was possible to even out the word count for the last part of the fifteenth century. In the sixteenth century, the word counts drop because the HCOS samples are shorter. Expanding the database with the Wgt corpus allowed me to achieve a better coverage of the sixteenth century, although admittedly the word counts are still lower than for the earlier dates. Due to the impossibility of designing the corpus in a balanced way in terms of time coverage, all the chronological counts that follow in the subsequent sections and chapters will be normalized per 10,000 words.

8.3. Lexical Bundles: A New Methodology in Historical Linguistics

Corpus searches are no novelty in historical linguistic studies as all collections of texts, also handwritten or printed, can be broadly defined as corpora. The giant leap in methodology happened with the introduction of computer tools for corpus analysis, which allowed the processing of large amounts of data easily, efficiently, and quickly. This new technology has dramatically changed the character of historical studies. The availability of new tools has prompted scholars to produce electronic versions of historical texts, which raises its own methodological and editorial issues (see e.g. Robinson and Solopova 1993), and allowed them to employ computerized searches in their research methodology. The searches can be based on two principles: they can be either corpus-based, where a hypothesis is postulated first and then checked in the corpus, or corpus-driven, where there is no a priori assumption what will be found in the corpus. As explained in section 3.7, the lexical bundles approach belongs to the second type of research.

Links between words have been explored by means of corpus tools for a long time. Lewandowska-Tomaszczyk gives an overview of lexical relations research with corpus methodology, listing lexical bundles as a relatively new tool (2005: 154; see also section 4.4). In historical linguistics, the first monograph with a whole chapter based on lexical bundles was published by Culpeper and Kytö (2010). The authors suggest that "it is worth reflecting on the general relevance of the notion of lexical bundle for historical studies" as "[n]umerous historical studies tend to be atomistic in approach, that is to say, they take as their object of study a particular structure, morphological inflection or word" (2010: 141). What follows is that historical corpus studies have tended to be corpus-based, rather than corpus-driven. It is typical to investigate a feature that the researcher expects to find or even knows that it occurs in the data, which has its own merits for understanding language change. However, with lexical bundles the texts speak for themselves and the atomistic approach is avoided.

8.4. Preparing the Data: Artificial Standardization of Spelling

8.4.1. SPELLING VARIANTS ELIMINATION

The greatest obstacle in automatic bundle extraction is spelling variation in historical texts which pre-date the standardization of spelling. In a pilot study to the present analysis run on the lemmatized version of ECOS (Kopaczyk 2012), I tried to overcome this problem by extracting repetitive series of lemmas—which have a single spelling—rather than word forms. The reliability of such "lemmatic bundles" depends on the consistency and availability of lemmatization, though. While lemmatization was available only in ECOS, the present larger project has used three different corpora whose transcription procedures vary. For example, ECOS uses <Y> for the thorn grapheme <þ>, while HCOS transcribes it as <+t>. Variants make it impossible to gauge the actual number of repetitive lexical strings, unless the software could recognize which of the variants represent the same lexical item. In (1) below, the range of spelling variants of the word *failzeand* 'failing' has been presented. Spelling variation in Middle Scots is quite impressive; suffice it to say that *failzeand* and its variants can hardly be called an extreme example of this variation in EdHeW.

(1) FAILzEANDE FAILLAND FAILzAND FAILz^EAND FAILzE+ANDE
FALEzAND FALY+AND FALYAND FALYHANDE FALYHEAND
FALzAND FALzANDE FALzE\AND FALzE-\AND
FALzE+AND FALzEAND FALzEANDE FA[I]LzEAND
FA[L]zEAND FAYLzHANDE FELzAnD = *failzeand* 'failing'

Consequently, spelling variation in the bundles will be even more extensive: sometimes one letter will cause a bundle to be listed separately, instead of being added to other occurrences of the same lexical-form strings. The example in Table 8.2 illustrates the extent of spelling variation in EdHeW data. Notice how automatic extraction lists all these strings separately, even though this is one and the same lexical bundle. Furthermore, the three corpora use different transcription notations and pay attention to handwriting features in a different degree of detail (hence various additional diacritics, like ^ or +, and differentiation between small and capital letters in ECOS), which introduces even more transcription variants. It is remarkable how spelling variation causes vast discrepancies in bundle counts: the most common spelling of the bundle in Table 8.2 renders 950 tokens, the least common is used just once, while all variants added together give the actual number of instances for this particular string. The bundle *of ye said* in fact appears 2,157 times in 3-grams extracted from the EdHeW data above the cut-off point, and 2,183 times counting all the instances (see the procedure below).

To find standardizing lexical patterns in this proliferation of spelling variants, one has no option but to accelerate the standardization of spelling artificially. This way one also gets rid of any editorial idiosyncrasies and prepares material from three different corpora for processing with the same extraction software. Present-day research which uses automatic extraction devices does not encounter such problems precisely because spelling standardization has already happened, and a given bundle will always look the same in a printed format. In historical texts one needs to combine the artificial standardization of spelling, which had not yet happened in the manuscript material, with the emergent standardization of lexical patterns in specialized discourse texts, which occurs regardless of the variation

TABLE 8.2

Spelling variation and bundle counts

A sample bundle	Number in EdHeW
OF YE SAID	950
OF Y^E SAID	464
OF THE SAID	396
OF YE SAIDE	182
of +te said	52
OF Y^E SAYD	46
OF YE SAD	44
OFF THE SAIDE	40
OFF THE SAD	8
off ye said	1
	2,183

in spelling (cf. the discussion of linguistic standardization on different levels of language in section 3.5).

As extraction of lexical bundles is one of the newest trends in historical corpus linguistics, it is important to summarize the current solutions to the spelling variation problem for the benefit of scholars who would like to try out this method. Culpeper and Kytö (2010: 138) overcome the problem of spelling variation by using a regularization program VARD (*Variant Detector*), and it is to this approach that the authors attribute the uniqueness of their study. VARD was developed by Dawn Archer and Paul Rayson at the University of Lancaster (Archer and Rayson 2006), with the assistance of Alistair Baron (Baron, Rayson, and Archer 2009; Baron and Rayson 2009). The program works on the basis of tools developed for spell-checking software, using a previously compiled "dictionary" of spelling variants and other variant-elimination algorithms.[4] Unfortunately, this software proved unsuitable to work with EdHeW files straight away. The texts here are written in Scots and start at an earlier period than the Early Modern English corpora, for which VARD has separately established lists of variants and letter replacements, as well as a target dictionary of modern English word forms. The program can be trained to work with other data, too, but the Scots files proved too messy to undergo a fully automatized spelling unification. It was therefore necessary to compile lists of spelling variants manually for each of about 14,000 lexical entries from EdHeW. Each of these entries had from one up to eighty spelling variants,[5] caused both by the unstandardized spelling of Middle Scots and by the different editorial procedures of each subcorpus.

Those manually compiled lists of variants now had to be represented by a single word form, to which all instances of a given word in the corpus would be changed automatically by VARD. In artificial spelling standardization one is forced to take an arbitrary decision about the target spelling. This decision, however, should not be completely random in order not to introduce even more chaos, nor should it represent modern spelling tendencies (as is the case in VARD), because this procedure would destroy the historical character of the corpus material. It is best to work with what the corpus itself offers as a clue to spelling standardization, and back it up with historical dictionary information. I therefore used a rationale based on three steps: first, spelling variants were checked for the number of their occurrences and were assigned values on a scale; when selecting the target variant, the variant from the top of the scale was chosen; finally, if two variants were in the same scale range, the *DSL* and/or *CSD* were checked for this entry and the dictionary form was chosen as the target variant. The lists of variants and spelling targets thus achieved were installed as working dictionaries in VARD, and the EdHeW corpora were then subjected to artificial spelling standardization.

8.4.2. WORD DIVISION ISSUES

With regard to spelling variation, we must also consider word division. Over forty years ago, the first corpus lexicographers drew attention to the problems of automatized searches which take a string of alphanumeric characters between spaces to be treated as a graphic word form (Kucera and Francis 1967: xxi). Youmans concludes that "[s]uch a definition can introduce statistical errors because [it] reflects editorial conventions rather than genuine differences in vocabulary" (1990). Nevertheless, in present-day work on lexical bundles, graphic words are indeed taken as the basis for extraction (Biber et al. 1999; Biber, Conrad, and Cortes 2003). It is worth considering the consequences of such an approach, especially as in historical texts variation in word division is greater and less predictable. As intimated above, the practical approach of a computer program treats any string of signs between spaces as a lexical item. When *because* is spelled as a single word, *because of them* would constitute a 3-gram; when spelled with an alternative space in *be cause*, it would turn into a 4-gram in the 'eyes' of the software. The bundle methodology assumes that in writing the spaces are used to delimit lexical units graphically; that there is an agreement as to how compounds should be spelled or whether there should be a space between "in" and "to" in the word *into*. In historical texts such agreements are only visible to a certain extent because spelling standardization was not fully in operation yet. Nonetheless, in their work on Early Modern English, Culpeper and Kytö adopt a mechanical definition of a word form, describing it in a footnote as "a string of letters bounded by spaces" (2010: 142 n. 2). This is a convenient solution because it assumes that the data counts will not be significantly affected. If one can avoid a potential risk of skewing the extraction results, and the amount of material is manageable, the word divisions should be scrutinized and unified, as a logical consequence of overall spelling regularization.

For that reason, it was decided to make two manual amendments to the corpus spelling practices. In cases where variation in spelling resulted in a compound word spelled either as two separate words (e.g. *fless prisaris* 'valuers of meat') or continuously (e.g. *flessprisaris*), I kept the continuous spelling for all instances. The target form was then checked in the *DSL* and/or *CSD*. Such a choice of (dis)continuous spelling was also available for some grammatical words, like prepositions or pronouns, indicating their status on the way towards full grammaticalization (e.g. *be fore* and *be cause*). Some similar items were spelled separately even though they had already been grammaticalized in the Old English period—or started, in fact, as single word forms (e.g. *be tuix* or *be hind*).[6] In all such cases, in order to unify the practice across the corpora, I made a decision to follow the *DSL* and accept the most frequent spelling and spell the grammatical words and prepositions together, as in the case of lexical compounds.

The second amendment involved introducing additional word divisions. Ambiguous word divisions were a problem in the Wgt corpus, where the scribes often linked a noun with the preceding article (e.g. *aboll* for *a boll* or *anox* for *an ox*). This is a spelling feature, possibly reflecting a prosodic structure of the nominal phrase, and it is not indicative of a single morphological or lexical unit. I did not register any such cases in the other two corpora, which may mean that the editors had done this regularization beforehand, or that this problem did not present itself there. I searched the Wgt corpus manually and introduced word divisions wherever an article was added to the noun in spelling.[7]

8.4.3. PUNCTUATION FEATURES

As with spelling, manuscript punctuation is not represented in a consistent manner throughout the corpora. The editorial practice of corpus compilers introduces, modernizes, or skips punctuation features, and that had been done differently for all three corpora combined in this study. In order to prepare the data for automatic bundle extraction, I decided to eliminate all punctuation from the EdHeW material. Other studies working with lexical bundles (e.g. Biber et al. 1999; Culpeper and Kytö 2010: 113) were designed so that a bundle would not span a punctuation mark. In my view, this approach may have eliminated bundles which were, for example, arbitrarily divided by a comma when the handwritten or spoken text was being digitized. In fact, Biber and Barbieri (2007: 268 n. 3) suggest looking at lexical bundles which span across punctuation marks as a future research topic. Before its fully standardized usage, punctuation was by no means predictable in its full range of forms and functions, nor was it used consistently, so allowing an arbitrary punctuation mark to work as a boundary for bundling becomes deceptive.

Of course, the texts were not devoid of endings and beginnings, and they did not run in a stream-of-consciousness fashion without existing or potential punctuation marks. Indeed, the marks of sentence or paragraph beginnings and endings may, in another project, be valuable for a study of lexical bundles used in that specific position in texts. The bundle methodology has, in fact, revealed patterns of fixed lexical strings stretching on both sides of a sentence break or a paragraph break, or indeed any other potential punctuation mark—a comma, a colon, a dash, as I discuss in the next chapters, for example, *curt ye samyn day* (see other formulaic sequences under Type N2d in section 9.2) or *plege his hand ye samyn day* (section 11.3.2). Importantly, in a corpus where fixedness occurs across such breaks, repetitive lexical bundles will appear in these very places and may be numerous enough to make it into the analysis (which always requires a set threshold of occurrences). Therefore, if anything interesting were to occur, it would do so regardless of the presence or absence of punctuation.

8.5. Extracting Lexical Bundles

8.5.1. DEDICATED SOFTWARE

Modern corpus research can use ready-made functions extracting lexical bundles in existing software (for a useful survey of lexical bundle extraction software, see Ari 2006).[8] As explained above, in the case of Scottish medieval and early modern material, artificial spelling standardization was needed first before other editorial issues could be addressed. Then, because of the fact that this investigation is based on three different corpora, with three different annotation styles, it was necessary to create dedicated software, customized to handle this specific material. Another reason why computer programs such as *WordSmith* tools could not be applied in this research was that I wanted to sort the results chronologically, regionally, and textually, to enhance explanatory factors in data interpretation. That could not be achieved with any software on the market so a dedicated computer program which would fulfil the demands of this project had to be created.[9] Developing software from scratch clearly had its advantages, especially because the programmer could tailor the tool along the way to target specific questions which arose during preparatory stages. The new software allowed me to search for bundles in EdHeW between 3- and 8-grams, to record the number of types and tokens and the number of texts with a given bundle, and to sort them according to the time of file compilation and the place where the text was written.

8.5.2. BUNDLE LENGTH

In this study an attempt is made to break the legal discourse of the past down to the lexical bundles making up that discourse. The idea is to look for textual standardization, indicated by repetitive strings of words. Consequently, the longer such strings, the more fixed and standardized the text(s). It follows that a study of textual standardization should concentrate on the longest bundles. What does "the longest" mean in this context? Recurrent word strings constitute a "predictable characteristic of different text types" and provide "evidence of units of routine language use" (Stubbs and Barth 2003: 62). Those authors set a threshold for length at five elements in a bundle, admitting that longer strings will be characteristic of more formulaic genres.[10] Stubbs and Barth (2003: 77) make a note of repetitive

7-grams in the Bible and liturgical texts, for example, *and the Lord spake unto Moses saying*; *the word of the Lord came unto*; *shall know that I am the Lord*; *and it came to pass in the*; *and it shall come to pass in*, taken from the King James translation. This text has a 0.85 million word count, with 260 7-grams occurring ten times and more, and 65 7-grams occurring twenty times and more. As Stubbs and Barth admit, "[m]any instances of these chains are parts of still longer recurrent chains" (2003: 77). Since text-type fixedness in very formulaic genres, such as the Bible, is visible in bundles around seven items in length, I made a decision to extract 6-, 7-, and 8-grams from the corpus and analyse them to reveal textual standardization patterns in Chapter 12. In case of even longer repetitive strings in the texts, automatic extraction results should indicate what these longer bundles are (on bundle overlap, see section 8.5.5, and the discussion in Chapter 12).

To invite comparisons and reveal parallels with other projects based on lexical bundles, extracting short bundles becomes indispensable. The majority of studies using this methodology concentrate on bundle lengths from 3- to 5-grams (Table 8.3). Also, the only historical study of lexical bundles so far (Culpeper and Kytö 2010) concentrates on 3-grams; in some cases, however, these bundles are too short to capture the whole meaning of a chunk, which may distort the picture of fixed patterns for specific functions. For example, TO SAY THAT was classified by Culpeper and Kytö according to function as Textual (narrative-related), while individual examples and longer contexts point towards speech acts ((10) "I regret to say that") and modality ((11) "I have to say <pause> that") (2010: 126–127). Similarly, the authors sometimes have to conflate two 3-grams because only a 4-gram serves as a satisfactory illustration of a given aspect, for example, GIVE AN ACCOUNT OF (2010: 127) or WITH ALL MY + ALL MY HEART (2010: 132). They acknowledge towards the end that "a full account... would need to look at bundles of other lengths too" (2010: 140), admitting the preliminary and exploratory nature of their work.

This book concentrates on textual standardization in legal discourse, which is why it should make provisions for the typical features of this discourse, as recognized by previous scholarship. Binomials (as in *husband and wife*, *stated and ordained*, *to have and to hold*, etc.), typically strings of three to five elements, are characteristic for the language of the law, as Chapter 2 explained. With the help of lexical bundles, one can extract binomials and multinomials from a corpus in a systematic manner, which is one more reason to include short bundles, 3- to 5-grams, in the research queries. In order to explore the fixed strings in EdHeW thoroughly, I thus decided to run searches for bundles from three to eight items in length. The findings were split between several chapters because the analysis presented in each one is targeted towards a different research question: the formal characteristics of short bundles in Chapter 9, the forms and motivations behind binomials and multinomials in Chapter 10, the functions of short bundles in early legal Scots in Chapter 11, and finally the symptoms of standardization to be gleaned from long bundles in Chapter 12.

8.5.3. SETTING THE FREQUENCY THRESHOLD

The lexical bundle method is, to date, the most robust tool for extracting repetitive strings. Running the EdHeW material through bundle extraction software results in a pool of lexical bundles, most of which are one-off accidentals of the automatized search without further value (Kopaczyk 2011a: 8). The overall number of bundles depends on the corpus size; after all, every string within a required length is recorded. The question remains as to how to correlate the fact that certain lexical strings repeat with the formulaic nature of discourse and with text type standardization. The first indicator of text-type standardization and discoursal formulaicity is the sheer numeric count of repetitive elements in the corpus. The second step is to narrow down the extracted data to capture the formulaicity in qualitative terms.

In order for the data to start revealing textual standardization patterns, a threshold for interpreting results needs to be established. There is no uniform practice in lexical bundle studies when it comes to setting the threshold, or the cut-off point below which the data is deemed unimportant. The decision depends on the length of the corpus, the length of the studied bundles, and the type of texts in the corpus. Every researcher takes an informed but idiosyncratic decision. Illustrating this, Table 8.3 presents the cut-off points in several selected studies on lexical bundles.

Fletcher (2003/2004) designed a search engine to run searches on the 100-million-word British National Corpus. His cut-off point was three occurrences for *n*-grams between one and eight elements in length. The enormous wealth of data and search combinations thus available entail a problem: "it is difficult to know what level of delicacy is appropriate in making generalizations across so much data. The only realistic strategy is to start small" (Stubbs 2007: 92). This assertion is valid for the present research, which is carried out on a specialized historical corpus of a relatively small size (although it is larger than other specialized corpora subjected to bundle extraction; Table 8.3). The study is not impeded by factors such as register, level of formality, style, addressee, conditions of writing, writing-versus-speech issues, and other considerations which go hand in hand with large multi-genre representative corpora. For anyone interested in applying the lexical bundles in textual analysis, this corpus can be used to trace numeric changes in the data as the threshold increases.

The first threshold was set at more than five occurrences of a given bundle in the corpus. This procedure was more or less in accordance with Biber et al.'s original cut-off point of ten occurrences per million (1999: 992).[11] For my research questions, I introduced another parameter into pruning the data: the textual spread, so that only the bundles which occur in more than five texts were taken into consideration. Biber et al. also employ this second parameter to "exclude individual speaker/writer idiosyncrasies" (1999: 993). The amount of bundles selected in this manner was large (Table 8.4), which in itself suggests a substantial degree of repetition in the corpus. Consider, for instance, the 857 types of 8-grams which

TABLE 8.3

A comparison of lexical bundle cut-off points in selected studies (1998–2010)

Author(s) and date	Type of texts in the corpus	Corpus length(words)	Length of the selected bundle	Number of instances at cut-off point
Altenberg (1998)	PDE: spoken	0.5 million	1- to 8-grams	10
Biber et al. (1999)	PDE: conversation, fiction, press, academic discourse	40 million	3- to 6-grams	10/5per 1 million in ≥5 texts
Biber, Conrad, and Cortes (2003)	PDE: conversation, academic discourse	7 million + 5.3 million	4- and 5-grams	20 per 1 million
Biber, Conrad, and Cortes (2004)	T2K-SWALspoken and written academic language	2 million	4-grams	40 per 1 million
Cortes (2004)	PDE: academic vs. student writing	2 million vs. 0.9 million	4-grams	20 per million in ≥5 texts
Goźdź-Roszkowski (2006)	PDE: legal discourse	0.3 million	4-grams	15
Biber and Barbieri (2007)	PDE: T2K-SWAL + LSWE subsection: spoken and written academic language	c.7.9 million	4-grams	40 per 1 million
Hyland (2008b)	English for Academic Purposes	3.5 million	4-grams	20 per 1 million in ≥10% of texts
Culpeper and Kytö (2010)	EModE playsEModE trials[a]	0.22 million 0.25 million	3-grams	10
This study	Middle Scots legal texts	0.6 million	3- to 8-grams	≥10 in ≥10 texts

[a] Two genres from the CED: EModE trials (252,607 words) and EModE plays (221,196 words) plus comparative PDE corpora of British trial proceedings and drama, not easily accessible, but through the BNC—126,271 words of trials and 38,190 words of direct speech from plays (2010: 111–112).

appeared in exactly the same wording in more than five texts. This is a confirmation of the initial hypothesis about the texts composed for legal purposes and their formulaic character and it will be given more space in Chapter 12.

The second stage was to cut down the amount of data in order to extract the most formulaic bundles for a qualitative analysis. A new threshold was set at ten or more instances in ten or more files, and these bundles served as input data for formulaicity factor counts (section 8.5.4). Table 8.4 summarizes the final counts of the lexical bundles analysed in this study.

As there are no studies of lexical bundles in medieval and early modern texts, apart from Culpeper and Kytö (2010) who do not comment on the overall proportion of bundles in their corpus,[12] it is impossible as yet to draw any historical comparisons, even cross-linguistic—English vs. Scots. It may nonetheless be worth noting that Biber et al. (1999: 993–994), using practically the same cut-off point as the present study, found that 3-grams constitute around 25% of the whole word count of their conversation corpus, and 18% of the academic prose corpus of present-day English. 4-grams were strikingly less attested, with 3% of the total word

TABLE 8.4

Lexical bundles in EdHeW—final data counts

	> 5 tokens + > 5 files		≥ 10 tokens + ≥ 10 files		Final top 10%	
	All types	All tokens	All types	All tokens	All types	All tokens
3-grams	7,269	166,401	3,535	135,243	354	54,307
4-grams	4,145	80,317	1,913	61,847	191	22,934
5-grams	2,552	43,817	1,142	32,449	114	11,133
6-grams	1,682	26,549	722	18,921	72	6,229
7-grams	1,205	17,388	495	11,837	50	3,841
8-grams	857	11,222	321	7,098	32	2,051

TABLE 8.5

Token counts and word count percentages in EdHeW

	> 5 tokens + > 5 files		≥ 10 tokens + ≥ 10 files	
	All tokens	% total word count	All tokens	% total word count
3-grams	166,401	29	135,243	24
4-grams	80,317	14	61,847	11
5-grams	43,817	8	32,449	6
6-grams	26,549	5	18,921	3
7-grams	17,388	3	11,837	2
8-grams	11,222	2	7,098	1

count for conversations and 2% for academic writing. (The authors did not comment on the coverage by other bundle lengths in the corpus.) Table 8.5 presents the percentage of total word count for each length of lexical bundles in EdHeW, both for the lower and the higher cut-off point. It is remarkable that recurrent 3-grams constitute between 24% and 29% of the whole collection of administrative and legal texts from medieval Scotland.

Even more striking is the relatively large portion of the corpus made up of 4-grams and longer lengths. In fact, it seems that Scottish burgh clerks and notaries compiled 7-gram bundles to roughly the same extent as modern users compile 4-grams in conversation and in academic writing—around 2–3%. The appearance of such long recurrent strings in a relatively large number is attributable to the requirements of legal discourse (cf. Chapter 2) and points towards standardization of textual patterns. As signalled above, longer bundles (6- to 8-grams) are therefore the subject of a separate discussion in Chapter 12.

8.5.4. THE FORMULAICITY MEASURE

Given the large amount of data, for the qualitative analysis it was decided that the top 10% of the most formulaic bundles from each group would be examined in detail and classified into grammatical and functional categories (cf. Fig. 9.1 in the next chapter). Now the question was what would count as 'most formulaic'. My definition of formulaicity presented in section 4.2 links to repetition and frequency in texts. A bundle which simply repeats many times and has many tokens in the corpus is a good candidate for a formulaic sequence. However, there are also other factors to consider when one wants to measure formulaicity. The most important factor is the token-to-file ratio—in other words, in how many different files a particular bundle appears. It can safely be postulated that a bundle which has 200 tokens in 50 files is more formulaic than a bundle which has 200 tokens in 200 files. The token-to-file ratio cannot, however, be the only factor to include in the search for formulaicity. If 3-grams were ordered by token-to-file ratio, in the top-ten there we would find bundles like *aker set to* 'acre (of land) set to' (46 tokens in 6 texts, first rank) or *oxgang set to*[13] (38 tokens in 8 texts, eighth rank), which seem to be coincidental and linked to a very specific small group of texts within the whole corpus of 1,818 files. These expressions are very formulaic indeed, but they stem from a specific group of files, dealing with the issue of land divisions, which is rendered by means of other expressions in the rest of the corpus. In fact, paying sole attention to token-to-file ratio promotes low numbers of files, which can be massively populated by relatively infrequent bundles (e.g. 6 texts with 46 tokens of the same bundle cited above). At the same time, this procedure misses such bundles which are characteristic for the whole corpus and repeat hundreds of times, even when spread over a larger number of files. A good example is *ye wrangus haldin*, with 525 tokens in 207 files, which would rank 121 according to the above procedure.

Clearly, the sheer number of tokens should be considered, too. A formulaic bundle should have a high token-to-file ratio (many tokens in few texts), while at the same time it should be very frequent in the corpus. This approach would promote a bundle like *ye wrangus haldin*, while at the same time it would discard items like *aker set to*. The second threshold was thus designed to cut off those bundles which would not qualify as formulaic according to the adopted restrictions. It was necessary to narrow down the material by excluding the bundles below ten instances and ten texts. Bundles with lower presence in the corpus could not really compete in terms of formulaicity (Table 8.6).

The final aim was to construct a mathematical formula which would rank the bundles according to their formulaicity factor (henceforth FF).[14] Following the rationale presented above, the formula combines two indices: the bundle count and the token-to-file ratio. The highest number of tokens constitutes three-quarters of the final factor value, while the highest token-to-file ratio gets one-quarter of that value. All the bundles of a given length are assigned values relative to the top scores in each index, according to function x^4, which sufficiently highlights the difference between the top scores and the lowest scores. The final factor value is a number between 0 and 100—the higher the number, the higher the formulaicity factor. I will be using the FF values in the remaining discussion. The FF values were calculated in the same manner for all bundle lengths, 3- to 8-grams.

TABLE 8.6
Numeric counts and average FF for top 10% in each bundle length

	Final top 10%		
	All types	All tokens	Average FF
3-grams	354	54,307	29.73
4-grams	191	22,934	46.10
5-grams	114	11,133	47.94
6-grams	72	6,229	46.15
7-grams	50	3,841	46.76
8-grams	32	2,051	47.47

The discrepancy between formulaic 3-grams and longer bundles in terms of the average FF value can be explained by looking at the sheer number of bundles which qualified for the top pool. 3-grams are to be found very often in texts but they are more diverse in nature than longer bundles, geared towards a specific text type as the length increases. This is why short bundles are less formulaic on average, according to the adopted measurement.

8.5.5. BUNDLE OVERLAPS

The software extracts lexical bundles from the corpus moving according to the n + 1 algorithm—one word boundary at a time. This means that there are two potential types of overlap between bundles. First of all, as a consequence of a linear arrangement of text, the next bundle contains a part of the previous bundle, which I will call *syntagmatic overlap*; secondly, longer bundles contain shorter bundles or their elements (*paradigmatic overlap*). This issue has not been acknowledged sufficiently in previous studies[15] even though it has a bearing on the reliability of data counts and quantitative interpretations.

When it comes to the syntagmatic overlap, consecutive bundles of a given length start at a different word boundary. Even though there is an overlap of some lexical items in two consecutive bundles, their counts in the whole corpus may differ, and *will* differ in the majority of cases, because the items at the respective beginnings and endings of the bundles will vary. This means that regardless of the syntagmatic overlap, the same-length bundles will represent different structural types, presented in detail in the next chapter. Some of them will then have more instances and those types will be interesting to explore further. For example, it may turn out that fixed nominal phrases are less numerous than prepositional phrases, as in *of the same* and *the same letter*. Those bundles which are more frequent than their further overlaps will also point towards their own characteristic discoursal functions, for example, *Item the burgh council* may be frequent because it launches a record entry, as opposed to *the burgh council was*, which has a referential function. The question of function constitutes the core of analysis in Chapters 11 and 12. It is clear that frequency of occurrence will indicate those bundles which are more important for discourse structure, regardless of their potential overlaps.

With paradigmatic overlap the situation is different. One can expect a 'matryoshka doll' effect, whereby the shorter bundles are included in the longer ones. The frequency counts of the bundles which have, say, the same beginnings but various lengths will be inversely proportional to the length of the bundle: the shorter the bundle, the more frequent it will be. A short bundle should be more frequent than any other in which it is included. However, the actual differences in frequency cannot be calculated in a predictable manner. There is no way of telling how a particular bundle is going to be expanded with the next item and whether that expansion will indeed be frequent enough to make it to the pool of repetitive bundles. What is possible, however, is to analyse bundles of a given length separately, and after that, to compare the results. This procedure will reveal which lexical combinations are relatively stable only up to a prescribed length, and which constitute elements of longer standardizing patterns. As I am interested in symptoms of textual standardization, the paradigmatically overlapping long bundles will indicate which parts of discourse and which meanings were conveyed in an unchanging manner. In fact, as Chapter 12 will show, by putting together parts of overlapping bundles we may discover even longer repetitive patterns than those originally included in the research plan of this project.

9

The Grammar of Lexical Bundles in Early Legal Scots

9.1. Introduction

One of the aims of this book is to investigate textual standardization in early legal Scots texts from a structural point of view. The previous chapter explained in detail how the stable, frequently repeated fragments of texts were extracted from the EdHeW corpus, to create a data pool of lexical bundles. Before the discussion moves on to the functions of these repetitive chunks of Scottish legal discourse, it is necessary to pay attention to their form. The most striking result of this study is that automatically extracted lexical bundles reveal the lack of connection between formulaicity in language and phrasal or clausal completeness. In fact, this observation is as valid for lexical bundle extraction from robust present-day corpora (as in Biber et al. 1999), as it is for a historical study of legal discourse in Scotland. As put forward by Sinclair in his idiom principle discussed in section 4.2.1, there is a large amount of prefabrication in language. He talked about "semi-preconstructed *phrases*" (1991: 110, emphasis added), while the stable chunks of language do not seem to be limited to phrasal constituents, as lexical bundles indicate.

Structural characteristics of lexical bundles are diverse because of the extraction method. As explained in Chapters 4 and 8, the very essence of this methodology is not to assume what structures will actually be most frequent but to allow these structures to emerge from the corpus. Automatic extraction discovers repetitive strings which are not necessarily phrasal, and thus reveals formulaic patterns in discourse beyond the phrase, or within the phrase. Bundles of different lengths will have different structural preferences. The discussion in the present chapter is centred on the shorter bundles, from 3-grams to 5-grams. Longer bundles are discussed in Chapter 12, as they are structurally more complex and should be considered separately. The bundles selected for the discussion are the top 10% from the FF rankings for each bundle length (see Chapter 8 for specific procedures and counts).

In their pioneering work on recurrent grammatical structures in present-day English, Biber et al. (1999) paid considerable attention to the structural types of lexical bundles in their corpus. Their categorization was sensitive to the incomplete phrasal status of the majority of strings and was later fine-tuned to focus on three major types of recurrent expressions: the verb phrase fragments, the dependent clause fragments, and the noun and prepositional phrase fragments (Biber, Conrad, and Cortes 2004: 381). Drawing on this approach, the subsequent discussion will centre on these three major groups of bundles, albeit with an amended inventory of subtypes to suit the characteristics of the EdHeW material. The prepositional phrase fragments, for instance, are given attention in a separate section (9.3). The order of the structural types also differs from the writings of Biber and his associates, as they typically concentrate first on clauses and verbs because these constructions feature more prominently in their material. In the typology below, I start with noun phrase fragments and I use capital letters to indicate whether the type in question is related to nouns (N), prepositions (P), verbs (V), or clauses (C).

In the medieval and early modern Scots legal documents, nominalizations and fragments of noun phrases and prepositional phrases are the most formulaic elements of discourse.[1] The following structural subtypes of lexical bundles will be discussed further in the chapter:

Type N1
: Noun phrase fragments (NPs)[2] with *of*-phrase fragment (e.g. *tolbuth of ye samyn, three estatis of, ye makin of thir*)

Type N2
: Other noun phrase fragments (e.g. *ye samyn day, james be ye, ye said landis and*)

Type N3
: Date and number fragments (e.g. *lord a thousande, a thousande four hundereth, god a thousande four*)

Type N4
: Personal pronouns[3] + (Conj) + (NP) (e.g. *me and myn, me myn airis and, ws or oure*)

The elements of the bundle given in parentheses are optional. It is important to note the separate category for the *of*-phrase fragments (Type N1) which have been singled out because in the texts from Scottish burghs they form stable connections with NPs to a much larger extent than other prepositional phrases (see section 9.2 for further examples). Sinclair (1991, 1994) also drew attention to the special behaviour of *of*, which typically functions as a noun-group extender, and not a clear-cut preposition. Bearing this in mind, *of*-phrase fragments have also been listed separately in the next group—the prepositional phrase fragments (section 9.3):

Type P1
: Prepositional phrase fragments with *of*-phrase fragment (e.g. *of that ilk, in witnes of, of vsuale mone of*)

Type P2
: Other prepositional phrase fragments (e.g. *for ye wrangus, in that tyme and, on ye west part on*)

In the case of verb phrase fragments and clauses it may be difficult to label a specific string of three or four elements without further context. Following Biber et al. (1999), I have divided the bundles incorporating a verb into two groups: bundles containing fragments of verb phrases and bundles containing clause fragments. Finally, the bundles introduced by an adverbial have been grouped into a separate type. In the verb phrase fragments the following subtypes were distinguished (section 9.4):

Type V1
: Verb phrase fragments with a passive verb or a present participle (e.g. *it is statut, and that was giffin for, remanand with ye said*)

Type V2
: Verb phrase fragments with a non-passive verb (e.g. *strekit a borch, pay for his, sal pay for his*)

The following clause fragments were identified (section 9.5):

Type C1
: *this/that* clauses (e.g. *and this is, this is ye first curt, that ye said*)

Type C2
: (Conj/*that*) (Verb) + *to*-clause fragments (e.g. *is to say, to be haldin, and to ferm*)

Type C3
: Adverbial clause fragments, including *if*-clauses (e.g. *as said is, efter ye forme, and gif it happinis*)

There is one more group of strings which was separated from the rest of the top formulaic bundles. These were coordinated constituents of the same grammatical category, as in *statut and ordanit, erd and stan, ye accion and cause, ye said abbot and conuent*. The decision to extract these phrases and separate them from the rest of the material was driven by one of my research aims: to identify binomial and multinomial patterns in early legal discourse. As signalled above, a detailed analysis of these constructions characteristic of legal discourse will follow in Chapter 10. In the sections below, the discussion will focus on the structural patterns identified above for 3-, 4-, and 5-grams, with the aim of highlighting the grammatical chunks most prone to formulaicization in legal discourse. To indicate the importance of a given string in the

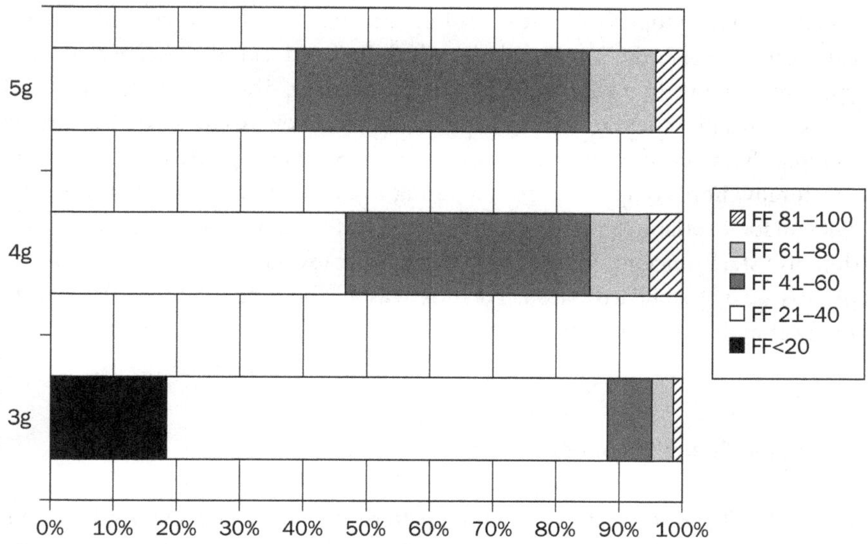

FIGURE 9.1 Formulaicity thresholds in the most formulaic short bundles

corpus material, I will employ the following benchmarks of formulaicity[4] in the examples below:

FF 80–100	***
FF 60–80	**
FF 40–60	*
FF 20–40	^
FF > 20	(not marked)

Each string in the discussion has been marked with an appropriate label. The examples constitute the top 10% of most formulaic lexical bundles of a given length (for exact counts see Chapter 8); the higher their FF score, the more frequent and structurally stable they are. In the sections below, the lexical bundles have been arranged from the most to the least formulaic. Those which have the most stars constitute indispensable ingredients of early legal vernacular texts in Scotland.

The overview of the whole pool of formulaic sequences in Figure 9.1 draws attention to the scarcity of the most formulaic strings. A clear majority of top formulaic lexical bundles ranges between FF = 21 and 60 on the formulaicity scale, while in 3-grams the largest group can be placed between FF = 21 and 40. The chart supports the decision to limit the qualitative analysis of formulaicity in bundles to the top 10%.

The longer the bundle, the more difficult it becomes to create exactly the same lexico-syntactic patterns, hence fewer discernible lexical bundles with enough tokens to qualify into the formulaic pool. To turn this around, when a scribe *does* produce a long string with enough frequency to make it through the formulaicity thresholds (section 8.5), it means that a given bundle constitutes a retrievable and indispensable element of the text. 5-grams are the last bundle length which renders variety in topics of these more fine-grained formulaic ingredients of legal texts. They are also the last bundle length to be fitted into the twelve structural types listed above in a relatively comfortable manner. The structural analysis of 3- to 5-grams presented in the subsequent sections allows us to notice the heavily nominal character of early legal discourse. From 6-grams upwards, the strings are structurally more complex, often containing two or more embedded phrases and syntagmatic overlaps signalled to the left and to the right of a particular bundle. They also start concentrating around very specific textual functions, which points towards textual standardization. For this reason, the longer bundles have been treated separately in Chapter 12.

9.2. Noun Phrase Fragments

It is a difficult task to specify a structural pattern for incomplete phrases. However, using the structural frames suggested by Biber et al. (1999), one may classify the material on the basis of the common characteristics of the most formulaic bundles. In Type N1, which gathers fragments of noun phrases combined with the preposition *of*, there is a discernible difference between these bundles which start with a definite determiner[5] (a), and those which do not (b). The word order Det + N + P, as in *ye yhere of* (FF = 74), is a non-phrasal 3-gram pattern contained within a larger unit. The preposition *of* closes this bundle most typically (cf. Type N2b below for other PPs), pointing to a possessive nominal complement to follow, which becomes visible in 4- and 5-grams with a syntagmatic overlap (e.g. *ye yhere of + god*, *ye burgh of + peblis*). This empirical observation, based on the extracted bundles, suggests that the boundary of a repetitive structural unit may not fall between the NP and the preposition.

Type N1

Noun phrase fragments with *of*-phrase fragment

(a) Det + N + *of*

3-grams: ye yhere of**, ye landis of**, ye monath of*, ye handis of*, ye pain of*, ye burgh of^, ye tenement of^, ye sum of^, ye lord of^, thre estatis of^, ye king of^, ye tyme of^, ye terme of^, ye date of^, ye fest of^, ye termis of^, ye chalans of^, ye tenour of^, ye act of, ye bischop of, ye lordis of

4-grams: ye yhere of god***, ye xxti day of**, ye yhere of oure**, and ye landis of**, ye said landis of*, ye makin of thir*, all ye dayis of^, xxti day of ye^, ye xxvi-ss day of^, ye said sum of^, ye landis of ye^, ye tolbuth of ye^, ye burgh of peblis^, ye thre estatis of^, ye said john of^, ye said erle of^, ye lordis of consail^

5-grams: ye yhere of oure lord**, ye yhere of god a**, ye yhere of god ane*, ye xxti day of ye monath*, ye tolbuth of ye samyn*, ye borow curt of wigtoun^

The structure identified in Type N1a always requires a possessor complement. Thus, the structure is built of the following elements: Det + N + *of* + xNP, where the last element xNP is a free position slot, easily filled with various complements (which becomes apparent in syntagmatic overlaps, see the 4- and 5-grams above). What is interesting for legal discourse of the day is that some of these complements were more frequent than others. In fact, reference to the year of the document is a highly formulaic bundle, even more so in its longer 4-gram version: *ye yhere of god* (FF = 83). It is because the 3-gram opens up another possibility for year reference, as visible in the competing 5-gram option—*ye yhere of oure lord* (FF = 76). In the majority of cases, however, the shorter bundle does not expand into equally formulaic longer bundles, leaving various options to the free position xNP in a less formulaic manner, for example, *ye sum of* (+ xNP), *ye lord of* (+ xNP), *ye pain of* (+ xNP), etc.

Another feature to observe is that the bundles with an initial determiner do not always have syntagmatic counterparts. In fact, bundles may enter the formulaic pool without the determiner, as illustrated below. In this structural type syntagmatic continuations of Type N1a can be noticed. If we look at the most formulaic lexical bundles, *yhere of god* and *yhere of oure lord* (FF = 65 and FF = 66) are in the top range again.

(b) N + *of*-phrase fragment

3-grams: yhere of god**, day of ye*, xxti day of*, yhere of oure^, vsuale mone of^, mone of scotland^, king of ingland^, landis of ye^, part of ye^, duc of albany^, said erle of^, erle of ye^, lordis of consail^, said landis of^, and stan of^, markis worth of^, schillingis of annuel^, schir john of^, albany erle of, auise of ye, curt of ye, erle of march, george erle of, langar lefar of, lefar of thaim, sid of ye, tenour of ye

4-grams: haldin fra him of***, day of ye monath***, yhere of oure lord**, yhere of god a**, vsuale mone of scotland**, yhere of god ane^, haldin fra hir of^, and sesing of ye^, ye said sum of^, tolbuth of ye samyn^, albany erle of march^, xxti day of ye^, februar ye yhere of^, may ye yhere of^, nouembre ye yhere of^, juli ye yhere of^, aprile ye yhere of^

5-grams: wrangus haldin fra him of***, day of ye monath of***, yhere of god a thousande**, witnes of ye quhilk thing**, yhere of oure lord a*, part and ye landis of*, stan in ye handis of*, tolbuth of ye samyn be*, curt of wigtoun haldin in*, borow curt of wigtoun haldin^, curt of newburch haldin^, wrangus haldin fra hir of^, james be ye grace of^, may ye yhere of god^, februar ye yhere of god^, juli ye yhere of god^, nouembre ye yhere of god^

The bundles in (b) may constitute syntagmatic extensions of bundles in (a), but not always. For instance, the date is a very formulaic element of legal texts also with regard to a specific day, *day of ye monath (of)* (FF = 82), and the names of the months (e.g. *may ye yhere of, nouembre ye yhere of*, etc.). These bundles are not introduced by a determiner because there are many possibilities for what may precede them, for instance, in the form of Latin digits or lexical ordinal numerals before *day*. The bundles in question open a formula which refers, in the first case, to a choice of twelve months, and in the second case to the year of the proceedings, which in turn continues into a further specification of a particular year.

Apart from bundles which refer to date (the day, the month, the year), two nominal bundles starting directly with a modifier are worth a closer look: *wrangus haldin fra him of* 'wrongful holding/taking[6] from him of' (FF = 94) and *vsuale mone of scotland* 'usual money of Scotland' (FF = 67). The first bundle is a highly overlapping 5-gram, both syntagmatically and paradigmatically (cf. Type N2a–b, Type P2a–b), and it remains within the most formulaic elements of discourse regardless of extracted bundle lengths (see how it re-emerges in the discussion of 6- to 8-grams and textual standardization in Chapter 12). It makes reference to the offence of stealing, indeed, stealing from a man, which was apparently frequent enough to trigger one of the most formulaic lexical strings in the corpus. Stealing from a woman—*wrangus haldin fra hir of* (FF = 36)—was less common in the texts, although also formulaic enough to make it to the top 10%. A closer look at the syntagmatic overlaps allows us to say that if the bundle is preceded by a definite article *ye* 'the', its formulaicity increases, cf. *ye wrangus haldin fra him* (FF = 98), *ye wrangus haldin fra hir* (FF = 43) (Type N2a), and is increased even further when the whole NP becomes a complement of the preposition *for*, where the length of the 5-gram excludes the pronoun reference at the end: *for ye wrangus haldin fra* (FF = 100) (Type P2a). The preference for a definite article at the start of the NP makes it clear that the activity is not discussed in generic terms, as in 'stealing from people is punishable by law', but rather the grammatical structure indicates the definiteness of the act.

The other selected bundle, making a specific reference to Scottish money, points to the importance of currency distinctions as a frequent element of legally confirmed transactions. It is a syntagmatic overlap with a prepositional bundle *of vsuale mone of (scotland)* 'of usual money of (Scotland)' (Type P1a below), which indicates a measure preceding this formula, most probably containing the actual sum to be paid. It is worth noting that partitives or expressions of quantity were also found by Culpeper and Kytö in their top frequency bundles from PDE trials: 'part of the' and 'a number of' (2010: 116–117). The former is also present in the top 10% formulaic lexical bundles in EdHeW (Type N1b, 144 times in 106 texts, FF = 24), while *ye nomer of* appears only 12 times in 10 texts, barely making it through the cut-off point but not into the most formulaic pool.

Type N2
Other noun phrase fragments
(a) Det + Mod + N

3-grams: ye samyn day***, ye said landis**, ye wrangus haldin**, oure souerain lord**, ye said john**, ye said lord*, ye said ser*, ye said william*, thir present letteris*, ye said burgh*, ye xxti day*, the quhilk day*, ye said day^, ye first day^, ye said balze^, ye said shir^, ye forsaid ser^, ye said erle^, ye forsaid erle^, ye said abbot^, ye said partis^, ye thre estatis^, this present parliament^, oure said souerain^, oure souerain lordis^, oure souerain lady^, ye said adam^, ye said alexander^, ye said dauid^, ye said davy^, ye said elizabeth^, ye said george^, ye said gilbert^, ye said james^, ye said jonet^, ye said marion^, ye said nichol^, ye said patrik^, ye said robert^, ye said thomas^, ye saidis william^, ye said master^, ye borow curt^, ye first curt^, ye nexit curt^, ye saidis landis^, ye forsaid landis^, ye said sum^, ilk mannis richt^, ye west part^, ye est part^, ye south raw^, ye hail curt, ye langar lefar, ye north raw, ye said andro, ye west sid, my said lord

4-grams: ye wrangus haldin fra***, ye samyn day ye**, ye quhilk day ye*, ye samyn day thom*, ye samyn day john*, oure souerain lord and*, oure said souerain lord*, oure souerain lord ye*, ye said abbot and*, ye said landis and*, that ta part and*, thir present letteris me^, ye said landis with^, ye west part on^, ye est part on^, ye balzeis and ye^

5-grams: ye wrangus haldin fra him***, oure souerain lord ye king*, ye wrangus haldin fra hir*, ye samyn day thom logan^, oure souerain lord and his^, ye said landis with ye^, that ta part and ye^

The example *ye samyn day* is, in fact, the most formulaic lexical bundle and the second most frequent 3-gram of all extracted from the corpus;[7] *ye samyn day* appears 1,655 times in 485 texts (FF = 99). It indicates the fact that legal discourse makes necessary connections within the text to sustain the coherence of documents and accounts by frequent links to preceding information. This point will be taken up again in the functional analysis of the top bundles in Chapter 11. The importance of formulaic date reference was mentioned above. Still, that initial date formula, as in *day of ye month (of)* (Type N1b), may include various combinations of the day, month, and year, whereas a subsequent link may simply occur in one formulaic format. The lexical bundle *ye samyn day* saves space and effort because the clerk does not have to meticulously repeat information about the date already provided.[8]

The same strategy is observable in the choice of the modifier. The most common modifier in the Det + Mod + N construction is *said*. It can very frequently modify a person's name (as in *ye said william*), whereby we learn about the popularity of specific names in the texts, or a common noun (as in *ye said landis*), which indicated the most frequent items or possessions under discussion in legal texts. Indeed, land transactions are among the most frequent topics in the documents and many formulaic strings pertain to this semantic area. The adjective *said* can also be pluralized, as in Older Scots there was a plural concord between adjective and noun (King 1997: 173–174). These modifiers, supplying coherence within the text, surface also in other types of nominal constructions, as illustrated in Type N2d below.

(b) N + PP

3-grams:	chalans for ye***, wrangus haldin fra**, haldin[9] fra him*, and stan in^, stan in ye^, landis with ye^, balze in that^, all men be^, west part on^, curt for ye^, sesing with erd^, est part on, james be ye, penny in-to ye
4-grams:	chalans for ye wrangus***, wrangus haldin fra him***, all men be thir*, men be thir present*, balze in that tyme*, stan in ye handis^, landis with ye pertenencis^, wrangus haldin fra hir^
5-grams:	chalans for ye wrangus haldin***, men be thir present letteris**

In general, there is a tendency for a nominal component to be followed by a prepositional complement, so that the preposition becomes part of the formulaic string. The actual prepositional phrase may or may not be equally formulaic. Some such bundles display a syntagmatic overlap but some show that it was possible to use a few typical nominal constructions with a specific preposition (most often *of*, see Type N1 above) and then add to this formulaic frame whatever information was relevant.

Again, one of the most formulaic lexical bundles in this structural pattern is *wrangus haldin fra (him)*, which, in fact, overlaps syntagmatically with the 5-gram *chalans for ye wrangus haldin*. These strings have been mentioned before as they typically extend with an *of*-phrase (5-grams in Type N1), pointing to the actual object of stealing.

(c) (Conj) + NP + (Conj)[10]

3-grams:	and ye said*, and his airis*, his airis or*, his airis and^, or his airis^, airis executouris or^, and myn airis^, myn airis and^, myn airis or^, airis executouris and^, son and apperand^, and apperand air^, souerain lord and^, or souerain lord^, lord and his^, lord erle and^, said abbot and^, ye aldirman and^, ye balzeis and^, balzeis consail and^, ye king and^, and ye landis^, said landis and^, and biggin with^, part and ye^, ye accion and^, but fraud or, balzeis and ye, his landis and, and his successouris, saidis william and
4-grams:	and stan in ye*, part and ye landis*, souerain lord and his*, his airis executouris or^, sesing with erd and^
5-grams:	and stan in ye handis*, balze in that tyme and*, and apperand air to ye^

This type of formulaic construction indicates the importance of conjunctions, and especially *and*, in legal texts. The role of conjunctions has not been noticed in other studies using the bundle methodology. However, the special character of *and* in discourse has already been signalled by Schiffrin (1985), and also explored with other corpus tools and in various genres and registers, historical and modern. The observations made by Biber et al. (1999: 79–84) indicate that it is academic discourse and prose which contain most *and* coordination. A more fine-tuned analysis into phrasal and clausal *and* reveals that different registers have different preferences here: academic discourse prefers phrasal *and* while conversation uses more clausal *and* (Biber et al, 1999: 81). This point was pursued by Culpeper and Kytö (2010: 160–183) in their investigation of *and* as a cohesive device in various Early Modern speech-related text types. Their study supported earlier findings that phrase-level *and* features more prominently in didactic texts, while clause-level *and* is a characteristic feature of speech-related text types, especially witness depositions (Culpeper and Kytö 2010: 183). Lexical bundles drawn from EdHeW material are most often instances of the phrasal *and*, at least in the most formulaic noun phrase fragments (see examples of Type N2c), which brings the documents closer to the instructive and narrative styles, rather than interactive trial language.

Interestingly enough, these 3-grams which start and finish with *and* do not overlap syntagmatically with longer bundles. The only two examples of such an overlap are *souerain lord and (his)* and *(part) and ye landis*. This means that one part of a coordinated construction was more formulaic than the other. For example, there may have been more possibilities to start a bundle which typically finished in *and his airis*, *and myn airis*, *and apperand air*, or other fragments listed in (c) above. Similarly, more options were available to finish a bundle which started in *his airis and*, *myn airis and*, *ye balzeis and*. In fact, some of these formulaic parts of *and*-coordinated phrases will indeed be binomial pairs or multinomials.

As a whole, a binomial seems to be less formulaic than its parts. This point will be further explored in Chapter 10. It is worth signalling at this juncture that there are also instances of initial *and* in verb phrase fragments, which points to single formulaic uses of the clausal *and* (see Types V2 and C1 below).

(d) other

3-grams:	samyn day ye^, quhilk day ye^, samyn day thom^, samyn day john^, curt ye samyn^, elizabeth his spouse^, john ye wath^, laurence lord oliphant^, robert lord fleming^, said souerain lord^, said ser william^, said lord erle^, oure lord a^, souerain lord ye^, his airis executouris^, men be thir^, scottyn lottyn wakyn^, ye mononday ye^, ye curt for^, said lord his, lord his airis, saidis william and
4-grams:	curt ye samyn day*, souerain lord ye king*, hand ye samyn day^
5-grams:	samyn day thom logan officer^

In the remaining noun phrase fragments, we find overlaps with more prominent constructions discussed above. Some such bundles come from paradigmatic overlaps, as in *samyn day ye* or *samyn day thom* being parts of more formulaic 4-grams *ye samyn day ye* and *ye samyn day thom* (Type N2a). What is striking about this varied group is that it contains bundles which were generated across sentence boundaries, or even paragraph boundaries. As I explained in the methodology section 8.4.3, the corpus files were stripped of all punctuation, so that the bundle extraction was not withheld by punctuation marks. As a result, the search rendered interesting examples of formulaicity across clause or paragraph boundaries. When we superimpose paragraph marks, two such examples can be seen here: *curt* || *ye samyn (day)* and *hand* || *ye samyn day*. Of course, *ye samyn day* is the most formulaic 3-gram in the corpus (Type N2a). But what is now visible is what often preceded this formulaic starting sequence: in 144 cases in 105 texts the clerks finished their previous paragraphs mentioning the dealings of the court, while in 79 cases in 60 texts they finished off writing about the hand, probably in the context of testifying with their own hand. And then they moved on to the next entry.

Type N3

Date and number fragments

3-grams:	god a thousande^, thousande four hundereth^, a thousande four^, lord a thousande
4-grams:	a thousande four hundereth**, god a thousande four*, oure lord a thousande*, lord a thousande four*
5-grams:	lord a thousande four hundereth*, god a thousande four hundereth*, oure lord a thousande four*

One of the most conspicuous formulaic patterns is the reference to the date of the document. In various chunks, it surfaces in all bundle lengths and becomes most prominent in its full span in the longer bundles (Chapter 12), once the rest of the shorter repetitive strings have been sifted off. In Culpeper and Kytö's findings, in the top twenty bundles from PDE trials there are also several references to the date: 'in nineteen eighty', 'nineteen eighty eight', 'nineteen eighty five', 'on the twenty' (2010: 116–117).[11] Of course, in Scots historical material the bundles will reflect the time of corpus composition, cf. the most formulaic 4-gram in the group, *a thousande four hundereth* (256 occurrences in 235 texts, FF = 65). There are also two competing options when it comes to the year of the document: *god a thousande four hundereth* and *oure lord a thousande four (hundereth)*. This rivalry has already been pointed out in other structural bundle types (Type N1); in fact, the preference for one or the other seems to be chronological (Fig. 11.1).

Interestingly, date reference did not make it to the top frequency range in EModE trials (Culpeper and Kytö 2010: 116–117), even though EModE trials have identified 'at that time' as one of the most frequent bundles. This lack of formulaic reference to date contrasts with legal Scots documents. As pointed out above, the EdHeW material is heavily nominal in nature, and therefore informative. It seems to have been crucial to provide a time frame for a given legal act, either to keep the order of entries in place, or to provide a point for future reference.

Type N4

Personal pronouns + (Conj) + (NP)

3-grams:	me myn airis^, him and his^, him and til^, ws and oure^, i ye said^, me and myn
4-grams:	him and his airis^, me myn airis and^, me and myn airis^
5-grams:	me myn airis and assignais^

Considering Type N4 lexical bundles, we move from lexical nominal phrase fragments to personal pronouns. These are less frequent in bundles but such strings with personal pronouns which do conform to the criteria point to two interesting formulaic trends.

First, personal pronouns often feature in bundles with the coordinating device *and* (e.g. *me myn airis and (assignais), me and myn airis*). They signal important personal relationships of the people involved in legal action, typically from the first person perspective. It is the central figure, the owner of property, the head of the family, who creates legal discourse in the document. We also find third person reference, *him and his (airis)* (the 3-gram appears 146 times in 100 texts, making it to the pool of most formulaic variants), and a much less frequent feminine pronoun reference: *and hir airis* (22 occurrences in 12 texts), *hir and hir (airis)* (14 occurrences of the 3-gram in 11 texts) and also *of hir husband* (13 occurrences in 10 texts), and *of hir said husband* below the bundle threshold (8 times in 8 texts). In general, women do feature in early legal Scots documents but not frequently enough to inspire a special formulaic bundle. The findings go hand in hand with historical accounts of the position of women in medieval and early Renaissance Scotland. Women are mostly referred to through sons and husbands, but some of them were self-sufficient, especially widows who could inherit property (for more on the social relations in the burghs, see section 6.3; for the legal provision for widows, see section 7.3.1 on burgh laws). From a purely structural side, the determiner (here in the form of a possessive pronoun) extends ambiguous scope over coordinated NPs. In *me myn airis and assignais* the pronoun *myn* may introduce one and the same referent—the people who are both heirs and assignees at the same time. In an alternative reading, this construction may mean 'my heirs and other people who are my assignees'. The problem of which reading is correct is unsolvable, as Scots allows determiner scope over coordinated NPs. The only solution would be to refer to the external circumstances for the composition of a particular document.

The other personal pronoun usage which comes across as formulaic is the plural self-reference *ws and oure*. This bundle is an example of the royal plural, and it could be the king who refers to himself by means of a distal plural form to stress royal authority, but the pronoun may also be used by someone who wants to create an impression of distance and legal authority. There are more examples of this usage in longer formulaic bundles, as explored in Chapter 12.

9.3. Prepositional Phrase Fragments

The second major group of the most formulaic bundles are prepositional phrase fragments.[12] They typically overlap with nominal phrase fragments discussed in section 9.2 above. Here I have also decided to separate the bundles beginning with the preposition *of* in order to investigate possessive relationships among lexical bundles and nominal complementation patterns. The pattern in Type P1a includes *of* followed by a noun phrase fragment where a noun is preceded by a modifier, while Type P1b lists the remaining *of*-phrases.

Type P1

Prepositional phrase fragments with *of*-phrase fragment

(a) *of* + Det + Mod + (N)

3-grams: of ye said***, of ye samyn**, of ye forsaid*, of that ilk^, of ye saidis^, of his realme^, of ye thre^, of annuel rent^, of vsuale mone^

4-grams: of ye said landis***, of ye said burgh**, of vsuale mone of*, of oure souerain lord*, of ye samyn be^, of ye said sum^, of ye said ser^

5-grams: of vsuale mone of scotland*, of ye said landis with^, of ye quhilk thing to^, of ye said landis and^

Among phrase fragments which can be expanded to a longer unit, the pattern of a preposition, determiner, and modifier stands out very clearly. It is most numerous in terms of tokens (there are 8,190 tokens of this word order in the top formulaic 3-grams, which constitutes 15%), while the actual types of constructions are relatively few. This points to a high level of formulaicity. In fact, a member of this subgroup, *of ye said* 'of the said', is the most formulaic 3-gram in the whole EdHeW corpus. It appears 2,157 times in 773 texts (FF = 97), which gives roughly three occurrences per text. If normalized per million words, this particular expression would render over 3,753 instances. Suffice it to say that the most common 3-grams in present-day English academic prose formed a group with "over 200 occurrences per million words" (Biber et al. 1999: 994); the discrepancy between the figures is striking and brings emphasis to the degree of formulaicity in early legal Scots. *Of ye said* is only slightly less formulaic than *ye samyn day* (FF = 99) commented on above (Type N2a) but performs a similar function: it provides cohesive links within a text. This characteristic feature is also visible in the next string starting with the preposition *of*, namely *of ye samyn* (560 occurrences in 360 texts, FF = 62), which may be either the beginning of a longer nominal phrase, or a substantivized adjective. This second option is signalled by the formulaic 4-gram *of ye samyn be*, where another prepositional phrase attaches itself at the end. There is also a less frequent option *forsaid* and an enumerative *ilk* 'each' in the same discourse function.

The ubiquity of *said* and *samyn* as nominal modifiers is dictated by the requirements of legal discourse for explicit cohesive links within the text. It appears that the compilers of the documents were constantly reminding the reader what a given piece of information refers to and where else it has already been presented. The structural monotony of these expressions, repeated over and over again, does not pose a problem, stylistic or otherwise. What counts is a clear and unambiguous link to preceding discourse. Also the nouns which are 'said', belong to the most formulaic inventory, for example, *of ye said landis*, *of ye said burgh*, *of ye said sum*, *of ye said ser*, listed above.

Finally, a curious case of one specific numeral, 'three', appearing in a formulaic lexical bundle *of ye thre*, requires a comment. The choice of this particular numeral is dictated by the fact that the bundle (most often)[13] refers to the Three Estates of the Scottish Parliament (section 7.2.4), as illustrated above with syntagmatically overlapping bundles *ye thre estatis* (Type N2a) and *thre estatis of* (Type N1a).

(b) *of* + NP

3-grams: of ye monath*, of god a^, of ye toune^, of ye burgh^, of ye curt^, of ye landis^, of this realme^, of ye realme^, of parliament maid^, of ye king^, of oure souerain^, of oure lord^, of ye levinax^, of albany erle, of thaim twa

4-grams: of ye monath of***, of god a thousande**, of oure lord a*, of ye landis of*, of ye burgh of*, of wigtoun haldin in^, of albany erle of^, of februar ye yhere^, of may ye yhere^, of juni ye yhere^, of juli ye yhere^

5-grams: of oure lord a thousande*, of god a thousande four*, of februar ye yhere of*, of may ye yhere of*, of juni ye yhere of*, of juli ye yhere of*, of aprile ye yhere of^, of nouembre ye yhere of^, of march ye yhere of^, of albany erle of march^, of wigtoun haldin in ye^

The *of*-phrase fragments without a modifier seem more diverse but, in fact, the major formulaic strings convey reference to the date of a given document. Indeed, if a 5-word string were to start with a preposition, in the same form over and over again, it would most probably be the reference to the month, followed by a chunk of the nominal phrase referring to the year. The actual months in the bundles reveal most frequent times of document composition. As the majority of the documents were compiled during burgh court proceedings, the times of the year when the most important courts were held become prominent. Interestingly enough, the months when the head courts would be held are not to be found among these formulaic constructions. As pointed out in section 7.3.2, the three most important meetings of a burgh court, the head courts, were convened at Michaelmas, Yule, and Pasch. The months which could therefore be expected to surface most often would be September, December, and March/April. Even though the spring months feature in the most formulaic structures, the other months do not. It is most probably due to the fact that these special days had their own very well-known lexicalized labels and needed no further specification of the month.[14]

In the PP-fragments beginning with *of* there are overlaps with NP bundles identified above, as the *of*-phrases constitute the most typical complements of the NP (e.g. Type N1a *ye yhere of* + Type P1b *of oure lord a thousande*).

Type P2

Other prepositional phrase fragments

(a) P + Det + Mod + (N)

3-grams: for ye wrangus***, to ye said***, be ye said*, in ye said*, with ye said^, in this present^, for ye said^, at ye said^, to ye forsaid^, be thir present^, on ye west^, on ye est^, on ye north^, on ye south^, to oure souerain^, within ye said, to ye nexit

4-grams: for ye wrangus haldin***, be thir present letteris**, on ye toyer part*, on that ta part*, on ye west part*, on ye est part*, on ye west sid*, to ye said lord*, to ye said ser*, to ye said john^, to ye said william^, to oure souerain lord^, to ye nexit curt^, in this present parliament^, within ye said burgh^, on ye est sid^

5-grams: for ye wrangus haldin fra***, all men be thir present**, on that ta part and**, on ye est part on*, on ye west part on*, be thir present letteris me*

The word order P + Det + Adj + N is most frequent and displays the greatest variety of types. Apart from *of*-phrases, there are other highly formulaic prepositional sequences in the corpus. The two most formulaic 3-grams require a separate comment. The discussion above has already touched upon the 'wrongful activity', referred to frequently in the documents and stemming from the traditional reference to law-breaking in Scotland, as reviewed in section 7.2.3. Type N2a structures had among them *ye wrangus haldin* (525 times in 252 texts, FF = 71), pointing to a specific wrongdoing. When we shift the bundle boundary to the left and include the introductory preposition *for*, we open space for more nominal complements to occur. Therefore *for ye wrangus* is more frequent and more formulaic (803 times in 280 texts, FF = 85). The overlapping 4-gram, *for ye wrangus haldin*, is a highly formulaic expression (FF = 99), found 509 times in over 200 texts. Other nominal complements found in the corpus are diverse but much rarer: *ye wrangus takin* (38 items in 31 texts), *ye wrangus occuping* (15 times in 12 texts), *ye wrangus selling* (12 times in 12 texts), and some from below the bundle threshold: *ye wrangus borch* (*DSL* 'something given or offered as a pledge', s.v. *borch(t)* n 2, 12 times in 9 texts), *ye wrangus wythaldyn* (9 times in 7 texts), *ye wrangus distroublance* (8 times in 6 texts), *ye wrangus slaing* (6 times in 6 texts), and *ye wrangus trublance* (6 times in 6 texts). All of them could be potential expansions of the formulaic *for ye wrangus* but cannot be treated as formulaic on their own. The extension into a 5-gram adds another prepositional element, *fra*, which indicates the person who suffered a loss of property. As the discussion below will show (Type P2b), the continuation was also highly formulaic when it concerned a man, and less so when a woman was involved.

Another feature of prepositional fragments is the appearance of the cohesive modifier *said* and its less popular, but still formulaic counterpart *forsaid*. The textual function of these bundles has been discussed in detail under Type P1a above because fragments with *said* and *samyn* constitute a characteristic feature in *of*-phrase fragments. Nevertheless, there are other prepositions which happily take a nominal complement with a cohesive modifier, for example, *to ye said* (1,469 tokens in 630 texts, FF = 93), *be ye said* (310 tokens in 214 texts, FF = 43), *in ye said* (291 tokens in 190 texts, FF = 42), and so on. Some of these expand syntagmatically to typical contexts and produce formulaic 4-grams (e.g. *to ye said lord*, *within ye said burgh*).

In this structural group there is another 4-gram which attracts attention: *be thir present letteris* (247 times in 178 texts, FF = 73). The prepositional construction is equipped with a deictic element *thir* 'these' which sets a given communicative situation in time and space by making direct reference to the document which is in front of the reader at this very moment. This is a direct link to the oral features of early laws, reinforced by the adjective *present*, another reference to the document itself. When the document speaks for itself, 'by these present writs', commanding people to obey a certain law, it is actually the town crier who is reading it out for the audience assembled around the tron in a medieval Scottish town (section 6.3.3). The prepositional fragment in question will, in fact, expand into one of the most standardized formulae of the EdHeW corpus: *be it kend til all men be thir present letteris* 'let it be known to all men by these present writs' (for details, see Chapter 12).

Finally, in the prepositional phrase-fragments there are a number of bundles referring to official transactions and hereditary arrangements. As indicated in section 6.4.2 on burgh economy, it was land that constituted the most frequent object of transfer, which finds confirmation in the frequent reference to measurements and the geographic position of a given tenement: *on ye west*, *on ye est*, etc. Other expressions connected with transactions, including land transfer, as well as with other agreements consist of various overlapping sequences of a longer structural frame: ___ *on that ta part and* ___ *on the tothir part*. The *DSL* defines *ta* as 'the one (of two); chiefly in opposition to *the tother*' (s.v. *ta* 1.), with a specific application in the legal context where it refers to one of the 'two parties involved in an agreement' or 'the boundaries of a piece of land' (s.v. *ta* 2.). Of course, the modifier *the tothir* is an example of a word-boundary reanalysis in *that othir*. In the corpus there are many types of lexical bundles extracted from and overlapping with these expressions.[15] It seems that the formula could have had many incarnations, and no specific single phrasing became the stylistic norm. However, the individual prepositional fragments are to be found among the top 10% of formulaic structures in the corpus.

(b) P + NP

3-grams: fra him *of***, and to ye*, for all ye^, and for ye^, for his fredom^, for faut *of*^, for scottyn lottyn^, for ye tyme^, and at ye^, in that tyme^, in tyme to^, in ye yhere^, vnder ye pain^, be ye king^, befor thir witnes^, to ye chalans^, in witnes *of*^, in ye tolbuth^, in amersyment for^, in ye handis^, in-to ye handis^, betuix ye landis^, betwene ye landis^, with auise *of*^, with erd and^, with ye pertenance^, with ye pertinencis^, in all punctis^, in like wise^, with thare pertenance^, to ye king^, til all men^, and til his^, til his airis^, with consent *of*, for a yhere, at ye fest, in amersyment *of*, saiffand ilk mannis

4-grams: vnder ye pain *of***, in tyme to cum**, in ye handis *of***, in-to ye handis *of**, in ye tolbuth *of**, with erd and stan*, betuix ye landis *of**, for all ye dayis*, til all men be*, and til his airis*, in amersyment for ye^, at the fest of^, in that tyme and^, to ye king and^

5-grams: till all men be thir*, for all ye dayis *of**, in that tyme and than*, in ye tolbuth *of* ye^, in amersyment for ye wrangus^

Other frequent prepositions at the beginning of most formulaic bundles include *for*, *be* 'by', *in*, *with*, and *til*. These prepositions introduce a range of formulaic nominal complements, whose content is dictated by the legal character of the corpus. The most formulaic 3-gram in this group is *fra him of* (415 tokens in 184 texts, FF = 61), which typically continues the frequently repeated accusation of stealing and other unlawful deeds (Type P2a). The masculine pronoun is certainly the most common referent, which implies the imbalance in legal involvement between males and females. The feminine counterpart *fra hir of* can be found 83 times in 60 texts, so it is not that rare but definitely less prominent.

The generic use of the lexical item *men* is visible in the repetitive bundles starting with the preposition *til* 'to': *til all men (be) (thir) (present) + letteris*, the final element belonging to formulaic overlaps discussed in Type P2a. All the burgesses were included in this generic address, regardless of the fact that women were also entitled to burghal privileges (Chapters 6 and 7). *Til* typically introduced NPs denoting human beings, as in the other formulaic example *til his airis* 'to his heirs' (84 tokens in 50 texts). To continue the comparison of male and female presence in the records, *til hir airis* does not surface in the bundles at all.[16]

Another frequent preposition at the start of formulaic strings is *in*. It often introduces reference to time as in *in that tyme (and) (than)*, *in tyme to cum*, *in ye yhere*. Culpeper and Kytö (2010: 116–117) have *at the time* and *at that time* in their top-20 bundles drawn from present-day trial material. The importance of date has been mentioned before, but in the second example another aspect of legal texts comes to the fore. The power of a court record or another official document to establish frames of acceptable social activity or to recognize somebody's claim to a given property reaches into the future. It is embedded in a formulaic sequence *in tyme to cum*, which appears 272 times in 171 texts (FF = 80). Other phrase fragments in *in* make reference to practices and rituals at court, for example, bringing the earth and stone (*erd and stan*, one of the most formulaic binomials discussed in Chapter 10) *in ye handis* or *in-to ye handis* of a new owner (cf. the 4-gram *stan in ye handis*, Type N2b). Of course, other objects could possibly be placed in the same hands but the connection with ancient custom involving earth and stone is clearly the most prominent employment of this 3-gram. Also the physical location for legal proceedings gets to the most formulaic pool: *in ye tolbuth* (186 tokens in 168 texts, FF = 24), as well as reference to discourse structure *in all punctis* (36 tokens in 13 texts, FF = 25) and *in like wise* (39 tokens in 15 texts, FF = 25). It is already visible that specific discourse functions come to the fore in the most frequent bundles; this point will be explored in Chapter 11. The same chapter will devote closer attention to other prepositional beginnings, typically pertaining to legal discourse, as in *befor thir witnes*, *to ye chalans*, or *vnder ye pain*.

To follow up the discussion of most formulaic nominal components, perhaps a general observation to be made on the basis of the material extracted by the lexical bundle methodology, is that phrasal bundles expand to non-phrasal ones. Conversely, non-phrasal bundles point to syntagmatic overlaps with longer structures, which may render a phrasal expression again. Another point, to which I return in the general conclusions at the end of this chapter, is that the bundles suggest a fixed structure with exchangeable elements preceding/following in a free position. What should be noted, though, is the fact that due to expansion, formulaicity may become reduced. Thus, some formulaic 3-grams are continued in formulaic 4-grams, some 4-grams in 5-grams, and so on, but not all strings keep their formulaic nature when expanded simply because expansion may involve rarer items. A good illustration of this phenomenon is the formulaic reference to the date of composition of a given text, discussed from various angles above. The Type P1b 3-gram *of ye monath* 'of the month' occurs 552 times in 442 texts (FF = 57). When expanded with the beginning of the next prepositional phrase, *of ye monath of* 'of the month of' it still can be found in the range of most formulaic 4-grams (484 tokens in 408 texts, FF = 81). However, if we look further into formulaic 5-grams, the expanded version does not make it to the top 10% of formulaic strings anymore. We still see the same bundle, expanded with different names of the months, in the remaining repository of lexical bundles, however not in the most formulaic range. So up to four elements the bundle repeats in exactly the same form very frequently, but once a reference to a specific month is added, the frequency drops, for example, *of ye monath of juli* 'of the month of July' appears 52 times in 43 texts, *of ye monath of nouembre* 'of the month of November'—47 times in 39 texts, or *of ye monath of februar* 'of the month of February'—35 times in 25 texts. Moreover, that 4-gram does not even need to be expanded with a specific month; the expanded string could well be 'of the month of this year', 'of the month of the same (year)', 'of the month of heavy floods', and so forth.

9.4. Verb Phrase Fragments

Moving on to the verb phrase fragments, the first observation should be that they are much less numerous in types than the NPs and PPs. For the lack of similar studies from the medieval and early modern period in Scotland, the only point of reference is either modern English data, or Culpeper and Kytö's study on early modern English dialogues. It has been suggested on the basis of lexical bundles that in historical trials there were more repetitive verb phrases than nominal ones, which has gradually given way to the opposite preference in PDE material (2010: 118). This could be seen as a counter-trend to Biber and Finegan's claim (1989, 1992) that various registers in English drifted from more literate (more nominal and informational) to more oral styles (more verbal and interactive). However, it should be pointed out with force that these studies were not all based on the same genres and registers. In fact, when Biber and Finegan expanded their database (1997) to include professional expository texts, the opposite tendency manifested itself. Professional expository texts seem to have shifted towards a more literate style in English within the last 400 years. As Chapter 11 will show, such a long diachronic trend cannot be observed on the basis of my data, nonetheless in the whole corpus the formulaic verbal element is definitely less numerous. When it comes to the degree of formulaicity, there are some very formulaic verbal lexical bundles which can be connected to the requirements of legal discourse. This point will also be followed up in Chapter 11.

The categorization of verb phrase fragments poses a major difficulty because the formulaic sequences are, most often, incomplete or the verb forms are ambiguous in structure. In short lexical bundles there is no context to disambiguate the forms of verbs; there are, however, formal similarities between various types among 3-, 4-, and 5-grams which allow us to group them according to common features. The distinction into passive versus non-passive verbs within verb phrase fragments, also employed to some extent by Biber, Conrad, and Cortes (2003: 381), has proven most useful. Parts of *that*-clauses and *to*-clauses have been classed separately (Types C1 and C2), as have adverbial clauses (Type C3), which conclude the list of structural types.

Type V1

Verb phrase fragments with a passive verb or present participle

(a) (*be*) + passive verb

3-grams: be it kend^, kend til all^, that was giffin^, was giffin for^, giffin for dome^, it is statut^, is statut and^, and ordanit that^, it is accordit^, is accordit that^, contenit in ye^, day was maid^, was maid burges^, ye sutis callit^, sutis callit ye^, callit ye curt^, callit to ye^,[17] ye curt effermit^, callit and nocht^, and nocht comperit^, callit nocht comperit^, comperit in curt^, haldin in ye^, maid *of* befor^, is contenit in, it is thocht, ordanit that ye

4-grams: sutis callit ye curt**, ye sutis callit ye**, it is statut and**, be it kend til*, it kend til all*, kend til all men*, that was giffin for*, and that was giffin*, ilk day was maid*, day was maid burges*, callit ye curt effermit*, callit and nocht comperit*, callit nocht comperit and^, nocht comperit and this^, comperit and this ye^, comperit in curt and^, callit to ye chalans^, yheris ye sutis callit^, curt of wigtoun haldin^, haldin in ye tolbuth^, it is accordit that

5-grams: ye sutis callit ye curt**, sutis callit ye curt effermit**, be it kend til all**, kend til all men be*, it kend til all men*, that ilk day was maid*, ilk day was maid burges*,

> haldin in ye tolbuth of*, yheris ye sutis callit ye*, callit to ye chalans of*, callit nocht comperit and this*, nocht comperit and this ye*, and that was giffin for*, that was giffin for dome^, day ye sutis callit ye^, callit ye curt effermit and^

At first sight, there are numerous verb phrase fragments with passive elements. On closer inspection, however, two aspects require further consideration. First of all, what looks like a passive verb may, in fact, be an adjectival passive. The distinction is subtle, as in *They were married (by the priest)*, which uses a passive verb, and *They were married* with a predicative adjective, as in *They were nice*. To test whether the construction involves a passive verb or an adjective, one can exchange the verb 'to be' with 'remain' or 'stay', which points to an adjectival reading (e.g. *They remained nice to us*). When we replace the ellipted *were* in *sutis callit* with *remane* 'remain', the structure becomes ungrammatical: **ye sutis remanyt callit*. Hence, the classification as a verb phrase fragment is justified in this case. However, with the verb *ken* 'know' the situation is not as straightforward. It seems possible to accept a rephrased version of *be it kend til all* 'let it be known to all' as *it remanyt kend til all* 'it remained known to all' but the corpus material did not render such constructions to support the grammaticality of the rephrased version. For this reason I have decided to keep such ambiguous cases in verbal structural types, with an important caveat about the categorial status of such expressions. Suffice it to say at this juncture that the status of a predicative adjective for *kend* would shift the balance in structural types even more to the nominal group.

Secondly, the degree of syntagmatic overlap within a specific bundle length and of paradigmatic overlap between shorter and longer bundles is substantial. This fact points to longer formulaic sequences, which indeed incorporate the shorter chunks identified among short lexical bundles. These longer sequences will be interpreted as indicators of standardizing textual patterns in Chapter 12. The overlapping 3-gram sequences in Type V1 are close to the lower part of the formulaicity scale—for the majority the formulaicity factor moves between 21 and 40 (see the explanation of thresholds above and Fig. 9.1), which means that there were many other, more formulaic 3-grams in the corpus. Interestingly, 4-grams built with a passive verb are more frequent. It was often enough to add one element of a phrase to boost the formulaicity, as in the case of *ye sutis callit* (FF = 31) expanded to *ye sutis callit ye* (FF = 64). It is necessary to remember that 3-grams are much more numerous than 4-grams, which is why a bundle requires more tokens to climb to the top formulaicity levels. Most of the 3-grams, however, do not expand into longer strings. If it happens, it means that this specific sequence of lexical items lends itself to formulaicization, possibly also textual standardization.

Among the most formulaic 4-grams in this type there are several typical verbs in the passive form: *callit* 'called', *comperit* 'appeared as a formal act', *effermit* '(about a court) fenced, formally opened', *statut* 'stated', *giffin* 'given', and *kend* 'known' (however, see the comments on its categorial status above). In terms of meaning and discourse function, which constitute the core of discussion in Chapter 11, all of the verbs answer to the requirements of the legal contexts. In constructions with the first three verbs, we find a typical ellipsis of the copula *be;* instead of 'the suits *were* called and *were* entered as a formal act in court', the records prefer *ye sutis callit and comperit/nocht comperit in curt.*[18] The same situation is visible in *ye curt effermit* 'the court (was) fenced'. In fact, these two elliptical passives are found in close proximity, if not directly following one another, as suggested by a very formulaic 5-gram *sutis callit ye curt effermit* (191 tokens in 175 texts, FF = 69). The verb *to be* is invisible on the surface but the construction is clearly passive and it points to syntagmatic overlaps to the left and to the right. Of course, at this stage the potential longer multi-element structures are gleaned from overlapping short bundles. But this specific elliptical word order is to be found among 6-, 7-, and 8-grams, pointing to one of the most standardized formulae in the corpus (section 12.2).

Interestingly, in *ye sutis callit ye* 'the suits called the', there is, in fact, a formulaic arrangement of coordinated, paratactic clauses. The final *ye* 'the' in that 4-gram is the beginning of another NP and there would be a comma in front of it, had the punctuation not been removed. Instead of a comma there could also be a coordinating device *and* (see the discussion of clausal *and* in section 9.5 below). The syntagmatic expansion of this bundle can be seen in the most formulaic 5-grams and upwards (section 12.2).

Other passive constructions are introduced with the verb *to be*, as in *it is statut (and)* (138 times in 48 texts, FF = 67). The conjunction typically expands this bundle into a binomial *statut and ordanit*, which will be discussed with the rest of the coordinated pairs in Chapter 10. It is due to this fact that the bundle *(and) ordanit that (ye)* '(and) ordained that (the)' has been classified among passive constructions, even though at first sight the verb form seems ambiguous. After investigating overlaps and numeric counts it turned out that this particular usage is always a past participle, coordinated with *it is statut.*[19] In terms of short bundles there is some competition between *it is statut* (144 times in 52 texts, FF = 39) and *it is accordit* (97 times in 42 texts, FF = 30; Fig. 11.3) but once the length of the extracted string is increased, the version with *statut* expands in a more predictable manner, with less formal variation and therefore with a higher formulaic score. Another budding formula can be predicted from the bundles with *kend* 'known'. The shorter chunks overlap and expand, to give several formulaic 5-grams which, in turn, point to a longer repetitive string: *be it kend til all (men) (be)* 'let it be known to all men by', the only imperative construction within the top formulaicity range. This is already a potential 7-gram, and once the most formulaic prepositional fragments starting with *be* 'by' are consulted (Type P2), it appears that the bundle expands further, without losing its formulaic character. MacQueen (2002a) suggests that this particular string was modelled on the Latin of earlier documents, which would explain the propensity for fixedness in the case of this bundle. This interpretation is confirmed by the analysis of the longest extracted lexical bundles in Chapter 12.

(b) present participle

3-grams:	remanand with ye^, lyand in ye^
4-grams:	remanand with ye said^, followand ye date of^

The few constructions with present participles which were most frequent among short bundles have prepositional and nominal complements, depending on the properties of the verb. The bundles pertain to a current position, usually of a tenement plot, and to situating the events in time. This deictic function will be explored in Chapter 11.

Type V2
Verb phrase fragments with a non-passive verb
(a) non-passive lexical verb

3-grams:	pay for his^, strekit a borch^, and gaif to, and obliss me, witnes ye hail
4-grams:	pay for his fredom*

Verbs in the active form are comparatively few when considered against the passive forms in Type V1. Altogether, the individual occurrences of active verbs in the top formulaic 3-gram range of the corpus amount to 289 instances, compared to the total count of passive 3-grams, which equals 3,316 tokens. Clearly, the documents have a preference for passive constructions. From a semantic point of view, all of these verbs pertain to legal activities at court, especially *to streke a borch* 'to put forward a pledge or surety' (*DSL* s.v. *strek(e* v. 3d). A more detailed functional analysis follows in Chapter 11.

(b) modal verb

3-grams:	and sal pay^, sal pay for^
4-grams:	and sal pay for*, sal pay for his*
5-grams:	and sal pay for his*, sal pay for his fredom*

Only one modal verb, *sal* 'shall', appears in the top formulaic range of the corpus, and indeed in combination with only one lexical verb—*pay*. All of the shorter chunks in Type V2b link up to create the relatively formulaic 5-gram *(and) sal pay for his fredom* (54 instances in 18 texts, FF = 50), with clausal coordination to the left. When it comes to the actual amount of the payment—the direct object of the verb *to pay*—this piece of information is not formulaic as it may have differed from one court ruling to the next.

(c) *be* + (potential complement)

3-grams:	ilk day was^, alswa it is
4-grams:	that ilk day was*

A free range of complements could also follow the verb *to be*, which is why several short bundles finish in this verb, without a further extension. However, on closer inspection of bundle overlaps, it turns out that the extension of *(that) ilk day was* is, in fact, a past participial construction *maid burges* (see Type V1a above, and section 6.3.2 on attaining burgess-ship). A much less formulaic *alswa it is* 'also it is' opens more possibilities to the right, but only 35 times in 18 texts (FF = 19).

9.5. Clause Fragments

Clause fragments come across as an important feature of legal discourse, with several very formulaic bundles. Type C1 (*this/that* clauses) has been separated from Type C2 (*to*-clauses), even though they both sometimes share the pronouns *that* or *this*. The separation was done in order to highlight *to*-clauses, which may have also been introduced with *this is to* or *that is to*. Whenever a *to*-clause appeared, it was classified as Type C2, regardless of the introductory part.

Type C1
this/that clauses
(a) (Conj) + (indicative *this/that*) + *be* + (Noun)

3-grams:	and this is^, this is ye^, is ye first^, and that was^, and this ye^
4-grams:	and this is ye**, this is ye first*, is ye first curt^
5-grams:	and this is ye first*, this is ye first curt*

(b) relative *that*-clause fragments

3-grams:	that ye said*

Clause fragments frequently begin with the conjunction *and*. The special connection of this element with different registers has already been mentioned in the discussion of Type N2c noun phrase fragments in section 9.2. So far the discussion of lexical bundles in the corpus has pointed to the ubiquity of nominal phrasal coordination, which characterizes an informational style of formal writing. At this juncture it is worth pointing out that the formula preferred by the clerks for closing and summarizing the dealings of a given court session starts with a clausal *and*. This clausal conjunction is followed by an indicative clause *this is ye first curt*, or the elliptical *this ye first curt* (only the initial part of this bundle has made it to the top formulaic pool). The bundle material has revealed that clausal *and* helps to bring sequences of discourse to a closure, as in *and this is ye* (157 tokens in 100 texts, FF = 62), where the nominal complement was typically *first curt*, but also *sycund curt*, *tyrd curt*, and *ferd curt*. In this context, *and* may even be considered a discoursal conjunction, operating on a level higher than a clause. On the basis of witness depositions, Culpeper and

Kytö (2010: 183) have noticed the frequent use of clausal *and* in speech-related text types. Scottish administrative and legal documents do not follow the same practice but the employment of summative *and* at the end of chunks of discourse bears traces of a narrative. I return to this point in the analysis of the textual function in section 11.3.2.

In PDE trials Culpeper and Kytö note instances of frequent 3-grams with the existential *there*—'there was a', 'there is a', 'there was no'. Sometimes these bundles overlap with *that* as a complementizer: 'that there was', 'that there is' (2010: 116–117). Such constructions also surface as the most frequent bundles in EModE trials: 'there was a', 'that he was', and may remind the reader of the clause fragments with elements of narration identified above.

Type C2
(Conj/*that*) (Verb) + *to*-clause fragments

3-grams:	that is to**, is to say**, it is to^, is to remember^, to remember ye^, to be payd^, to be maid^, to be haldin^, tyme to cum^, and to ferm, and to be
4-grams:	that is to say***, it is to remember*, is to remember ye*, followis that is to^, is to say that^
5-grams:	it is to remember ye*, followis that is to say*, that is to say that*, that is to say ye*

The fragments of *to*-clauses are an important element of legal discourse, especially when introduced with the relative pronoun *that*. Built out of two overlapping formulaic 3-grams, the bundle *that is to say* appears 592 times in 395 texts (FF = 89), which gives it the sixth place on the list of formulaic 4-grams. It plays a crucial role in providing coherence to legal discourse by introducing an explanation, further details or clarification to the matter unfolded earlier. Using such linguistic means, the compilers of legal texts aimed to guarantee greater comprehensibility of their produce.

To-clause fragments contain parts of orders and refer to the most typical legal activities like paying a fine or remembering a particular court decision or parliamentary statute. These orders are phrased in an indirect, impersonal manner, as if to convey the distance between the legislative authority and the burgesses. Links to indirect speech acts, a device typical for legal discourse (see sections 2.2 and 2.4.3), are also noticeable, something which will be further explored in Chapter 11. By way of concluding the discussion of verb phrase fragments, let me once again point out the formulaic nature of passive constructions and the cohesive devices, holding the text together in the form of verb phrase fragments with clausal coordination or by means of *that*- and *to*-clauses.

The final structural type of lexical bundles in Scots legal texts, Type C3 includes adverbial clause fragments and *if*-clauses.

Type C3

Adverbial clause fragments, including *if*-clauses

3-grams: that ilk day*, item it is^, item that ilk^, item ye same^, as said is^, as to ye^, efter ye forme^, and gif it^, and than ye^, than ye said^, and than incontenent^, than incontenent ye^, inconenent ye said^, triis callit nocht^, than ye balze^, than ye balzeis, all ye dayis, and gif ye, efter ye tenour, as is befor

4-grams: item it is statut*, item that ilk day*, and than incontenent ye*, than incontenent ye said*, incontenent ye said balze*, triis callit nocht comperit*, item ye same day^, item it is accordit^, and than ye said^, efter ye tenour of^, efter ye form and^, efter ye forme of^, all and hail ye^, and gif it happinis^, samyn day thom logan^

5-grams: item it is statut and*, and than incontenent ye said*, than incontenent ye said balze*, triis callit nocht comperit and*, efter ye form and tenour*, efter followis that is to^, as efter followis that is^, item that ilk day was^, that tyme and than incontenent^, tyme and than incontenent ye^, oft tymis callit and nocht^

The first adverbial which frequently introduces a new entry in the documents is *item* 'in the next place, likewise, also' (*DSL*, s.v. *Item* adv.), a borrowing or code-switching from Latin.[20] Historical dictionaries attribute the use of *item* in vernacular writings to the late 1390s, when it is still difficult to decide whether the Latin adverb has become fully integrated into the vernacular lexicon of Scots (or English, for that matter). It is necessary to recall in this context the close connection of Scots law with civil law, based on the traditions of ancient Rome, and also the impact of Latin as a medieval lingua franca in the legal domain (for further discussion see Chapter 7). There is no native competitor for *item* in the top formulaic bundles but in fact other options, albeit less formulaic, were in use, too. For example, *in like wise* appears 39 times in 15 texts, *alswa it is*—35 times in 18 texts, which contrasts starkly with *item it is* used 151 times in 54 texts. The latter bundle typically expands with a very formulaic *statut and ordanit*, visible in longer bundles in Type C3. Nevertheless, with reference to previously supplied information the native adverbial seems to compete with the Latin borrowing in a more or less equal manner: *alswa ye said* was used 27 times in 16 texts, while *item ye said*—21 times in 14 texts (both too rare to get into the top 10%). Constructions with the modifier *samyn* seem to prefer the Latin adverbial: *item ye samyn* was used 64 times in 36 texts, while *alswa ye samyn* has been found below the threshold specified for lexical bundles, at 8 tokens in 6 texts.

Another important group of bundle-initial adverbials are temporal expressions with *than* and *than incontenent* 'then at once, immediately' (*DSL* s.v. *incontinent* adv.). These bundles stem from narrative contexts in legal texts and describe a sequence of events. A similar function can be seen in various adverbials of manner, describing for instance how many times a case was called before the court: *triis* 'thrice' or simply *oft tymis* 'frequently'. The manner of entering the case in writing is also formulaic in nature: *efter ye forme* and *efter ye tenour* surface separately as 3-grams but also link up in one of the top 5-grams: *efter ye form and tenour* 'following the form and substance/importance (of a legal document)'. Finally, a few initial fragments of conditional clauses have made it to the top formulaic range, for example, *and gif it (happinis), and gif ye,* preceded again by the clausal (or discoursal) coordinating *and*. The further chunks of discourse introduced in this manner were too diverse to surface in the formulaic pool.

9.6. Conclusions: Structural Properties of Lexical Bundles in Early Legal Scots

The analysis of structural types allows us to make several general points on the nature of lexical bundles and their employment in early legal documents in Scotland. First, even though the structures are often incomplete, they suggest a formulaic frame with free positions to be filled in with a predictable syntactic element. For instance, Type N1a, as in *ye yhere of*, may be treated as a complete structure on the basis of the recurrence of this specific constituent arrangement, with a semantically varied and contextually determined complement, which nevertheless will always be an NP. This approach intersects with the idea of Part-of-Speech grams (PoS-grams), where the attention is shifted from the lexical content of a bundle to its structural components and the recurrence of a specific arrangement of parts of speech (Fletcher 2003/2004; Stubbs 2007). To continue the discussion of *of*-phrases, some partitive expressions Det + N + *of* + Det + (N) refer to a relationship between two NPs and are biphrasal (e.g. *ye king of ye cuntre* 'the king of the country'), whereas some similar structures are pseudopartitives Det + N + *of* + N, as in *ye king of* scotland 'the king of Scotland'. The latter example would, in fact, be analysed as monophrasal in syntactic accounts, going back to Selkirk (1977). This underlying distinction may suggest that partitives would produce bundles out of the first or the second NP and would be more frequent among short lexical bundles, while pseudopartitives would standardize in a wholesale manner and will surface more often among longer bundles. This point remains to be investigated further.

Returning to the structural nature of lexical bundles in the EdHeW corpus, it is interesting to observe that nouns, adjectives, verbs, and adverbs—open grammatical classes—still produce very formulaic sequences. The requirements of legal discourse prevent lexical creativity and promote stability in order to inhibit manifold interpretations of the text. In closed classes, such as prepositions and pronouns, their inventory is limited even further in the most formulaic strings. The special importance of the preposition *of* (Type N1, Type P1, Type P2b) is also worth stressing. On a similar note, the comparison between nouns and verbs highlights the preference for nominal bundles of all kinds, even though both grammatical classes are open. It is crucial to remember, though, that nouns have less variety in their grammatical forms than verbs, which also impacts on bundle extraction.

Nevertheless, the difference in frequency between nominal and verbal phrase fragments is not just due to the range of available forms. Nouns, prepositions, and attributive adjectives have been identified by Biber (1988) as indicators of the informational character of a text, as opposed to verbs, especially in present tense, which indicate involved production. The proportions of such features may change in time for a given genre. Biber and Finegan (1989, 1992) have postulated that, diachronically speaking, written registers "drift" towards orality because the language is becoming increasingly involved.[21] When their corpus database was expanded, it became apparent that some written texts were not part of this process. These were specialist expository texts, including legal prose, which tended towards a more nominal, informational style (Biber and Finegan 1997). Of course, those studies were carried out on material which is fundamentally different than the present corpus in terms of the chronological period and linguistic variety, not to mention its sheer volume, as well as the multiplicity of genres.[22] However, the linguistic choices characteristic for written and spoken genres identified by Biber have already been taken as a useful reference point in historical studies of English. In their work on EModE and PDE trials, Culpeper and Kytö (2010) have found that the former were more interactive in nature, while the PDE corpus preferred a more nominal style. "[T]he text type has acquired its legalistic, bureaucratic and not at all speech-like flavour over the last 400 years at least in part through the frequent use of a particular set of lexical bundles", say Culpeper and Kytö (2010: 130). Their results go hand in hand with Biber and Finegan's (1997) observations on specialist exposition; the present study allows the same conclusions for medieval and early modern Scots legal discourse.

A more systematic comparison of EdHeW bundles with Culpeper and Kytö's recent findings is not without problems. Even though a part of their study on a corpus of EModE and PDE trials was based on lexical bundles, the results of extraction differ in some important aspects from the material in the Scots legal and administrative corpus for several reasons. First, the underlying spoken and interactive character of courtroom discourse produces a different inventory of lexical bundles. In Culpeper and Kytö's material, the top twenty examples of the most frequent 3-grams typically contain fragments of questions and reported speech constructions, as in 'do you know', 'I did not', 'he told me' (2010: 116–117). Very few and infrequent structures of this kind surface in EdHeW bundles in the whole formulaic inventory cut off at 10 instances in 10 texts (for data preparation procedures, see especially section 8.5.3). This discrepancy points to different styles and genres within legal discourse (cf. section 2.4.2 and Bhatia 1993: 101); Culpeper and Kytö's corpus is speech-oriented whereas EdHeW relies on the conventions for written texts. The spoken residue of earlier oral legal practice is also visible in written texts, for example, in the form of a narrative, but the lexical bundle method has shown that there are few elements of interaction as such, if any. Events are reported not as somebody described them but as the court saw them, in an authoritative manner.

Another point of difference which inhibits a systematic comparison between the two studies is the temporal discrepancy. Even if we wanted to engage in cross-linguistic and cross-cultural comparisons of Scots and English legal texts, they would have to represent the same period. Unfortunately, this research path cannot be followed at present. Culpeper and Kytö's corpus takes up where EdHeW leaves off. There is no corpus of Early Modern dialogues in Scots to enable a comparative study. Conversely, for Middle English there is a comprehensive digital edition of the Rolls of the English Parliament (1272–1504)[23] (Given-Wilson et al. 2005) but no similar resource for local court records and municipal documents. Therefore, any comparisons between the English and Scots corpora can only point to interesting phenomena which should be investigated in a more controlled environment in due course, when more data becomes available.

The third difficulty lies in the research methodology. Even though this study and Culpeper and Kytö's study both use the lexical bundle method, different decisions were made as to the extraction procedures: the choice of software, the cut-off points, and the investigated bundle length. These choices, naturally, depended on the research aims and the array of tools selected to answer the research questions. The employment of lexical bundles by Culpeper and Kytö is not as extensive and comprehensive as in the present project; it was just one of the corpus tools employed in their research.

Coming back to the structural characteristics of lexical bundles in Scottish legal texts, there are many more bundles related to the nominal phrase than to the verb, which places the corpus clearly in the area of written discourse even in this early period. This feature once again highlights the difference between trial proceedings and legal documents—the latter are not written to be "devoured by an eager public" (Culpeper and Kytö 2010: 119), as was the case with famous trials,[24] but rather to provide a repository of court rulings, statutes, and notarial instruments for future reference, which brings the texts towards a more informational style. The most formulaic nominal phrase fragments in EdHeW refer to the date of the proceedings, people involved, and the legal activities performed in court, such as bringing 'earth and stone' to legitimize land transfers (section 7.3.4). Types N1 and N2 together incorporate 172 types of 3-grams with almost 25,000 tokens, which constitutes almost half of the top formulaic 3-grams (Table 8.4). Lexical bundles starting with a preposition (Type P1 and P2) are the second most numerous category with 80 types and almost 16,000 tokens. The most formulaic examples are openings of prepositional phrases which refer to NPs found earlier in the text, thus providing cohesive links between nominal elements of discourse. The most formulaic nominal phrases never start with an indefinite article, always making reference to situational circumstances which have been previously defined or which are clear from the context of situation, or the context of the text. For example, the bundles often result from meticulous attention paid to the date in the documents, as pointed out earlier in the chapter. Added together, nominal and prepositional phrase fragments account for around 75% of the top formulaic 3-grams in EdHeW. Moreover, even verb phrase fragments have a nominal feel to them because they come across as potential predicative adjectives, as in *ye sutis callit* 'the suits called'. The copula, invisible on the surface, has to be reconstructed in order to classify such cases as verb fragments.

Having said that, one would still expect some prominence of verb phrases in creating legal and administrative documents given the oral legacy of law. Indeed, the verb phrase fragments in Scots texts, although fewer in number, constitute some of the most formulaic bundles and perform communicative functions indispensable in the legal context. They are not dialogic, as is the case with bundles from early modern depositions and trials, which often functioned as utterance launchers and adjacency pairs (Culpeper and Kytö 2010: 127, 140). Rather they reflect the performative character of the law through indirect speech acts (*it is statut* 'it is stated', *it is ordanit* 'it is ordained', *be it kend* 'let it be known'), as well as building a coherent sequence of events in a document through narrative techniques, with the help of adverbial clauses (*and this is ye first curt* 'and this is the first court', *that ilk day* 'that same day', *then ye balzeis* 'then the bailies'). This final point makes it clear that specific structural patterns visible in lexical bundles will correlate with a specific range of discourse functions. Because the overwhelming majority of lexical bundles are nominal in nature, we may expect the referential function to be most prominent in these texts. On the other hand, the material made of verb phrase fragments also renders formulaic sequences which create the functional core of legal texts. These functional considerations will be taken further in Chapters 11 and 12.

10

Binomials and Multinomials in Early Legal Scots

10.1. Introduction

As signalled in previous chapters, we now make a detour into a specific structural type of construction emerging in lexical bundles, deemed as one of the most characteristic ingredients of legal texts. This important position of binomials and multinomials has already been indicated in Chapter 2 on the language of the law and in Chapter 4 on repetitive constructions (see especially sections 2.4.3 and 4.5). These phrases, composed of two or more coordinated elements: *A and/or B*, as in *will and testament*, *heirs or assignees*, or *give, devise, and bequeath*, are most often perceived as a consequence of the multilingual environment in which official documents were produced in medieval and early modern times. According to this view, it was not enough to express a concept in one language, especially the vernacular, but a sort of "translation" had to be provided for clarity's sake. There are examples of binomials and multinomials, though, which are devoid of the non-native element or those which are built solely from borrowings. The "translation" hypothesis does not tell the whole story.

This chapter begins with detailed remarks on the extraction of binomials from the EdHeW corpus (section 10.2), to follow up the outline of extraction methodology presented in Chapter 8. I consider the grammatical properties of binomials in early legal Scots discourse and then investigate the reasons why specific lexical items were paired up and coordinated. The motivations fall into two groups: semantic and non-semantic. First, I discuss binomials where the semantic properties of the lexical items motivate their coordination: complementation (as in *abbot and conuent*), contiguity (as in *kepe and defend*), cause and effect (as in *summond and process*), hyponymy (as in *consail and comonite*), and antonymy (as in *men and women*). The other group, which I have termed binomials proper (Kopaczyk 2009) because of their semantically repetitive nature, are motivated by phonology (as in *consent and assent*) and etymology, where one of the pair members seems to have been clarified or even translated with its co-member (as in *bind and obliss*). In this context, the discussion makes reference to orality and memory aids (Chapter 2), as well as the history of the language of the law in Scotland (Chapter 7). A careful reader will notice that in some cases more than one motivation behind a binomial could be postulated, semantic factors competing with phonological and etymological ones. In each debatable case, I assumed the primacy of semantic motivations, which add to the clarity and all-inclusiveness of the law; for instance, *consail and comonite* could be treated as an instance of alliteration, and thus a reflection of orality in legal discourse (see section 2.3). This particular binomial, however, occurs in the texts to spell out who was involved in a given legal activity, to give the text its comprehensive reading, so the coordinated pair relies more on semantics than on phonology. Throughout this chapter, I will offer a similar commentary about the decisions taken in dubious cases.

The corpus search proves that some binomials allow the reversal of their constituents (e.g. *yhere and day* as well as *day and yhere*). I take a closer look at the constituent order, before moving on to the extended version of binomials, multinomials, in section 10.3. The EdHeW corpus search renders several interesting multinomials and indicates extended strings of multiple coordinated sequences. It should be borne in mind that the Scots material displays its own preferences and lexical choices, even though it may contain some expressions common to English legal texts.

10.2. Binomials

10.2.1. EXTRACTING BINOMIALS FROM THE CORPUS

With the help of corpora, it should be possible to extract binomials in a comprehensive fashion, especially when the methodology employed is corpus-driven.[1] Biber et al. warn, however, that "[m]ost binomial phrases occur too infrequently to be considered part of recurrent lexical bundles" (1999: 1031), at least in a general corpus. Previous research shows that coordinated phrases often appear just once in a given collection of texts. The question then lies in whether to accept them as fixed phrases when their fixedness cannot really be judged. In legal discourse, binomials constitute one of the most conspicuous lexico-syntactic elements, adding to the formulaicity of the text (section 4.5). In the present study the binomials had to be present more than five times in more than five texts, so the problem of hapax legomena is not relevant. At the same time, this procedure may have left out some less frequent constructions which, under different criteria, could qualify as binomials.

At first sight, binomials still seem relatively rare in the corpus of all lexical bundles from EdHeW (when the cut-off point is set at 5 tokens in 5 texts, Table 8.4), amounting to 3% of all types and 3% of all tokens in 3-grams. On closer inspection, this is a large group of expressions, with 179 different types, represented by 5,239 tokens, and with roughly two instances of binomials on average in each text in the corpus.[2] They also differ from a typical 3-gram because they are always phrasally complete (see section 9.1 and the discussion of the structure of formulaic 3-grams throughout Chapter 9) and they appear at crucial junctions of legal discourse: in reference to dates, people involved, and objects. Some binomials get repeated more often than others but the construction itself is repetitive, too; after all, the same or a similar concept is expressed twice and coordinated. Structural repetition is the essence of a binomial—the same category gets repeated and coordinated. Through repetition, the formulaic nature of binomials is enhanced.

To extract binomials, the software was set to search for 3-grams with *and* or *or* in the last-but-one lexical slot. The list had to be pruned manually to eliminate instances where different categories were coordinated (e.g. *part and ye* 'part and the'). These discarded 3-grams, if formulaic enough, would have still made it to the pool of repetitive constructions discussed in Chapters 9 and 11. Furthermore, I decided to discard some instances of same-category coordination, such as numerals (e.g. *thirty and seven*), names (e.g. *william and john*)[3] and coordinated personal pronouns (e.g. *him and thaim*). These coordinated structures are either too specific and context-bound, as in names and numerals, or too broad, as in the case of pronominal reference. It seems that Bhatia's definition (1993), quoted in section 4.5.1, needs revising, since it accepts all instances of same-category coordination as a binomial, while the semantic properties of coordinates, as well as their scope, should be considered as well.

The next step was to categorize binomials according to grammatical category to identify the preferences of medieval and early modern clerks in coordinating specific parts of speech (section 10.2.2). Then the material was divided into thematic groups to facilitate the search for motivations behind the pairs.

10.2.2. GRAMMATICAL PROPERTIES OF BINOMIALS

Binomials constructed out of coordinated nouns outnumber verbs and other categories (Table 10.1), which supports earlier findings on binomials as markers of nominal style in the language of the law (Gustafsson 1984). Among coordinated nouns, one-third are in plural form. Gerunds have been grouped together with

TABLE 10.1
Binomial counts in EdHeW, according to grammatical category

	Tokens	Types	Most frequent type(number of tokens)
Nouns	3,181	101	*erd and stan* (318)
Verbs	1,020	53	*statut and ordanit* (191)
Adjectives and nominal modifiers	734	14	*all and sindry* (209)
Adverbs	284	9	*lelely and treuly* (101)
Prepositions	20	2	*in and to* (14)
Total	5,239	179	

nouns; in Scots it is easy to distinguish them from present participles because of different morphological marking, for example, *obseruing and kepin* (gerunds) vs. *obseruand and kepand* (present participles, King 1997: 179–180).

The most popular binomials have also surfaced in lexical bundles at the top of the formulaicity range: *erd and stan* (FF = 55), *statut and ordanit* (FF = 44), *all and sindry* (FF = 34). As explained in section 8.5.4, the formulaicity scale is counted on the basis of frequency together with the text spread, which means that formulaic lexical bundles, binomials among them, were used all over the corpus, in many different texts. All binomials found in the top 10% of formulaicity range are shown in (1).

(1) binomials in the top formulaicity range

abbot and conuent (FF = 35)	*erd and stan* (FF = 55)
accion and cause (FF = 29)	*executouris and assignais* (FF = 34)
airis and assignais (FF = 44)	*executouris or assignais* (FF = 22)
airis or assignais (FF = 42)	*fraud or gile* (FF = 27)
aldirman and balzies (FF = 29)	*landis and biggin* (FF = 29)
all and hail (FF = 26)	*landis and tenement* (FF = 40)
all and sindry (FF = 34)	*statut and ordanit* (FF = 44)
consail and comonite (FF = 27)	

When it comes to binomials coordinated with *or*, the numbers are much lower. In fact, only twelve such constructions were found among the 3-grams. Again, it is nouns which are most often coordinated with *or*, and the two most frequent constructions are *fraud or gile* 'fraud or deceit' (FF = 27) and *airis or assignais* 'heirs and assignees' (FF = 44). Reference to assignees appears in one more coordinated pair, *executouris or assignais* (FF = 22; its counterpart coordinated with *and* appears 157 times in 82 texts, FF = 34).

It turns out that the majority of very frequent binomials are nouns referring to the people who take part in legal procedures: those who inherit property or are involved in its transfer, the members of the burgh council or burgh court, or simply "everybody"—*all and sindry*—who witness a given case or who should pay heed to a given regulation. It is interesting to note that the most frequent lexical bundles from present-day political speeches also contain a binomial related to people in general—*men and women* (Bastow 2010). In EdHeW, among the most formulaic expressions there are also references to legal rituals (*erd and stan*) and the most prominent property under transaction—land. In the sections below I explore the motivations behind why the coordinated pairs were formed and suggest explanations for the most formulaic ones among them.

10.2.3. SEMANTIC MOTIVATIONS

Let us start with binomials whose primary motivation is semantic. In his early paper on binomials and the order of constituents, Malkiel warned about "the fluidity of any semantic classification" (1959: 129), which is even more arbitrary when dealing with historical material. To achieve a trustworthy semantic interpretation, the division into semantically motivated subgroups was supported by the _DSL_ and, in the case of incomplete information, by the _OED_. In the presentation of EdHeW binomials, I have listed the pairs alphabetically and indicated their frequency in the corpus with tags in order to signal which constructions are to be found most often, and which were less numerous. The scale is as follows:

> 120 tokens	***
70–119 tokens	**
30–69 tokens	*
10–29 tokens	^
< 9 tokens	no mark

The first subgroup contains binomials motivated primarily by complementation. Here, both elements—coordinated lexical items denoting objects, people, concepts—contribute to the overall meaning of a pair. This relationship can be presented by means of a formula borrowed from mathematical operations on sets—here, we deal with the union of two sets of meanings, $A \cup B$. In this group in EdHeW we find:

(2) nominal binomials with complementation

abbot and conuent**
aldirman and balzies***
aldirman and consail^
baronis and commissaris
charter and possession^
charter and sesing^
charteris and euidentis^
_day and plas_*
erd and stan***
executouris and assignais***
fader and conuent^
forme and manner^
_forme and tenour_*
gold and siluer^
_hand and gudis_*
hesp and stapyll^
_landis and biggin_*
landis and gudis^
landis and tenement**
letter and sele
_maner and forme_*
martinmes and witsunday
notar and witnes^
_provost and balzeis_*
realme and liegis^
tyme and plas^
_witsunday and martinmes_*
_yhere and plas_*

Some of the most common binomials are included in this group, for example, _aldirman and balzeis_ (to refer to the local government), _executouris and assignais_ (to include both the people who administer the inheritance process and those who inherit), and _erd and stan_ (the symbolic token of land transfer). I also listed here _charter and possession_ and _charter and sesing_, because the document and the right to possess property complement each other.[4] From among the less frequent complementation binomials, the pair _hesp and stapyll_ requires a comment, as the reference to a "contrivance for fastening a door or lid" (_OED_, _hasp_, n. 1a) at first sight does not seem to be motivated by the context of legal documents. However, the handing over of the actual metal implement for locking the door of a property was yet another customary and symbolic action performed when giving sasine in medieval and early modern Scotland (*DSL*, *hesp* n. 1), similarly to *erd and stan*, as explained in section 7.3.4. The pair *notar and witnes* is also embedded in burgh court discourse and draws attention to the two functions of the person who wrote the text: compilation and authentication (section 7.4).

(3) verbal binomials with complementation

command and charge	*herd and saw*
*constitut and ordanit^*	*ordanit and statut*
creat and ordanit	*statut and ordanit****
decretit and ordanit	*warnit and chargit^*
grantit and promittit	

Here I included all the combinations which represent two complementary speech acts: a representative in stating something and a directive in ordering something, for example, *decretit and ordanit*, *constitut and ordanit*, *statut and ordanit* (for syntagmatically overlapping lexical bundles, see section 11.3.3 on interactional functional elements). The last binomial is the most frequent coordinated verbal expression, appearing almost 200 times in the same form in the corpus (Table 10.1).

(4) other grammatical categories with complementation

*gud and vsuale**	*nobil and michty**
honorabil and worschipful	*purely and simply**
honorabil and michty	*quhen and quhar^*
*in and to^*	*spirituale and temporale^*
*nerrast and lawful**	

It is clear that binomials can also act as formulaic modifiers. The adjective *vsuale* typically modifies the noun *mone* 'money' (see section 11.3.1), which opens a possibility of a syntagmatic overlap with the binomial *gud and vsuale*. Similarly, *nerrast and lawful* extend to *nerrast and lawful air* 'nearest and lawful heir', *nobil and michty* take the complement *lord* or *lordis*, and *purely and simply* modify the verb *resignit* 'resigned property'. However these extended bundles were not frequent enough to enter the discussion in Chapter 11 wholesale, which points to the fact that the binomials were more formulaic than their combinations with nouns or verbs.

Among binomials which share some part of meaning, there are coordinated nouns where one represents a metonymic extension of the other. This group will be motivated by semantic contiguity: the meaning of A overlaps with some meanings of B, A ∪ B. In EdHeW the following instances were found:

(5) nominal binomials with contiguity

*auise and consent^*	*faith and treuth**
*dayis and termis^*	*forme and stile*

fulfillin and kepin
*kepin and fulfillin^*
*nam and behalf^*
resonis and allegacionis
richt and titill
*son and air**
*wakyn and wardyn^*
*yhere and terme^*
yheris and termis

Some overlaps of meaning are less transparent to the modern eye. For example, *auise and consent* may be rephrased as "opinion and consent" (*DSL avise* n1, 1), which share the element of stating one's position. Keeping watch and guard, *wakyn and wardyn*, combines being awake (*DSL wa(l)kin(g* vbl n.[1], 1, cf. 5) with guarding (*ward* v[1], 1a). This was one of the basic duties of burgh inhabitants. Talking about such obligations in section 6.4.1, I have pointed out that this expression often followed another binomial, *scot and lot* 'a yearly rent', which is classified below as a phonologically motivated pair (section 10.2.4). In fact, one could postulate that the whole sequence is phonologically motivated due to rhyme in *scot and lot* and alliteration in *wakyn and wardyn*. I would add, though, that in the first pair one cannot discern individual meanings in the pair, whereas in 'being awake' and 'guarding' there are two related but separate meanings, whose coordination is then enhanced by alliteration.

(6) verbal binomials with contiguity
decretis and delíueris
kepe and defend
*kepe and fulfil^*
resauit and admittit
*sald and analiit^*
warand and defend

In verbs, one of the meanings of *deliver* in Older Scots was "to give a decision or judgement" (*DSL deliver* v, 3a), so it shares some part of its meaning with *decrete* "to make or pronounce a decree" (*DSL decrete* v, 3). As above, the coordination was given an additional boost from alliteration. When it comes to the verb *warand*, it had a specialized legal meaning of "to guarantee the security of the tenure" and, according to the dictionary, it was chiefly combined with *acquiet* and *defend* (*DSL*, *war(r)and* v, 2). Here, we have *kepe and defend* as well.

(7) other grammatical categories with contiguity
*all and sindry****
all and quhatsumeuer
*aucht and wont^*
befor and aganis
*gud and sufficiand^*
lawful and honest
othir and sindry

The expression *all and sindry* requires comment, as it is one of the most frequent binomials in the corpus (over 200 instances). The adjective *sindry* meant "different, distinct, separate" (*DSL*, *sindry* adj, 1, cf. 5) and could enter into other pairs, synonymous or contiguous: *mony and sindry*, *divers and sindry*, *uther and sindry*, the last one attested in EdHeW. The dictionary gives the binomial *all and sindry* with reference to every individual—or all people—who were under a certain obligation or were supposed to acknowledge a legal act. The collective nature of the determiner *all* overlaps with reference to the individual ingredients of the whole—*sindry*. Thus the requirement of comprehensive reference in the language of the law is more than satisfied. Another contiguous pair, *aucht and wont*, is built out of coordinated past participles, denoting an action which is "due and customary" (*DSL aw*, v, 5b, *won(e* v^{1}, 4).

The next group involves nouns which stand in the relation of cause and effect. In other words, the presence of one thing brings about the other: $A \leftarrow B$ or $A \rightarrow B$. The order of constituents does not have to be linear as the effect may well precede the cause. The binomials motivated in this manner in EdHeW are the following:

(8) nominal binomials with cause and effect

*accion and cause**	*forme and effect**
*alienacion and resignacion^*	*help and supple*
*cause and querellis^*	*resignacion and sesing^*
*costis and expensis^*	*richt and clame*
*costis and scaithis^*	*scaithis and expenss*
expenss and interes	*vtilite and profeit^*

The expression *forme and effect* has a strong presence in the texts, because it encapsulates the two crucial aspects of the documents: their formal properties and the effects that they generated. Similar binomials with *forme* have been listed above under complementation (2)—*forme and tenour* and *forme and manner*. These, however, refer to the properties of the documents rather than to their results.

(9) verbal binomials with cause and effect

acquite and defend	*deliuerit and laid^*
*appointit and accordit^*	*fand and deliuerit*
appointit and concordit	*maid and giffin^*
*apunctit and accordit^*	*maid and led^*
chosin and sworne	*raisit and takin^*
*comperit and folowit^*	*summond and process^*
*contenit and payd**	

The most frequent binomial in this group, *contenit and payd*, is a coordination of two subsequent activities: first an amount of money is *contenit*, included in a document (*DSL contene* v^{1}, 3b), and then paid. The dictionary also notes a combination of the verb *appunct* (and its cognate *appoint*, both from medieval Latin *appunctuare*) with *accord*, *concord*, or *aggre* (*DSL appunct* v); the first two appear in the EdHeW material.

Another semantic relationship to be found in binomials is hyponymy. A larger concept is coordinated with a more specific, related lexical item, which is contained in the one with the broader meaning, $A \subseteq B$ or $A \supseteq B$. Norrick (1988: 85) considers such examples to be species-genus synecdochic binomials.

(10) nominal binomials with hyponymy

accionis and querellis^	*manrent and seruice*^
balzeis and comonite^	*monath and yhere*^
*balzeis and consail**	*possessionis and gudis*^
*consail and comonite****	*sesing and coniunctfeftment*^
day and yhere^	*stat and coniunctfeftment*
*fee and heritage**	*stat and possession**
help and supple	*stat and sesing**
man and seruand	*yhere and day*^

Here, the attention to detail is visible. It seems that in legal texts it was not sufficient to write 'actions' but the kind of action had to be specified. To turn this around, it was not enough to say 'quarrels' but it was also necessary to add that a quarrel is a type of action. Reference to burgh government is frequently conveyed in hyponymic binomials, for example, *balzeis and comonite*, where bailies are special members of the community, or *balzeis and consail*, where the council is made up of the bailies (see section 6.3.3 for details of burgh government). The most frequent binomial in this group is *consail and comonite* 'council and community', with 125 instances in the corpus.

(11) verbal binomials with hyponymy

assithit and payd	*pay and assith*
committit and done^	*payd and assithit*^
haldin and had^	*refound and pay*

Among verbs, the most versatile hyponymic binomial is *payd and assithit* (*DSL assith* v, 1. "to satisfy,[5] especially by the payment of compensation"), with two more forms used in the material: a reversed word order and a present tense. Again, it seems not to have been enough to state that the dues were simply paid, but more informative to add that is was a special type of payment.

The final group of binomials motivated by semantics displays antonymy or contrast between the members of the pair. In EdHeW, the following examples have been found:

(12) nominal binomials with antonymy or contrast
bakland and forland
ische and entre^
men and women

(13) other grammatical categories with antonymy or contrast
*mouabil and vnmouabil**
*coniunctly and seueralie**

Antonymy and contrast are not very frequent in terms of binomial types. No such binomials are built of verbs. Among nouns the most frequent is *ische and entre* (*DSL isch(e* n, 1. "the action of going out, egress"), with 15 tokens in the corpus, most probably referring to the freedom of movement into and out of a property. The two remaining pairs, one made of adjectives, the other of adverbs, answer to the requirement of comprehensiveness in the language of the law. The *DSL* notices that *conjunctly* often collocated with *severally*, to mean both "jointly" and "separately", and thus cover all the options. It is interesting that the first Scots quote of *conjunctly* comes from 1428, while it seems to have entered the English lexicon only in the subsequent century (*DSL conjunctly*, adv [EModE (1514) from the adj]).

In Chapter 7, I laid out historical reasons for the individual character of Scots law. This research reveals further arguments of linguistic nature: the legal vocabulary which is either limited to Scots or was used in Scots texts earlier than in English texts. Supported by etymological information and quotations from the *DSL* and the *OED*, this discovery points to the separate character of the language of the law in Scotland and its innovative features in a wider geographic context.

10.2.4. MOTIVATIONS BEHIND BINOMIALS PROPER

Apart from the conspicuous group of binomials which rely on a whole range of semantic relationships between constituents, in the corpus there were examples of binomials with semantic repetition (Wang 2005). I refer to such phrases as *binomials proper* (Kopaczyk 2009: 91). The constituents are, in fact, different lexicalizations of the same concept so, in Norrick's terms, together they constitute a single sememe—an 'iterative' binomial (1988: 72, 77). They may also be considered to be a version of the so-called 'echoic' binomials (Norrick 1988: 76–77), such as *more and more* or *stronger and stronger* (Bastow 2010: 149),[6] with one of the items replaced with a synonym. For this reason, motivations for binomials proper should be sought outside semantics: in the phonological shape of the pair, in the etymologies and the 'translation hypothesis', or in calquing from a different language. In the case of early Scots legal texts, the most prominent source will be Latin, whose intricate relationship with the vernacular was mentioned several times in Chapter 7.

The discussion in this section concentrates on these very motivations. Why repeat the same concept when the same meaning could be conveyed by a single lexical item? Legal requirements of clarity and comprehensiveness do not have a full explanatory force in this respect, but they do link to different etymological backgrounds of some binomial pairs (see (19)–(22) below), where one item seems to be a translation of the other. Some of the repetition is conditioned stylistically: through alliteration, rhyme, or prosody.

Binomials proper constitute a formulaic ingredient of legal discourse because they are used repeatedly in the same form. Previous analyses have supported this claim, showing the fewest hapax legomena among binomials proper, if compared to other, semantically motivated pairs. It means that semantic motivations produce more varied binomials than stylistic reasons (Kopaczyk 2009: 93–94). The lexical bundle methodology adopted in this book precludes research into hapax legomena (cf. frequency cut-off points in section 8.5.3), however, it is a worthwhile direction for future inquiries.

10.2.4.1. Phonological Motivations

Phonological reasons for binomial coordination may be diverse: from alliteration and assonance, to rhyme and prosodic structure (Bugaj and Włodarczyk 2006: 91–92). Among nouns, rhyming patterns seem to have inspired the coinage, echoing the oral ritualistic practices of pre-chirographic law, expounded in Chapter 2.

(14) phonologically conditioned nominal binomials proper

*art and part^*	*scot and lot^*
*assent and consent^*	*ward and dome*
*consent and assent***	

Still, the phonetic motivation may run even deeper into history, as the binomial *art and part* illustrates. The Scots expression had been borrowed from Latin *ars et pars* which, according to the *DSL*, "used to denote participation in crime" (*art* n^1, 2). Clearly, the phonetic motivation had initially inspired the Latin binomial, and later may have facilitated the adoption of this phrase in vernacular legal texts. Moving to the next binomial, in Older Scots, *assent* meant as much as 'agree', which is why *consent and assent* and its swapped counterpart were included among binomials proper, motivated by the rhyme. The Old Norse term for 'shot, portion'—*skot*—seems to have merged with *skattr* 'tax, tribute' and inspired a rhyming phrase *scot and lot*, used commonly, as the *DSL* puts it, in reference to municipal taxes (*scat(t* n. 2).[7] The pair *ward and dome* exhibits semantic repetition; in the *DSL ward* is defined as "a decision in court, chiefly in collocation with *dome*", a "judicial decision" (*ward* n^2; *dome* n.). The phonological motivation relies here on the assonance of the final and initial consonants, creating an emphatic effect.

Among verbs, one alliterative pair is present in several different grammatical forms and in swapped word order.

(15) phonologically conditioned verbal binomials proper

giffand and grantand	*giffis and grantis^*
*giffin and grantit^*	*grantit and giffin^*

Alliteration provides a powerful means to achieve a poetic quality in the utterance and to make it stand out (section 4.5.1). Its use in legal discourse links back to the oral practices, aiding the memory, on the one hand, and adding solemnity, on the other. *DSL* lexicographers mention the binomial in the entry for *grant* (v 6), marking it as 'occasional'.

Binomials proper have also been found among other grammatical categories in the form of two rhyming pairs:

(16) other phonologically conditioned binomials proper
*all and hail****
*ay and quhill**

The first pair is one of the most frequent binomials in the corpus (see (1) above), serving to ensure comprehensive reference through repetition of the same concept. The pairing is more attractive because of the closeness of the vowels—*all* would have been pronounced with /a/ and *hail* 'whole'—with /aː/, vowels 12a and 4, respectively, in Aitken's analysis (1977) of Middle Scots phonology. The other pair, *ay and quhill*, is not even analysed into separate lexical items in the *DSL*, but appears as one of the typical phrases with the meaning 'always, ever, continually' (s.v. *ay* adv, 2b). Around the mid-fifteenth century, the members of the pair came close in pronunciation of the root vowel, when *ay* had raised to /ɛi/ and *quhill* developed a diphthong (Aitken 1977: 6–7).

The general phonological rule established for the order of constituents within a binomial pair stated: "short before long" (Cooper and Ross 1975; Gustafsson 1974). For the lack of other potential motivations, several pairs have been treated as representatives of this particular trend. The pairs in (17) and (18) have a feel of coordinated pairs of fancy new words, doubled just for the stylistic effect with a prosodically heavier (near-)synonym.

(17) nominal binomials proper motivated by prosodic structure (short + long)
act (OF 14) *and statut* (OF 14)^
actis (OF 14) *and statutis* (OF 14)^
airis (OF la14) *and successouris* (OF 14)^
punctis (med L 14) *and articlis* (OF/L 14)^
rentis (OF la14) *and possessionis* (OF la14)^
vse (OF e15) *and consuetude* (OF/L 15)

(18) adjectival binomials proper motivated by prosodic structure (short + long)
ferm (OF 14) *and stabil* (OF/L 14)*

The chronological details in brackets indicate that both elements of the pairs entered Scots more or less simultaneously from the same Latinate background, so these binomials cannot be classed as motivated by chronology and the need to clarify meaning.

10.2.4.2. Etymological Motivations

The next group of binomials proper are those which may have been coined for the sake of clarity. The members of the pair come from different etymological backgrounds, so that they come across as stylistic doublets, or even triplets, along the lines of *meeting* (OE)—*assembly* (OF)—*congregation* (L), known in both Scots and

English. At the same time, the native and the borrowed form may have already developed new shades of meaning, which pushes the pairs in the direction of contiguity rather than semantic repetition (see section 10.2.3 above on semantic motivations). On the basis of lexical information from the *DSL* and the *OED*, I gauged the discrepancies in meaning and decided to keep the examples in (19) to (22) as binomials proper, motivated by different etymological backgrounds of the constituents.

(19) nominal binomials proper of different etymological backgrounds
brukin (OE) *and joysing* (OF 14)
compt (OF/L 15) *and reknyng* (OE)
dampnage (med L 15) *and scaith* (ON)
liberte (OF/L 16) *and fredom* (OE)
obseruing (OF/L 15) *and kepin* (OE)
staff (OE) *and bastoun* (OF 15)
strenth (OE) *and effect* (OF/L 15)^
vse (OF e15) *and wont* (OE)

Some of these binomials were conspicuous enough to make it into *DSL* definitions, for instance, *bruke* (v[1], 1) is "frequently associated with other verbs of similar meaning, esp. *jois*". For *baston* (n, 1b), the dictionary provides the following further information: "[c]oupled with *staf* (also *fust*), to render the L. *per fustem* (or *fustum*) *et baculum*, denoting the symbols by which the possession of land was resigned". The procedure of land transfer, together with its necessary attributes, was presented section 7.3.4. The related binomial shows a calque from Latin, where one of the pair members is translated into the vernacular (*staff*) while the other also leaves the Latin original and resorts to a later borrowing.

(20) verbal binomials proper of different etymological backgrounds
askit (OE) *and requirit* (OF/L 14)
bind (OE) *and obliss* (OF 14)^
bindis (OE) *and obliss* (OF 14)**
bruk (OE) *and joyss* (OF 14)^
bundin (OE) *and obleist* (OF 14)*
contenis (OF 14) *and beris* (OE) ^
obleist (OF 14) *and bundin* (OE)
obleist (OF 14) *and sworne* (OE)^
obserue (OF/L 15) *and kepe* (OE)^
obseruit (OF/L 15) *and kepin* (OE)^
obseruit (OF/L 15) *and kepit* (OE)^
proportis (L 14) *and beris* (OE)*

The definition of *bind* in the *DSL* (*bind* v, 3) explains that the word means "[t]o put (oneself or another) under a bond or obligation (to do something); to constrain or restrict in respect of action" and that in legal texts it is "frequently combined with other verbs, esp. *obliss*, and common in the pres. tense or the past participle". In the corpus, we find a representation of both the present tense and past participle, in accordance with the dictionary information, and the reversed word order has also been found (see (20)). Another versatile pair in terms of grammatical forms is *obserue and kepe*, used by the clerks in the present, past, and past participle (cf. Giammarresi 2010 and the present-day versatility of *come and go*). There are also two binomials which coordinate a foreign synonym with the Germanic verb *to bear*: *contenis and beris* and *proportis and beris*. As a synonym of *bear*, the former may refer to conveying a statement in a document (*DSL contene* v^1, 3, *bere* v^1, 6) or—especially in reflexive contexts—to behaving, bearing oneself in a specific manner (*DSL contene* v, 1, *bere* v^1, 5). The latter is a direct loan characteristic for Scots in the legal context, meaning "to convey to the mind, to set forth (that something is the case); to express; to state" (*DSL proport* v. 1a; cf. *bere* v^1, 6). Both foreign counterparts also serve to construct a trinomial, see section 10.3 below. What should be noticed in etymologically conditioned binomials is that the order of elements in the pair does not proceed in any specific direction; there is no indication that the native element would come first or second in the pair.

(21) adjectival binomials proper of different etymological backgrounds
lele (OF 15) *and trew* (OE)*
opin (OE) *and manifest* (OF/L)
nexit (OE) *and immediat* (med L 15)*

(22) adverbial binomials proper of different etymological backgrounds
lelely (OF 15) *and treuly* (OE)**

The combination of the foreign *lele* 'loyal' and the native *trew* 'true, loyal, firm in allegiance' (*DSL trew(e* adj, A1) appears in adjective and adverb form. The binomial *nexit and immediat* in legal context refers to someone who is next in the line of succession (*DSL immediat* adj, 1), while *opin and manifest* does not seem to be limited to legal contexts. The *DSL* gives a quotation with this binomial from Henryson's *Testament of Cresseid*, underscoring the poetic echoes in legal discourse. But to turn this around, it was legal coinage that inspired Henryson in his lexical choices (Sellar 2007: 240), for instance, to include more legal binomials and multinomials in that very poem, such as *reull and steir*, or *seen, heard, and understood* (Mathews 2002: 51, 53).

To continue the etymological considerations, there was a group of same-source lexical items which had been borrowed by Scots at two different points in time, much as *warrant* and *guarantee* were in the history of English. I list them under etymological motivations because one of these lexical items must have already been much more embedded in the vernacular than the other at the time of writing, see (23)–(24).

(23) nominal binomials proper including borrowings from different periods
airis (OF la14) *and assignais* (OF e15)***
force (OF 14) *and effect* (OF/L 15)^
fraud (OF 14) *and gile* (OF 13)*
pain (L 13) *and charge* (OF 14)^
possession (OF 14) *and sesing* (med L 13)^
sesing (med L 13) *and possesion* (OF la14)*
stile (OF 14) *and forme* (OF 15)^

(24) verbal binomials proper including borrowings from different periods
quitclamis (OF/L 14) *and dischargis* (OF 15)^
quitclame (OF/L 14) *and dischargis* (OF 15)

In these examples, there is usually a gap of a century between the two borrowed items, which means that they cannot be treated as equally assimilated into the vernacular. The same concept is thus conveyed twice, through an earlier and a later borrowing. It is worth noting that only Romance borrowings constitute such chronological pairs, which testifies to the importance of this etymological background in the continuous lexical enrichment in the field of Scots law.

10.2.4.3. Other Factors

Finally, example (25) seems not to have been motivated by any of the factors discussed above. The etymological reasons are not decisive, so possibly, the pair was motivated by the assonance of the plural marker to enhance the weight of the phrase. The last explanatory resort may be lexical transfer from Latin originals of early laws and the influence of continental legal writing.

(25) binomials proper motivated by other factors
commoditeis (OF 14) *and esementis* (OF 14)^

The binomial in (25) was conspicuous enough to be noticed by *DSL* lexicographers, who commented on the collocational preferences of the noun *esement* thus: "[u]sually coupled with synonymous terms, esp. *commoditeis*, *fredomis*, or *profittis*" (*DSL es(e)ment* n.1). In fact, this binomial may be a paradigmatic overlap with the trinomial *fredomis commoditeis and esementis*, see section 10.3 below.

Turning now to binomials coordinated with *or*, they could imply two interpretations: the inclusion of both options, or, the exclusion of one of the options. In the corpus, the first interpretation is valid.

(26) nominal binomials with 'or'

*airis or assignais****	*in or to^*
*ane or ma**	*juge or jugis*
*fraud or gile****	*person or persons**
*executouris or assignais**	*spirituale or temporale^*
*heris or seis^*	

The choice of one option does not preclude the other. In fact, both elements of the pair are equally important. The striving for all-inclusiveness, characteristic of legal discourse, is best illustrated in the two binomials with coordinated singular and plural forms of the same noun, reminiscent of 'echoic' binomials. It would suffice to write *persons*, as it would to write *jugis*, because a singular 'person' or 'judge' would nevertheless be subsumed under the plural form.[8] The requirements of legal discourse cause the same lexical item to be doubled.

10.2.5. CONSTITUENT ORDER

As outlined in Chapter 4, binomial material often comes across as 'frozen' and irreversible, when gathered intuitively. Corpus searches prove that one order usually dominates (see the recent study on reversibility of binomials drawn from the BNC, Mollin 2012), but the overall situation looks more diverse. The irreversibility of binomials in EdHeW is contradicted by the existence of nominal and verbal combinations which allow constituent swap.

(27) nominal reversible binomials
yhere and day (29 tokens, 15 texts)
day and yhere (10 tokens, 10 texts)

witsunday and martinmes (68 tokens, 61 texts)
martinmes and witsunday (9 tokens, 9 texts)

sesing and possession (42 tokens, 35 texts)
possession and sesing (24 tokens, 12 texts)

kepin and fulfillin (11 tokens, 11 texts)
fulfillin and kepin (6 tokens, 6 texts)

maner and forme (68 tokens, 61 texts)
forme and maner (17 tokens, 14 texts)

consent and assent (82 tokens, 62 texts)
assent and consent (10 tokens, 8 texts)

It should be pointed out, though, that in each case one of the combinations is clearly more frequent. In verbal coordinated pairs, the following were reversed:

(28) verbal reversible binomials

statut and ordanit (191 tokens, 71 texts)
ordanit and statut (7 tokens, 6 texts)

bundin and obleist (62 tokens, 58 texts)
obleist and bundin (8 tokens, 8 texts)

giffin and grantit (16 tokens, 15 texts)
grantit and giffin (15 tokens, 13 texts)

payd and assithit (10 tokens, 10 texts)
assithit and payd 'satisfied and paid' (6 tokens, 6 texts)[9]

The preferred constituent order seems to rely on various factors. One explanation may lay in a modified version of the Me-First constraint (section 4.5.2; Cooper and Ross 1975), whereby the native word, like *bundin*, *giffin*, *kepin* is closer to the experience of the user and therefore comes first. Similarly, borrowings which had already established themselves in the lexicon would have priority, as in *sesing* or *pay*. Another reason may be the pattern 'from short to long' (Cooper and Ross 1975). There is no single explanation both for the reversible binomials, and for those which have surfaced in the corpus in one order.

10.3. Multinomials

10.3.1. EXTRACTING MULTINOMIALS FROM THE CORPUS

In order to extract multinomials with stacked coordinated elements, the bundles were screened for 4- to 8-grams with 'and' and 'or' in the last-but-one lexical slot. This procedure rendered various expressions which could not be classified as multinomials, for example, *his spouse and gaif* 'his spouse and gave' (in 4-grams), or *ye est part and ye* 'the east part and the' (in 5-grams), so again the results had to be pruned manually. During this procedure it became apparent that 4-grams and longer lexical bundles provide interesting collocational information about the grammatical and semantic context in which binomials will typically be found. For instance, one can learn from this material that the binomial *erd and stan* 'earth and stone' is most often modified by *ye said* or becomes part of the prepositional *with*- and *of*- phrases (see also the discussion of structural types in Chapter 9). It is most often the object of the verb *bring*, which links to the ritual of bringing a clod of earth and some stones to court to settle a land transaction (Chapters 6 and 7). Conversely, the reference to somebody *taking* the earth and stones is much less frequent, which may indicate that the action of taking was not as salient as the act of bringing and giving. These observations may serve as a starting point for a more detailed inquiry into the collocational behaviour of binomials. In this part of the investigation, however, the main aim was to extract multinomials—extended coordinated versions of binomials.

The procedure rendered 25 different trinomials and 9 different quadrinomials[10] (coordinated with *and* and *or*[11]). When it comes to grammatical categories, coordinated nouns clearly prevail, see examples in (29).

(29) trinomials with 'and' and 'or'

*airis executouris and assignais****
*airis executouris or assignais**
*balzeis consail and comonite**
clame properte and possession
constitut creat and ordanit
costis scaithis and expenss
*day yhere and plas**
*delay fraud or gile^*
foreuer all and hail
*forme strenth and effect^*
*fredomis commoditeis and esementis^*
him his airis and assignais
*landis rentis and possessionis^*
*lottyn wakyn and wardyn^*
*maid constitut and ordanit^*
*maner forme and effect^*
*me myn airis and assignais**
me myn airis or assignais
monath yhere and plas
obseruing kepin and fulfillin
proportis contenis and beris
*provost balzeis and consail^*

*rentis possessionis and gudis^*	*stat sesing and possession^*
*sesing stat and possession^*	*warand acquite and defend*
*stat possession and sesing^*	*yhere* day *and plas^*

All trinomials extracted from the corpus are extended versions of binomials, discussed above. The shorter versions, however, are more frequent. Sometimes, the majority of binomials overlapped, in fact, with trinomials, as in *executouris and assignais* (157 tokens in 82 texts) and *airis executouris and assignais* (126 tokens in 68 texts). More typically, however, a binomial would appear without the extension, for example, *consail and comonite* (125 tokens in 76 texts) and *balzeis consail and comonite* (66 tokens in 39 texts), or *day and plas* (65 tokens in 53 texts) and *yhere day and plas* (16 tokens in 16 texts).

In two cases, dictionary information indicated the possibility that a lexical item would be used in a trinomial. The noun *esement*, defined as "[a] material convenience or advantage, esp. in connexion with the occupation of land or houses", was equipped with a note that it is "[u]sually coupled with synonymous terms, esp. *commoditeis*, *fredomis*, or *profittis*" (*DSL*, *es(e)ment* n.1). Indeed, on several occasions in the corpus this noun formed a trinomial with the first two. The other indication of a potential trinomial was found in the entry for *warrand*, "chiefly [in the construction] warrand, acquiet and defend" (*DSL*, *war(r)and* v, 2). This trinomial was used 7 times in the corpus.

(30) quadrinomials
*provost balzeis consail and comonite**
*scottyn lottyn wakyn and wardyn^*
day monath yhere and plas
*landis rentis possessionis and gudis^*

Among 5-grams, four quadrinomials were encountered. The most frequently used quadrinomial (34 tokens in 22 texts) referred to the government of a burgh, starting with its highest member, the provost, and then moving to the lower levels of collective burghal representation. Compared with the number of texts where this specific wording was not used, this quadrinomial does not come across as a standardized pattern. Nevertheless, the decision to express a particular meaning, using a combination of four lexical items in one specific order, cannot be a simple coincidence. There are also 5-grams which, actually, render tri- and not quadrinomials, because one of the elements is modified and takes up two lexical slots (e.g. *him his airis and assignais*). This indicates that in future research the extraction procedure should allow for constituent modification within a coordinated phrase.

Coming back to the question of unit arrangement in multinomials, within coordinated structures of three elements there was also a degree of freedom, for example, *day yhere and plas* vs. *yhere day and plas*, or *stat possession and sesin*, where three possible arrangements were found with a relatively similar frequency. From a semantic point of view, it can be postulated that in multinomials the order of importance of individual referents becomes more pronounced. In *balzeis consail and comonite* the order proceeds from the most powerful individuals, through the larger governing body, to the general burgh community at the end. When the provost is also mentioned, the trinomial becomes *provost balzeis and consail*, and the quadrinomial becomes *provost balzies consail and comonite*, indicating the priority of the provost before the bailies and everybody else. Significantly, these orders do not get mixed or reversed. This structural stability is also the case in *scottyn lottyn wakyn and wardyn*, built out of two binomials which may occur independently (sections 10.2.3 and 10.2.4), but when they are used together, the order is always the same (see also section 6.4.1 on the obligations of the burgesses).

10.3.2. LONGER BUNDLES AND MULTINOMIAL STRINGS

Longer multinomials were not found among EdHeW lexical bundles. Bundles of 6 elements and more only provide context for shorter binomials and multinomials. The longest coordinated structure was a 6-gram *me myn airis executouris and assignais*, which should nevertheless be treated as a quadrinomial because four nominal units are coordinated. There are also cases among 6-, 7-, and 8-grams where two shorter coordinated constructions, discussed above, are linked into one string. The strings found in EdHeW are the following: *deliuerit and laid ye said erd and stan* (2 + 2, 12 tokens in 12 texts), *resignacion and sesing was maid and giffin* (2+ *to be* + 2, 12 tokens in 11 texts), *airis and assignais all and hail* (2 + 2, 9 tokens in 9 texts), *landis rentis possessionis and gudis mouabil and vnmouabil* (4 + 2, 9 tokens in 9 texts), *lelely and treuly bindis and oblissis* (2 + 2, 6 tokens in 6 texts). Dossena (2001) paid attention to the same phenomenon in letter writing, treating it as an intensification device (see section 4.5.1 on motivations for binomials). This practice of stacking coordinated structures answers to the requirements of the language of the law, but at the same time it appears infrequently, compared to the extensive employment of repetitive strings which are not phrasal, let alone coordinated in nature (see the discussion of other lexical bundles in the remaining chapters).

10.4. Conclusions: Binomials and Multinomials in Early Legal Scots

Looking for binomials in Scots legal and administrative texts, one comes across pairs unaccounted elsewhere in literature on binomials. This chapter has provided abundant examples of such unfamiliar phrases, for instance, *erd and stan*, *aldirman and balzies*, *fraud or gile*, and also confirmed the recurrent use of more typical expressions, such as *grant and give* or *all and sindry*. While answering to general demands of legal discourse, binomials and multinomials in EdHeW grow out of the individual characteristics of medieval and early renaissance

Scottish legal culture. The most conspicuous binomials are those referring to the ritual character of land transfer (*erd and stan*, contextualized further in section 6.4 on burgh economy) and to people involved in inheriting possessions, titles, and land (*airis and/or assignais*, see also section 6.4.2). The hierarchical representation of burgh inhabitants in the records, described in detail in section 6.3, also comes to the fore in such binomials as *aldirman and balzeis* and *consail and comonite*. When it comes to the most formulaic verbal binomials, the expression *statut and ordanit* points towards giving out directives in the name of law, the importance of which has been captured in this recurrent pair. Everyday life in the burghs is reflected in the binomial and multinomial strings, too, for example, in reference to the important market and court days (*witsunday and martinmes*), and to the daily obligations of the inhabitants (*scottyn lottyn wakyn and wardyn*).

The search within EdHeW lexical bundles has proven that, when systematically extracted from frequent repetitive material, binomials emerge as an important part of legal and administrative texts. The majority of the pairs are semantically motivated, that is, their constituents stand in some kind of a semantic relationship, such as complementation, contiguity, cause and effect, or antonymy (see the discussion in section 10.2.3). In most cases, the pairs were composed of one lexical element complemented by the other, which goes hand in hand with the all-inclusiveness requirement of legal discourse (Chapter 2). It is among semantically motivated pairs that the most formulaic binomials were found.

The ubiquity of nouns and nominal modifiers in binomial pairs contributes to the nominal style of the language of the law, as is the case with other lexical bundles (see the discussion of grammar in Chapter 9). The verbs are doubled in important speech acts, which will be further addressed in Chapter 11. Binomials and multinomials are repetitive in nature from a structural point of view, but also from a semantic angle, which is visible in binomials proper in EdHeW. In these coordinated pairs, the repetition can be traced back to the oral and ritualistic legal practices, explained in Chapter 2. It was stylistic reasons, mostly phonological or etymological, that caused repetition here, although without a single or prevalent explanatory factor (see the discussion in section 10.2.4). Moreover, the study has contradicted the irreversibility of binomial pairs, at least as an absolute defining feature of binomials.

Binomials and multinomials gathered from EdHeW lexical bundles are mostly referential in nature, since they are typically built of nouns. Most coordinated verbs express a performative meaning, answering to the demands of legal discourse (e.g. the directive *command and charge* or the commissive *bind and obliss*). The functions of fixed and repetitive elements of discourse will be further explored in the final two chapters, Chapter 11 dealing with short lexical bundles and Chapter 12 devoted to long lexical bundles. The most frequent binomials will also surface in this discussion again.

11

Short Bundles

FUNCTIONAL PROPERTIES

11.1. Introduction

The ultimate goal in extracting lexical bundles from corpus material is to discover what parts of early legal discourse become fixed and repetitive, and what important communicative functions are present in these repetitive chunks. Thanks to dedicated software, it is also possible to trace preferences for bundles carrying a specific function on a time axis. At the stage of data collection, the decision was made to split short bundles (3- to 5-grams) from long bundles (6- to 8-grams) for the functional analysis. Shorter bundles offer more general observations on the repetitive functional elements in early legal texts and their diachronic distribution. They are more numerous, more varied, and constitute the smallest recurrent building blocks of medieval and early modern Scots documents. Another reason to separate them from longer bundles is that practically all studies on lexical bundles so far have concentrated on 3- to 5-grams (Table 8.3), so we can draw careful comparisons on the basis of these studies as to the nature of legal texts in Scotland, for example, considering the oral residue in medieval and early modern documents.

To address the functions performed in historical legal texts by these short recurrent strings, this chapter draws on the Hallidayan functional framework expounded in Chapter 3 and lays out the principles of the functional classification of short bundles in section 11.2. In the section 11.3, the three major functional classes, the referential, textual, and interactional, serve as a frame for data analysis. The short lexical bundles are further divided into a range of relevant subtypes within each general function, to highlight the diversity of contexts which promote textual fixedness. Longer bundles will be, in turn, discussed in Chapter 12 to illustrate the standardizing textual tendencies of legal discourse and to show which chunks of substantial length tended to reappear in exactly the same form throughout the corpus.

11.2. Functional Classification

 The functional framework adopted in this chapter follows on from the Hallidayan tradition of treating language as a communicative tool, dependent on the situational context, on the requirements of the discourse itself, and on the characteristics of the participants (section 3.3). The sections below will thus present the findings under three respective headings: the referential (section 11.3.1), the textual (section 11.3.2), and the interactional (11.3.3). The functions performed by text fragments within each functional category may be subdivided further into smaller context-dependent and data-driven subtypes.

As was the case with structural classification, the functional categorization of lexical bundles poses obstacles which need to be considered before the actual analysis is performed. These obstacles, however, are of a different kind. The issue to consider is the multifunctionality of linguistic elements making up a text. In his initial considerations on language functions, Halliday (1978: 112) observed that a text is a product of all three functions: ideational, interpersonal, and textual, working simultaneously towards the meaning of a text. In fact, one can often see each function even within a single segment of a text, and lexical bundles are no exception here. Biber, Conrad, and Cortes (2003: 79) point out that "some lexical bundles are multifunctional" and this is perhaps the major problem in striving to achieve replicable results in functional research. This observation was repeated in Biber, Conrad, and Cortes (2004: 383); to overcome this difficulty, in both papers the authors decided to list each bundle under what they deemed its primary function. In their classification, the researchers admit that they simply followed "the most common use" (2004: 384). Culpeper and Kytö (2010: 113–114) approached this problem by paying attention to the functional equivalence of each bundle in context, and cross-checked their respective categorizations. In the present work, some of the functional categorization was performed in view of earlier scholarship and the decisions taken there. However, large parts of the material did not have direct counterparts in earlier analyses, which is why an inductive approach had to be adopted, and the context in which a given bundle appeared was carefully scrutinized. At one point, I decided to devote a separate section to the bundles which share a secondary function of textual cohesion (section 11.3.2.2) but in general each bundle was classified according to a single major function.

The data presentation in this chapter has been designed along similar lines as in Chapter 9 on the grammar of lexical bundles. Each lexical bundle has been allocated within a formulaicity benchmark, which is expressed by the following symbols:

FF 80–100	***
FF 60–80	**
FF 40–60	*
FF 20–40	^
FF >20	(not marked)

In other words, the more stars accompany a given lexical bundle, the more frequent it was, both in sheer numeric terms, as well as in the range of texts (for the formulaicity measure FF, see section 8.5.4).

11.3. Short Bundle Functions in EdHeW

11.3.1. REFERENTIAL BUNDLES

The *referential* function is performed by bundles which make reference to the extralinguistic circumstances of a given communicative situation. In medieval and early modern Scots texts this is the primary role of repetitive chunks—to convey information about the external circumstances in a non-arbitrary manner. As I have pointed out earlier (section 2.3), by repeating the referential chunks in an unchanged form, the documents attain institutional fixedness; the text evokes a feeling of authority by promoting stability over variety. The text should sound the same every time one hears it (or reads it). What is unchangeable is supported by tradition and transmission. In longer bundles, I look for symptoms of textual standardization on the basis of such unchanged strings. Here, however, the shorter bundles give a glimpse onto a range of frequently repeated external references, helping to build a picture of Scottish legal affairs in medieval and early modern times.

There are eight subsections in this discussion. The subdivision was data-driven and was applied to the material found in the lexical bundles *post factum*, that is, once it became apparent which themes and references tend to be conveyed in an unchanging form in the corpus. In the analysis of each functional group attention was paid to the diachronic preferences of the clerks for specific bundles, depending on the subperiod. In this manner we can see which fixed arrangements of words were in use earlier, and which ones started to develop at a later point in time.[1] Each subsection lists the most popular lexical bundles according to the point of reference: (a) date and time, (b) collective reference to the authorities, (c) collective reference to other community members, (d) reference to named individuals, (e) reference to unnamed individuals, (f) action, (g) location, and (h) object.

(a) date and time

3-grams: ye samyn day***, ye yhere of**, yhere of god**, day of ye*, of ye monath*, ye monath of*, that ilk day*, xxti day of*, ye xxti day*, ye quhilk day*, god a thousand^, tyme to cum^, in that tyme^, in tyme to^, ye said day^, thousand four hundreth^, ilk day was^, yhere of oure^, samyn day ye^, quhilk day ye^, samyn day thom^, ye tyme of^, ye fest of^, for ye tyme^, a thousande four^, ye terme of^, ye termis of^, in ye yhere^, ye mononday ye^, ye date of^, ye first day^, samyn day john^, all ye dayis, for a yhere, at ye fest

In a diachronic perspective, the most frequent bundle in the earliest period is *ye yhere of*, which keeps the first position practically throughout the corpus. Reference to the day (*day of ye*) and the month of the document's compilation (*of ye monath, ye monath of*) also gain formulaicity around the first half of the fifteenth century and they continue to be employed until the 1500s, when their frequency plummets. Interestingly, around that time another bundle, with a cohesive link to preceding discourse: *ye samyn day*, seems to be taking over the formulaic date reference. The bundle used to be modestly present in earlier documents but at the beginning of the sixteenth century it becomes hugely popular. Other interesting referential bundles from the first part of the corpus include *ye terme of* and *at ye fest/ye fest of*, all of which are rarely used after 1470. They make reference to the special dates of local court hearings, which at the same time were Christian holidays and market days in medieval Scotland (section 7.3.2).

4-grams: ye yhere of god***, day of ye monath***, of ye monath of***, yhere of god a**, of god a thousande**, ye yhere of oure**, yhere of oure lord**, in tyme to cum**, a thousande four hundereth**, ye xxti day of**, ye samyn day ye**, curt ye samyn day*, ye samyn day john*, that ilk day was*, ye quhilk day ye*, oure lord a thousande*, lord a thousande four*, god a thousande four*, for all ye dayis*, februar ye yhere of^, ye xxvi-ss day of^, of februar ye yhere^, of may ye yhere^, may ye yhere of^, juli ye yhere of^, of juni ye yhere^, of juli ye yhere^, aprile ye yhere of^, nouembre ye yhere of^, yhere of god ane^, followand ye date of^, all ye dayis of^, xxti day of ye^, at ye fest of^, in that tyme and^, that tyme and than^, hand ye samyn day^, item ye samyn day^

5-grams: day of ye monath of***, yhere of god a thousande**, ye yhere of god a**, ye yhere of oure lord**, yhere of oure lord a*, of oure lord a thousande*, oure lord a thousande four*, lord a thousande four hundereth*, ye yhere of god ane*, of god a thousande four*, god a thousande four hundereth*, for all ye dayis of*, ye xxti day of ye*, xxti day of ye monath*, of februar ye yhere of*, of may ye yhere of*, of juli ye yhere of*, of juni ye yhere of*, in that tyme and than*, of aprile ye yhere of^, of nouembre ye yhere of^, of march ye yhere of^, may ye yhere of god^, februar ye yhere of god^, juli ye yhere of god^, nouembre ye yhere of god^, ye samyn day thom logan^, item that ilk day was^

More types of 4-grams and 5-grams referring to date and time have qualified into most formulaic bundles because they constitute syntagmatic overlapping strings, and in fact they reappear in the form of longer bundles (Chapter 12). The most established lexical bundles were those pointing to the month and the year of compilation in a given document. This size of the bundle has allowed us to observe a rivalry between two ways of expressing reference to the year of compilation of a given document. It turns out that clerks all over Scotland would prefer to write

FIGURE 11.1 Diachronic trends in year reference (normalized per 10,000 words)

about *ye yhere of oure lord* until the mid-fifteenth century, and then switched to *ye yhere of god* around the same time (Fig. 11.1).

It is intriguing that reference to "our lord" in the documents practically disappears from use and that the same function is taken over by a direct reference to God. The change in preference cannot be attributed to dialectal choices and the possibility of convergence to some emerging local norm. The mid-eastern area can be considered the centre of standardization (section 12.3), but documents from this area do not favour either of the bundles. Could the reason then be the revival of the Roman and canon law in the fifteenth century, as discussed in section 7.2.1? Could it have caused the departure from metaphoric references to the deity by feudal earthly terms—*oure lord*, which in its time was calqued on the Latin *Anno Domini*? In any case, the switch to 'the year of God' caught on in Scotland and remained as the only recurrent option to introduce the year of the document well into the sixteenth century.

(b) collective reference to the authorities

3-grams: ye thre estatis^, thre estatis of^, aldirman and balzeis^, ye balzeis and^, balzeis consail and^, consail and comonite^, lordis of consail^, ye first curt^, ye nexit curt^, ye curt for^, curt ye samyn^, curt for ye^, of ye curt^, this present parliament^, of parliament maid^, ye borow curt, curt of ye, balzeis and ye, than ye balzeis, ye hail curt

References to the authorities are found in several formulaic 3-grams, but none of them are formulaic enough to be recorded in the bundle material prior to the period 1411–1440. In this period, we witness formulaic reference to *aldirman and balzeis* (179 tokens in 125 texts), also in a 4-gram equipped with a determiner, as well as to *consail and comonite* (141 tokens in 76 texts). These two bundles are also examples of binomials, discussed in terms of structure and motivations in Chapter 10, and they remain in use until the end of the period under scrutiny. In the second half of the fifteenth century, an explicit mention of the Three Estates in the Scottish parliament is made: *ye thre estatis (of)*. The fact that the reference to the structures of the parliament appears in the most formulaic 3- and 4-grams (on the Three Estates, see sections 6.5 and 7.2.4), testifies to the importance of this theme: the representation of the burghs in the country's government. As the majority of the documents come from burgh courts, we can, in turn, observe how the institution of the court was addressed in a typical fashion. In fact, for the compilers of the documents it was important to note at which session of the court a specific case was presented (*ye first curt*), what the plans for future sessions were in view of current events (*ye nexit curt*), what rank a given court had (*ye borow curt*), and whether decisions were made and witnessed unanimously (*ye hail curt*). The bailies—members of the burgh government, having a say in the court proceedings (for details, see sections 6.3.3 and 7.3.3)—are also typically included in such referential bundles.

4-grams: ye aldirman and balzeis*, ye borow curt of*, balzeis consail and comonite^, ye balzeis and ye^, ye lordis of consail^, to ye nexit curt^, ye thre estatis of^, in this present parliament^, curt of wigtoun haldin^

All 4-grams related to authorities are syntagmatic extensions of the shorter patterns. The most formulaic one, *ye aldirman and balzeis*, gains currency after 1410 and steadily rises in frequency towards the end of the corpus. The multinomial *balzeis consail and comonite* enters the formulaic pool in the mid-fifteenth century and steadily grows in popularity (on multinomials, see section 10.3). It may be the case that in the fifteenth century the institutions and authorities in royal burghs reached a stage when the major offices had crystallized, duties and rights had been assigned and document writers could then "agree" on a uniform label, repeated in more and more documents (on the early burgh officials, who were often given several different labels, see sections 6.3.3 and 7.3.2–7.3.3). The second most formulaic bundle may be expanded with the name of any royal burgh, for example, Wigtown, which appears frequently enough to be listed in the top range of 4-grams.

(c) collective reference to other community members

3-grams: ye handis of*, and his airis*, airis and assignais*, airis or assignais*, his airis or^, befor thir witnes^, his airis and^, abbot and conuent^, in ye handis^, all and sindry^, executouris and assignais^, me myn airis^, airis executouris and^, oure souerain lordis^, myn airis and^, in-to ye handis^, all and hail^, his airis executouris^, ws or oure^, til all men^, myn airis or^, all men be^, airis executouris or^, executouris or assignais^, til his airis^, or his airis^, men be thir^, and myn airis^, and his successouris, lord his airis, ye lordis of, of thaim twa, ye hail toune

This group is a bit more varied and its top members are more formulaic than the preceding one. The bundles which make reference to human collectivity, but not necessarily to official authority, tend to appear earlier. For example, in the earliest documents in the corpus, the most prominent group of people involved in the proceedings are heirs and assignees, as well as executors of wills and orders. Bundles with reference to these participants of legal affairs continue to be found throughout the corpus, which clearly indicates the preoccupation with inheritance issues in the documents. The important position of witnesses in the records comes across through the bundles *before thir witnes* (310 tokens in 256 texts) and *all and sindry* (209 tokens in 138 texts), where the public is called to witness a specific legal act. Both bundles are most popular between 1411 and 1500. In this subgroup of referential bundles I have also included those connected with the ritual of bringing earth and stone to court because these objects (see (h) below) were placed *in ye handis (of)* the people engaged in the transaction. The formulaic reference to the hands gains most popularity towards the end of the fifteenth century.

4-grams: in ye handis of**, his airis and assignais**, his airis or assignais**, airis executouris and assignais*, all men be thir*, men be thir present*, til all men be*, in-to ye handis of*, and til his airis*, said abbot and conuent*, him and his airis^, myn airis and assignais^, airis executouris or assignais^, me myn airis and^, myn airis or assignais^, me and myn airis^, his airis executouris or^, all and hail ye^

5-grams: all men be thir present**, til all men be thir*, ye said abbot and conuent*, me myn airis and assignais^, his airis executouris or assignais^, his airis executouris and assignais, his airis or his assignais^

Longer syntagmatic extensions are again indicative of multinomial constructions preferred for collective reference (e.g. *airis executouris and assignais*). While in the corpus the term *airis* 'heirs' is used in the most versatile manner on its own, the bundles show that it typically collocates with *assignais* 'assignees' (see examples (1) and (23) in Chapter 10), and, if the binomial is extended, the term *executouris* always comes in between. The most formulaic overlapping 5-grams in this group, *(til) all men be thir present (letteris)*[2] '(to) all men by these present (letters/writs)', suggest a longer formulaic sequence, which in fact constitutes one of the most standardized ingredients of the documents, especially in the fifteenth century (see also the chronological preference for the directive *be it kend* 'let it be known', which introduces the referential part of the repetitive string, section 11.3.3.1).

(d) reference to named individuals

3-grams: ye said john**, ye said william*, ye said robert^, ye said james^, ye said thomas^, ye said alexander^, ye said gilbert^, ye said dauid^, ye said davy^, said ser william^, ye said adam^, ye said george^, duc of albany^, ye said patrik^, john ye wath^, ye said marion^, ye said nichol, laurence lord oliphant^, ye said jonet^, elizabeth his spouse^, robert lord fleming^, schir john of^, ye said elizabeth^, ye saidis william, saidis william and, albany erle of, of albany erle, ye said andro, james be ye, george erle of

In fact, the most formulaic reference to a person's name, *John*, gains popularity only from 1410s onwards. Earlier, the most frequent names in bundles are *William* and *Davy*. There is also a repetitive reference to *Duke of Albany* towards the end of the fifteenth century, which is probably due to the current political events in the country (section 5.4.4). The first reference to a female to make it to the pool of most formulaic 3-grams is *ye said marion*, appearing often enough in mid-fifteenth century and modestly continuing in later texts.

4-grams: ye samyn day thom*, to ye said william^, to ye said john^, ye said john of^, of albany erle of^, samyn day thom logan^, albany erle of march^

5-grams: samyn day thom logan officer^, of albany erle of march^, james be ye grace of^

Longer bundles do not offer as many repetitive chunks, but there are a few paradigmatic overlaps with 3-grams. There is also an interesting reference to the Scottish king, *james be ye grace of* 'James by the grace of' (56 instances in 42 texts, FF = 30), which may refer to any of the Jameses on the Scottish throne during the period in question (section 5.4). A closer look at the chronological distribution of the bundles with the name *James* shows that this name was collocated with 'grace' between 1441 and 1500, so the kings in question may have been James II (section 5.4.3), James III (section 5.4.4), or James IV (section 5.4.5). There is also another option for kingly reference, *james through ye mercy* (28 instances in 20 texts, outside the top formulaic range), used especially between 1411 and 1440, which implies King James I (section 5.4.2). It is important to note that there were other formulaic ways of referring to the monarch, not only by his (or her) first name, as the section below illustrates.

(e) reference to unnamed individuals

3-grams: oure souerain lord**, ye said lord*, ye said ser*, ye said balze^, ye aldirman and^, of oure souerain^, of oure lord^, ye lord of^, souerain lord and^, to ye king^, ye said schir^, of god a^, or soureain lord^, ye quenis grace^, ye said erle^, of ye king^, said souerain lord^, lord and his^, oure said souerain^, said erle of^, said abbot and^, said lord erle^, balze in that^, to oure souerain^, oure souerain lady^, ye said abbot^, ye king of^, king of ingland^, ws or oure^, erle of ye^, ye said master^, ye forsaid erle^, lord erle and^, ye king and^, son and apperand^, and apperand air^, be ye king^, oure lord a^, than ye balze^, erle of march, souerain lord ye, ye forsaid ser, said lord his, my said lord, langar lefar of, lefar of thaim, ye langar lefar, ye bischop of, saiffand ilk mannis

In the earliest texts there is only one referential bundle from this group which marks its presence in the formulaic pool—*ye lord of*. It remains in use in later periods, joined by other bundles with a similar function and a noun modifier which makes reference to preceding discourse (see the textual function in section 11.3.2 below): *ye said lord*, *ye said ser*, *ye said erle*. An interesting development can be observed in bundles referring to the monarch: *oure souerain lord* is especially popular in the late fifteenth century, together with its textually connected version *oure said souerain (lord)*. The change of the king to queen also becomes visible at a relevant point in time, when *ye quenis grace* and *oure souerain lady* enter the formulaic pool in the last period in the corpus (1531–1560) and coincides with the ascension of Mary to the throne (section 5.4.7). The latter bundle appears also between 1441 and 1470, probably as a reference to the Queen Mother who was acting as Regent in James III's minority (section 5.4.4). There is enough talk about *(ye) king of ingland*, especially in the time spans 1380–1410 and 1471–1500, for this bundle to make it to the top 10% of formulaic 3-grams (cf. the struggles in the Borders and James IV's marriage with the Tudor princess—perhaps the most prominent Scottish-English affairs in the respective periods, see sections 5.4.1 and 5.4.5).[3]

Another range of bundles deserving a comment, not because of their ubiquity but due to the referents, is the syntagmatically overlapping *(ye) langar lefar of (thaim)* 'the one living longer of them two'. This is a reference to a married couple who enter an agreement as to the fate of their common property in case one of them dies earlier. Incidentally, the very same phrase was adopted by Ewan (2005) in the title of her analysis of medieval Scottish marriage economy, which stresses the salience of this particular expression in historical documents. Yet another illustration of the preoccupation with inheritance matters, this bundle also points to the relatively comparable standing of men and women in such situations. This repetitive reference to the one who simply happens to outlive the spouse does not differentiate between the husband and the wife (even though the legal status of husbands and wives was not equal, see Sanderson 2002: 99–134, Ewan 1992, and section 6.3 above). Of course, specific arrangements for the heirs were also made, which is indicated by relevant referential bundles (see (c) above and the discussion below).

4-grams:	of our lord a*, of oure souerain lord*, to ye said lord*, balze in that ye* oure souerain lord and*, son and apperand air*, ye said abbot and*, souerain lord and his*, our said souerain lord*, to ye said ser*, oure souerain lord ye*, incontenent ye said balze*, souerain lord ye king^, to oure souerain lord^, ye said erle of^, of ye said ser^, to ye king of^
5-grams:	oure souerain lord ye king*, balze in that tyme and*, son and apperand air to^, oure souerain lord and his^, and apperand air to ye^

Among longer bundles, one notices the attention paid to clarity of reference, even at the cost of saying the same thing twice, as in *oure souerain lord ye king*. The disposition of legal language towards wordiness (section 2.4.3) comes to the fore again. Similarly, in inheritance documents, the heir was meticulously specified, as in *son and apperand air* (96 tokens in 64 texts, FF = 45)[4] or in *airis executouris and assignais*, discussed above.

The sheer number of lexical bundles in subsections (b)–(e) indicates how important it was to refer in a formulaic manner to people in their various capacities in the legal context. These findings have prompted further research which addresses the question of text community formation (Kopaczyk, forthcoming; see also section 3.6). It turns out that around 30% of all 4-grams in the corpus contain reference to community members, which is quite a remarkable ratio for a single referential theme. Historians have stressed that keeping legal and administrative records in medieval European towns was instrumental in the creation of the common memory of the citizens and their shared identity as a group (Butcher 2004; Ketelaar 2010). Our modern understanding of records attaches a rather passive role to texts in the archives. In the fifteenth and early sixteenth century, however, the texts were very much an active part of legal and administrative proceedings: they were read aloud to the public, they were retrieved from repositories for scrutiny to resolve conflicts and claims, and they could serve as blueprints for similar texts. Formulaic reference to the people who took part in these public affairs conveyed a sense of authority and solemnity, on the one hand, and on the other, it created a point of reference for the community members. People's awareness of their public roles was enhanced through the features of the texts.

(f) action

3-grams: for ye wrangus***, chalans for ye***, ye wrangus haldin**, wrangus haldin fra**, haldin fra him*, ye pain of^, vnder ye pain^, in amersyment for^, ye accion and^, accion and cause^, fraud or gile^, in witnes of^, to ye chalans^, ye chalans of^, remanand with ye^, haldin in ye^, for scottyn lottyn^, scottyn lottyn wakyn^, but fraud or, in amersyment of, ye act of

The most formulaic bundles in the subgroup of legal action, incorporating the adjective *wrangus*, refer to wrongful deeds, taken to court, and the challenge against the wrongdoers. These bundles constitute syntagmatic overlaps and make up a longer standardizing formula, discussed in section 12.2.4. Their presence is especially striking in the sixteenth-century part of the corpus, even though occasional instances were recorded in the first half of the fifteenth century and later. A differently phrased reference to the challenge presented in court, *to ye chalans (of)*, is popular between 1411 and 1440. Other repetitive bundles, more stable throughout the corpus, include *(but) fraud or gile* 'without fraud or deceit'—a safeguarding expression against potential dishonest intentions or activity, *vnder ye pain (of)*—introducing a specific penalty, and *in witnes of*—making reference to the act of witnessing.

4-grams: chalans for ye wrangus***, for ye wrangus haldin***, ye wrangus haldin fra***, haldin fra him of***, wrangus haldin fra him***, vnder ye pain of**, but fraud or gile*, ye makin of thir*, to ye chalans of*, in amersyment for ye^, ye accion and cause^, is ye first curt^, wrangus haldin fra hir^, haldin fra hir of^, remanand with ye said^, haldin in ye tolbuth^

5-grams: for ye wrangus haldin fra***, chalans for ye wrangus haldin***, ye wrangus haldin fra him***, wrangus haldin fra him of***, ye wrangus haldin fra hir*, wrangus haldin fra hir of^, in amersyment for ye wrangus^

The syntagmatic overlaps visible in longer bundles clearly point towards a much longer formulaic string with reference to the wrongful deeds brought to court, and especially the *haldin*, or taking something from someone. This specific construction will be given more attention in Chapter 12, as it is one of the most standardized lexical bundles in the corpus.

(g) location

3-grams: ye said burgh*, of ye toune^, ye burgh of^, on the west^, on ye est^, lyand in ye^, of ye realme^, of ye burgh^, of this realme^, betuix ye landis^, on ye north^, and at ye^, of his realme^, in ye tolbuth^, west part on^, ye south raw^, ye est part^, on ye south^, of ye levinax^, est part on, ye west sid, ye north raw, sid of ye

In the next subgroup of referential bundles, pertaining to location, the most formulaic one denotes the burgh in which a given legal activity took place—*ye said burgh*. Interestingly, there is a rivalry between two *of*-phrases referring to the urban centres: *of ye burgh* and *of ye toune*. Even though *toune* in Scots started as reference to a farm settlement (*DSL* s.v. *toun*, n), it features in the burgh records quite prominently. In the bundle beginning with *of*, it was generally more numerous and even increased in popularity towards the end of the studied period. The word *toune* was frequently employed in reference to burghs also in other contexts. In the documents we find reference to the *stroublans of ye toune* 'causing public disorder in the town' (47 tokens in 36 texts). As the bundle material shows, some burghs were referred to as *toune* in the records: *toune of edinburgh* (14 tokens, 13 texts; cf. *burgh of edinburgh* 19 tokens, 11 texts), *toune of berwik* (9 tokens in 7 texts), and *toune of lech* (9 tokens in 6 texts). A wider contextual application is visible in *this gud toune* (17 tokens in 15 texts) and *ye gud toune* (12 tokens in 9 texts). These bundles are outside the formulaic pool but they show a degree of lexical freedom in reference to urban centres in Scotland in that period.

The rest of the bundles referring to location are concerned with land measurements and the position of a given plot—a frequent object of inheritance or transactions in the records. Hence the appearance of prepositional phrases with *on*, *in*, and *betuix* 'beween' (compare the prepositional phrase fragments, discussed in section 9.3), and references to directions.

4-grams:	of ye said burgh**, that ta part and*, of ye burgh of*, betuix ye landis of*, on ye toyer part*, on that ta part*, in ye tolbuth of*, on ye west part*, on ye est part*, on yw west sid*, ye west part on^, ye tolbuth of ye^, ye est part on^, within ye said burgh^, tolbuth of ye samyn^, on ye est sid^, of wigtoun haldin in^, ye burgh of peblis^
5-grams:	on that ta part and**, part and ye landis of*, haldin in ye tolbuth of*, ye tolbuth of ye samyn*, on ye est part on*, on ye west part on*, tolbuth of ye samyn be*, curt of wigtoun haldin in^, in ye tolbuth of ye^, curt of ye newburch haldin^, that ta part and ye^, of ye said landis with^, ye borow curt of wigtoun^, borow curt of wigtoun haldin^, of ye said landis and^, of wigtoun haldin in ye^, ye said landis with ye^

In a few cases, individual location names were used in such a repetitive format that they have entered the range of formulaic bundles. This tendency to spell out the name of the burgh, and place it in the records in an immutable manner, is most striking in Wigtown. The texts from Wigtown (Map 1), situated in Galloway in the south-west (Map 2), were included in the corpus to boost its regional coverage and complement the sixteenth-century data from the HCOS (section 8.2). In longer repetitive chunks, this particular place name features prominently in a number of overlapping strings (see also Chapter 12). Other recurrent place names include *newburch* 'Newburgh' in Fife, *peblis* 'Peebles', and *levinax* 'Lennox', and their appearance may be linked to local standardizing procedures in making reference to the place of document compilation or other legal activity.

(h) object

3-grams: ye said landis**, ye landis of**, erd and stan*, thir present letteris*, vsuale mone of^, landis and tenement^, and ye landis^, with ye pertenencis^, landis of ye^, mone of scotland^, and stan in^, part and ye^, with erd and^, ye said partis^, for his fredom^, ye said sum^, landis and biggin^, of ye landis^, stan in ye^, ye sum of^, of ye thre^, of annuel rent^, with ye pertenance^, sesing with erd^, ye saidis landis^, said landis and^, part of ye^, landis with ye^, with thare pertenance^, ilk mannis richt^, said landis of^, schillingis of annuel^, ye tenement of^, of vsuale mone^, markis worth of^, and stan of^, and biggin with^, for faut of^, ye forsaidis landis, betwene ye landis, penny in-to ye, his landis and

The actual objects of legal action, most commonly found among the bundles, are as follows: a plot or plots of land (*ye said landis*, *ye landis of*, etc.), any buildings which may be situated there (*landis and tenement*, *landis and biggin* 'lands and building'), and additional real property (*with ye pertinencis*, *with ye pertenance*, etc.). At the beginning, *ye forsaid landis* is preferred but after 1410 the modifier *said* becomes dominant. Physical objects which could, and often should, be brought to court included *erd and stan* 'earth and stone' (see section 7.3.4 for the ritualistic residue in medieval court practice), often found in texts from 1440s onwards. A reference to Scots money—*(vsuale) mone of scotland*—was made in a relatively stable manner throughout the corpus. Other bundles referring to money behaved in a similar way (e.g. *schillingis of annuel*, *of annuel rent*, *ye said sum*, or *ye sum of*). More abstract concepts, like freedom or right, were also conveyed by means of lexical bundles (e.g. *for his fredom*, *ilk mannis richt*).

4-grams: of ye said landis***, be thir present letteris**, vsuale mone of scotland**, and ye landis of*, with erd and stan*, of ye landis of*, part and ye landis*, of vsuale mone of*, erd and stan in*, ye said landis and* ye said landis of*, and stand in ye*, stan in ye handis^, of ye said sum^, ye landis of ye^, ye said landis with^, with thare pertenencis^, thir present letteris me^, ye said sum of^, sesing with erd and^, landis and biggin with^, erd and stan of^, and sesing of ye^

5-grams: men be thir present letteris**, of vsuale mone of scotland*, erd and stan in ye*, and stan in ye handis*, stan in ye handis of*, be thir present letteris me*, sesing with erd and stan^

Among 4-grams, the bundle *of ye said landis* is clearly the most formulaic one, with 264 tokens in 147 texts (FF = 82). Together with *of ye said burgh* (see (g) above), these are the most formulaic syntagmatic extensions of the top 3-gram *of ye said* (FF = 97, section 11.3.2.1), which shows that location and land as a commodity were the most crucial themes of medieval and early modern legal texts in Scotland. Larger repetitive chunks of discourse concentrate around a different aspect, namely the objects or instruments of legal ritual. And so, the physical carrier of the legal act, the 'letter', is referred to in a formulaic format which indicates further syntagmatic overlaps and a longer standardized bundle (Chapter 12). The objects brought to court in relation to land transfers, *erd and stan* 'earth and stone', become a part of longer formulaic chunks as reference is made to the act of giving—the act of handing them over as a token of transaction (for more historical context, see section 7.3.4).

(i) ambiguous cases

3-grams: fra him of*, for all ye^, and for ye^, and to ye^, and til his^, him and til^, him and his^, me and myn

It is always the case that some chunks of language escape straightforward classification. For the lack of context, the 3-grams in (i) may be syntagmatically expanded into bundles of various functions, for example, *and for ye* may get expanded into *for ye time* (11.3.1a), *for ye wrangus* (11.3.1f), which are both referential bundles of different kinds, or into a textual bundle *for ye said* (11.3.2.1). The situation is the same with the other short bundles starting with a preposition. There are also bundles made up of personal pronouns, where the ambiguity of function stems from the lack of context. Nevertheless, such bundles point to stable ingredients of text which construct a mould to be filled with interchangeable elements depending on the context. These particular bundles made up of personal pronouns will most likely surface in referential contexts and serve as deictic pointers towards the people involved.

11.3.2. TEXTUAL BUNDLES

Lexical bundles which are used in the records to provide links within discourse and thus maintain coherence in the text have been grouped under the *textual* function. Here I have also included bundles which make logical connections within the text on the basis of extralinguistic referents, for example, by means of sequencing the events, which is an addition to the traditional Hallidayan textual function.[5]

The textual bundles have been subdivided into five subcategories recognized in the material. The first two kinds are both incarnations of textual cohesion. In 11.3.2.1, we have bundles whose primary function is to provide cohesion by means of modifiers making reference to previous discourse (*said*, *samyn*, etc.). However, these are not the only bundles which serve to make connections within the text. Bearing in mind Halliday's statement about linguistic multifunctionality and recognizing the important nature of cohesive devices in early legal texts in Scots, I sifted through all formulaic bundles in search of cohesive modifiers frequently found in the corpus. I compiled a list of bundles whose primary function was different, for example, referential, but which still possessed an overt element of cohesion. This list is discussed separately in 11.3.2.2, where the material has been arranged according to the common cohesive element (e.g. *said*, as in *ye said landis*). The next group of textual bundles are those which convey narration (11.3.2.3), with a very visible role of adverbials and coordination. Section 11.3.2.4 focuses around intertextuality as expressed in bundles which reach outside the situation of a given text, to other texts and other areas of knowledge. Finally, clarification, an important feature of legal discourse, is illustrated in section 11.3.2.5.

11.3.2.1. Cohesion (Primary)

3-grams:	of ye said***, to ye said***, of ye samyn**, and ye said*, that ye said*, be ye said*, of ye forsaid*, in ye said*, of that ilk^, be thir present^, with ye said^, i ye said^, for ye said^, at ye said^, to ye forsaid^, of ye saidis^, within ye said, to ye nexit, in this present, alswa it is, as is befor
4-grams:	of ye samyn be^

The most numerous and most formulaic 3-gram, *of ye said*, belongs in this group. It appears over 2,150 times in more than 40% of texts in the corpus (FF = 97). Figure 11.2 shows that in the early texts this expression was not so widespread yet. There was also another formulaic expression, *of ye forsaid*, employed to carry the same reference to previous information in the text. In time, however, the popularity of the first expression grew, while the other bundle diminished in number (note that it was still frequent enough to make it to the top 10% of most formulaic 3-grams). A similar pattern is observed in a different pair of prepositional phrase fragments: *to ye said* and *to ye forsaid* (Fig. 11.2), where the latter is even the preferred option to start with, but gradually falls out of favour.

Another important textual bundle is *of ye samyn*, 'of the same', which gradually rises in popularity throughout the corpus, to become the second most frequently employed bundle at the beginning of the sixteenth century. Earlier research has shown that *of the samyn* was a versatile construction in Older Scots (Bugaj 2006b: 181–182), and one of its functions was closely linked with the lack of a possessive neuter pronoun (King 1997: 170). In modern Scots (or English) one can simply use *its* in the same cohesive function, or *his/her* if the nominal antecedent is [+human] (Purves 2002). In Older Scots the most common carriers of this function were *of the samyn* and *thairof*, especially in formal registers. The

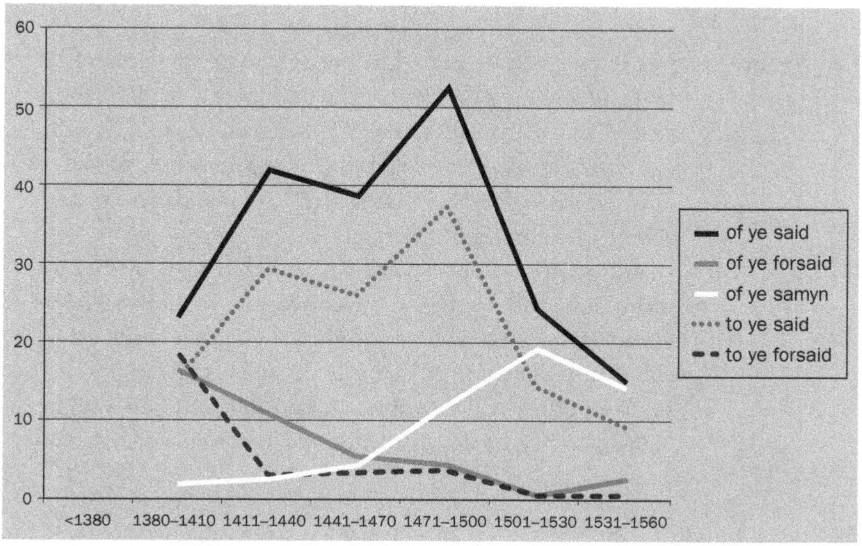

FIGURE 11.2 Three cohesive modifiers (*said, forsaid*, and *samyn*) in prepositional phrase fragments (normalized per 10,000 words)

former gradually diminished in currency, especially after the synthetic pronoun *its* entered the scene in the second half of the seventeenth century (Bugaj 2006b: 196), so the EdHeW material in fact captures the heyday of *of ye samyn* and its frequent employment in legal texts (although the frequency does drop slightly in the sixteenth century, Fig. 11.2).

Textual lexical bundles also signal the continuation of previous information in relative and coordinated clauses, as in *and ye said* (FF = 59) and *that ye said* (FF = 56), which were most formulaic 3-grams in their respective structural types: Type N2c and Type C1, see Chapter 9. Other bundles in this group are typically made of a preposition and a chunk of a nominal phrase, where the modifier points to previous discourse. The tendency to form repetitive chunks out of the beginnings of prepositional phrases has already been noticed in section 9.3. Apart from the bundles discussed above, also *be ye said* and *in ye said* show a substantial degree of formulaicity, FF = 43 and FF = 42, respectively. The cohesive modifiers found in the bundles, apart from *said, forsaid* and *samyn*, include *present, quhilk, ilk*, and *nexit*. The same modifiers will be part of the multifunctional bundles discussed below.

11.3.2.2. Cohesion (Function Overlaps)

Among the lexical bundles with overlapping textual function, the most common modifier is the participial adjective *said*, meaning 'aforesaid, previously mentioned' (*DSL* s.v. *said* ppl adj 1).

(a) *said* 'said'

3-grams: ye said landis**, ye said john**, ye said lord*, ye said ser*, ye said william*, ye said burgh*, ye said robert^, ye said balze^, ye said james^, ye said thomas^, ye said alexander^, ye said day^, ye said schir^, ye said partis^, ye said sum^, ye said erle^, ye said gilbert^, ye said dauid^, ye said davy^, ye said abbot^, ye said adam^, ye saidis landis^, ye said master^, ye said george^, ye said patrik^, ye said marion^, ye said nichol^, ye said jonet^, ye said elizabeth^, ye saidis william^, as said is^, incontenent ye said^, oure said souerain^, said abbot and^, said erle of^, said landis and^, said landis of^, said lord erle^, said ser william^, said souerain lord^, saidis william and^, ye said andro, my said lord, said lord his, than ye said

The lexical bundles with *said* are overwhelmingly referential, going outside the text to the external reality (section 11.3.1), but at the same time they make links to the known information within the text—the previously mentioned people, activities, or dates. Here, the most formulaic bundle refers to the lands, which had already been introduced in an earlier part of the document. Now, thanks to text-internal cohesion devices, the lands need not be described again. In a simple fashion, the cohesive link is provided by means of the participial adjective *said*. What is interesting to notice, and what goes back to the oral quality of legal discourse (section 2.3), is that this widespread adjective is a form of the verb *to say*, clearly reflecting the conceptualization of the written text as a reflection of spoken communication.

4-grams: of ye said landis***, of ye said burgh**, to ye said lord*, ye said landis and*, ye said abbot and*, than incontenent ye said*, incontenent ye said balze*, oure said souerain lord*, to ye said ser*, ye said landis of*, said abbot and conuent*, and than ye said^, ye said landis with^, of ye said sum^, ye said sum of^, to ye said john^, to ye said william^, ye said john of^, within ye said burgh^, ye said erle of^, remanand with ye said^, of ye said ser^

5-grams: and than incontenent ye said*, than incontenent ye said balze*, ye said abbot and conuent*, of ye said landis with^, of ye said landis and^, ye said landis with ye^

In comparison to shorter bundles, 4- and 5-grams do not contain as many personal names in reference to people already mentioned in the text. The balance is shifted more towards titles and status markers: *lord*, *abbot*, *erle* 'earl', or *balze* 'bailie'.

(b) *forsaid* 'aforesaid'

3-grams: ye forsaid erle^, ye forsaid landis^, ye forsaid ser^

Similarly, the adjective *forsaid* contains an oral ingredient. As explained above (Fig. 11.2), its popularity waned in time but this cohesive link still appears in three of the most formulaic 3-grams.

(c) *samyn* 'same'

3-grams: ye samyn day***, curt ye samyn^, samyn day john^, samyn day thom^, samyn day ye^, item ye samyn^
4-grams: ye samyn day ye**, curt ye samyn day*, ye samyn day john*, ye samyn day thom*, hand ye samyn day^, tolbuth of ye samyn^, samyn day thom logan^
5-grams: ye tolbuth of ye samyn*, tolbuth of ye samyn be*, ye samyn day thom logan^, samyn day thom logan officer^

The textual cohesion signalled by means of *samyn* is most often centred on the date of the proceedings and the resultant documentation. The bundle *ye samyn day* is in fact the most formulaic 3-gram in the corpus (FF = 99), which emphasizes the importance of the textual function in legal Scottish documents of the time. The repetitive character of this bundle stems from its typical employment at the beginning of each entry and results in a stable, institutionalized frame to be filled in with further information. The end of an entry is often formulaic too and leads on to the same beginning, as in *curt* | *ye samyn* (cf. the structural discussion in Chapter 9). In fact, in the documents an entry would often end with *witnes ye hail curt*, which was formulaically followed by *ye samyn day*. The decision to ignore punctuation marks in bundle extraction allowed for this corpus-driven discovery (see section 8.4.3 on methodology). Another such case is *hand* | *ye samyn*, which can be syntagmatically extended to *plege his hand* | *ye samyn day*, which does appear as a 6-gram in the corpus.[6]

(d) *quhilk* 'which' and *ilk* 'this, that, the very same'

3-grams: that ilk day*, the quhilk day*, quhilk day the^, ilk day was^, of that ilk^, item that ilk, saiffand ilk mannis
4-grams: the quhilk day the*, item that ilk day*, that ilk day was*, ilk day was maid*
5-grams: witness of ye quhilk thing**, in witnes of ye quhilk thing*, that ilk day was maid*, ilk day was maid burges*, of ye quhilk thing to^, item that ilk day was^

Textual cohesion is also provided by the use of modifiers *quhilk* 'which' and *ilk* 'that, the same one', which in essence link back to a previous nominal phrase or a clause. They could be exchanged in the same context with the above-mentioned adjectives *said* and *samyn* or indicative pronouns *this* or *that*. But as the clerks had not decided on a single choice yet, these rarer modifiers made their way to the formulaic bundles in the corpus, too.

(e) *present* '(this) same, the (one) in hand'

3-grams:	thir present letteris*, in this present^
4-grams:	be thir present letteris**, men be thir present*, thir present letteris me^, in this present parliament^
5-grams:	all men be thir present**, men be thir present letteris**, be thir present letteris me*

The adjective *present* most often provides reference to a document, and indeed to the very document in which it appears. This instance of self-reference has been classed as a textual function because of the broad definition of text adopted in this book (section 3.3.1): text as a unit of meaning. Through reference to itself in the adjective *present*, the text keeps the internal semantic unity. A slightly different application is found in the bundle *in this present parliament*, where reference is made to the situational context. The documents are written in this very place, in this very assembly, so the function of the bundle is primarily referential but it also makes the text coherent with the context.

(f) *nexit* 'next'

3-grams:	ye nexit curt^
4-grams:	to ye nexit curt^

Finally, the last bundle whose secondary function is textual in nature is *(to) ye nexit curt* '(to) the next court'. Similarly to the previously discussed modifier *present*, this choice of modifier is dictated by the external circumstances. The text simultaneously informs readers about the continuity of discourse and makes a link to potential further documentation.

11.3.2.3. Narration

Among textually-oriented bundles, there are those which introduce elements of narration and turn parts of legal discourse into a story made of consecutive elements. Narratives are central to court proceedings, by telling and retelling, constructing and reconstructing a course of events in front of a jury (Jackson 1988; see Archer (2005) for the late modern and contributions to Cotterill (2003) for present-day courtroom discourse). In real-time, the narration is spoken. When recorded, it becomes a part of written documentation. As Culpeper and Kytö observe, "narrative is fundamental also to history of writing" (2010: 174). In legal discourse, the features of orality, narrative among them, manifest themselves in recurrent constructions such as those providing links between events or maintaining the sequence of events.

3-grams:	item it is^, in like wise^, than incontenent ye^, and than incontenent^, incontenent ye said^, and than ye^, and this is^, and that was^, this is ye^, and this ye^, is ye first^, and that na, and gaif to
4-grams:	and this is ye**, and than incontenent ye*, this is ye first*, item that ilk day*, than incontenent ye said*, and than ye said^
5-grams:	and than incontenent ye said*, than incontenent ye said balze*, and this is ye first*, this is ye first curt*, that tyme and than incontenent^, tyme and than incontenent ye^, brocht erd and stan of^

The role of adverbials, such as *than* 'then', *incontenent* 'immediately', or their combination, is to take the reader (or listener) through the progression of events. These expressions were in use mostly during the fifteenth century and are not to be found in frequent repetitive structures in the later parts of the corpus. On the other hand, the adverbial *item* 'likewise, moreover', borrowed or code-switched from Latin, regains popularity at that time. Altogether, *item it is* can be found 151 times in 54 texts, but there is every reason to suspect that *item* on its own, without the bundle context, is even more frequent.[7]

The group of narrative bundles makes use of the coordinating conjunction *and*, which builds a paratactic sequence of clauses, trying to mirror the sequence of events at the same time. The frequent use of clausal *and* has been identified as a feature of spoken language (Chafe and Danielewicz 1987), however Biber et al. (1999) have shown that it is also an important ingredient of procedural written texts and fiction. In early legal texts *and* is a frequent initial element of recurrent lexical strings (sections 9.2 and 9.5). It is used in several formulaic bundles which close the preceding discourse with a summative clause: *and this is*, *and this ye*, or *and that was*. Each of these initial 3-grams may overlap syntagmatically with further bundles to inform which court hearing has been referred to in the text. Only the reference to the first court, *this is ye first curt*, has become formulaic enough to enter the top 10% of 5-grams.

11.3.2.4. Intertextuality

3-grams:	in all punctis^, efter ye forme^, ye tenour of^, forme and tenour, tenour of ye
4-grams:	efter ye forme of^, efter ye tenour of^, ye forme and tenour^
5-grams:	efter ye forme and tenour*, ye forme and tenour of^, of ye quhilk thing to^

In this subcategory of textual bundles, we find references to other texts—to previous writings, previous legal decisions, to tradition. One of the themes in Chapter 2 was the transmission of linguistic patterns which had been created in early law by pre-chirographic societies, and later on continued in writing. Scots law enjoys its independent history, as expounded in Chapter 7, and it is no wonder that documents should contain an intertextual reference to previous documentation and legislation. The nouns *forme* and *tenour*, surfacing in a variety of overlapping bundles, make reference to the model format of a given document and to the substance of a relevant legal provision. The overlapping bundle *ye tenour of (ye)* dates from the earliest period onwards (1380–1560); however, the binomial *forme and tenour* starts appearing in texts from the 1470s till the end of the corpus. A fuller version of this bundle—*efter ye form and tenour*—already reaches the formulaicity level of FF = 41, which places it among top formulaic 5-grams (cf. Fig. 9.1). One more intertextual 3-gram, *in all punctis* 'in all points', gains popularity from mid-fifteenth century onwards and acts as a link to the necessary points to be met in legal action.

11.3.2.5. Clarification

The final subcategory of textual bundles is lexical bundles employed to provide, or rather introduce, a definition or explanation. Due to the clarity requirement of legal discourse (section 2.4), the bundles appear in the text in a formulaic fashion to signal that the previous statement is now going to be rephrased, clarified, and repeated for the benefit of those who had not grasped it before, or to reinforce the message.

3-grams:	that is to**, is to say**, as said is^, it is to^, as to ye
4-grams:	that is to say***, followis that is to^, is to say that^
5-grams:	followis that is to say*, that is to say that*, efter followis that is to^, as efter followis that is^, that is to say ye^

The 3-gram *that is to* is high on the formulaicity scale (618 tokens in 410 texts, FF = 65), because it can take various complements apart from *say*. Similarly, *is to say* (599 tokens in 399 texts, FF = 64) may be preceded by a different pronoun.[8] Together, they form a top formulaic 4-gram *that is to say* (FF = 89), which is a key ingredient introducing clarification in the corpus, especially in the fifteenth-century texts.

11.3.3. INTERACTIONAL BUNDLES

The last function identified in the lexical bundles extracted from early legal Scots texts is the *interactional* function. It corresponds to the interactional function in Halliday's framework (1978) and the subsequent adaptations of this category in Biber's and Culpeper and Kytö's works. As explained in section 3.3.2, the label 'interpersonal' could not be adopted because legal and administrative discourse is institutional in nature. It is not limited to taking place between individual people but also emerges between people and institutions. In essence, bundles from this group emerge in discourse in the context of interaction. They may be related to speech acts performed by either participant in the communicative situation. They may also carry modal meanings and express attitudes. Contrary to other studies of lexical bundles, which were mostly concerned with features of dialogue and spoken interaction (Biber, Conrad, and Cortes 2003, 2004; Culpeper and Kytö 2010), in top formulaic bundles in EdHeW there are no examples of epistemic and boulomaic modality, hedges, or politeness strategies. There are, however, bundles carrying deontic modality and fragments of such speech acts which are crucial for legal discourse, for example directives (section 2.4). These functional elements have been grouped together under the interactional label because they originate either as a result of interaction between discourse participants or they do so in order to create interaction.

The first four subgroups within this category stem from the speech act framework[9] and contain bundles which carry action by means of words, although mostly in an indirect manner (Searle 1976). Indirectness may be achieved by using utterances devoid of the required illocutionary force in a neutral context. Blum-Kulka and House see indirectness as "a measure of illocutionary transparency" (1989: 133). Thus, "It's cold in here" may be interpreted as a genuine statement of fact in some situations, or it may become an indirect request to close the window. The study of this phenomenon on the basis of historical texts presents its own methodological challenges, as Culpeper and Archer point out (2008: 56–60). Searle's exposition of indirect speech acts is based, among other things, on the fact that the remodelled speech acts are conventionally phrased in a limited number of most recurrent, typical options, recognized by language users in spite of the lack of a direct correlation between the semantic content and the illocutionary force (Searle 1976: 66). Culpeper and Archer find formulae problematic in their study of early modern trial requests (2008: 59), because formulae may simply act as support moves and may not represent the actual indirect speech act. What is crucial for our discussion, though, is that recurrence and repetition of specific wordings in legal documents lead to the establishment of fixed text fragments which may or may not utilize a specific performative verb, but nevertheless carry the binding force of a legal act. The formulae are then understood as intended speech acts, remembered, and transmitted to the next generation of texts.

The indirectness in the bundle material below has one more characteristic trait. Here, the written mode requires the speech acts to be reported and the actual utterances to be rephrased. Some of these indirect speech acts may in fact have the form of what Finegan (1982: 119) called *postponed performatives*. The felicity conditions were there at the time of speaking but the illocutionary act was not completed immediately but was conditionally suspended, as in *be it kend til all men* 'let it be known to all people'. The various strategies emerging in the form of bundles are discussed in sections 11.3.3.1 to 11.3.3.4 below. The last group includes bundles which convey modal meanings. Such meanings are also generated in an interpersonal perspective and relate to the speaker's (or writer's) attitude towards the proposition. This is the subject of section 11.3.3.5.

11.3.3.1. Directive Bundles

Directives are essentially about "getting the hearer to do something" (Searle 1976: 11). The addressee of the message is expected to react to the proposition and, in the case of legal texts, to comply with it. In the recurrent lexical bundles gathered from EdHeW there are few direct speech acts of this kind—only those with *sal* 'shall' and the main verb, which will be discussed under deontic modality in 11.3.3.5. All the other instances of ordering and directing are phrased in a non-personal manner, mostly by means of passive constructions.

3-grams:	statut and ordanit*, it is statut^, is statut and^, and ordanit that^, it is accordit^, be it kend^, is accordit that^, kend til all^, ordanit that ye
4-grams:	is statut and ordanit**, it is statut and**, statut and ordanit that**, be it kend til*, kend til all men*, it kend til all*, item it is statut*, it is accordit that^, item it is accordit^, statut and ordanit be^
5-grams:	it is statut and ordanit**, is statut and ordanit that**, be it kend til all**, it is to remember ye*, kend til all men be*, it kend til all men*, item it is statut and*

The chronological preferences for expressing a directive present an interesting picture (Fig.11.3). At the beginning, a very popular bundle was *it is accordit*, found 97 times in 42 texts in the earlier part of the corpus. In time its popularity dropped, while at the same time a new construction was on the rise: *it is statut* (potentially overlapping with *and ordanit*), which steadily rises from the mid-fifteenth century onwards. The third prominent directive bundle, *be it kend* 'let it be known', is typically found in texts from the middle part of the corpus, but it completely disappears from use in the sixteenth century. A shift of focus is visible here. Rather than continue to refer to the cognitive powers of the audience, a strategy originating in an underlying Latin expression (MacQueen 2002a), the clerks worked out an impersonal formula which linked the speech act force to the activity of the court.

The bundles show that two elements of the directive may separately become formulaic. The introductory part of the illocutionary act lends itself very well to formulaicization, especially in *it is statut and ordanit*, which is one of the most formulaic 5-grams (FF = 80). This is where the actual speech act is performed by means of directive verbs *state* and *ordain*, albeit in an impersonal construction to emphasize deferential distance towards the source of the law. The binomial *statut and ordanit* (FF = 44) is relatively high on the scale of formulaicity among 3-grams. As visible above, the more this bundle is extended, the more formulaic it becomes. It means that when a clerk was compiling a text, he had a wider range of recurrent

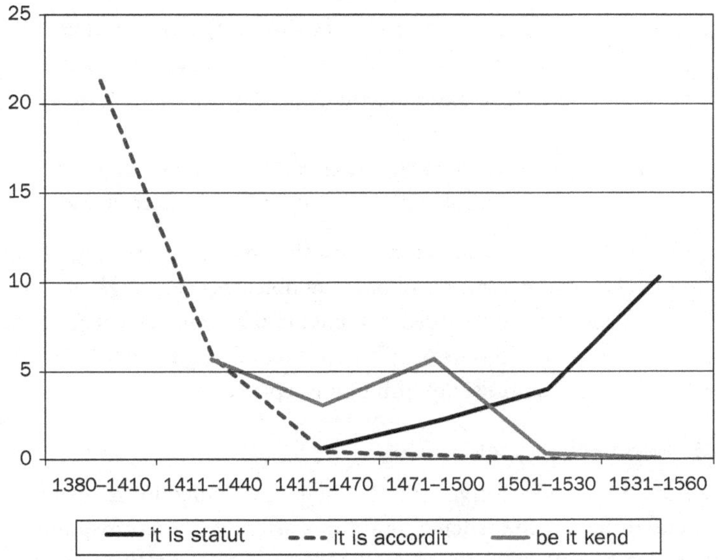

FIGURE 11.3 Preferences in the most formulaic 3-gram directives (tokens per 10,000 words)

3-element strings at hand, but there was less variety as the repeated strings became longer. This issue will be further expanded in the next chapter (Chapter 12), with due attention paid to the directives.

The other part of a directive—the "what is to be done"—has a modal meaning and constitutes the actual obligation. This part should be more varied and therefore less formulaic but makes it in one case to the pool of recurrent bundles. It is the reference to the obligation of payment: *sal pay for his fredom* 'shall pay for his freedom', which has been classified as an expression of deontic modality in 11.3.3.5 below.

11.3.3.2. Representative Bundles

Representatives were identified by Searle as "commit[ting] the speaker (in varying degrees) to something's being the case, to the truth of the expressed proposition" (1976: 10). Thus, the interpretation is moving on a scale from true to false, as decided by the speaker (or writer), whose words may be rephrased as "I *verb* (that) + S" (Searle 1976: 18). Such instances of indirect speech acts have also been found among formulaic bundles in EdHeW, especially in relation to the activity of the court. The first representative verb is *efferme* or *afferme* which is employed in order to formally establish the official status of a court hearing (*DSL* s.v. *afferm(e* v tr, 1b 'to fence a court'). The bundle *ye curt effermit*, following a declarative *ye sutis callit* (section 11.3.3.3), becomes an important ingredient of longer strings summarizing legal activity at a given point in the document.[10] This formulaic 5-gram, listed under representatives because of its focal element, appears in an unchanged form 191 times in 175 texts (FF = 69), starting from the mid-fifteenth century onwards.

3-grams: ye curt effermit^, was giffin for^, contenit in ye^, that was giffin^, it is thocht, is contenit in, giffin for dome
4-grams: callit ye curt effermit*, and that was giffin*, that was giffin for*
5-grams: sutis callit ye curt effermit**, and that was giffin for*, that was giffin for dome^, callit ye curt effermit and^

Other representative bundles are centred on the concept of passing a judgement. The verb *gif* may take non-material or abstract objects (*DSL* s.v. *gif* 'give', v 2), so *gif for dome* means roughly 'give judgement, pass judgement, state'. The expression *it is thocht* 'it is thought' also has its source in the act of judging, while *(is) contenit in (ye)* refers to the act of stating something in the proceedings.

11.3.3.3. Declarative Bundles

The core function of declaratives is to bring about change in the external conditions. Provided that all the felicity conditions are met, the corresponding aspect of reality is changed by the propositional content of a declarative (Searle 1976: 13). The result may be a new appointment, a resignation, a marriage, and so on. In the corpus, the lawsuits are typically *callit* 'called' and *comperit* (or *nocht comperit*). The first verb can be classed as an indirect declarative because it reflects a speech act which could well be phrased as 'I hereby call the suit'. The second verb is a participial form of *compere* 'to put in appearance as a formal act, esp. in a court of justice' (*DSL* s.v. *compere* v[2], 1 intr.). It thus has a meaning similar to 'declare' or 'show'. One should not be misled by the English cognate 'to compare', even though both may be traced back to the Latin source *comparāre* 'to bring together' (*OED* s.v. *compare,* v[1]). This is an example of differences in the lexical enrichment of Scots and English due to language contact with the Romance language family (see section 1.4 and 7.2.2 for the differences in the language of the law).

3-grams: comperit in curt^, ye sutis callit^, callit ye curt^, sutis callit ye^, callit to ye^, callit nocht comperit^, and nocht comperit^, triis callit nocht^, day was maid^, was maid burges^, maid of befor, callit and nocht
4-grams: sutis callit ye curt**, ye sutis callit ye**, triis callit nocht comperit*, callit and nocht comperit*, ilk day was maid*, day was maid burges*, yheris ye sutis callit^, callit to ye chalans^, callit nocht comperit and^, nocht comperit and this^, comperit and this ye^, comperit in curt and^
5-grams: ye sutis callit ye curt**, yheris ye sutis callit ye*, triis callit nocht comperit and*, callit to ye chalans of*, callit nocht comperit and this*, nocht comperit and this ye*, that ilk day was maid*, ilk day was maid burges*, day ye sutis callit ye^, oft tymis callit and nocht^

In the formulaic range, we also find infelicitous declaratives. Because of external reasons, a court case or a litigant could fail to appear and be formally recognized—*nocht comperit*. Bundles with this ingredient are still potential declaratives, however negated in this particular situation. Suffice it to say that non-appearance has been identified as a notorious obstacle in smooth operations of burgh institutions (section 7.3.4), something which has now found confirmation in the most formulaic bundles.

Another formulaic declarative was used when a prospective burgess was recognized as such, see *was maid burges* and its syntagmatic extensions. In section 6.3, the issue of attaining burgess-ship was discussed in more detail, however at this point it is worth remembering that the more people had the status of a burgess, the more money flowed annually into the municipal chest (see section 6.4.1). Non-existent as bundles up to the mid-fifteenth century, such declaratives must have been performed by means of non-repetitive constructions. It would be unreasonable to suspect that there were no means for declaring someone a burgess in earlier texts at all. Nevertheless, only the texts from after 1440 contain *was maid burges*, and indeed as many as 94 tokens in 34 files, so this bundle seems to have caught on quite fast.[11]

11.3.3.4. Commissive Bundles

When a commissive speech act is perpetrated, the speaker commits himself or herself "to some future course of action" (Searle 1976: 11). Echoes of such spoken commitments can be gleaned from several formulaic 3-grams, where somebody at court puts forward a pledge (*to streke a borch*, *DSL* s.v. *strek(e* v. 3d), gives advice, obliges himself or herself to doing something, bears witness to a course of action, and agrees to a proposition.

3-grams:	strekit a borch^, with auise of^, auise of ye, and obliss me, witnes ye hail, with consent of
5-grams:	witnes of ye quhilk thing**

The activity of witnessing a case in court gave rise to longer formulaic strings, frequently employed especially in the first half of the fifteenth century. More discussion of this issue will follow in Chapter 12.

11.3.3.5. Modal Bundles

The final subcategory of interactional bundles contains constructions which convey or introduce modality, as is the case with *if*-clause fragments. In studies on spoken discourse this group of bundles is usually well-represented because conversation is rich in expressions of stance, prediction as well as volitional utterances. Among the most formulaic bundles in EdHeW, few such bundles have been found. The prevailing modality is deontic—connected with obligation, which is unsurprising in legal texts. The only modal verb which has made it to the top formulaic bundles is *sal* 'shall'. It is typically used to refer to the obligation of payment *sal pay for his fredom* 'shall pay for his freedom', where 'freedom' refers to being free from financial dues. The bundle may appear in a specific context of a given court case but also in a generic sense, to inform how a person may legally regain financial independence. Other indicators of obligation have the form of infinitival complements with *to*: *it is to remember*, *to be maid*, *to be payd*, and so on.

3-grams:	and gif it^, and gif ye, and sal pay^, is to remember^, pay for his^, sal pay for^, to remember ye^, to be maid^, to be payd^, to be haldin^, and to be, and to ferm
4-grams:	it is to remember*, is to remember ye*, and sal pay for*, pay for his fredom*, sal pay for his*, and gif it happinis^
5-grams:	and sal pay for his*, sal pay for his fredom*

In the documents, the beginning of an *if*-clause comes across as a modalizing strategy. However, this is not an epistemic use, as in introducing speculation, but rather an obligation to do something under a certain condition. The appearance of *if*-clauses in the bundle material is not a surprise, as strong presence of *if*-constructions in legal texts has already been noticed by Finegan (1982: 116–117). He found around 26 tokens of *if*-clauses per one hundred sentences in wills, which was five times more than instances of *if*-clauses in the control corpus. In the Scottish documents the *if*-clause fragments are typically preceded by the conjunction *and*, serving to connect paratactic clauses (see the discussion of clausal coordination in section 9.5). Thus, the secondary function of these bundles is also textual.

11.4. Conclusions: Short Bundles in Context

Before I move on to conclusions proper, it is crucial to realize the importance of the very fact that a string of lexical items repeats in an unchanged form throughout a collection of texts. Repeated elements become a recognizable part of a given genre and help to construct the 'horizon of expectations', shared by the participants of a communicative situation (section 3.4). Halliday (1978) treated repetition itself as a textual functional component because it provides cohesion in the text and makes connections between the elements of discourse. It is also a mnemonic device to enhance the replicability of a given text in similar contexts, which is a requirement of a legal setting. In smaller repetitive elements, especially 3-grams, we can recognize the building blocks of text-type characteristics: Biber's research has shown how institutional writing scores high in terms of informational density, complex noun phrases, and passive voice (2003: 59–61). All these characteristics emerge also in medieval and early modern legal texts written in Scots, in the form of lexical bundles.

Repeated chunks of language, extracted here by the lexical bundle methodology, have revealed the core substance of early legal texts in the Scottish vernacular. This chapter has given insight into the functional characteristics of the most formulaic bundles in the EdHeW corpus, following the division into referential, textual, and interactional categories. The findings point to the major role of external circumstances in creating legal discourse. Referential bundles are clearly dominant, regardless of their length (Fig. 11.4.–11.6) and regardless of the subperiod. They make up more than 40% of the most formulaic 3-grams, and over 70% when counted together with referential bundles whose prominent but secondary function is textual.

The textual function is carried by around 20% of the most formulaic 3-grams, which may be extended to include the referential overlaps in expressions such as *ye samyn day* or *ye said landis*. As discussed above, these are clearly referential but at the same time they construct a network of cohesive links, pointing towards elements of previous (or forthcoming) discourse. Overall, cohesive strategies, primary or secondary, constitute a considerable share of most formulaic short bundles, around 40% of the data. Thus, the referential and textual bundles together leave only around 10% for interactional 3-grams in early legal Scots documents. What is interesting to note at this juncture is that the employment of recurrent interactional patterns seems to be on the rise towards the end of the studied period, as if the actual speech acts were also bending towards a uniformity of practice. Also, the longer the bundle, the more prominent the interactional aspect becomes (Fig. 11.5–11.6).

As discussed in Chapter 8, the most formulaic 4-grams are less than half as numerous as 3-grams, and 5-grams are, in turn, half as numerous as 4-grams

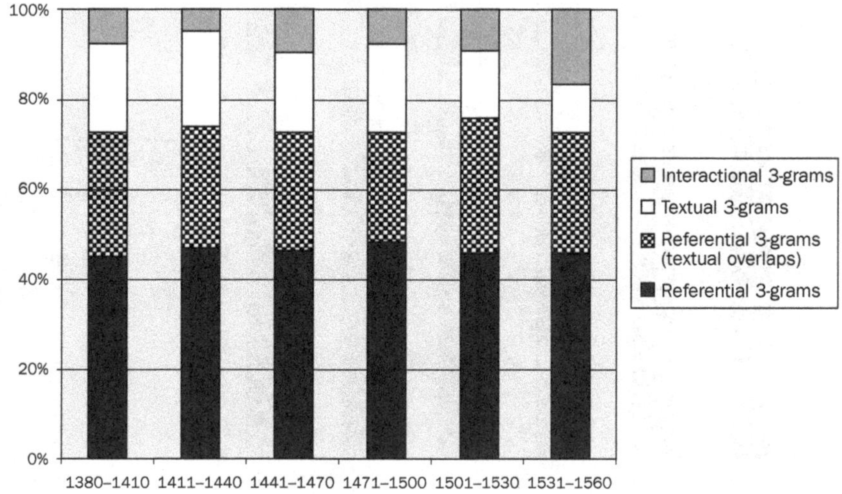

FIGURE 11.4 Chronological distribution of top formulaic 3-grams according to function (token frequency normalized per 10,000 words)

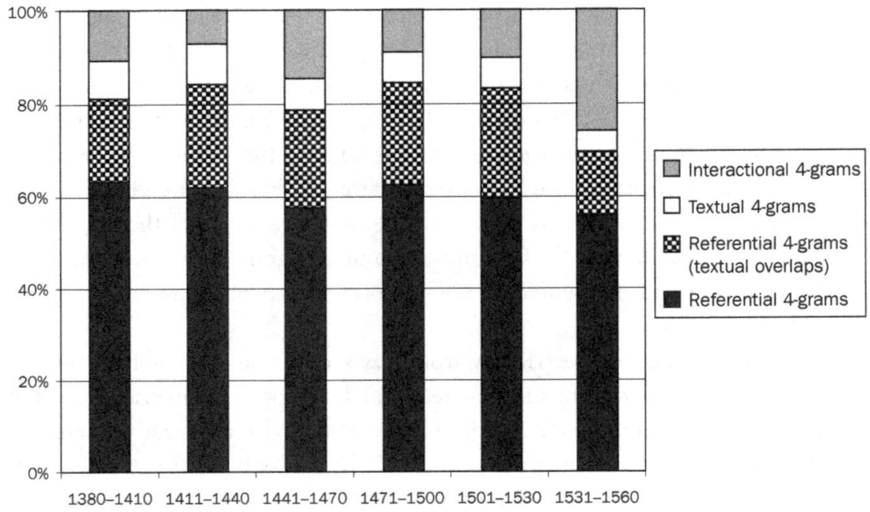

FIGURE 11.5 Chronological distribution of top formulaic 4-grams according to function (token frequency normalized per 10,000 words)

(Table 8.5). This is connected with the fact that short bundles may be employed in a wider variety of syntactic frames, serving as a paradigmatic element inserted whenever the context requires it, and may therefore repeat in an unchanged form much more often. It is harder to repeat a 4-word chunk with the same frequency as a 3-word chunk, and still harder to put five consecutive elements in a row in a similarly unchangeable manner. This issue is crucial in the interpretation of functional

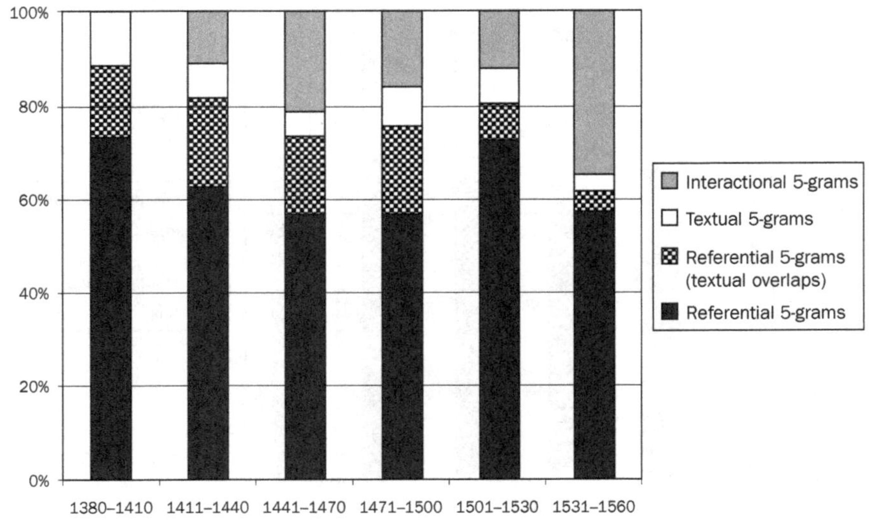

FIGURE 11.6 Chronological distribution of top formulaic 5-grams according to function (token frequency normalized per 10,000 words)

characteristics of longer bundles and will be even more pronounced in Chapter 12, where 6- to 8-grams are taken into consideration.

In 4- and 5-grams, the important position of referential bundles is confirmed (Fig. 11.5–11.6). They are in clear majority among repetitive discourse elements. A closer look at the two remaining functions allows us to conclude that the interactional bundles grow in importance with the length of the bundle. And they also grow in importance as the time progresses.

In the earliest documents in the corpus, interactional 5-grams hardly appeared at all, suggesting that there were no stable linguistic patterns which would render speech acts and modality at length in early legal Scots. Of course, these functions must have been present in the texts, according to the requirements of specialized legal discourse, but the clerks hardly ever employed the same lexico-syntactic strings of more substantial length to carry them (cf. short bundles where the interactional component does surface in around 10% of the earliest texts). In time, more and more interactional 5-grams become repetitive, to reach over a third of the most formulaic 5-grams in mid-sixteenth century. In other words, it seems that compositional variety in longer interactional bundles was becoming supressed, contrary to the referential, and especially the textual bundles, which seem to have opened for more structural variety at that time. The question of whether the longest bundles confirm this tendency remains to be explored in the next chapter.

The final point to make about the functional characteristics of 3- to 5-grams is that the functional types show a correlation with structural types, discussed in detail in Chapter 9. The mutual relationship between form and function lies at the foundation of the functional approach towards language (Halliday 1978), even though the correspondence between the two may not be straightforward (Culpeper and Archer 2008: 58). Nevertheless, in earlier lexical bundle research, Biber, Conrad, and Cortes (2004) have empirically shown, for instance, that prepositional phrases most typically make up referential bundles. In EdHeW, the referential function is typically carried by nominal phrase fragments, but the employment of prepositional phrases to the same effect can also be observed (Fig. 11.7).

The world outside the text is built out of nominal repetitive patterns, including prepositional phrases which are also nominal in nature—they relate to entities rather than to actions and states. The textual 3-grams, providing cohesion within the text and coherence with the external circumstances, often have the form of prepositional phrase fragments, as in *of ye said* or *of ye samyn*, discussed in detail above. A clear verbal component is present in the textual and even more so in the interactional lexical bundles. Although the formulaic elements of interaction in the corpus are typically verbal in nature, it is important to remember that these are mostly passives and reported speech constructions which diminish the immediacy of communication.

The present chapter has shown that fixed functional elements emerge in discourse in an orderly fashion—that there are correlations with structural types and consequences of the length factor in extracted fixed chunks. I have also discussed

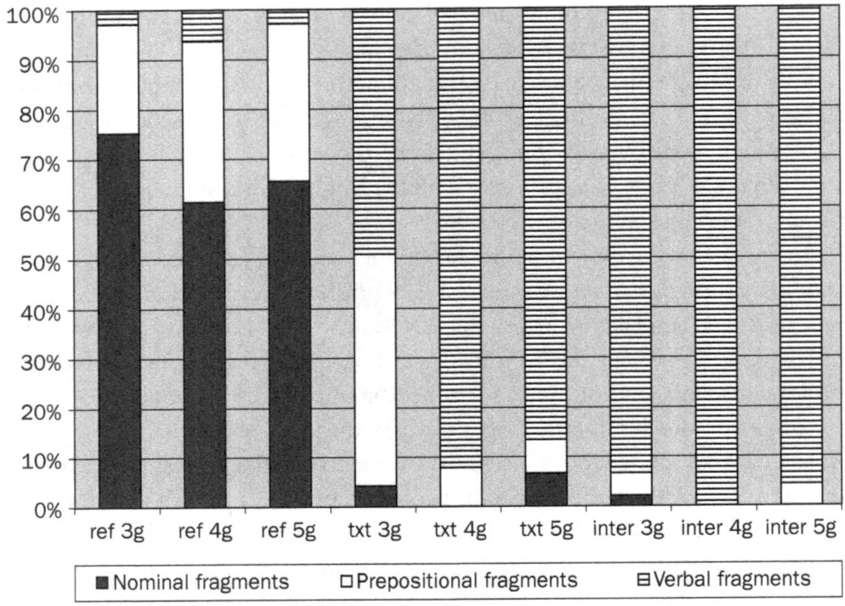

FIGURE 11.7 Functional and structural characteristics of 3- to 5-grams

The structural types N1–N4, identified in Chapter 9, have been grouped under *nominal* bundles, *prepositional* bundles include types P1–P2, while *verbal*—V1–V2 and C1–C3.

individual bundles whose function went hand in hand with frequent employment in the corpus. This research thus substantiates the suggestion that "lexical bundles should be regarded as a basic linguistic construct with important functions for the construction of discourse" (Biber, Conrad, and Cortes 2004: 398). Moreover, the extraction software has made it possible to trace developments in bundle formation and selection as time progressed. The most important trends here will be the growth of interactional bundles in the sixteenth century Scots documents and the dominant position of referential bundles throughout the corpus.

Finally, the functional analysis presented in this chapter clearly indicates that the extracted bundles bear straightforward connections to the socio-historical background in which the texts were created. The micro-linguistic patterns in the form of 3- to 5-grams reflect and enact the legal and institutional setting, presented in Part Two of the book. Referential bundles contain fixed date formulae, creating a clear temporal frame and a point of reference for future users of a given document. As pointed out in Chapter 2, the medium of writing enabled keeping a careful record of legal activities and regulations; the fixed reference to the date is therefore unsurprising and appears to be one of the crucial elements of early Scots legal discourse. Within this function, one finds fluctuating trends, which might be connected with a larger socio-historical context. For example, the legal reforms of James I and his son (sections 5.4.2 and 5.4.3) may have created a favourable milieu for textual standardization of the date in the documents (as well as other patterns of text), while at the turn of the sixteenth century the date formula was not as frequently repeated in its entirety but limited most often to *ye samyn day* (section 11.3.1). The intriguing switch of preference from 'the year of our Lord' to 'the year of God', emerging in the bundles (Fig. 11.1), could be taken to illustrate a departure from the feudal conceptualization of the deity and the Latin calque on *Anno Domini*.

The bulk of referential bundles concern people involved in legal discourse: the authorities, other collective bodies, and various individuals, whose names recur in the texts. The hierarchical government of a Scottish burgh, described in sections 6.3 and 7.3, is reflected in important repetitive strings, such as *ye aldirman and balzeis, lordis of consail*, or *ye borow curt of*. Throughout Part Two, I showed how active the burghs were in national (and international) politics as one of the Three Estates in parliament and as financial supporters of the Crown; now lexical bundles reveal that in legal and administrative documents the talk of *ye thre estatis* was frequent, indeed, and that the word *parliament* is found at the core of several repetitive strings. The documents also make formulaic reference to the monarch, both at home (*oure souerain lord*) and abroad (*king of england*). Burgh inhabitants populate the most formulaic bundles as well (e.g. *all and sindry*, *ye hail toune*, or the frequently mentioned Johns and Williams). In reference to individual people, one finds historical figures like the Duke of Albany, whose turbulent relationship with the Scottish Crown (section 5.4.4) secured him space among the most formulaic lexical bundles. The extracted formulaic sequences draw attention to people involved in typical legal activities of the day, especially land transactions and other inheritance-related activities. This is why the records abound in patterns like *his airis and assignais*, *airis executouris and assignais*, or *ye handis of*. As suggested above, these bundles create a frame for the emergence of a text community. The participants of legal discourse recognize their own role through stable referential patterns and thus are able to place themselves in the context of the legal action. Their public identity is sanctioned by the contents of the texts.

Some information on gender issues can also be gleaned from the lexical bundles. One should remember that the material discussed here constitutes the pinnacle of formulaicity in the corpus, as explained in Chapter 8. Therefore, even occasional lexical bundles discussed here testify to the presence of women in the world of medieval legal discourse. They are represented by formulaic reference in various capacities: as participants in court activity (e.g. *ye said marion*), as relatives of male burgesses (e.g. *elizabeth his spouse*), or, by implication, as a spouse who can outlive the other and thus inherit property: *ye langar lefar* 'the one living longer' (section 11.3.1). Women could also claim their right to possessions or land taken from them: *wrangus haldin fra hir* is less frequent than *wrangus haldin fra him*, but still makes it to the pool of the most formulaic bundles. The final note about female participants in legal discourse should be that the lexical bundles are coherent with the time of composition of the records and change the formulaic reference to the female monarch accordingly (*ye quenis grace* and *oure souerain lady*), towards the mid-sixteenth century (for Mary, Queen of Scots, see section 5.4.7).

Another area of formulaic referential function is the legal activity itself. The adjective *wrangus*, which most often describes the deed in question, bears a clear connection to the principles of medieval Scots law and its idea *thow salt dae na wrang* 'you shall do no wrong', as discussed in section 7.2.3. The bundles indicate the most common offences, such as theft, fraud, or non-appearance in court. Historical records discussed in Chapters 6 and 7 have already hinted at these and other daily concerns of Scottish burghs. Another major issue was land, the source of income and the necessary ingredient of burgess-ship (section 6.4.2). Among referential lexical bundles, *(of) ye said landis* and *ye landis of* score highest on the formulaicity scale, followed by other land-related strings: *landis and tenement*, *landis and biggin* 'lands and building', or *with ye pertinencis* 'with other landed property'. In connection with land and its transfer, the binomial *erd and stan* surfaces again (cf. sections 10.2.2–10.2.3), representing the physical props used in ritualized legal transactions (section 7.3.4). All in all, the most formulaic bundles with a referential function highlight the link between the linguistic fabric of the records and the extralinguistic conditions in which they were put down.

The second important functional group are the textual bundles, which create connections within legal discourse. As discussed at the beginning of the concluding section, these bundles are less numerous than the referential ones, but they include the most frequent and the most formulaic 3-gram of the whole corpus, *of ye said* (section 11.3.2.1). Other cohesive bundles are also very frequent and stable in form. The present study thus shows that early legal discourse relied heavily on cohesive connections within the texts, as well as took care to engage with the extralinguistic context in a stable manner. It is especially visible in the bundles which combine the textual and the referential function. This functional duality is best illustrated by *ye said landis* or *ye said burgh*, where the adjective *said* creates a cohesive link to preceding discourse, while the modified noun relates to an important aspect of extra-textual reality. Numerous other bundles of this kind relate mostly to people involved in legal affairs. Among textual bundles, a less prominent but important part is played by narrative, intertextual, and clarifying sequences (especially the highly formulaic 4-gram *that is to say*), whose employment answers to the requirements of legal discourse, presented in Chapter 2.

The final functional group contains interactional bundles. Research into historical legal discourse typically concentrates on genres which give us the key to the patterns of interaction in the past (cf. Kryk-Kastovsky 2000, 2006b; Culpeper and Archer 2008; Culpeper and Kytö 2010). As pointed out several times in the present discussion, this study looks at legal documents, whose central focus is not interactive; it follows that the interactional function will not be represented in large quantities among the lexical bundles. Indeed, the bundles which encapsulate speech acts and modality are limited in number, as the detailed proportions discussed above have shown. Still, reference to the main legal activities of burgh courts is carried by fixed and stable patterns (e.g. *it is statut and ordanit*, or *be it kend til*), which will show a propensity towards textual standardization and become part of even longer strings in the next chapter. The Scottish medieval context is responsible for such representative bundles as *that was giffin for (dome)* and *callit ye curt effermit*: the first bundle completes the record of a certain punishment or duty, while the latter makes reference to the activity of fencing the court, the formal opening of the proceedings (section 7.3.4). The latter example also points towards syntagmatic extensions to the left, where a declarative *ye sutis callit* would typically be found (see also section 12.2.3 for the emerging formulaic 6-gram). The data show that interactive elements in early legal documents were typically unidirectional; the formulae inform about the dealings of the court or carry orders for discourse participants, but no response-related bundles can be observed. This textual behaviour diverges from the findings on trial proceedings and builds a case for a separation of documents and records within the field of legal discourse. This specialized field is constructed out of texts which show a close relationship to the extralinguistic, institutional context of medieval and early modern Scotland, as demonstrated throughout the chapter. At the same time, the language of these texts contains an impressive degree of structural repetition, creating stable linguistic patterns and enhancing the authority of the written word.

12

Long Bundles

FUNCTIONAL PROPERTIES AND STANDARDIZATION

12.1. Standardization Triggers and Long Formulaic Bundles

Texts written by notaries and burgh scribes display an extraordinary stability of wording preferences for several reasons. It all began with education and tradition. An apprentice clerk or a student of law must have consulted formularies to acquaint themselves with the legally binding forms of texts, initially inspired by medieval continental practices in Latin, as signalled throughout Chapter 7. Traditions had to be preserved and followed in order to ensure the institutional power of the text. Notaries and clerks had access to earlier products of their trade in the form of protocol books (Donaldson 1952; Symms 1993; cf. Gouldesbrough 1985), or watched their masters compose texts in a workshop (Durkan 1983: 29–30). This community of practice shared resources and worked towards a common public goal in very specific circumstances of a medieval burgh, well-known to the community members. In this way, the external context of text production helped to reach large degrees of unanimity in many aspects of wording and form.

The scribes worked within the field of legal discourse, whose nature from the very beginning was formulaic and repetitive, as manifested in Chapter 2. Further chapters in this book have argued that repetition bears a direct connection to fixedness, which, in turn, may be considered one of the elements of standardization. When it comes to the content of legal documents, the writings concerned similar topics, making certain pieces of information bound to recur. This is why textual standardization is best observable in specialized discourse rather than in balanced multi-genre corpora, where topics and formats vary. The corpus-driven lexical bundles method, applied to a specialized corpus, reveals recurrent patterns which constitute the core of specialized discourse. In the present project, due to the text mark-up and the settings of the extraction tool, it was also possible to trace the patterns which become more and more popular in time, as well as those which are repeated in the same manner throughout the country.

This chapter concentrates on the longest investigated lexical bundles—6- to 8-grams—as they are considered to be tokens of textual standardization. Before the bundles could make it into this discussion, they had to be sifted according to

TABLE 12.1
Long lexical bundles in EdHeW—final data counts

	> 5 tokens + > 5 files		≥ 10 tokens + ≥ 10 files		Final top 10%	
	All types	All tokens	All types	All tokens	All types	All tokens
6-grams	1,682	26,549	722	18,921	72	6,229
7-grams	1,205	17,388	495	11,837	50	3,841
8-grams	857	11,222	321	7,098	32	2,051

their formulaic quality. The most formulaic 10% of the material was accepted for further analysis, using the methodology described in detail in Chapter 8. Table 12.1 shows in numeric format how much repetition was encountered among long lexical bundles in the corpus.

When the length parameter is set at six consecutive elements, repeated in the same order, there are 722 types of such constructions (up from 10 tokens in at least 10 texts), with almost 19,000 individual tokens. With 7-grams, the numbers drop but still the amount of repetition is impressive, compared, for example, to findings on long repetitive strings in the Bible (0.85 million words). In the King James Bible (1604–1611), there are 260 7-grams with ten or more occurrences (Stubbs and Barth 2003: 77; section 8.5.2), which would correspond to around 184 occurrences in a corpus of the same length as EdHeW (0.6 million). Scots legal texts render 495 bundles with seven consecutive elements, and even when one more element is added, the 8-grams are still more numerous than the 7-grams in the Bible. For the lack of other points of reference, it is impossible to draw more cross-generic comparisons. However, the corpus material in EdHeW clearly comes across as very standardized and formulaic, which is supported by its numbers of the longest repetitive bundles.

To illustrate how frequent a specific bundle had to be in order to make it to this chapter, suffice it to say that the most formulaic 6-gram was *chalans for ye wrangus haldin fra* 'charge for the wrongful taking from' with 401 tokens in 161 texts, FF = 99. The 6-gram closing the top 10% is *on that ta part and ye* 'on that side and the', with 40 tokens in 30 different texts, FF = 32. The list of most formulaic 6-grams has seventy-two types of lexical bundles (Table 12.1), each repeating well over 30 times in at least 10 texts. For 7- and 8-grams the numbers go down for the obvious reason that it is less likely to repeat a longer string of words in exactly the same order. Still, if such long strings recur word-by-word in a given discourse situation, they can be treated as symptoms of textual standardization. In the top 7-grams there are as many as fifty different lexical bundles, the most formulaic being *chalans for ye wrangus haldin fra him* 'charge for the wrongful taking from him' (317 tokens, 149 texts, FF = 98) and the list is closed by *ye monath of juli ye yhere of* 'the month of July the year of' (37 tokens, 29 texts, FF = 33). In the top 8-grams there are thirty-two different bundles, with the syntagmatic extension of the most formulaic 7-gram, *chalans for the wrangus haldin fra him of* (297 tokens,

146 texts, FF = 100). At the bottom of the most formulaic 8-grams there is *curt of ye newburgh haldin in ye chapel* 'court of Newburgh held in the chapel' (48 tokens in 46 texts, FF = 37).

In the discussion below, due to a large degree of syntagmatic overlap, the bundles from 6- to 8-grams will be analysed together, on the basis of the longest distinguishable sequence to which they contribute. Standardization involves convergence on some selected variant, which may be approached from at least three angles: diachronic—tracing the emergence of patterns in time, diatopic—identifying regional areas of convergence, and diastratic—looking at the specific groups of users who advance standardization (cf. Garvin 1970). The diastratic perspective may be applied to groupings of texts when tracing the source of linguistic standardization, for example, in morphology or syntax, among various genres and registers. Textual standardization, however, happens within a specialized context, so that other genres become irrelevant. The present chapter thus adopts the first two perspectives. First, the analysis will focus on the diachronic employment of long bundles in the texts and will address their function and structure, as well as highlight their connection with the context of Scottish burghs and their legal institutions (section 12.2). The regional distribution of the most repetitive bundles is brought to focus in section 12.3. Short bundles have been added to complement the emerging picture and achieve a full overview of the diatopic standardizing tendencies. The discussion will thus indicate the core areas in Scotland where textual patterns were undergoing the process of standardization. The final part of the chapter, section 12.4, returns to the symptoms of textual standardization in a more comparative and contextualized perspective.

12.2. Emergent Standardizing Patterns: The Diachronic Dimension

12.2.1. DIACHRONIC TRENDS IN THE LONGEST BUNDLES

We find waxing and waning trends for individual long bundles from the top range of formulaicity scores. To get a perspective on the diachronic preferences, the frequencies of occurrence were normalized per 10,000 words and the data was sorted by a specific time-frame. In order to compare and conflate the normalized frequencies for the longest bundles, the sum of normalized occurrences for each length was counted in a given period, and then divided by the number of types in a given bundle length. For instance, in 6-grams, the normalized frequency between 1380 and 1410 was 22.39, divided by 72 types, equals 0.31. In 7-grams, for the same period we have 16.99 in normalized frequency, divided by 50 types of most formulaic 7-grams, equals 0.33, and so on (Fig. 12.1).

In general, among the most formulaic 8-grams, 7-grams, and 6-grams, there are two visible patterns. The first is the rise in frequency of several bundles in the period 1411–1440 and their subsequent decline. The bundles which first gained and then gradually lost popularity can be grouped thematically, which is also because

FIGURE 12.1 Diachronic presence of long lexical bundles in EdHeW (normalized per 10,000 words)

some of them form syntagmatic and paradigmatic overlaps. The second trend is a growth in popularity of some bundles in the final part of the corpus, between 1500 and 1560. The sections below will concentrate on these two groups of long bundles according to chronological tagging and discuss their structural and functional properties, with an interlude in 12.2.3 to present the less prominent bundles which were used in the late fifteenth century, between the standardization peaks.

12.2.2. LONG LEXICAL BUNDLES—THE EARLY FIFTEENTH CENTURY

Long bundles overlap and extend into even longer strings. In the presentation of data, the sequences which remain unchanged regardless of bundle length are placed in the centre, while all the optional extensions available in the top formulaic material are indicated with brackets. The lengths range from 6- to 8-grams. The first thematic group encodes reference to the date of the document, which was an "elaborate" (Murray 1910: 17) and indispensable element of every legal document. Durkan (1983: 25) notes that the dates of documents were given with maximum precision.

(1) {6g–8g} (ye) (yhere) (of) oure lord a (thousande) (four) (hundereth) (thirty) (and)

(2) {6g–7g} (ye) xxti day of ye monath (of)

(3) {7g–8g} (day) of ye monath of may ye (yhere) (of)

The syntagmatic overlaps indicate increasing fixedness of the arrangement of lexical items in the date, and also a reference to a specific chronological period—1400s, or even 1430s, as the 8-gram in (1) shows. In terms of function, these are clearly referential bundles (section 11.3.1), anchoring the documents in a specific time slot. In section 5.4.2, I drew attention to the fact that the early fifteenth century was a time of revival for Scotland under James I. This monarch had a strong ambition to regulate the laws and to implement efficient methods of taxation and government. Interestingly, the documents compiled during his rule exhibit the most uniformity when it comes to dating, as if fulfilling the requirements of neat documentation. This fact cannot be due to the imbalance in word count from specific periods, and a potential overrepresentation of the early fifteenth century, because the frequencies of occurrence were normalized. Thus, the reforms of James I may explain why dates were recorded in a standardized manner during his time, while for other periods they varied in format. Summarizing the presence of long bundles in EdHeW, Figure 12.1 shows a peak of formulaicity between 1411 and 1440, and here it is the standardized date reference which is responsible for this trend. Of course, we should not be surprised that the 1400-bundles declined when the period of reference was over. Indeed, in the sixteenth century another fixed reference to the date emerges (examples (27–28) below).

The bundles show that clerks kept to the rules of legal document compilation and authorization by including a reference to God in the date (cf. Durkan 1983: 25). It transpires that they most often chose the wording "the year of our Lord" in longer formulaic strings, even though there was another option available—"the year of God" (see Fig. 11.1 for the swap in scribal preferences in respective 3- and 4-grams). That phrase does exhibit formulaic features because it is recurrent; however, it does not display a standardizing tendency within longer strings at that particular time. From the 1440s onwards, however, the reference to "God" rather than to "our Lord" exhibits a steady rise (examples (9)–(11) below). Considering the date from the structural angle, it is a compilation of nominal and prepositional phrase fragments, which confirms the tendency for fixing and stabilizing nominal expressions, observed earlier in shorter recurrent strings (section 9.6).

Another theme in the mid-fifteenth century in the long fixed bundles is establishing the force and scope of the documents.

(4) a. {6g–8g} (be) (it) (kend) (til) all men (be) (thir) (present) (letteris) (me)
b. {7g–8g} (be) (it) (kend) (til) all men (be) (thir) (present) (letteris) (ws)

Clearly, there is also a large degree of syntagmatic overlap, where one item is added at a time, while the bundle remains in the top formulaic patterns. The standardizing formula emerging in (4) is: *be it kend til all men be thir present letteris me/ws* 'let it be known to all men by these present letters I/us', which spreads over eleven elements and keeps repeating in the same form in early fifteenth-century documents. Structurally speaking, this bundle is built out of an imperative verb phrase with two prepositional phrases acting as complements. From a functional point of view, this is a longer version of the recurrent directive *be it kend*, discussed in section 11.3.3.1, supporting the conspicuous position of directives in EdHeW.

This formulaic string, extracted by means of bundle methodology was, in fact, recognized by contemporaries as a characteristic feature of legal jargon even one century later. The following mock-poem, making fun of legal writings, was jotted down on the fly-leaf of a register by an Edinburgh clerk in the mid-sixteenth century (Sanderson 2002: 194):

> *Be it kend to all men*
> *be thir present lettres*
> *Ther would not be so much writing*
> *wer not all debtoris*

The best targets for mockery are well-known genres because one can easily recognize where conventions have been transgressed or warped (for the "horizon of expectations" see section 3.4). This little rhyme shows a meta-reflection on legal discourse and a self-awareness of a clerk with regard to his own job. The lexical bundle method has extracted exactly the same formula which the clerk had deemed emblematic for legal writings—perhaps a good testimony to the robustness of the corpus tool. MacQueen (2002a) has looked for the roots of this particular phrasing in the formal openings of many early Latin documents. Its subsequent entrenchment in vernacular legal texts is remarkable, indeed.

Coming back to the linguistic features of the bundle in question, it exhibits a similar preference for singular and for plural self-reference to the authority of the notary, or even to the monarch who was the ultimate source of laws and regulations. Earlier texts show a tendency for the royal plural, which slowly goes out of the most formulaic preference at a later stage. 7-grams ending in 'us' score 3.82 (per 10,000 words) between 1411 and 1440 and then decline to 1.22 by 1500, while those in 'me' score 1.21 in the earlier period and grow in popularity to 3.15 in the period 1471–1500. Also, the longer the bundle, the clearer the preference for the singular 'me' instead of the royal plural 'us'. Both forms were available, both were formulaic, but only one of them is used enough times and in enough texts to make it to the top pool of 8-grams.

Another bundle popular in the early fifteenth century performs the interactional function:

(5) {6g–7g} (iṇ) witnes of ye quhilk thing to

This particular construction refers to the interactive quality of legal discourse, where the act of witnessing and individual participation echoed the oral character of early law and gave force to legal proceedings (sections 2.3 and 7.3). This bundle is a commissive formula, whereby the persons concerned commit themselves to testifying to the authenticity of the event and the document. Structurally speaking, the bundle is made of two prepositional phrases. The possessive construction *of ye quhilk thing* 'of the which thing' is a typical Middle Scots pattern of a definite article preceding the relative pronoun (Moessner 1997: 144–149; on the function of relatives in Scots, see Meurman-Solin 2007b).

Returning to the long standardizing bundles with conspicuous nominal elements, there are two 6-grams and one 8-gram to be considered.

(6) {6g} to ye said abbot and conuent

(7) {6g} on ye ta part and ye

(8) {8g} james throu mercy of god prior of

Reference to the monastic neighbours of a burgh can be found in (6), and it is one of the bundles which combine a referential function with a cohesion device—"the said"—working within the textual function (see 11.3.2.2 on function overlaps and Fig. 11.2 on *said* as a cohesive modifier). The most formulaic fragment of land descriptions, *on ye ta part (...) on ye tothir part* 'on this side...on the other side', surfaced in (7), although only as the initial 6-gram. The 4-gram *on ye ta part* is typically followed by a coordinator and a definite article starting the next phrase (e.g. the dimensions of the plot), rendering a stable and formulaic six-word combination in the records. The second part of this expression does appear among shorter bundles (see 11.3.1g) but has little opportunity to expand into a longer formulaic string.

In (8), we witness an interesting case of cross-sentential formulae. As the data preparation included stripping the texts of all punctuation (see 8.4.3), there is no overt indication of sentence boundaries. However, among the top formulaic 8-grams of the early fifteenth century, the name *James* makes its appearance again. It may be reference to the king and his divine license at the end of one sentence, while the next sentence starts with *prior of*, which is in all probability a signature of a prior. It may also be the case that the prior's name was James, and his intense involvement with legal matters was captured in the formulaic string. It must have been a common enough textual pattern to reach the top formulaic 8-grams, so regardless of the interpretation of the name *James*, the church officials make their appearance in the fixed parts of discourse once more.

12.2.3. LESS FREQUENT LONG FORMULAIC BUNDLES—THE LATE FIFTEENTH CENTURY

Apart from the bundles which showed a frequency increase in the two identified sub-periods, there were other formulaic strings which were popular in documents only for a while. Since the previous section has dealt with bundles reaching their popularity peak in the early fifteenth century, the chronology takes the discussion now to the later part of the fifteenth century, to be followed by the early sixteenth century in section 12.2.4.

Again, let us start with date reference, which continues to be one of the longest strings undergoing standardization. Example (9) shows an intermediate stage in lexical preferences; as observed above, in the earlier part of the fifteenth century, the standardized reference to the year involved the phrase 'of our Lord' rather than 'of God', typical of the sixteenth century.

(9) {6g–8g} (ye) yhere of god a thousade four (hundereth)
(10) {8g} (day) of ye monath of februar ye yhere (of)
(11) {6g–8g} (day) (of) (ye) (monath) of juli ye (yhere) (of) (god)
(12) {8g} (day) of ye monath of nouembre ye yhere (of)

What examples (10)–(11) have in common is the initial 5-gram 'day of the month of', one of the most formulaic referential 5-grams (section 11.3.1), which gets specified in the remaining part of the bundles. Three specific months are referred to so frequently in the last part of the fifteenth century within the same lexical arrangement, that they become formulaic 8-grams. February can be explained as the first of the traditional quarter days in Scotland, a continuation of the Celtic festival of Imbolc, turned later into Candlemas Eve (Moffat 2005: 185–188). In fact, the next important month in the calendar would be May, with Beltane celebrations, and it does appear in the most standardized date reference in the earliest period in the records, see (3). The month of July (11) does not seem special in any way, unlike August, the month of the next quarter day—Lammas. It does not surface in the most formulaic reference, though. The month of November recurs in the documents because this is the time of the annual celebration of Martinmas, which was the fourth quarter day (see the discussion of Type P1b in section 9.3).

Reference to people was also prominent in the late fifteenth century. Participants in inheritance matters would typically be referred to with lexical bundles in (13) and (14).

(13) {6g} son and apperand air to ye
(14) {6g–7g} (to) ye langar lefar of thaim (twa)
(15) {6g–8g} (balze) (in) that tyme and than (incontenent) (ye) (said) (balze)

The bundle in (15) shows the involvement of the bailies in the court proceedings, and a formulaic way of talking about the sequence of their activities. Especially interesting are the time adverbials: 'in that time' gives a hint of the temporary nature of the official post of the bailie, and the reference to when another action was taken—*than incontinent* 'then immediately'—adds to the legal narrative by repeating the idea of a sequence twice.

Similarly to Wigtown in the sixteenth century, see (30) below, the burgh court of Newburgh was typically referred to by means of a long formulaic string somewhat earlier (16). We can also assume, judging on the basis of the repetitive sequence, that the proceedings typically took place in a chapel and not in a tolbooth, as would be the case in the majority of burghs (section 6.4.2).

(16) {6g–8g} (ye) (borow) (curt) of ye newburch (haldin) (in) (ye) (chapel)
(17) {6g–7g} (erd) and stan in ye handis (of)
(18) {6g} of ye said landis with ye
(19) {6g} of ye vsuale mone of scotland

Other referential bundles continued the patterns identified in shorter bundles (section 11.3.1), for example, in reference to the lump of earth and stone presented as a ritual token in land transactions (17), the reference to lands together with a cohesive premodifier *said* (18), and the full phrase making a link to the Scottish currency (19).

When it comes to textual bundles, one long *n*-gram exhibits stable employment in late fifteenth-century texts, (20).

(20) {6g–7g} (as) efter followis that is to (say) (that)

This bundle is built of two elements: 'as follows thereafter', which is both an example of a defining phrase and a cohesive link to forthcoming discourse, and 'that is to say that', which aims to clarify an earlier proposition, see section 11.3.2.5 for a separate discussion of both strings. The tendency to combine these two potentially separate expressions was present in late fifteenth-century texts.

The final group of long formulaic bundles at that time is interactional bundles. As explained in section 11.3.3.2, to *gif for dome* meant 'to pass judgement, to state', so this bundle can be qualified as a representative (21).

(21) {6g} and that was giffin for dome

It is worth noting the standardizing passive construction, typical of legal discourse, as well as the coordinating device *and*, which must have always linked that final phrase to the rest of the document.

There are also two standardizing declaratives, concerning the admission of new burgesses (22) (section 6.3), and the official calling of suits (23) (for the discussion of shorter paradigmatic overlaps, see section 11.3.3.3).

(22) {6g–7g} (item) that ilk day was maid (burges)
(23) {6g–8g} (ye) (quhilk) day ye sutis callit (ye) (curt)

The relative pronoun *quhilk*, preceded by the definite article, also acts like a textual cohesive device, as it connects to the previously mentioned date. Similarly, another interactive bundle, the commissive in (24), also refers to an earlier situation commented on in the records.

(24) {6g–8g} (in) witnes of ye quhilk thing to (thir)

In fact, this expression first became popular in the earlier part of the corpus, see (5), but it was retained by the scribes and rose in frequency again in the late fifteenth century.

The final standardizing pattern, found among long bundles, expresses deontic modality directed at somebody who is to be punished with a fine (25). A shorter version of this bundle has been discussed in section 11.3.3.5 in the context of other bundles which carry obligation.

(25) {6g} and sal pay for his fredom

Nevertheless, in a longer format we only find the bundle to do with payment.

12.2.4. LONG LEXICAL BUNDLES—THE EARLY SIXTEENTH CENTURY

The second group among long formulaic bundles with an increase in popularity are those which experienced a growing trend towards the end of the studied period, between 1500 and 1560. At that time, even at first sight, one can notice growth in the sheer number of formulaic types (Fig. 12.1). Some themes remained but changed the wording (e.g. the reference to date). In some bundles new topics came to the fore, mostly enhancing the institutional character of legal discourse. The most striking formulaic sequence is the specification of the challenge set against a wrong-doer in a burgh court, especially for the appropriation of somebody's possessions, very often a simple theft. In fact, the pronoun reference indicates that the victims were of both sexes; however, men feature more prominently in the records (cf. 26a and 26b).

(26) a. {6g–8g} (chalans) (for) ye wrangus haldin fra (him) (of) (ane)
b. {6g–8g} (chalans) (for) ye wrangus haldin fra hir (of)

The formulaic, stable pattern combines two types of action—the legal action of bringing a case to court (*chalans*), and the action deemed as wrongful by the law. Separately, both of them emerge as shorter bundles discussed in section 11.3.1f; however, there are more options as to the types of misconduct which recur in the documents. In the long recurrent versions, only *ye wrangus haldin*, the illegal 'keeping' or 'stealing', combines frequently enough with *chalans for* to enter the most formulaic pool. Structurally speaking, these fixed strings are made of nominal elements, also within prepositional phrases. What is interesting is that the formulaic string finishes with a preposition—an indication of yet another nominal complement, which, nevertheless, does not recur. This potential nominal complement is of a more varied kind because various possessions may have undergone *ye wrangus haldin*.

The reference to date had changed in the course of time. Apart from the obvious update of the century digit (27), in the sixteenth century the preferred formula referred to 'God' (28), and not 'our lord', as used to be the case (1). The two months which featured most prominently in the records of the time were February and May (28), both of which correlate with quarter days and dates of head courts discussed in section 7.3.2 and above.

(27) {6g–8g} (ye) (yhere) of god a thousande (v) (hundereth) (and)
(28) {6g} of februar ye yhere of god, {6g} of may ye yhere of god

The reference to the month of May was also found in formulaic strings in the earlier records (3), but it forms a stable combination with 'the year of God' only in the sixteenth century. As discussed above, here too the most frequently repeated fragments of the date are strings of nominal and prepositional phrases.

Reference to the place of the proceedings, and specifically to the tolbooth (sections 6.2 and 6.4.2), acquires a fixed character in the texts (29).[1] The extended version of the bundle *haldin in ye tolbuth of ye* 'held in the tolbooth of the' continues into a syntactic possessive frame *of ye samyn* 'of the same', which fulfils the role of a textual cohesive device (on short cohesive lexical bundles, see section 11.3.2). The proceedings were held in the tolbooth of a given burgh, whose name must have been mentioned before in the text. Anaphoric reference had to be realized in a periphrastic manner, by means of analytic constructions, because at the beginning of the sixteenth century the possessive pronoun *its* had not yet appeared in Scots (Bugaj 2006b).

(29) {6g–8g} (haldin) (in) (ye) tolbuth of ye (samyn) (be)

This standardizing sequence consists of a past participle and a string of prepositional phrases. Again, the preceding finite copula is missing, which suggests several possibilities of introducing the bundle: "is haldin", "was haldin", "to be haldin", "will be haldin", and so on. Shorter recurrent strings indicate, though, that the verbal character of this long bundle is misleading because the most frequent context for *haldin* is a nominal phrase post-modified by this past participle, as in *curt of wigtoun haldin* (section 11.3.1g). The form *haldin* originates in a verb, but in this longer context it becomes identifiable as a predicative adjective (see the discussion of Type V1 constructions in section 9.4).

One burgh turns out to be a local centre of formulaic legal writing at the beginning of the sixteenth century. The Wigtown Burgh Court Book, incorporated into the corpus material, as presented in section 8.2, shows a picture of idiosyncratic yet very formulaic usage. In (30), explicit reference to the burgh of Wigtown is made, and it is so fixed and so frequent that it has made it to the top pool of all most formulaic 6- and 7-grams in the sixteenth-century part of the whole corpus.

(30) {6g–7g} (ye) borow curt of wigtoun haldin (in) (ye)

As the texts from Wigtown constitute a large part of the sixteenth-century time-frame in the corpus, their striking formulaicity may be the effect of corpus composition. However, texts from elsewhere constitute another half of the material from the sixteenth century (1501–1560: WgtCtBk 77,640—other texts 75,462; see the word counts in section 8.2). It would then be possible for other place names to surface in the top lexical bundles, too. And surface they do (e.g. Peebles or Newburgh) but in earlier time-frames. This is an indication of the especially formulaic nature of the Wigtown material, which indeed gets confirmation in the regional spread of the bundles (section 12.3).

The sixteenth century also marks a more rigid formulation of the openings involving a binomial expression *statut and ordanit* 'stated and ordained', in (31). A longer bundle provides a standardized context for the binomial; it turns out that it was typically introduced by the adverbial *item* (on its textual function, see section 11.3.2.3) and a dummy subject with the copula verb. The binomial introduces a relative clause, whose subject is most often defined with the definite article. It was to be expected that the nominal phrase, which should follow, would contain diverse content and would not become part of a long standardized sequence.

(31) {6g–7g} (item) (it) is statut and ordanit (that) (ye)

From the functional angle, this standardizing bundle is a directive. As pointed out in section 11.3.3.1, some directives are built of two elements: the performative verb and the proposition—the actual command. In short bundles, one order was recurrent enough to enter the pool of formulaic 3- to 5-grams—*sal pay for his fredom*. In longer strings only the beginning of the directive expression enters the path of textual standardization and may be found in a larger number of texts in an unchanged form, to be completed with a variety of possible continuations.

Another binomial expression which rises in popularity at the beginning of the sixteenth century is (32):

(32) {6g} efter ye form anformed tenour of

This binomial construction refers to the authority of a textual legal instrument, which stems from its form and meaning (*tenour*). Throughout Chapter 2, I presented the reasons why form in legal texts is so important. Stability of form assured the same, unaltered readings and evoked trust in the text. It also continued the oral, mnemonic residue of early legal codes in the new, institutionalized setting. One could always refer to the 'form and tenour' of legal texts in need of formal support for one's legal actions. It is worth pointing out that this bundle is another example of a long standardizing string with a binomial expression in the centre (cf. (6) and (31) above).

Other discourse fragments, connected with the institutionalization of legal discourse, also feature in the top range of standardizing expressions.

(33) {6g–8g} (yheris) (ye) (sutis) (callit) ye curt (effermit) (and) (absentis) (demyt) (in)
(34) {6g–7g} (triis) callit nocht comperit and this (ye)
(35) {6g} oft tymis callit and nocht comperit

Examples (33)–(35) list fragments which can be found at the beginning of burgh court proceedings: the suits were called, the court was fenced (*effermit*), the absences were noted (*demyt*). The passage usually continues with *amerciamentis*, or fines for being absent at court (section 7.3.4). On the whole, (33) is an interactional bundle and it marries two specific functions: the declarative and the representative (see sections 11.3.3.2 and 11.3.3.3 for the shorter paradigmatic overlaps of the same bundle). The part "the suits were called" is a reported version of how the court proceedings were declared open. In the discussion of shorter bundles, it emerged that this specific declaration could be followed by another declarative—that the suits were entered (or not) into a formal act—*(nocht) comperit*. However, this combination does not repeat often enough within some longer unchangeable context. On the contrary, the opening formula which makes reference to *curia firmata* recurs as a 6-gram: *ye sutis callit ye curt effermit* "the suits were called and the court was fenced (affirmed)" (183 tokens in 168 files, FF = 71), which is expanded even further with reference to the absentees (33). What draws attention from the structural side is the missing copula *be* in the passive, which may be taken to represent a certain structural shortcut, eliminating the verbal props and leaving the nominal contents. Another intriguing ingredient of this string of overlapping formulaic bundles is the word *yheris*, appearing before the formulaic opening of the proceedings. This is the final part of the date reference, for example "the year of our lord one thousand four hundred thirty and five *yheris*".[2] A bundle search within the top formulaic pool does not reveal the left-hand context for "years" but clearly shows—due to the elimination of the punctuation marks—that to the right this particular word formed a formulaic string with "the suits". It is thus possible to establish that the typical pattern of a medieval Scots legal or administrative document started with date reference (with a large degree of formulaicity, too, see (1)–(3) and (27)–(28) above) and was followed by a formal declaration of opening the court proceedings. Among less stable patterns, one finds the left-hand context for *yheris*—this word is most often found in a frame *and* + NUM + *yheris* (e.g. *and fif yheris*), which confirms the date interpretation.

The bundles in (34) and (35) show another frequent phrasing which reflects court reality—that the lawsuits were often continued for a longer period of time. The word *comperit* in this context means 'was put down as a formal act' (*DSL*, *compere* v[2], 1. 'to appear, put in appearance, as a formal act, esp. in a court of justice'). What draws attention is the fact that reference to the third calling of a given lawsuit was formulaic enough to be extracted from the corpus, even though there were even up to four sessions before the burgess was severely punished for non-appearance (section 7.3.4). Another adverbial, *oft tymis* in (35), is less specific but it also indicates multiple entries of the same case in a medieval burgh court. All the long bundles in (33)–(35) have a verb in the past participle form as their core element. To build a string as long as eleven consecutive elements, see (33), coordination was necessary. The clerks stacked paratactic elliptical clauses (note that the copula is missing again) and repeated the same format in many documents. From a functional angle, these strings all perform declarations (cf. section 11.3.3.3).

Often at the end of these formulae one could find a closing statement, which also grew in popularity in the sixteenth century:

(36) {6g} and this is ye first curt

This 6-gram is a conflation of shorter formulaic fragments (section 11.3.2.3). For example, *and this is* could well introduce other nominal phrases, as in *and this is ye first day* (27 tokens in 17 texts), *and this is ye sicunt curt* (20 tokens in 19 texts), *and this is ye tyrd curt* (12 tokens in 12 texts). However, only the pronouncement of the first court emerges in a longer formulaic string, adding to the most conventional narrative of the court proceedings.

The entry in the documents continued then in a customary way, which is visible in an overlapping formulaic 6-gram, spreading across sentence boundaries.

(37) {6g} ye first curt ye samyn day

The last part of the bundle in (37) is the beginning of another entry in the records. The popularity of this initializing 3-gram can be supported with evidence from the corpus; *ye samyn day* is, in fact, the number one formulaic bundle of its length (1,655 tokens in 485 files, FF = 99, see also section 9.2). However its apparent connection with the closing words of *ye first curt* would have remained unknown, had the present methodology not been used. Thanks to eliminating the punctuation marks and treating the corpus as a running text, it was possible to fish out such formulaic groupings. Their presence points to textual coherence in legal discourse, which can be achieved by repeating the same pattern of sentence endings and subsequent beginnings.

12.2.5. GENERAL PATTERNS

The presentation of the longest recurrent bundles emerging in EdHeW allows us to make several conclusions. First of all, the sheer numeric counts should be considered. In the corpus comprising c. 0.6 million words, stable combinations of six and more lexical elements can be found in impressive quantities. As summarized in Table 12.1, Scottish scribes and notaries produced identical 6-element strings about 19,000 times, and 8-element strings over 7,000 times, with parameters of lexical bundle extraction set to ten (or more) tokens in ten (or more) files. The most formulaic of these strings fall into 72 types for 6-grams, 50 types for 7-grams, and 32 types for 8-grams, which opens an intriguing possibility of investigating the meanings and functions of these long unchanging strings in early legal discourse, and allows us to draw conclusions about the areas of textual standardization. As the corpus material covers more than one century, the decision was taken to concentrate also on the diachronic trends in the formation of long formulaic strings. The normalized counts for individual bundle lengths per period show that the most formulaic 6- to 8-grams were present throughout with a more or less equal frequency, with a slight preference for the shorter bundles in the sixteenth century (Fig. 12.1). We should not forget, however, that these strings overlap with one another extensively, and often contribute in an overlapping fashion to still longer, stable lexico-grammatical arrangements.

At the beginning of this chapter, Figure 12.1 also indicated two moments when long bundles were repeated in the records the most: the early fifteenth and the early sixteenth centuries. The first peak was due to very formulaic and stable reference to the date of the document—a practice which did not continue with as much uniformity in the rest of the corpus. The second peak marks the growing recurrent use of long bundles in various contexts, as illustrated in section 12.2.4 above. This situation may be taken to imply that early documents followed formularies to some extent but not always to the letter.

Structurally speaking, the long bundles which contribute towards textual standardization are typically built of nominal and prepositional phrase fragments, which continues the trend observed in short repetitive chunks (section 9.6). The investigation shows the large extent of nominalization in early medieval legal discourse and a tendency to stack prepositional phrases one after another, often with an indication of yet another prepositional phrase to follow, whose varied content did not allow for textual standardization, as in *haldin in ye tolbuth of ye samyn be* (29). Other bundles with a series of prepositional phrases were presented in (3–5), (10–12), (16–19), (24), (26–30). These and other extended bundles, discussed in this chapter, were used in exactly the same wording throughout the corpus.

The third observation concerns the functional value of the longest standardizing bundles. The majority of the long strings are referential, which was to be expected on the basis of their structure (for the connection between functions and structural types, see Fig. 11.7). The points of reference may change but the tendency to convey this specific function by means of a standardized sequence remains, as is the case with dates, people, objects, and places in the whole material. There were single examples of textual bundles in a long standardized format, especially those which introduced clarification (20) and those which involved intertextual connections (32). When it comes to interactional bundles, at the beginning just two long standardized strings carried this function in the form of a directive and a commissive speech act: (4–5). In time, more interactional bundles developed a stable format, for example, the directive in (31), or the declaratives in (33–35).

MAP 2 Dialectal areas, based on Robinson (1985: xxxi–xxxii)

12.3. Emergent Standardizing Patterns: The Diatopic Dimension

Meurman-Solin has pointed out that "[l]egal texts, especially public documents, usually offer good *prima facie* evidence for localization 'in space'" (2004a: 31). Due to the fact that the texts in the corpus were tagged for county of compilation as a part of the *Linguistic Atlas of Older Scots* (Williamson 2008), the popularity of a given bundle in specific regions can be traced. Scotland is typically divided into seven dialectal areas: Orkneys and Shetlands (only the former present in the corpus), northern, north-eastern, mid-eastern, mid-western, mid-southern, and southern regions (Robinson 1985: xxxi–xxxii, see also Johnston 1997: 55–63), with thirty counties submitting texts for the EdHeW corpus. The boundaries of the dialectal areas (Map 2) may be compared with Map 1 in Chapter 5, which illustrated the location of royal burghs throughout the kingdom.

Discrepancies in word count available from each area in EdHeW are substantial—from just over 1,200 words from Orkney, to over 304,000 words from the mid-east. These are much larger gaps than in the case of chronological subdivisions (cf. Fig. 8.1), where this problem could be overcome by normalization of counts per 10,000 words. Here, even if individual bundle counts were normalized, it would be ineffective to look for quantitative comparisons between regions. What is feasible, though, is a qualitative analysis of the presence of a given bundle in the texts written in a specific area. As in the rest of the chapter, the bundles I examined from the diatopic angle came from the top of the formulaicity scale—they showed most fixedness and repetition throughout the corpus.

It is natural to assume that the Scottish Lowlands, especially the mid-east, will be the centre of textual standardization, for the historical and political reasons described in Part Two. This is a place where urbanization was most rampant and where the most ancient and most developed burghs were based (sections 5.2–5.4). It includes the county of Fife and crucial centres of trade with the Continent, as well as the first university town—St Andrews. The mid-east also incorporates Peeblesshire with one of the most important market centres in Peebles, Perthshire with the traditional coronation venue at Scone, and one of the richest burghs, Perth. It also includes the strategically important Stirlingshire and Berwickshire. Edinburgh in Midlothian rose in importance throughout the fourteenth century (Fox 1983: 83) and enjoyed a dominant status since at least James III's times (section 5.4.4). It was a "magnet for people looking for work" (Sanderson 2002: 178), and the centre of legal activity in the kingdom (Finlay 2000: 96); this is where the kingdom's capital was ultimately based. The mid-east was where parliaments typically gathered (e.g. in Edinburgh, Stirling, and Perth) (see Map 1), where the administration for the whole kingdom was centred, and where the medieval peripatetic Scottish court would sojourn most typically and carry out judicial duties, as well as other activities (Wormald 1981: 24).

From a general linguistic angle, several scholars have pointed out the apparent uniformity in Middle Scots texts (Macafee 1989: 429; Agutter 1990: 1). Even though Görlach (2002: 181 n. 4) talks about the beginning of Edinburgh norms after 1500 as a characteristic development in Scotland before the Reformation, the norms may not have been fully formed yet, at least not on the graphophonemic level of personal genres, such as correspondence (Meurman-Solin 2000a: 251). Studies of uniform usage in Scots on other levels of language and on the basis of other genres are still to be written. When it comes to legal writing, the prestigious mid-central region could provide a forum for sharing and maintaining the textual patterns and norms, for example, by the professional community of burgh clerks and notaries. It remains to be examined below whether the regional distribution of the most formulaic lexical bundles supports this assumption.

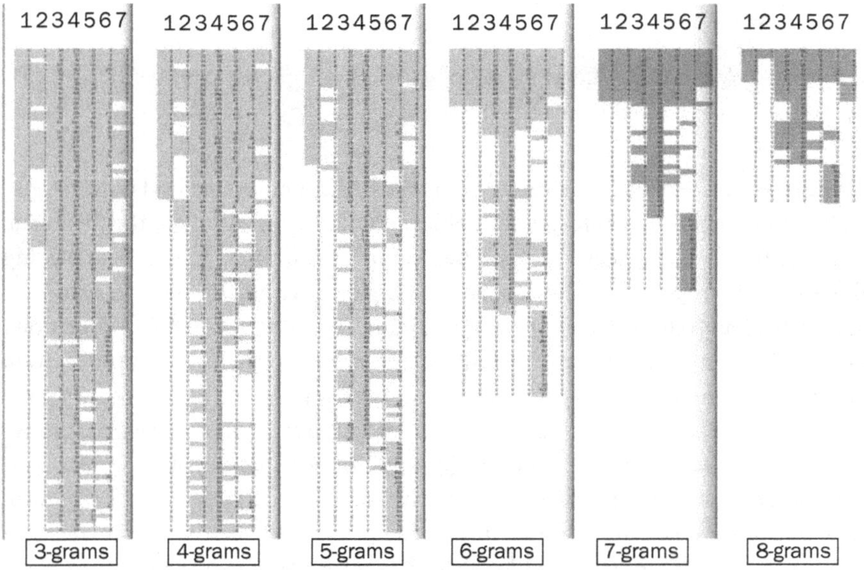

FIGURE 12.2 Geographical distribution of the top 100 *n*-grams in EdHeW (1—Orkneys, 2—North, 3—North-East, 4—Mid-East, 5—Mid-West, 6—Mid-South, 7—South)

In Figure 12.2 all bundle lengths have been presented together according to their employment in specific regions, marked with numbers from 1 to 7. The grey cells indicate that a bundle did appear in texts from a given area. Because shorter bundles are much more numerous, the chart includes the top 100 formulaic bundles from 3- to 5-grams, and the top 10% of 6- to 8-grams.

The figure shows that several bundles were present everywhere—this is the top grey range of the charts. Burgh clerks and notaries in at least six, and most often in all seven regions, used the following *n*-grams (with overlaps):

- referential

(38) {3g–4g} (ye) xxti day (of), {3g–5g} (day) of ye (monath) (of), {3g–7g} (ye) yhere of (god) (a) (thousande) (four), {3g–8g} (ye) (yhere) of oure (lord) (a) (thousande) (four) (hundereth)

(39) {3g–4g} (in) tyme to (cum)

(40) {3g} all and sindry, {3g} befor thir witnes, {3g} executouris and assignais, {3g–5g} (oure) souerain lord (ye) (king)

(41) {3g} ye said william, {3g} ye said robert, {3g} ye said lord

(42) {3g–4g} (of) ye said landis (and), {3g–5g} (of) (vsuale) mone of (scotland)

(43) {3g} for all ye

- textual

(44) {3g} of ye said, {3g} be ye said, {3g} to ye said

(45) {4g} that is to say

- interactional

(46) {3g–8g} (it) (kend) til all men (be) (thir) (present) (letteris) (me/ws)
(47) {5g} (in) witnes of ye quhilk thing

These repetitive sequences extracted using the lexical bundle method indicate special requirements and characteristics of legal discourse. First of all, the formulaic shape of the date (38) seems to have been employed by all clerks, as was placing the text in time (39). Typical discourse participants (witnesses, assignees, and the authorities) are referred to in a uniform manner (40), while textually embedded personal reference points to recurrent names in all regions (41). Another group of bundles recurring all over Scotland are references to objects featuring in legal transactions (42). One also notices the formulaic character of prepositional phrase fragments, or at least their beginnings (43–44). These short recurrent strings convey the general characteristics of formal written discourse (e.g. the important function of prepositional phrases in providing links between nominal constituents). Similarly, all the clerks employ a clarification device (45) to safeguard against possible comprehension problems. The most formulaic interactional bundle, present in documents all over the country, is (46)—a directive required to establish the force of the document, with a meta-reference to itself, see the discussion in (4). The final bundle popular among all notaries and scribes is (47), which commits the participants to witnessing a legal act, most probably the actual event rather than the document itself.

Sorted by regions, the most formulaic 3-grams are spread more or less evenly across the whole corpus (saving the smallest samples from Orkney and the north, Columns 1–2, Fig. 12.2). From 4-grams upwards the situation starts changing and the position of the mid-eastern region becomes more pronounced, supporting the earlier assumption. The graphs show the largest degree of formulaicity in the texts from that region (Column 4)—the most formulaic bundles which have been found in the corpus originate there, and may or may not have been used elsewhere. Thus, the mid-east comes across as the centre of textual standardization in medieval legal Scots. Given the similar background of the early men of law (section 7.4) and the contacts between burgh officials and inhabitants (section 6.5), it is possible that some of these typical ways of phrasing the documents would permeate to other regions. In every location, after all, the same situations were becoming part of legal discourse: land and property transfer, everyday misconduct of the burgesses, some more serious crimes, new laws and regulations, and so on. The records and documents needed to have the same force around the country. Even if the same meanings were not expressed in exactly the same wording everywhere, it did not undermine the validity of the documents, which relied to a large extent on external factors. However, the unification of procedures must have been a welcome trend. One may imagine an itinerant notary, travelling on the job throughout Scotland (Finlay 2009: 405–407), bringing his way of structuring the documents—within the limits of the Latin tradition, of course—and his signature to new places. The convergence on a textual norm could add to the legal force of documents, enhancing their stability and trustworthiness. The employment of exactly the same wordings as used in the centre of administration and power (Fig. 12.2) could be found in several other locations, too. Unfortunately, due to the anglicizing trends at least from 1540s onwards (Devitt 1989: 17) and the eventual removal of Scots from public discourse, we can only speculate on how the vernacular language of legal documents in Scotland would have turned out.

In longer bundles, indicating a high degree of textual standardization, one more region starts to emerge as a centre of developing norms for legal texts. It is the mid-southern region (Column 6), with three important burghs: Dumfries, Wigtown, and Kirkcudbright. The texts compiled in Wigtown are filled with highly formulaic and highly repetitive bundles. Nevertheless, the choices of those clerks do not overlap with choices from other regions (Fig. 12.2). This fact can be accounted for by the special, rather isolated position of the Dumfries and Galloway region on the historical map of Scotland. For a long time, it had been a largely autonomous area, with linguistic influences from Scottish Gaelic and Old Norse (Bugaj 2004b). The Cheviot Hills may have constituted a natural geographic barrier between the south-west (or the dialectal mid-south) and the influential mid-east. Still, the most prominent reason for the textual separation of Wigtown scribes from the rest of the clerks could have been a political barrier. That area had been governed for centuries by the notorious Clan of Douglas, who used to voice their claims to the Scottish throne and conspire against the rule of the Stewarts (sections 5.4.1 and 5.4.6; also Barrell 2000: 161–170, 206–208; Fox 1983: 81). The existence of a separate legal tradition in Galloway could be gleaned from James I's efforts to introduce his legal reforms there (section 5.4.2). This instance of local autonomy may have encouraged individual interpretations of practice in legal text compilation in the early sixteenth century. The existence of a different centre of local standardizing practices than Edinburgh is not strange. Meurman-Solin has often pointed towards other urban norms, existing outside the influence of the metropolitan area (2000a, 2000b, 2004b), and suggested a potential rivalry between those local centres and the capital. The evidence drawn from the lexical bundles points in the same direction, although apart from the south-west, other areas do not exhibit a tendency to produce standardizing patterns out of their own accord.

12.4. Symptoms of Textual Standardization

Textual standardization has been linked in this book to the presence of recurrent lexical bundles, following the investigation of different bundle lengths and their behaviour in early legal documents from Scotland. As discussed in the previous

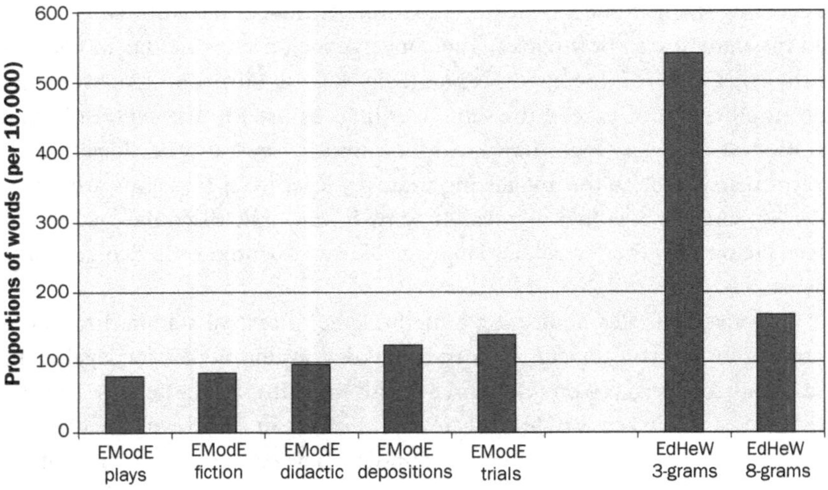

FIGURE 12.3 The comparison of formulaicity in five speech-related text types from Culpeper and Kytö (2010: 136) and the legal documents from EdHeW

chapters, bundle length is conversely proportionate to the number of formulaic types, which means that formulaic 3-grams are much more numerous in types than formulaic 8-grams (Table 8.4). One should nevertheless remember that the longer the bundle, the more difficult it was to create its exact copy in another text—they must not differ by any single word or even in the order of constituents. Thus, it is the longer bundles that point towards textual standardization, especially when they appear several tens of times in an unchanged form in a large number of texts from all over the country, or just in the hub of standardization—the mid-eastern region.

The question which can be posed at the end of these investigations is how formulaic Scots legal discourse was in general. Finding a point of reference to judge the level of formulaicity is difficult because such investigations into historical discourse have only just begun. Culpeper and Kytö (2010) measure the formulaicity of their text types using the proportion of words involved in the most frequent lexical bundles. They define formulaicity in the following manner: "[T]he greater the proportion of the words of a text-type belonging to fewer different lexical bundles the more formulaic that text-type is" (Culpeper and Kytö 2010: 135–136). I have employed Culpeper and Kytö's method[3] to gauge the formulaicity of EdHeW texts, which made it possible to draw comparisons with the profiles emerging from different studies. The results of the juxtaposition of the Scots language of the law and other text types from the history of English are presented in Figure 12.3.

This data presentation does not claim to draw any mutually dependent comparisons between the corpora because they have very different characteristics and it would be difficult to find a valid *tertium comparationis*. The graph simply shows a striking discrepancy between the speech-related English material and the texts from EdHeW in terms of formulaicity, measured with the same tools. Expressed by means of exactly the same formula, formulaicity in the legal texts from Scottish burghs, calculated on the basis of 3-grams, is at least four times greater; it is only with the longest bundles, the 8-grams, that the proportions of words used in the bundles start to become more similar, although the Scots material still scores higher. At first sight these results look too far removed. But when one considers the fact that the most frequent 3-gram in EModE trials, *do you know*, has a raw frequency of 182 tokens, and normalized frequency (per 10,000 words) of 7.2 (Culpeper and Kytö 2010: 116), and the most frequent 3-gram in EdHeW, *of ye said*, has a raw frequency of 2,157 tokens, and normalized frequency (per 10,000 words) of 37.5, then the bars in the chart become persuasive.

These results are the best confirmation of the repetitive and formulaic character of early legal documents. It is true that trials and depositions also belong to legal discourse but their interactive character allows for more variety nevertheless. The oral residue in notarial documents, burgh court records, and other texts from EdHeW is of a different kind: it goes back to mnemonic devices and ritualized solemnity. Another formulaicity booster is the fact that these texts had developed in the written format, aiming for the stability of expression, often on the basis of classical formularies, but also of local patterns, handed down from one professional to the next. All these aspects cause the amount of structural repetition in these texts to be truly remarkable. The findings also corroborate the choice of lexical bundles as a corpus tool fit to investigate textual standardization. Lexical bundles, and especially the long ones, comprising over six consecutive elements, capture the stable parts of text and reveal their socio-historical themes and functional characteristics. From these kernels of textual standardization, we can glean the importance of such extralinguistic aspects of legal discourse as the time-frame and location. Formulae referring to the participants also come to the fore, especially in the context of land transfer and inheritance matters. They all form part of the referential core of the documents and recur in large numbers in the corpus. Less numerous in types, but very formulaic and frequent in tokens, are bundles bearing connection to the interactive aspect of legal discourse, such as directive speech acts, the famous *be it kend til all men*... serving as the prime example of a standardizing chunk of early legal text. Standardization happens also in the purely textual domain, where providing cohesive links and defining the scope of propositions in a formulaic manner constructs the skeleton of legal discourse. Owing to the rich historical background sketched in Part Two of this book, it was now possible to interpret corpus data in relation to the social conditions and legal practices of medieval and early modern Scotland. The emerging standardizing patterns in the legal language of Scottish burghs have now been traced and contextualized, forming a coherent pragmaphilological picture of textual standardization in the legal domain.

PART THREE

General Conclusions

The study of standardizing patterns in legal documents from medieval and early modern Scotland proceeded from theoretical considerations and external background to the analysis of corpus data. Now we can reverse this structure and formulate general conclusions which follow from the empirical part of the book, in relation to the introductory discussion presented in Parts One and Two. It should be remembered that this book pays attention to written discourse and its specific nature. The majority of historical corpus studies have been exploring spoken features embedded in written texts, also in legal discourse. This project appreciates the fact that orality characterizes many social activities, including legal rituals from the past, and it may have left a residue in written texts, but at the same time our focus has been placed on the properties of the written language and its formulaicity. From this angle, the "bad" historical data does not seem so deficient. Single-register corpora, such as these comprising specialized texts, provide ample material for a rigorous study of historical discourse. In our case, the EdHeW compilation allowed us to investigate the degree of formulaicity and textual standardization in early Scottish legal and administrative writing.

The first major aim of the book was to identify standardizing patterns in historical legal texts. Drawing on the theoretical Part One, the conclusions formulated below will start with structural considerations and technical findings, paying due attention to the fresh insights into linguistic formulaicity and repetitiveness achieved through the analysis of EdHeW data. Then the discussion will move on to address the second research question raised in the Introduction: the relationship between the repetitive chunks of texts and textual standardization. The final comments will address the last aim of the book, which was to recognize and understand the connections between the language of early legal Scottish texts and the external conditions of their creation, illuminated by the extensive historical background presented in Part Two and reflected in the lexical bundles drawn from these texts.

There were two issues to consider when setting out to identify standardizing patterns: how to define standardization, and in what manner to extract chunks of text which answer to this definition. The distinction between language standardization and linguistic standardization, introduced in Chapter 3 effectively narrowed down the scope of the phenomenon in question. Standardization on the level of text is visible in the formal stability of recurrent strings and a high frequency of their occurrence in an unchanged form. The question of fixedness and repetition formed the core of Chapter 4, leading on to the selection of a corpus method which could identify such strings in an objective manner. The lexical bundles method, a new tool in historical linguistics, was borrowed from applied linguistics, specifically from research on recurrent chunks of spoken and written texts. Its application to the historical corpus of Scottish texts required a range of adjustments, reviewed in Chapter 8. The major technical problem facing corpus linguists who work with historical texts is the lack of standardized spelling. For artificial spelling unification of a complex corpus of early legal texts written in Scots, a combination of methods had to be used: from automatic generation of lists with all the spellings, through manual attribution of spelling variants to their headforms and compilation of a variant dictionary, to the final upload of the dictionary into the VARD program for automatic recognition and substitution of spelling variants. The texts were then ready for lexical bundle extraction. Lexical bundles of three to eight lexical elements were drawn from the EdHeW corpus by means of dedicated software, together with chronological and geographic information to enable further diachronic and diatopic analyses. Admittedly, extracting lexical bundles from modern corpora is a much more straightforward enterprise. In spite of certain methodological hurdles, the lexical bundles proved to be a transferable tool and rendered abundant and fascinating material which formed the core of the present study. The sheer amount of fixed lexical strings, even if compared against modern specialized corpora, was impressive and testified to the textual standardization and to a certain maturity of early Scots legal discourse.

With 3- to 8-grams extracted from the texts, the discussion could proceed to the analysis of structure and function of the most frequent and stable elements of text. In addition, I designed a formulaicity measure (FF), based on the frequency and textual spread of the bundles, to place every extracted lexical bundle on a scale of fixedness. The decision to consider short and long bundles separately helped to achieve a more focused picture of structural types: phrase fragments making up the shorter repetitive chunks on the one hand, and extended multi-phrasal fragments on the other, pointing towards the most conspicuous places in a legal document where the text becomes fixed and standardized. In Chapter 9, short lexical bundles showed that legal discourse is built of recurrent structural frames which may be filled with members of a given grammatical category, especially with nouns. The most abundant structural types were nominal and prepositional phrase fragments, which links to the informational style identified by Biber and his followers. In the bundles, I also observed the tendency to include an element of coordination, the coordinating conjunction *and*, employed to join phrases rather than clauses. This paratactic arrangement of phrases is a feature which indicates aiming for coherence within the texts under scrutiny, as well as all-inclusiveness and informational style of legal discourse.

Coordination was also observed in other structures. Lexical bundles extracted from EdHeW are objectively characterized by a large degree of recurrence in the corpus, and what is recurrent, is indispensable for a given type of texts. Previous studies of legal discourse considered binomials and multinomials (coordinated phrases made of members of the same grammatical category) to be such indispensable elements, so I expected to find them among the lexical bundles. Indeed, as discussed in Chapter 10, binomials and multinomials recur in early Scottish legal documents and their presence is motivated by stylistic, as well as semantic factors. Many binomials identified in EdHeW were culturally bound and very specific to the nature of the documents and their Scottish background. It is visible in a high incidence and high formulaicity scores of coordinated pairs stemming from specifically Scottish legal regulations and customs practised in the burghs, for example, *erd and stan*, *fraud or gile*, *airis and assignais*, *aldirman and balzies*, whose background was richly documented in Part Two of the book and will be given more space below.

From the functional perspective explored in Chapter 11, a striking degree of fixedness was found in the referential bundles, especially in reference to the date and place of document compilation and to the people involved in legal procedures. This fact makes the EdHeW material radically different than other incarnations of legal discourse, for example, depositions and trial proceedings, where the interpersonal functions come to the fore, as identified by Archer (2005), Kryk-Kastovsky (2006a), or Culpeper and Kytö (2010). Interestingly, on the basis of different lengths of lexical bundles, it was possible to observe the increasing formulaic character of interactional bundles towards the end of the period under study. I noted the correlation between structural types of lexical bundles and their functions, whereby referential bundles are typically made of nominal and prepositional phrase fragments, and interactive ones are made of verbal fragments. The same correlations can be postulated for any kind of discourse but more work is needed on the structural characteristics of the textual function. In the discussion, I also drew attention to changing preferences in selected bundles performing the same discourse function, for instance, a date reference or a directive speech act, which would not have been possible to observe without the automatic extraction of repetitive chunks of discourse. Indeed, lexical bundles should prove helpful in function-to-form mappings—one of the two trends in diachronic pragmatics identified by Jacobs and Jucker (1995), usually shunned by historical pragmaticians. It is less problematic to start one's research with a given linguistic form and trace its functions through time (form-to-function mapping) than to look for all exponents of a given linguistic function and consider the changing forms through which it could be carried. Lexical bundles reveal the most important functional elements in discourse, leaving room for the scholar to interpret the linguistic means which express a given conspicuous function.

The data discussion concluded in Chapter 12 with symptoms of textual standardization found in the long bundles in EdHeW. There was a considerable degree of overlap between the longest extracted bundles. All of them showed a numeric increase towards the sixteenth century, which I interpreted as a standardizing tendency of legal documents in Scotland at that time. There were two frequency peaks, which could be due to the external conditions of the production of legal texts elucidated in Part Two: first, a stable reference to the date of the document, established as a standard procedure on the wave of legal reforms in the early fifteenth century, and second, the appearance of standardizing bundles in more contexts towards the sixteenth century. Apart from the diachronic dimension, it was also possible to trace symptoms of standardization diatopically, thanks to the geographical tagging of EdHeW files and special settings of the dedicated software. The expected influential position of the mid-east, with Edinburgh and other important burghs, was confirmed. Nevertheless, another area of potentially standardizing usage was identified in Galloway, signalling a degree of separation of that area from the rest of the kingdom, which finds support in the historical context. In general, the burghs have come forth as venues both for language standardization, through the promotion of the vernacular in official contexts, and for linguistic standardization, as visible in the stable repetitive fragments of legal and administrative texts.

It is through the historical background, discussed in detail in Part Two, that this book provides the indispensable contextual framework for data analysis: from the historical circumstances in which early urban centres grew, through their social organization and conditions of living, to the unique Scots legal tradition and its institutions in the burghs, and finally to the texts—the legal documents and the specialized discourse community of their compilers. Thus, the study has offered a fresh and comprehensive perspective on the language of a unique legal tradition in a British and European context. The Scottish dimension did not use to be very conspicuous in the general discussion of the language of the law in the Anglo-Saxon world, let alone from a historical angle. This picture is currently being revised, also in view of the present-day developments in the language of the Scottish Parliament, which regained its independent status after the devolution referendum in 1997. As one of the government documents has it, "[t]he establishment of the Scottish Parliament has presented an opportunity for divergence in the style of Scottish legislation" (Office of the Scottish Parliamentary Counsel 2006: Chapter 2), a conscious linguistic effort which goes hand in hand with the Plain Language movement (Williams 2011: 141–142). The official language of law and administration in today's Scotland is, of course, English, but the Scots residue of the past remains conspicuous. For instance, one of the language features currently in decline is the cohesive modifier *said* (Williams 2007: 112–113), so vividly present in the EdHeW lexical bundles (see especially Chapters 9 and 11).

The historical investigation offered in the present study creates a solid backdrop for today's developments and allows for a better grasp of the specific Scottish legal discourse. Due attention has been given to the external conditions which influenced Scots law and its language in their formative stages. Shaped within the parameter of continental civil law influence, and at the same time sensitive to legal requirements of feudalism, Scots legal practice developed its own procedural and linguistic traditions. The relationships between people were captured in documents such as bonds of manrent, marriage contracts, or other notarial instruments, carefully crafted and filled with formulaic expressions, for instance, *be it kend til all men be thir present letteris*, or *I sal be lele and trew* (see the specific examples in Chapters 9–12). The context of medieval and early modern Scottish burghs (Chapters 5–6) brought explanation to the recurrent stable references to various actors in legal discourse: the bailies, the community, the testators, and assignees. In fact, the abundance of lexical bundles connected with land transfer and inheritance can only be fully understood in view of the preoccupation of medieval Scots with land as the token of status and burgess-ship, and a source of financial security. The elaborate land-transfer rituals, which continued the pre-chirographic forms of legal proceedings, have been captured in such formulaic expressions as *in ye handis of* or the binomial *erd and stan*. On closer inspection, one begins to notice the Germanic character of Scottish legal discourse reflected in the vernacular legal formulae. The verbs *ken* 'know', or *bruke* 'enjoy', the nouns *scaith* 'damage' or *scot and lot* 'financial contribution', or even the most common modifier *said*, as in 'of the said lord', all reflect the indigenous legal culture and make up the most recurrent and stable fragments of text.

It is not to say, however, that Scottish legal discourse was free of foreign touch. Quite the contrary. Continental influences, and especially the impact of Latin through civil codes and canon law, together with drafting traditions and educational channels, can be seen in the etymologies of typically Scottish legal expressions in the corpus. By this token, terms such as *effermit* 'confirmed, fenced (about a court)', *comperit* 'put down as a formal act', *incontenent* 'at once', or *dampnage* 'damage, injury', testify to the separate history of language contact and legal transmission in Scotland, adding to the common pool of Romance vocabulary which had entered both English and Scots. Notaries and clerks, responsible for the vocabulary choices and linguistic patterns emerging from the records, appear to the modern eye as a special type of a professional community who had been trained to conform to specific discourse rules and traditions, and who could be trusted with important documentary tasks. Working within a peculiar milieu of a Scottish burgh, they created, disseminated, and stored legal and administrative texts full of stable lexico-syntactic patterns, and in this manner contributed to the textual standardization in progress.

The interdisciplinary character of this book allowed for establishing the connection between the language of the law and the external conditions in which it was produced. It would be interesting to carry out similar research on English data, or, indeed, on any other historical corpus of legal texts, which become increasingly available in the digital format. This project also opens a forum for methodologically compatible studies of other specialized discourse areas, in order to achieve a larger picture of formulaicity in various communicative contexts. It should become a more frequent practice to answer the requirements of interdisciplinary research in a thorough manner, and to delve deeper into the context of language use by engaging with historical primary sources and critical analyses. Such are also the requirements of pragmaphilology, the study of language use in historical context. Only then can electronic compilations of historical texts become windows onto the societies of the past and enable us to understand their specific linguistic practices and choices of the writers more profoundly.

NOTES

Chapter 1

1. In fact, Brinton listed "fixed phrases and clauses" (2001: 144) as a potential area of interest for historical discourse analysis proper.

2. The genetic status of Pictish has not yet been established in a satisfactory manner (Price 2000).

3. The most important earlier sources on the history of Scots include Templeton (1973), Murison (1979), Aitken (1979), Romaine (1983), and Aitken's historical introduction to the *Concise Scots Dictionary* (Aitken 1985). Since the detailed overview of English in Scotland by McClure (1994), the most comprehensive linguistic description of Older Scots was compiled by the contributors to the *Edinburgh History of Older Scots* (Jones 1997). Recently, several general publications on Older and Modern Scots have appeared, including Görlach (2002), who offers a history of the language observed through its employment in different text types and genres; a historical and linguistic outline of Scots in the long-awaited final volume of the *Dictionary of the Older Scottish Tongue* (Macafee and Aitken 2002); Jones (2002) with an overview of Modern Scots sounds, grammar, and usage; and Corbett, McClure, and Stuart-Smith (2003), who give a useful introduction to Older and Modern Scots on the most important levels of linguistic analysis, as well as from selected extralinguistic angles. For a critical view on the last forty years of discourse concerning the history and status of Scots, see Costa (2009). Scots also features in several edited collections on regional varieties of the British Isles and on the history of English, for example Smith (2000) and Millar (2012).

4. The term *nation* applies here to "a self-aware ethnic group" (Connor 1978: 388), a community which draws this common awareness from tradition, history, and experience even without immediate mutual contacts between all members, as in Anderson's *imagined community* (1991). For this self-aware grouping, Millar adds the "belief in their right and ability to govern themselves" (2005: 28), which fits the situation in medieval Scotland at least from the Wars of Independence of the late thirteenth–early fourteenth century.

Chapter 2

1. See the classic case for the independent nature of writing and the study of written texts in Romaine (1982: 14–21).

2. For an overview of research on courtroom discourse, see Doty (2010). The "bad data" problem, flagged up by Labov (1972a: 100), will be addressed in a separate discussion on historical corpus studies in section 3.7.

3. As Ong ([1982] 2002: 2) points out, humans developed literacy relatively recently (around 6,000 years ago), which makes the 30,000–50,000 years of the history of *Homo*

sapiens exclusively gestural and oral. What is more, "of all the many thousands of languages—possibly tens of thousands—spoken in the course of human history only around 106 have ever been committed to writing to a degree sufficient to have produced literature, and most have never been written at all" (Ong ([1982] 2002: 7). We should bear this observation in mind in the context of legal traditions other than Western European, to which Scots law belongs.

4. Rituals did not have to rely on oral transmission and may have appeared earlier than the oral stage. Evidence from Neanderthal behaviour shows that ritual was possible without speech, which suggests that ritualistic behaviour is older than speech and not directly dependent on it (Danet 1997: 20). Bax (2010) provides the most recent overview of approaches to the study of ritual behaviour, also from a discourse-related and pragmatic perspective, and to the forms and functions of ritual. He concedes that in order to investigate historical rituals, one "needs to fall back on indirect sources" such as "written historical documents" (2010: 506).

5. See Stock (1983: 46–47) on the use of writing in the laws of the continental Germanic tribes in the fifth and sixth centuries.

6. On the interplay of literacy and traditional oral cultures outside Europe, see Goody (1968). In each geographical context, the contact with European colonists had a significant impact on oral cultures. For instance in New Zealand, the shift from oral to written (and printed) was very abrupt and loaded with missionary ideology (McKenzie 1985). The binary opposition of orality and literacy, and the implied superiority of the latter, has evoked criticism (e.g. in Teuton 2010). It is worth noting that in some parts of the world today there are still societies where the oral culture predominates, for example, in Africa (see e.g. Finnegan 1976) or south-east Asia and Oceania (Kemp 2004).

7. There were more curses in wills and land grants than in royal writs, the latter being more declarative than performative (Danet 1997: 27–28). The connection between words and magic reflects the orality of language, its dynamism, and performative nature (see Ong [1982] 2002: 32).

8. For more information on canon law as a vehicle for the Roman law in Scotland, see Robertson (1997); see also Helmholz (2008: 388, 391) on the import of canon law books to Scotland and England.

9. "In England, the printing of the law began in the 1480s with a relatively unknown printer, W. de Machlinia" (Collins and Skover 1992: 530); then more famous names appear: Pynson, Rastell, and Thomas More. "Their first law books were printed in Latin and French, as the vernacular was not yet the official language of English law" (Collins and Skover 1992: 531), which changed with the publication of the acts of Parliament in 1485 in English, and the enhancement of English in legal domain during the Tudor reign. There is a need for comparative work on this issue in the context of England and Scotland, and the mutual contacts and influences. The recent chapter on legal printing (Baker 2008) from the Cambridge history of the book in Britain is very detailed on the situation in England but adds little to the picture of legal printing in Scotland.

10. For further outlooks on historical and contemporary LSP, see the *Linguistic Insights* series edited for Peter Lang by Maurizio Gotti.

11. In his preface to the Polish edition of Jakobson and Halle's *Fundamentals of Language* (1964), Zawadowski sees no conflict between structuralism and functionalism, as both schools approach language as a system. For a critical discussion of Firth's legacy in the work of other linguists, also in Halliday's writings, see Kachru (2006).

12. It is interesting that in other specialized genres the need for clarity does not or, indeed, must not lead to repetitive and wordy style. For example, in the experimental essay, the need to render the procedure and results of an experiment in a detailed and clear manner did not lead to verbosity and redundancy, unless the author wanted to shun the possibility of being too brief and therefore unclear in his exposition (see, for instance, Gotti 2001: 226–227). The authors of early experimental essays positioned their writings between ornamented prose of the literary kind and "a dull mode of expression", and neither of these styles was encouraged, as one sees in Robert Boyle's reflections on scientific writing (Gotti 2001: 229). Robert Boyle advocated the use of language understandable for a common reader, "so that everybody can decode the contents" (Gotti 2001: 230), which in the end contributed to the formation of a specialist community (on discourse communities, see Swales 1990 and section 3.6 below).

13. For some criticisms of the methodology employed in previous research into specialized texts, for instance, the number of linguistic features taken into consideration, the number of texts, the generic bias, see Conrad (2001).

14. After explaining how legal English became recognized and important worldwide, and by whom it was spread, Frade says: "One of the most powerful properties of legal English is the non-attribution of authorship of written documents (other than cases wherein authors are explicitly mentioned) such as legislation and contracts. Due to their frozen, formulaic, and conventionalized properties, such genres may seem somewhat anonymous pieces of writing, as there are no linguistic signs to indicate who really wrote them" (2007: 50). This feature of modern legal language sets it apart from its past incarnations; see the discussion below.

15. Other studies taking Mellinkoff's lists as a point of departure include Danet (1980), Charrow, Crandall, and Charrow (1982), Hiltunen (1990), Tiersma (1999), Maley (1994), Mattila (2006). For a succinct overview of the characteristics of legal language, see Kryk-Kastovsky (2006a: 164–167).

16. The Standard Corpus of Present-Day Edited American English included 1 million words and was compiled in the 1960s out of 500 samples of different genres, 2,000 words each (Finegan 1982: 117).

17. Binomials used by Shakespeare to create legal references include such expressions as *bargain and sale, hue and cry, watch and ward, fine and recovery* (Sokol and Sokol 2000: 22, 60, 69, 122, 137).

18. This statement evokes the notion of prototypical semantics (Rosch 1983) and "penumbra" (Hart 1961: 126)—the meaning of a word is clearer in typical contexts rather than in untypical ones.

19. Passive voice was also used for standardized procedures in other specialized discourse, such as the language of science (Gotti 2001: 233).

20. A study of legal hearsay within speech act theory is offered in Schane (2006); on the legal speech act of decisions, see Kevelson (1982).

Chapter 3

1. For an overview of approaches to context, including philosophical, sociological, and literary angles, see Goodwin and Duranti (1991: 13–42). More recent work on context and its relation to micro and macro aspects of communication can be found in Fetzer (2007) and Fetzer and Oishi (2011).

2. Jucker (2005: 10) notices a progression from narrow to wide applications of the term *discourse*. The narrow understanding concerns spoken interaction between a small number of participants, while the widest application of this concept has to do with "a particular communicative domain". Legal discourse belongs on the wider side of the scale as it includes documents, reference sources, spoken exchanges in an institutional setting, verdicts, the metalanguage used by professionals to discuss their trade, and so on.

3. There is a cognitive basis for discourse organization and comprehension, to which one may add the visual aspect of discourse, "often ignored in discourse studies" (van Dijk 1997: 6). Even though this book relies on corpus methods and does not pay attention to the visual layout in quantitative terms, van Dijk's observation might well inspire some further qualitative observations about the textual instances of legal discourse in Scottish burghs.

4. Hoey (1991) talks about transporting old concepts onto a new paradigm in linguistic theory, namely the study of text. Such practices were conceptualized by Schon (1963) as *extension* or *displacement of concepts*.

5. The original concepts linking the situational context, the function of text, and its form were formulated by Halliday, McIntosh, and Strevens (1964: 90–94), as 'field of discourse', 'style of discourse', and 'mode of discourse', respectively.

6. For instance, Moon's (1994) research into the employment of fixed phrases in English, where she multiplies functional categories, has been critically reviewed by Culpeper and Kytö (2002, 2010).

7. Halliday's ideational function is adopted by Culpeper and Kytö (2010), who include topical and circumstantial elements into this category.

8. For instance, the bundle I THINK IT (WAS) is classified in Biber, Conrad, and Cortes (2004: 384–388) as a stance expression in the personal epistemic subgroup, while the same bundle is put in the group of interpersonal modalizing bundles by Culpeper and Kytö (2010: 121). I DON'T KNOW is classed in the first study as a stance expression in the personal epistemic subgroup, while the second study classifies the same bundle as textual and discoursal, in the subcategory of answers. These groups do not even go back to the same original function, as identified by Halliday, because stance expressions would fit best in the interpersonal category. Another problematic bundle is THE FACT THAT, classified by Biber et al. (1999) as impersonal epistemic stance, while Culpeper and Kytö (2010: 122) see it as an ideational bundle in the organizational function. In my view, the incomplete structure of lexical bundles (section 4.4.2 and Chapter 9) adds to the categorization problem.

9. Ure's "language-in-action" corpus (1971) rounds up to 42,000 words; cf. the volume of corpora employed to explore features of registers by means of modern computational tools (section 3.7 and Chapter 8).

10. See e.g. González-Álvarez and Pérez-Guerra (1998) in their discussion of five early modern genres on the basis of a 95,000-word corpus, or to some extent Culpeper and Kytö (2010). In her introduction to the issue of the *European Journal of English Studies* dedicated to new genre models, Moessner (2001) gives a useful overview of the terms *genre*, *text type*, *style*, and *register*.

11. Görlach (2004) lists about 2,000 labels for different conventionalized uses of language, according to a specific function in the mind of the writer and the expectation of the reader. Note that Görlach talks about written texts only.

12. Lee (2001: 270) provides a table with scores of core vocabulary for various text types, where legal presentation (82%) ranks higher than the language of tabloids (72%); cf. the early studies on lexical density by Ure (1971).

13. Hasan (1978) has proposed a framework of the so-called *generic structure potential*—GSP.

14. *Grapholect* was originally defined by Haugen as "a precise record of [the speaker's] idiolect" (1966: 53–54). As a written record, it is edited (free of false starts and other online production phenomena), analysed (given a written symbolic representation), delayed (secondary in acquisition to speech), and stabilized (capable of creating a repository for reference and transmission). The last feature "encourages repetition and stability in... form", which links to the idea of grapholects shared by members of a discourse community (section 3.6).

15. See, however, Meurman-Solin, who admits that features of spoken discourse can be extracted from texts "whose functionality derives from the needs of a tightly-knit speech community" (2001: 243). The most recent attempt to do this in historical texts is Culpeper and Kytö (2010).

16. Drawing on Hymes (1974a), Romaine's interpretation of *speech community* is also broader than Labov's: "[a] speech community would be characterized by both referential and stylistic features which must be considered with respect to structure on the one hand and use on the other" (1982: 7).

17. On other specialized discourse communities, for example, the scientific, literary, academic, or medical community, see Bazerman (1988, 1990, 1991), Bazerman and Paradis (1991), and Bazerman and Prior (2004).

18. Butcher (2004) also makes a case for medieval urban societies to be perceived as speech/text communities, calling for the reappraisal of urban records and their role in community creation. Using the material from the present study, I show how the scribes and notaries create the text community in the burgh. Fixed and repetitive reference to members of the community constitutes around 30% of the whole number of the lexical bundles extracted from the EdHeW collection (Kopaczyk, forthcoming).

Chapter 4

1. The labels for prefabricated and fixed structures, mentioned by Biber, Conrad, and Cortes (2003) include lexical phrases, formulae, routines, fixed expressions, prefabricated items (prefabs), and lexical bundles. See also the section on multi-word units below.

2. For an overview of fixed chunks from a language teaching perspective, see O'Keeffe, McCarthy, and Carter (2007). A detailed categorization of fixed expressions can be found in Fernando and Flavell (1981); Hudson (1998) provides a good guide to earlier research on fixedness, especially EFL contexts. Fixed units in spoken PDE were studied, among others, by Aijmer (1996), Altenberg (1998), Hudson (1998), and in Biber et al. (1999). Fixed units in written PDE were explored by Moon (1998), Biber et al. (1999), Biber, Conrad, and Cortes (2004). Biber, Conrad, and Cortes (2003: 71–72) give an overview of approaches to lexical fixedness with respect to five different criteria: research goals, methodologies of identification, kinds of multi-word units, corpus size, and inclusion (or not) of register comparisons.

3. Schmitt (2005) indicates that formulaic structures may vary in terms of their fixedness. The issue of variability of form within formulaic sequences falls outside the focus of this book. However, in the discussion of data (Part Three) some observations on variability will be offered.

4. For the role of frequency measurements in core vocabulary research, see Lee (2001).

5. A kind of repetition which works *within* a lexical unit is reduplication. Persson (1974: 6–7) offers criteria to distinguish between reduplication and repetition: type-setting (spaces between continuous units), prosodic, morphological (e.g. when the second element of a reduplicated sequence is inflected), and semantic. It may mean that some expressions, for example, *hear hear* in parliament, can arguably be treated as a single unit because they express a single idea, carry one linguistic function, and therefore should be classified under reduplication. Opponents may say that this case is an example of repetition because the unit *hear* is produced twice to form a pragmatic unit with a single meaning (see the discussion of pragmaticalization below), regardless of being written or pronounced separately.

6. The earliest research on the intensifying role of repetition was carried out by Fijn van Draat between 1910 and 1915. See Persson (1974: 5ff.) for a review of earlier scholarship on the issue.

7. Tannen (1987: 219) gives an overview of nomenclature for MWUs and idiomatic expressions. Erman and Warren (2000: 30) survey other studies of formulaic language. Wray (2002: 9) lists terms used with reference to formulaicity and includes various labels for MWUs. Linnel, Hofvendahl, and Lindholm (2003) concentrate on multi-unit questioning turns (MUQTs), which are more complex in nature than traditional speech-act theory models assume.

8. The study showed that around 55% of the material (spoken samples from the London-Lund Corpus and written samples from the Lancaster-Oslo-Bergen corpus) was made of prefabs. These findings offer "strong support to the idiom principle as formulated by Sinclair...and reveal that the proportion of prefabrication in language has generally been much underestimated" (Erman and Warren 2000: 50).

9. Hudson (1998: 156) introduces the terms *structuration* for situations where there is no change of word-class during fixing.

10. The term *pragmaticization* is also in use.

11. Lexical bundles have also been called *keyword clusters* (Scott 1997), *recurrent word-combinations* (Altenberg 1998), *conjoined phrases* (Tiersma 1999), *recurrent word-chains* (Stubbs and Barth 2003), *lexico-grammatical patterns* (Stubbs 2005), *contiguous formulaic strings* (Conklin and Schmitt 2008), *clusters* (Hyland 2008a), *computationally derived recurrent word-combinations* (Culpeper and Kytö 2010: 103), *lexical clusters* (Tyrkkö, Hickey, and Marttila 2010), or, simply, n-*grams* (Fletcher 2003/2004).

12. The pie-charts in Biber, Conrad, and Cortes (2003: 76) indicate that almost 80% of lexical bundles are non-recurrent in both conversation and academic prose. I discussed the counts of non-repetitive bundles in the ECOS and HCOS in a pilot paper to this project (Kopaczyk 2011a). The majority of lexical bundles were not repeated. For 3-grams, non-recurrent bundles amounted to around 60%; the longer the bundle, the larger the percentage, and the greater the numeric discrepancy between non-recurrent and recurrent bundles.

13. Since bundles in some kinds of specialized discourse may be rather long, including even over eight items, a question is raised about storing, processing, and retrieving such structures for efficient use. Schmitt's experiments with bundle recognition (2005) suggest that lexical bundles are not stored holistically. See also the discussion of long bundles in Chapter 12.

14. In Altenberg's study (1998), clause constituents were the most frequent structural types, accounting for 76% of the collected bundles.

15. On problems in bundle methodology posed by contractions and word boundaries, see section 8.4.2.

16. Although English is leading the way, cf. the recent two-volume overview of the field of corpus linguistics, edited by Lüdeling and Kytö (2008/2009), electronic corpora with the intention to represent actual usage and provide a base for the description of modern standard language are also produced for other languages. The Scottish Corpus of Texts and Speech (SCOTS) aims to represent the written and spoken registers of the Scots language in present-day times (after 1945) (http://www.scottishcorpus.ac.uk/). See also e.g. the National Corpus of Polish [Narodowy Korpus Języka Polskiego] (http://nkjp.pl/), the German Reference Corpus [Das Deutsche Referenzkorpus] (http://www.ids-mannheim.de/kl/projekte/korpora/), the Czech National Corpus [Český národní korpus] (http://ucnk.ff.cuni.cz/), the Russian National Corpus (http://www.ruscorpora.ru/), and the overviews by Xiao (2008) and Ostler (2008).

17. Other labels employed in the sense of binomials include *repetitive word-pairs* (Koskenniemi 1968), *freezes* (Oden and Lopes 1982; Alexander 1984; Pordány 1986; Fenk-Oczlon 1989), *doublets* (Raumolin-Brunberg 1991; Waldron 2001; Sauer 2013), *binominals* (Lee 1990; Bhatia 1993, Coulmas 1994; Bugaj 2006a; Mattila 2012; for a different meaning of this term, closer to compounds, see Bennett 1978), *fixed-order conjuncts*, *binomial fixed phrases* (Abu-Ssaydeh 2005), *twin formulae* (Sauer 2011, 2013).

18. I am grateful to the anonymous reviewer for this observation.

19. For the diverse educational and professional characteristics of medieval men of law, see section 7.4.

20. Consider, for example, the Plain Language movement (http://www.plainlanguage.gov/whatisPL/index.cfm); for the rationale behind the movement, an overview of its history, and tips for Plain Language drafting, see Adler (2012); for recent developments, see Williams (2011).

21. The medieval tendency to expand the Latin expression when translating into the vernacular has been noticed by Waldron (2001) and illustrated by numerous examples from Trevisa's *Polychronicon*.

22. This was not without precedence in the British Isles; on the Anglo-Saxon law-codes of Æthelberht, Alfred, and Ine, see Hough (2001: 170–187). The author also mentions scanty evidence of northern Anglian laws in the form of *Norðleoda laga*, 'Law of the North People'.

23. Frequent as the binomials were "only about a quarter of them occurred more than once" (Danet 1997: 28), cf. discussion of hapaxes among formulaic structures in 4.2.2.

24. It is not just in literature and legal texts that binomials and multinomials are employed as a significant discourse feature. Crawford et al. (1999) studied binomials in mental health nursing students' texts (e.g. *anxious/-iety and depressed/-ion*) and found that such constructions help to achieve technical accuracy with reference to a medical condition (cf. Gustafsson 1984: 134). What is more, binomials introduce variety and detail, which makes the accounts more vivid and convincing. In fact, the largest semantic field/relationship in nursing language binomials is 'Feelings and Assessment', as in *suicide or self-harm*, *low and depressed*, *confidence and courage*, and so on (Crawford et al. 1999: 335). The semantic criterion will, naturally, be responsible for different pairings of words depending on the type of discourse and its theme, even though the same bi- and multinomials could be used in a variety of contexts. In fact, cross-corpora studies have shown that binomials with the highest frequency do not result from corpus design (Giammarresi 2010: 266).

25. An interesting development in legal discourse is the invention of, what Malkiel (1959: 130) calls, "the artificial compromise formula *and/or*", which he deems recent at the time of writing.

26. Compare the discussion of Latin calques in Scots burgh laws in the preceding section and Kopaczyk (2011b).

27. Rules of politeness, for instance, may alter constituent order (e.g. *you and I*).

28. There is a problem with objectivity of judgement in this study as it is based on a single speaker.

29. Hudson (1998: 32) notes the need for more research in this particular area.

30. Therefore, Giammarresi (2010: 266) calls for the inclusion of the most fixed binomials in separate dictionary entries (e.g. *come and go*).

31. As observed above on the basis of Kopaczyk (2011b), many binomials in the earliest laws of Scottish burghs were calques from the earlier Latin version of the same text. The reverse direction of influence was also present in the laws, where a Scots binomial was incorporated into Latin. A more detailed investigation of the role of calquing in multinomial expressions is still to be conducted.

32. I am grateful to the anonymous reviewer for this suggestion.

Chapter 5

1. Even though related forms exist in medieval Latin *burgus* and Old French *bourg* (*OED*, s.v. *bourg* n.), it seems that the etymology is Indo-European, with cognate words relating to fortifications on a hill in different languages, then borrowed into Latin from continental Germanic. The earliest usage in the British Isles in the sense of 'a fortified town; a town possessing municipal organization' (*OED*, s.v. *borough* n. 2a) was recorded in c. 893 as *burg*. The meaning of a town recognized by the royal charter is an extension of that earlier meaning in feudal times. The *OED* gives the earliest evidence of this usage for English from the late fourteenth century in the spelling *burgh* or *borugh* (s.v. *borough* n. 3a), while the Scots data in the *DSL* point to early twelfth-century place names (*Rokesburgh*, 1120; *Edenesburg*, 1125; *Dryburgh*, c. 1150) and late fourteenth–early fifteenth-century documents. Murison (1979: 5–6) lists *burgh* among Germanic vocabulary items characteristic of early urban centres in Scotland. The etymology of *burgage*, a late medieval feudal concept, seems to go back to the Latin *burgagium*, and Old French, *bourgage*, derived from the earlier Germanic root.

2. The incursions made by the Romans into Scotland were of military character and no urbanization or long-term settlement followed (Hall 2002: 11).

3. In the case of monarchs, their dates of reign will be provided for reference.

4. Scottish coins were deliberately "of the same weight and fineness as English ones", which may suggest trade on a larger scale over the whole island. Nevertheless, historians note that "in the twelfth century transactions in cash must have remained unusual in most of Scotland, at least outside of the burghs" (Barrell 2000: 33). Several references to Scottish money have surfaced in the lexical bundles (e.g. *vsuale mone of scotland*), see the referential bundles pertaining to objects in section 11.3.1, and the standardizing long bundles in section 12.2.3.

5. One should remember, however, that there is "no documentary evidence at all for eleventh-century Scotland and very little written evidence of any kind" (Duncan 1975: 465).

We may infer that grants of urban property to the clergy suggest the existence of urban centres but this piece of evidence remains indirect.

6. For some burghs archaeologists have proven pre-burghal origins, for example, in St Andrews where a large religious centre existed, possibly with an attached lay settlement (Hall 2002: 10, 41–44).

7. Early *notitiae* of land grants by kings and other landholders, cleric and lay, survive in entries in the Gaelic *Book of Deer*, as well as in Latin registers, which pre-date extant charters (Donaldson 1970: 14).

8. Erection charters were not part of the EdHeW corpus, but among interactional bundles we find directives with the verb *ken* 'to know', letting the public know about the new legal decision, see section 11.3.3.

9. For instance, the Hundred Years' War, Henry V's and Henry VI's unsuccessful campaign in France.

10. King Robert the Bruce granted the whole earldom of Moray to Thomas Randolph, including three royal burghs of Elgin, Forres, and Nairn. The burgesses nevertheless kept their original privileges (Walker 1990: 421).

11. Dennison (2007) uses a separate term, *parliamentary burghs*, to refer collectively to the royal burghs and the few ecclesiastical burghs represented in the Scottish Parliament.

12. The presence of burgesses is acknowledged quite early, for instance in an indenture between Robert I and his parliament of Cambuskenneth (1326), which was aiming to introduce an extraordinary tax (Donaldson 1970: 59).

13. In contrast to his predecessor, he had twenty-one offspring, including seven illegitimate daughters and eight illegitimate sons (Bingham 1974: 269), which could (and did) present further problems in terms of inheritance and influence; see the historical sketch below.

14. Scotland was sparsely populated so the hardships after the Black Death were not so much connected with the loss of manpower, as with the loss of markets and demand for Scottish produce elsewhere.

15. The infamous 'Battle of the Clans' (1396) was no more than a mortal combat, whereby a clan feud was to be solved. Sixty men represented their respective clans. The king, Robert III (1390–1406), presided over this massacre, finishing it when only twelve men remained alive (Bingham 1974: 30).

16. Young James, heir to the Scottish Crown, was captured by pirates while on his way to France on a Danzig ship *Maryenknyght* (Bingham 1974: 32), to escape the tumults between his ruling father, Robert III, other potential heirs and the powerful family of Douglas. The pirates handed him over to the English, who kept James hostage for eighteen years, before favourable conditions for ransom presented themselves. The sum of 40,000 (Bingham has it at 60,000 marks, with 10,000 returned as the royal bride's dowry, 1974: 46) was not officially called ransom as James had not been captured in battle. "It was termed a payment for the hospitality" (Barrell 2000: 150, 153).

17. For instance, when the University of St Andrews was to be founded, James added his name to the petition sent to the Pope to obtain a bull of foundation (Bingham 1974: 39).

18. *Inglis* is a label still applied at the beginning of the fifteenth century to Scots, see section 1.4. James I's proficiency in the language of his childhood "was automatically fostered by the Scottish household which surrounded him throughout the years he spent in England and by the many visitors from Scotland" (Bingham 1974: 37–38).

19. Lairds were "the men immediately below the nobility in rank, who were of substance and influence in their own right and who could bring as adjuncts to the magnate's affinity their own circles of partakers." They could be identified by the characteristic form of their personal name, 'A.B. (name) of C. (place)'. Lairds "saw themselves... as 'natural counsellors' of the magnates just as the magnates saw themselves as 'natural counsellors' of the king" (Kelham 1986: 11). Dawson (2007: 100–105) provides a tabulated overview of the most powerful noble families and their politics during the Stewart rule.

20. Barrell advises greater caution "before we over-emphasize the impact of James's constitutional, legal and administrative reforms", as the quoted epithet "was a conventional way of expressing approbation" for a medieval king (2000: 155). He admits, however, that James's reforms were "on an unprecedented scale" so it seems that such a name was not just a matter of courtesy.

21. More information on Mons Meg at the official Edinburgh Castle website: http://www.edinburghcastle.gov.uk/index/tour/highlights/highlights-mons-meg.htm.

22. Those who persisted in playing golf or football paid fines. The money from the fines went to buy drinks for those practising archery, much to their amusement, no doubt. As Bingham notices, however, such measures did not cause Scots to divert en masse from their favourite sports (1974: 85).

23. A regality (see also section 5.3) was effectively a miniature of royal legal administration, with the power to try all cases except for treason. This system must have given way to abuse in the hands of unscrupulous local lords, craving power equal to that of the king.

24. James III's favourites caused so much distress that they were seized and hanged before the king's own eyes during a war council when the nobles became too agitated. The army was in field, marching to regain Berwick from the hands of the contriving Duke of Albany and his English supporters (Bingham 1974: 109). For the summary of how Berwick kept passing from English to Scottish hands and vice versa, see Walker (1990: 106–107, 119–120).

25. The recurrent bundle *duc of albany* (section 11.3.1) suggests frequent talk about the Duke in burgh records.

26. Pedro de Ayala was sent to Scotland by Ferdinand and Isabella of Aragon and Castile, who were eager to establish peace between Scotland and England. The Spaniards offered James IV the hand of a royal princess, but it soon transpired that all three royal Spanish daughters had already been promised to England, France, and the Holy Roman Empire. This trickery inflamed James who decided to wage war upon England in 1496. After a year of military cat-and-mouse between James IV and Henry VII, Pedro de Ayala successfully negotiated another truce between the two kingdoms (Bingham 1974: 131–132).

27. See also the section on the Highlands and Lowlands below, as well as section 1.4, for the status of Scots as a national tongue.

28. The strong position of Scotland on the map of early sixteenth-century Europe is confirmed by the fact that English nobles were uneasy about such a close royal connection. They feared that the Crown of England might fall into Scottish hands, should the first two royal sons predecease their sister, to which Henry VII prophetically, if somewhat boastfully, replied: "Since it ever happens that the less becomes subservient to the greater, the accession will be that of Scotland to England, just as formerly happened to Normandy" (Bingham 1974: 134; see Dawson (2007: 66) on the sumary of the succession implications).

29. Bingham (1974: 138) points out that "James III had indeed recognized [Edinburgh] as 'principalior burgus regni nostri'—the principal burgh of our realm—but since Stirling had been his favourite place of residence Edinburgh had scarcely functioned as a capital."

Dennison and Lynch (2005) discuss the rise of Edinburgh as the royal capital and the function of the adjacent Canongate as the seat of the urban court.

30. As recorded by a Scots vernacular chronicler, Robert Lindsay of Pittscottie: "For this Ship was of so great Stature, and took so much Timber, that...she wasted all the Woods in Fife, which was Oak-Wood, by all Timber that was gotten out of Norroway" (1565 [1728]: 107, EEBO). For the overall costs of the creation of a Scottish royal navy, see Dawson (2007: 76–77).

31. "It is stated and ordained throughout the realm that all barons and freeholders who are of substance should put their eldest sons and heirs to schools from the age of eight or nine; they should remain in grammar schools till they are competently educated and have a perfect knowledge of Latin, and thereafter remain at schools of arts and law so that they may have the knowledge and understanding of the laws" (translation mine).

32. The first extant printed Acts of Parliament go back to James V's Parliaments of 1535 and 1540, so maybe the Acts of James IV were never printed in the end (Bingham 1974: 144).

33. On printing and Scottish legal records, see Chapter 7; on its repercussions for the Scots language, see Chapter 1; on the general relationship between law, the printed word and standardization, see Chapter 2; on writing and printing in reconstructing the discourses of the past, see Chapter 3.

34. Interestingly, the home of the Douglases, Galloway in the south-west of Scotland, emerges as a separate linguistic area in the analysis of diatopic trends in the longest lexical bundles (section 12.3).

35. A death in the family was a doubly mournful occasion, for it was required that the dead person's bed be covered with 'upmost cloth' and 'a corpse-present beast', usually a cow, be paid to the priest upon burial (Bingham 1974: 178). In times of high mortality rates, people must have felt resentment towards the clergy who were preying on their loss.

36. By then Mary had become the Queen of France and resided in France together with her husband, François (on Franco-Scottish relations during this time, see Dawson 2007: 176–199). When he died in December 1560, Mary was left a childless widow. Her options were either to stay in France and rule as the Queen-dowager or go back to Scotland and be a Catholic ruler in a Protestant country (Bingham 1974: 201).

37. The king's official legislation was more lenient: for open and notorious rebellions the punishment was supposed to be "forfatour of lif landis and guidis" (Donaldson 1970: 76)—forfeiture of all lands and possessions to the Crown.

38. James IV had a keen interest in medicine and, following the medical faculty in Aberdeen, he set up the College of Surgeons in 1506 in Edinburgh. The king "was eager to try his own hand" at dentistry and surgery, and agreed for the College to perform one autopsy per year, on a body of an executed criminal (Bingham 1974: 142), a gesture truly ahead of his times. For instance, the well-known depiction of autopsy, *The Anatomy of Dr Tulp*, was painted by Rembrandt only in 1632, when one yearly dissection of a criminal's corpse was allowed by the Amsterdam Guild of Surgeons.

Chapter 6

1. There are exceptions to this pattern, for instance, in Peebles, where excavations so far have uncovered remains of stone buildings only. Stone could have been more readily available in the area, and such constructions may have been preferred for the risk of flooding (Hall 2002: 34).

2. The *OED* defines a *vennel* as "a narrow lane, passage, or thoroughfare in a town or city; an alley or wynd" and traces its etymology back to OF *venele, venelle, vanelle* (French *venelle*), from medieval Latin *venella*, diminutive of 'vein'. This expression is linked typically with Scottish townscape, which may give a hint about the Norman influence on urbanization in Scotland, especially on street layout.

3. The only medieval tolbooth in Scotland has been excavated in Peebles (Hall 2002: 34). Tolbooths in other towns (e.g. Glasgow, Culross, or Dunbar) date to later periods.

4. Important excavations started in Scotland in 1970s in Elgin, Aberdeen, Perth, and St Andrews. Recently, the largest urban archaeological project so far was completed at the building site of the Scottish Parliament, within the limits of the medieval burgh of Canongate, now incorporated into the city of Edinburgh (Hall 2002: 7, 21).

5. The Black Death, which is said to have claimed a third of Scottish lives, entered Scotland in 1349, most probably through contact with the English army (Hall 2002: 32).

6. In the 1960s it was suggested that a burgh needed a minimum population of 1,000 to be successful (Alauddin 1968: 40), but this viewpoint has been widely rejected as "too rigid a concept" (Symms 1986: 3–4).

7. Note the multinomial and formulaic nature of the phrase (for the analysis of binomials and multinomials in the EdHeW corpus, see Chapter 10). The editor of Glasgow charters explains that both in England and Scotland *natives* or *neyfs* designated people who were the original inhabitants of a place or descendants of such, and "had been reduced to serfdom, and were transferable by sale or gift along with the soil which they cultivated". He also claims that serfs of religious proprietors were generally better off than those of secular masters, in view of Glasgow being an ecclesiastical burgh (Marwick 1897: xii).

8. The post of the alderman was slowly renamed to that of a provost, but one still comes across the term *alderman* in the records of Glasgow (1453), Edinburgh (1456), Ayr, and Selkirk (till 1530s–1540s) (Pryde 1937: xxii, n. 7). Aberdeen council minutes record the term *provost* in 1506 for the first time (Booton 1987: 3).

9. For other competing translations of these terms into Scots, see Kopaczyk (2011b).

10. "[G]ood men of the town who ought to be loyal and of good reputation" (translation mine).

11. This practice develops by the sixteenth century. Surviving documents from Perth, however, suggest that beforehand rubbish used to pile up even in the streets, which jeopardised the town's safety and had to be controlled by means of special burgh laws (Hall 2002: 12).

12. On the basis of burgh records, Booton (1987: 59–95) gives an interesting overview of marriages, property dealings, and positions of power held by members of eleven most influential burgh families in Aberdeen in the fifteenth and early sixteenth century. For a first-hand account of merchant families and their daily life, one should consult *The compt buik of David Wedderburne, merchant of Dundee, 1587–1630* (Constable and Constable 1898), which contains forty-three years of business and family life affairs, as well as reflections from journeys to Flanders and Scandinavia.

13. Fig seeds were found at archaeological sites in Ayr (Hall 2002: 40).

14. The institution of a licensed beggar continued until the nineteenth century. The National Museum of Scotland in Edinburgh hosts an impressive collection of beggar badges from all over the country.

15. Burgh records of Selkirk show a gaping discrepancy in the numbers of admitted new burgesses: normally one–two people per year, and in the extreme years when the town needed money—even as many as 23 or 46 people (Symms 1986: 46).

16. In exchange for their extensive privileges in trade, burgesses all over Scotland had one more responsibility: a nightly watch (*watch and ward*) from every household to provide security for the town (*Leges*, lxxxi; Smith 1955: 606–607; Symms 1986: 40). Together with *scot and lot*, this expression is to be found among the most formulaic multinomials: *scottyn lottyn wakyn and wardyn* (section 10.3.1; see also section 10.2.3 for *wakyn and wardyn*). Notice how the most important concepts in the legal language of the burghs are carried through binomials (cf. Chapter 2 for binomials and the law, Chapter 3 for their semantic and formal properties, and the analysis of other binomials from EdHeW in Chapter 10).

17. This shift could happen relatively early. In Stirling, the feu charter, with characteristic burgh seals on the document, came in 1386 for an annual feu-duty at 16 pounds (Stirling records 1884: vi–vii).

18. As Pryde has it, "[t]he burghs felt impelled to protest against excessive custom-dues" (1937: lxx).

19. Interestingly, this lexical item is found in the compound *blackmail*, which was coined in Scotland and referred initially to money paid in order to protect someone's lands and property from "spoilation and injury" (*DSL*, s.v. *blak-maill* n.). For specifically Scots legal lexicon, see sections 2.4.3 and 7.2.2. The Scots word *maill* shares the same Germanic background with Old Norse *mál* 'agreement, speech' and, ultimately, 'language'. In the Viking sagas, it is also the word for a legal case or claim (Slusher 1991: 31), which shows once again the intricate connection between language and law in oral cultures, see Chapter 2.

20. In Edinburgh, this law applied to "all pedlars and vendors of produce" (Pryde 1937: xliv, n.7).

21. *Thirlage* was a type of feudal servitude. The *DSL* definition stresses "the right of a superior to such a servitude from tenants" (s.v. *thirlage* n. 2b), which means that by introducing thirlage, the burgh again acted as a corporate body in the possession of the land, to gain as much profit as possible from its cultivation.

22. English kings were unscrupulous, even during times of truce. However, they did not dare to declare open war with Scotland. For instance, historians write about Henry VII that "[u]nofficially sanctioned privateering and intrigues with Scots traitors were the limits of his anti-Scottish activity" (Bingham 1974: 125).

23. The strings such as *iii firlotis of*, *ellis of quhit* 'ells of white [fabric]' or *and stan of* 'and stone of' were too infrequent to qualify to the formulaic lexical bundles, but they did occur in the records.

Chapter 7

1. On the extent of legal book and document production in early medieval England and Wales, see Ramsay (2008); the volume on the earliest history of the book in Scotland is to appear (Mann and Mapstone 2013).

2. Chthonic law takes its name from the Greek word *χθόνιος—chthonios*, which means 'of the earth, from (below) the earth', thus making a connection with nature and the underworld. Law was not seen as a means of punishment or retaliation, but rather as a way of restoring balance to the community (Glenn 2007: 60).

3. "Handfasting was a form of provisional marriage dependant on the woman becoming pregnant during the probationary period—the object being to secure against a childless union" (Smith 1955: 605 n.7). Dodds (1927) brings into focus differences between Scottish and English law regulating marriage and family issues. Possibly connected to the Celtic 'handfasting', in Scotland the law recognized the so-called 'irregular marriage', whereby living together for an extended period of time gave the partners spousal status. The differences also concerned wills, hereditary rights, children's age of independence, and divorce and separation. Suffice it to say that in England even until the 1920s the man's adultery, as a reason for divorce, was only the case when combined with incest or cruelty; in Scotland, divorce could be granted if either party cheated on the other—clearly a more balanced treatment of the two sexes.

4. One of the incentives for the adoption of Roman law in Europe may have been the need for unity of legal procedures under the Muslim threat (Glenn 2007: 132–133).

5. I would like to thank Dr Edda Frankot (Erasmus Universiteit Rotterdam) for bringing this fact to my attention.

6. Visby, a city on the island of Gotland in Sweden, a UNESCO World Heritage Site (the best-preserved medieval town in Scandinavia).

7. *DSL*, s.v. *charter party*—'a deed (originally indentured) between owners and merchants relating to the hire of a vessel and the delivery of the cargo'. The use of this term in Scottish documents pre-dates the English use by more than one century (cf. *OED*, s.v. *charter-party* n.).

8. The most popular comparative dictionaries and glossaries include Beaton (1982), Duncan (1992), Stewart (1995), Styles and Whitty (2003), and O'Rourke (2004). Comparative legal studies mostly shed light on the discrepancies, see e.g. Cameron (2005) on a different treatment of nuisance in both systems.

9. "English legal language is rooted in the common law tradition, an endless string of stories, like one thousand and one nights, with a legal solution affixed to each one. Although the historical origin of a concept may not matter to a lawyer, the origin of a word may well determine its meaning. To use an English word having a specific meaning in common law to describe a vaguely similar civil law concept may produce a comparative law nightmare" (Rossini 1998: xxi).

10. Interestingly, even in present-day law, certain problematic cases on the English side are being solved by referring to Scots law. There are also voices saying that sooner or later the English law in general will, by necessity, fall back on Scottish solutions (cf. Birks 1995).

11. Murison notices an exception to this pattern: a dispute between Alexander III and Robert Bruce (mid-thirteenth century), documented in French. This language was also used by Scottish barons and nobles of Norman origin in correspondence, for example, with the English kings in feudal matters (Murison 1974: 77). Barrow asserts that "it was not uncommon for Latin charters of the twelfth century to show strong French influence in their choice of vocabulary and more especially in their spelling of proper names", but still "French remained an exotic language in Scotland" (1997: 138). MacQueen (2002a) argues for a reassessment of the French influence on the earliest Scottish legal texts in light of "the *oral* use of that language in legal business" (emphasis added), alongside even earlier Celtic terms. It appears that the default language of legal and administrative documentation was Latin, with an undercurrent of oral Gaelic and French, until Scots took over in the late fourteenth century, absorbing the waves of earlier linguistic and conceptual influence.

12. A *borgh*—a person standing as surety for another or something offered as a pledge (*DSL*, s.v. *borch* n., 1–2); *OED* lists *borgh* as a Scots counterpart to the obsolete English expression *to let to bail* (s.v. *let* v[1], 4c).

13. When the lairds became a part of the parliament towards the end of the sixteenth century, they tried to separate themselves from the higher nobles, and act as a discrete estate with its own interests. This is visible in the 1599 petition "for their own annual convention *like that of the burghs*" (MacDonald 2002: 29, emphasis mine; on the Convention of the Four Burghs, see section 6.5).

14. After continuous conflicts over the Borders with the English, the latter two were replaced in the Court of Four Burghs with Linlithgow and Lanark (see below and section 6.4; Walker 1995: 321).

15. For a linguistic comparison and the assessment of Latin influence on the Scots version of the *Leges*, see Kopaczyk (2011b). I would like to thank Dr Edda Frankot (Erasmus Universiteit Rotterdam) for helping me find the relevant manuscripts in the National Library of Scotland.

16. For breaking the set price, there was a punishment, executed through all the administrative levels, if not already applied to the 'brekaris' in the first place. The introduction of an elected warden was also aimed at reducing the possibility of secret conspiratorial meetings led by the deacons of crafts (Donaldson 1970: 76, 81).

17. Ovens were supposed to be located outside the town walls because of the obvious fire risk. A law forbidding swine to be kept by burgesses must have grown not only out of concern for health and safety but also for unpleasant smells and filth. Still, swine were allowed if the owner kept them in a sty, which indicates that such a practice was not regular (*Leges*, lxxxiv).

18. Beveridge notes that in the burgh of Dunfermline the admitted burgesses were female "in many cases" (1917: xviii). Ewan (1992) explores the position and roles of women before Scottish burgh courts in the fifteenth and early sixteenth centuries.

19. The Dunfermline records mention a particular case of 'strublans'—"breach of the peace, on one occasion 'in langagis'" (Beveridge 1917: xviii), which suggests that a loud mouth could earn its owner a lawsuit before a burgh court.

20. "[G]uiltiness of, or liability to a penalty for, bloodshed; an action against a person for bloodshed" (*DSL*, s.v. *bludewite* n. 1).

21. "[T]he crime of forcibly preventing an officer of the law from discharging his duty" (*DSL*, s.v. *deforcement* n. 1).

22. Such privileges were first given to the brethren of Scone, then to the burgh of Dunfermline (in the twelfth century) (Dickinson 1937: xii–xiii).

23. In the long run, this legislation caused the power to be centred in the hands of few, who could ensure the continuity of their own personal interests. "[M]unicipal power was concentrated in an oligarchy of leading merchants and master craftsmen", which Smith calls "a deplorable situation" and regrets that it had continued until 1833 (1955: 663).

24. Similarly, the parliament required fencing—"formal constituting"—before it could be opened (Mackie 1923: 27–32).

25. "[T]he condition of being subject to a pecuniary penalty at the discretion of the court or judge" (*DSL*, *amerciament* n. 1).

26. The expression *erd and stane* referred initially to the actual clod of earth and a stone taken from the plot under transfer. In some earlier records, two other expressions are used,

pertaining perhaps to slightly different particulars of the ceremony: *be hesp and stapil*—a bolt and loop for fastening (Beveridge 1917: xviii) and *wytht staf and bastone*, from Latin *per fustem et baculum*, used in the context of resigning land (*DSL*, s.v. *baston* n. 1b). The binomial nature of such expressions will be scrutinized in Chapter 10. The procedures outlined above were by no means limited to Scotland. In Anglo-Saxon England, the symbolic tokens of transfer used during the oral ceremony of passing on land could be "a clod of earth or a knife or sword belonging to the donor" (Danet 1997: 30). The 'hasp of the door of a house' is also mentioned by Rodger and Newman (1988: 51), as is a 'twig of a tree'. The authors draw attention to the fact that in England there was no intermediary of the feudal sovereign in the transaction between the granter and the grantee, whereas in Scotland the lord was either present or represented. In a burgh, the bailies performed the function of representing the feudal superior—the king.

27. "[B]y 1617 a general register of titles to land, the Register of Sasines, was established in Scotland, and has continued virtually uninterrupted until the present day" (Rodger and Newman 1988: 49).

28. The oath was very formulaic and full of repetition, see Finlay (2000: 5).

29. This special connection with continental law schools—and a reluctance to study in England—was continued in later times by such eminent names in Scots law as Craig, Mackenzie, Spottiswood, and Fountainhall, who "studied at Orleans, Poitiers, Bourges or Paris... despite the Union of the Crowns in 1603 and of the Parliaments in 1707" (Smith 1955: 619). Estimates indicate that there were about 1,600 Scottish students in Leiden alone (ibid.).

30. Some clerks also performed other duties for the community; for example, Ninian Bryden, the common clerk of the burgh of Selkirk, was appointed ale-taster in 1529 (Symms 1988: 286 n. 25).

31. Durkan (1983: 28–29) suggests that protocol books of deceased notaries were archived in burghs also to provide models to copy for new appointees.

32. Williamson (2002b) used the term *text community*, to underline the written character of the data produced by the notaries. Following Butcher (2004), I reserve this term for a community which constitutes itself through its involvement in and consumption of the texts, as was the case with Scottish medieval burgesses (Kopaczyk, forthcoming). Together with the community of practice which provides the texts, the human collective in a burgh can be conceived of as a discourse community in Swales's terms (1990).

33. I address the "bad data" problem (Labov 1972a) in section 3.7.

34. It is worth pointing out that the witnesses were called to authenticate the transaction or court ruling, not the notarial document (Sanderson 2002: 190).

Chapter 8

1. Trial records were excluded because of their dialogic and interactive character.

2. There were, in fact some 340 words of text written earlier in the fourteenth century, but I decided to include it in the first period in the final version of the chronological breakdown.

3. There was also a small textual overlap between ECOS and HCOS, but I have eliminated all overlapping samples from the final version of EdHeW.

4. I owe thanks to Alistair Baron for giving me access to the VARD 2.3 software and for answering a series of questions on how to adjust this tool to my data. The software has also

been used in other corpus projects, for example, the *Early Modern English Medical Texts* (see Lehto et al. 2010: 283–285). For more information, see Alistair Baron's homepage http://www.comp.lancs.ac.uk/~barona/vard2/.

5. The most varied spelling was encountered in the word *amerciament* 'the condition of being subject to a pecuniary penalty at the discretion of the court or judge' (*DSL*, s.v. *amerciament* n. 1), which had 78 different variants, due to graphemic variation, abbreviations, and manuscript-related transcription procedures.

6. I would like to thank Professor Rafał Molencki (University of Silesia) for more information about the grammaticalization of adverbial prepositions.

7. In addition, Culpeper and Kytö (2010: 114), as well as present-day studies, faced the problem of contractions, especially in the context of negation. Contractions typically turn two word forms into one, which affects the extraction of lexical bundles. This problem need not concern us here. The time span of this study allows us to assume that contraction with an apostrophe was not present in the EdHeW corpus because it is too early both for this feature of spelling (Cram 1989) and for *do*-support in negation (Nevalainen 2006: 108–110; Fischer and van der Wurff 2006: 154–158).

8. Culpeper and Kytö (2010) used *WordSmith Tools* v.3 and v.4 (Scott 1998/2007), as well as *Multilingual Corpus Tools* (Piao 2002). They looked for 3-grams and admit that the output files contained two-word clusters, too. They also note that each program rendered a different list of bundles, even if the discrepancies were small (Culpeper and Kytö 2010: 113 n. 11). To avoid similar difficulties, I opted for using software whose code I could adjust to my purposes and whose operation would be transparent to me.

9. The software, essentially, consists of a set of related scripts written in Python by Dariusz Stróżyński, who also worked on customizing VARD for the Scots data and prepared the corpora for automatic extraction.

10. This may be yet another argument for the division of the bundles into short (3- to 5-grams) and long (6- to 8-grams); see the rationale for chapter content in Part Three, presented in section 8.1.

11. Using Biber et al.'s cut-off point (1999) in a corpus of around 0.6 million words, I would have to eliminate all bundles below 5.75 occurrences.

12. The authors give information about "the proportion of words, per 10,000, accounted for by the ten most frequently occurring three-word bundles" in Early Modern speech-related genres and present-day English trials and plays for comparison (Culpeper and Kytö 2010: 136). I return to these findings in section 12.4 with a comparison of the Scots material.

13. *DSL* defines *oxgang* as "the extent of land calculated as the share of one ox in the land ploughed by the standard eight-ox team" (*oxgang* n.).

14. I am indebted to Jacek Głębocki (Poznań University of Technology) for suggesting a mathematical solution to the question of formulaicity levels dependent on two interrelated indices.

15. Culpeper and Kytö mention the overlap only in the context of selecting 3-grams as their focus, noting that "the shorter the bundle the more often they are incorporated into longer bundles...so it makes sense to avoid the shortest bundle (i.e. two-word)" (2010: 106). They do not explain, however, how 3-grams become part of 4-grams, and why it is necessary to resort to longer bundles for the sake of understanding the pattern which 3-grams may only hint at.

Chapter 9

1. Culpeper and Kytö (2010: 118) have also noticed informational style, based on nominal constructions, in PDE trials. I return to this point later in the discussion.

2. Similarly to English (as first proposed by Abney 1987), in Scots the noun phrase is in fact a determiner phrase (DP) with a potential space for a determiner. In spite of that, I refer to nominal phrases as NPs and indicate wherever an overt determiner is present in a bundle.

3. Pronouns and nouns share many syntactic properties and can therefore be grouped together. In fact, Huddleston and Pullum (2005: 17) have suggested a new categorization for modern English which incorporates personal pronouns into nouns and noun phrases. One should remember, though, that nouns are an open class with potential new members and are therefore more versatile and varied, while personal pronouns are a closed class, albeit with a similar syntactic behaviour.

4. Biber et al. (1999: 1001) used benchmarks based solely on the number of occurrences per million words. I have decided to rely on the formulaicity factor (FF) calculated on the basis of frequency but also textual spread, see section 8.5.4 for details.

5. By *determiners* I understand definite articles, possessive pronouns, numerals, and nominal negation. Curiously, indefinite articles never surfaced as the initial element in the top 10% of formulaic lexical bundles in EdHeW.

6. The *DSL* defines this specific meaning of the verb *hald* (s.v. 2a) as 'to keep for oneself, to retain as one's own'. There is evidence in the dictionary that this verb could actually have been used in active constructions, as in *He helde wragwisli frae him ane achtand part of ry* (Hay I. 205/15), however in the EdHeW corpus the most formulaic use of this verb was in fact a gerund—*haldin*, which serves as the head of a nominal phrase. The preference for nominalizations is a noteworthy trend in the material, as discussed throughout this chapter.

7. For *of ye said*, the most numerous 3-gram, and a runner-up in terms of formulaicity, see Type P1a below.

8. There are two other formulaic options, *ye quhilk day* and *ye said day*, however, these are much less popular (131 occurrences in 26 texts, FF = 41, and 168 occurrences in 95 texts, FF = 33). For these and other bundles with a cohesive function in the texts, see section 11.3.2.

9. The form *haldin* may be treated as a past participle of the verb *tae hald* 'to hold'. The overlaps with other bundles, however, disambiguate it as a gerund.

10. Here I grouped together two conjunction phrases: (NP1) + Conj + NP2, and NP2 + Conj + (NP3), where the NP in brackets is not visible in the bundle, even though it is an obligatory element of the construction; after all, coordination involves two elements of the same category. Thus, the bundle either starts or finishes in a conjunction.

11. Apart from self-evident date reference, in PDE trials there are some numeric expressions of quantity among the top frequency scores: 'a hundred and', 'hundred and twenty', 'hundred and fifty', 'hundred and thirty' (Culpeper and Kytö 2010: 116–117). They may conceivably refer to date as well.

12. Interestingly, prepositional phrases account for half of the top twenty most frequent 4- and 5-grams in the written texts from the *Cambridge and Nottingham Corpus of Discourse in English* (Carter and McCarthy 2006).

13. *Thre* can also modify other nouns, e.g. *thre hundereth markis* (21 times in 12 texts), or *and thre yheris* (22 times in 21 texts), which were too infrequent to qualify to the formulaic pool.

14. There are some less repetitive bundles which contain reference to other special days (e.g. to St Martin's day in November and Whitsunday in May), as visible in the following 3-grams: *martinmes in winter* (69 tokens in 58 texts), *and martinmes in* (43 tokens in 40 texts), *at martinmes nexit* (17 times in 14 texts), *martinmes next efter* (11 times in 10 texts), *and martinmes be* (10 times in 10 texts), and in *witsunday and martinmes* (68 tokens in 61 texts), *fest of witsunday* (31 times in 26 texts), *of witsunday nexit* (26 times in 21 texts), *witsunday nexit thareftir* (14 times in 12 texts), *witsunday nexit followand* (13 times in 13 texts), *witsunday nexit efter* (11 times, 11 texts), *ye witsunday nexit* (13 times in 12 texts), *(to) say witsunday and* (21 times in 21 texts), *at witsunday and* (15 times in 15 texts), *at witsunday nexit* (11 times in 10 texts), *at ye witsunday* (11 times in 10 texts), *yhere witsunday and* (15 times, 15 texts), *ye yhere witsunday* (12 times in 12 texts), *and witsunday be* (11 times in 11 texts). These two days in the Scottish calendar had a special significance, as they belonged to the so-called quarter days, or term dates, when new servants could be employed, accounts had to be balanced, and old debts had to be either paid off or officially prolonged. On the agricultural origins and later pagan and Christian adaptations of the four pivotal celebrations in a Scottish calendar, see Moffat (2005: 185–190).

15. For instance, there are combinations of this frame with reference to the geographic position and measurements of a plot of land, as well as to its owners or location. As the actual numbers and names vary, the bundles consist of frames easily filled with these specific details, for example, *that ta part and ye landis of* (25 times in 20 texts), *that ta sid and ye landis of* (11 times in 11 texts), *est part on that ta part and* (7 times in 6 texts), and so on. A rivalry between *part* and *sid* 'side' as the head noun is also observable.

16. A related bundle *and hir airis* was found 22 times in 12 texts, while *and his airis* appears in the top formulaic range (Type N2c) and scores 242 tokens in 116 texts (FF = 45).

17. Due to the incomplete structure of lexical bundles, in this one case the 3-gram escapes straightforward classification. The verb may be both active or passive, depending on the context (which is not provided because the bundle is too short). Looking at potentially overlapping bundles we may infer that *callit to ye* includes a past participle (cf. Type V1a *callit to ye chalans* 'called to the charges', 40 tokens in 15 texts). However, this 3-gram appears 67 times in the corpus in 32 texts, so it is impossible to decide on the basis of bundle overlaps whether the verb *callit* was also employed in active contexts.

18. Here an alternative reading could be a reduced relative clause—'the suits (which were) called', and so on—which would support the interpretation of *callit* 'called' as an adjectival passive. However, the context following never contains a verb phrase whose predicate would be 'suits' modified by the clause.

19. The forms *statut* 'stated' and *ordanit* 'ordained' could still be subject to the passive adjective interpretation, see above.

20. It is noteworthy that the *CSD* does not have an entry on *item* (adv), treating it most probably as an instance of code-switching to Latin. The *DSL* and the *OED* do include *item* (adv) in their lexicons.

21. They studied three selected parameters, the so-called *dimensions*, which distinguish oral production of language from the written mode (Biber 1988, Biber and Finegan 1992). In a paper revising the multidimensional framework, Biber (2003) included lexical bundle material in the search for newly defined dimensions of difference between oral and written modes of communication. It turned out that lexical bundles with verbs, *wh*-elements, and *it* in the initial position correlate positively with *oral* discourse, whereas those with

initial prepositions indicate *literate* discourse (Dimension 1, terms after Biber 2003: 55). Similarly, lexical bundles with initial prepositions and nouns are positively correlated with Dimension 4, Academic Stance.

22. Biber works on the 2.7 million-word TOEFL 2000 Spoken and Written Academic Language Corpus (2003: 49).

23. Substantial parts of this material are in Latin and French.

24. See also Archer (2005) for the characteristics of the language of the early modern courtroom. The EdHeW material suggests that everyday mundane cases did not attract that much public attention, hence the notorious fines for failure to appear in court, commented on in section 7.3.2.

Chapter 10

1. Bastow (2010) notes that Hatzidaki's unpublished dissertation (1999) is the first corpus-driven study into binomials.

2. For the sake of numeric comparison, suffice it to say that Benor and Levy (2006) found 3,680 binomial tokens in three combined PDE corpora (c. 5 million words, cf. EdHeW with 0.6 million words). After pruning them of personal names and vague extender phrases, such as "...and stuff", they were left with 411 types.

3. Benor and Levy (2006) did not include personal names, either. For a discussion focused specifically on constituent order in pairs of female and male first names, see Wright, Hay, and Bent (2005).

4. Alternatively, these binomials could be seen as 'cause and effect', as the document first had to be signed in order for the claim or right to be recognized.

5. As the anonymous reviewer points out, the verb *to satisfy* may mean 'to put to rest any legal claim'. If this interpretation were accepted, this binomial would qualify as an instance of cause and effect. In my analysis, I followed the *DSL*, which clearly sets this verb in the context of financial satisfaction.

6. No purely echoic binomials or multinomials were found in EdHeW, probably due to the specialized and written nature of the data (cf. Gustafsson 1975; Norrick 1988; Biber et al. 1999).

7. Interestingly, the *DSL* lists a reversed pair in two different spellings, *loth and scoth* (1297), *lote & scott* (1320), which have not been found in EdHeW.

8. Unless the coordination of singular *juge* and plural *jugis* indicated a choice between a single opinion and the opinion of several judges. I am grateful to the anonymous reviewer for this suggestion.

9. Note that only the more frequent order, *payd and assithit*, is found in a present tense form *pay and assith*. Similarly, *give and grant* renders other grammatical forms like the present tense (*giffis and grantis*) and the present participle (*giffand and grantand*).

10. Włodarczyk (2007b: 311) uses the term *tetranomials*, while Sauer (2013: 97) calls such strings *quadruplets*.

11. Another possible thread of future inquiry was suggested by a 4-gram *had has or may*, which clearly indicates a trinomial whose final coordinated element is built out of two lexical items: *may* and the missing *have*. Unfortunately the procedure used so far did not allow for extracting multinomials with the coordinating device in a different slot than the last-but-one, so such potential multinomials had to be set aside.

Chapter 11

1. Due to uneven word counts for each 30-year subperiod of the corpus (Fig. 8.1), all numeric counts were normalized per 10,000 words. All conclusions drawn in this chapter are based on these normalized frequencies.

2. The syntagmatic overlap *men be thir present letteris* has been classified in the category of 'object' because the letters are the focus of this bundle, see section (h) below.

3. The same bundle making reference to the home monarch, *(ye) king of scotland*, is rare—only 19 tokens in 8 texts, which did not allow for this bundle to be included in formulaicity calculations. More frequently is the monarch referred to as *king of scottis* (34 instances in 34 texts), but it remains outside the most formulaic pool, too. Clearly the document compilers saw fit to stress the mutual relationship between the Scottish monarch and his subjects in the legal documents by the use of the possessive pronoun *oure* 'our' and the title *souerain* 'sovereign'. Also the honorific term *grace* was employed, attached typically to the noun 'queen', as well as in reference to God (*grace of god*, 53 tokens in 50 texts). Another honorific, *ye king hienes* (14 tokens in 7 texts) or *ye kingis hienes* (7 tokens in 6 texts), was too infrequent to qualify in final bundle counts. One more royal reference is found in 3-grams—*king of france*, 16 instances in 7 texts, also below the bundle threshold.

4. In the most formulaic bundles, the adjective *apperand* 'apparent' is used only in the premodifying position. The other word order barely made it to the initial bundle search, with 6 tokens of *son and air apperand* in 6 texts.

5. Halliday (1978) placed such functional elements within the ideational function, see sections 3.3.1–3.3.2 for further details.

6. Forms with feminine and plural reference are also found, however, they are rarer: *plege hir hand* appears 15 times in 14 texts and 11 times it is followed by *ye*, while *plege thare handis* appears 33 times in 28 texts and is followed by *ye* in 22 texts.

7. For example, I have classified *item ye same* (64 tokens in 36 texts) and *item that ilk* (66 tokens in 27 texts) in the category of cohesive links but both contain the sequencing adverbial of narration, too.

8. A bundle which could well be a potential syntagmatic overlap is *is to remember* (133 tokens in 79 texts, FF = 29), which has a directive function, see section 11.3.3.1. Less frequent bundles include *is to put* (20 tokens in 16 texts) and *is to bere* (9 tokens in 9 texts), as in 'to bear witness'.

9. A separate analysis of legal speech acts, seen through the prism of modern Anglo-American common law, was presented in Kevelson (1982).

10. Notice that in both cases the auxiliary is missing—the lawsuits *were* called and the court dealings *were* affirmed (or the court *was* fenced), see also the structural discussion in Chapter 9.

11. A present tense counterpart *is maid burges* also appears in the corpus (16 tokens in 15 texts) but only in the sixteenth century.

Chapter 12

1. The burgh court could also gather outdoors, for example, on the plot of land under transfer (Hamilton-Grierson 1924). For more detail on burgh court venues, see section 7.3.4.

2. The position of the coordinating device *and* in numerals seems to be fluctuating at that time, something worth further investigation.

3. Culpeper and Kytö (2010: 137) use the following formula: the sum of instances of the top ten bundles, times 3 (because the bundles were 3-grams), divided by the corpus word count, times 10,000. Their top ten bundles were simply the most frequent ones. Consequently, I also chose the top 3-grams on the basis of sheer frequency counts, disregarding for a moment the formulaicity factor (FF) used in the rest of the discussion, which additionally incorporates the textual spread and the relative weight of more frequent bundles, see 8.5.4.

REFERENCES

Abney, S. P. 1987. "The English Noun Phrase in its Sentential Aspect." Ph.D. diss., MIT.

Abu-Ssaydeh, Abdul-Fattah. 2005. "Variation in Multi-Word Units: The Absent Dimension." *Studia Anglica Posnaniensia* 41: 125–146.

Adler, Mark. 2012. "The Plain Language Movement." In *The Oxford Handbook of Language and Law*, edited by Lawrence M. Solan and Peter M. Tiersma. New York: Oxford University Press. Accessed at Oxford Handbooks Online.

Agutter, Alex. 1990. "Restandardisation in Middle Scots." In *Papers from the 5th International Conference on English Historical Linguistics*, edited by Sylvia Adamson, Vivien Law, and Susan Wright, 1–11. Amsterdam: John Benjamins.

Aijmer, Karen. 1996. *Conversational Routines in English*. London: Longman.

Aitken, Adam J. 1971. "Variation and Variety in Middle Scots." In *Edinburgh Studies in English and Scots*, edited by Adam J. Aitken et al., 177–210. London: Longman.

———. 1977. "How to Pronounce Older Scots." In *Bards and Makars: Scots Language and Literature Medieval and Renaissance*, edited by Adam J. Aitken, M. P. McDiarmid, and D. S. Thomson, 1–21. Glasgow: Glasgow University Press.

———. 1979. "Scottish Speech: A Historical View, with Special Reference to the Standard English of Scotland." In *Languages of Scotland*, edited by A. J. Aitken and Tom McArthur, 85–118. Edinburgh: Edinburgh University Press.

———. 1983. "The Language of Older Scots Poetry." In *Scotland and the Lowland Tongue*, edited by J. D. McClure, 18–49. Aberdeen: Aberdeen University Press.

———. 1985. "A History of Scots." In *The Concise Scots Dictionary*, edited by Mairi Robinson, ix–xvi. Aberdeen: Aberdeen University Press.

Alauddin, Khan. 1968. "Scottish Burghs: Some Aspects of their Origins, Development and Plan." B.Litt. thesis, University of Glasgow.

Alexander, R. J. 1984. "Fixed Expressions in English: Reference Books and the Teacher." *ELT Journal* 38(2): 127–134.

Altenberg, Bengt. 1998. "On the Phraseology of Spoken English: The Evidence of Recurrent Word-Combinations." In *Phraseology: Theory, Analysis and Applications*, edited by A. Cowie, 101–122. Oxford: Clarendon Press.

Anderson, Benedict. 1991. *Imagined Communities: Reflections on the Origin and Spread of Nationalism*. London: Verso.

Archer, Dawn. 2005. *Questions and Answers in the English Courtroom (1640–1760): A Sociopragmatic Analysis*. Amsterdam: John Benjamins.

———. 2006. "(Re)initiating Strategies: Judges and Defendants in Early Modern English Courtrooms." *Journal of Historical Pragmatics* 7(2): 181–211.

Archer, Dawn, and Paul Rayson. 2006. "Dealing with Variation: Spelling." Invited talk at SCOTS Symposium on Linguistic Variation and Electronic Projects, University of Glasgow, April 28, 2006.

Ari, Omer. 2006. "Review of Three Software Programs Designed to Identify Lexical Bundles." *Language Learning and Technology* 10(1): 30–37.

Astill, Grenville. 2008. "General Survey 600–1300." In *The Cambridge Urban History of Britain*. Vol. 1, *600–1540*, edited by D. M. Palliser, 27–50. Cambridge: Cambridge University Press.

Baker, J. H. 2008. "The Books of Common Law." In *The Cambridge History of the Book in Britain*. Vol. 3, *1400–1557*, edited by Lotte Hellinga and J. B. Trapp, 411–432. Cambridge: Cambridge University Press.

Bald, Marjory A. 1928. "Contemporary References to the Scottish Speech of the Sixteenth Century." *Scottish Historical Review* 25: 163–179.

Baron, Alistair, and Paul Rayson. 2009. "Automatic Standardization of Texts Containing Spelling Variation: How Much Training Data Do You Need?" In *Proceedings of the Corpus Linguistics Conference, CL2009, University of Liverpool, UK, 20–23 July 2009*, edited by M. Mahlberg, V. González-Díaz, and C. Smith. Available at: http://ucrel.lancs.ac.uk/publications/cl2009/.

Baron, Alistair, Paul Rayson, and Dawn Archer. 2009. "Automatic Standardization of Spelling for Historical Text Mining." Poster session presented at Digital Humanities 2009, University of Maryland, USA.

Barrell, A. D. M. 2000. *Medieval Scotland*. Cambridge: Cambridge University Press.

Barrow, Geoffrey. 1997. "Non-literary Manuscript Production and Survival in Scotland." In *Pragmatic Literacy, East and West, 1200–1330*, edited by R. H. Britnell, 131–146. Woodbridge: Boydell Press.

Bastow, Tony. 2010. "The Rhetoric of Binomial Phrases in a Corpus of U.S. Defence Speeches." In *Perspectives in Politics and Discourse*, edited by Urszula Okulska and Piotr Cap, 143–154. Amsterdam: John Benjamins.

Bax, Marcel. 2010. "Rituals." In *Historical Pragmatics*, edited by Andreas H. Jucker and Irma Taavitsainen, 483–519. Berlin: De Gruyter Mouton.

Bazerman, Charles. 1988. *Shaping Written Knowledge: The Genre and Activity of the Experimental Article in Science*. Madison: University of Wisconsin Press.

———. 1990. "Discourse Analysis and Social Construction." *Annual Review of Applied Linguistics* 11: 77–83.

———. 1991. "How Natural Philosophers can Cooperate: The Literary Technology of Coordinated Investigation in Joseph Priestley's History and Present State of Electricity (1767)." In *Textual Dynamics of the Professions: Historical and Contemporary Studies of Writing in Professional Communities*, edited by Charles Bazerman and James Paradis, 13–44. Madison: University of Wisconsin Press.

Bazerman, Charles, and James Paradis, eds. 1991. *Textual Dynamics of the Professions: Historical and Contemporary Studies of Writing in Professional Communities*. Madison: University of Wisconsin Press.

Bazerman, Charles, and Paul Prior, eds. 2004. *What Writing Does and How It Does It: An Introduction to Analyzing Texts and Textual Practices*. Mahwah, NJ: Lawrence Erlbaum.

Beaton, John Angus. 1982. *Scots Law Terms and Expressions*. Edinburgh: W. Green & Son.

Beaugrande, Robert de. 1997. "The Story of Discourse Analysis." In *Discourse Studies: A Multidisciplinary Introduction*. Vol. 1, *Discourse as Structure and Process*, edited by Teun van Dijk, 35–62. London: SAGE Publications.

———. 2000. "Text Linguistics at the Millennium: Corpus Data and Missing Links." *Text* 20(2): 153–195.

Behaghel, Otto. 1909. "Beziehungen zwischen Umfang und Reihenfolge von Satzgliedern." *Indogermanische Forschungen* 25: 110–142.

Bennett, William. 1978. "Comparison of Predicative Binominals in French and English." *Linguistics* 16(1): 195–204.

Benor, Sarah Bunin, and Roger Levy. 2006. "The Chicken or the Egg? A Probabilistic Analysis of English Binomials." *Language* 82(2): 233–278.

Bergs, Alexander T. 2000. "Social Networks in pre-1500 Britain: Problems, Prospects, Examples." *European Journal of English Studies* 4(3): 239–251.

Bergs, Alexander T., and Laurel J. Brinton, eds. 2012. *English Historical Linguistics: An International Handbook.* Vol. 1. Berlin: De Gruyter Mouton.

Beveridge, Barbara. 2002. "Legal English—How It Developed and Why It Is Not Appropriate for International Commercial Contracts." In *The Development of Legal Language*, edited by Heikki Mattila, 55–79. Helsinki: Talentum Media.

Beveridge, Erskine, ed. 1917. *The Burgh Records of Dunfermline, Transcribed from the Original Manuscript Volume Courts, Sasines, etc. 1488–1584.* Edinburgh: William Brown.

Bex, Tony. 1996. *Variety in Written English: Texts in Society: Societies in Text.* London: Routledge.

Bhatia, Vijay K. 1993. *Analysing Genre: Language Use in Professional Settings.* London: Longman.

———. 2004. *The Worlds of Written Discourse.* London: Continuum.

———. 2008. "Genre Analysis, ESP and Professional Practice." *English for Specific Purposes* 27: 161–174.

Biber, Douglas. 1988. *Variation across Speech and Writing.* Cambridge: Cambridge University Press.

———. 1989. "A Typology of English Texts." *Linguistics* 27: 3–43.

———. 1994. "An Analytical Framework for Register Studies." In *Sociolinguistic Perspectives on Register*, edited by Douglas Biber and Edward Finegan, 31–56. Oxford: Oxford University Press.

———. 1995. *Dimensions of Register Variation: A Cross-Linguistic Comparison.* Cambridge: Cambridge University Press.

———. 2003. "Variation among University Spoken and Written Registers: A New Multi-dimensional Analysis." In *Corpus Analysis: Language Structure and Language Use*, edited by Pepi Leistyna and Charles F. Meyer, 47–69. Amsterdam: Rodopi.

———. 2004. "Lexical Bundles in Academic Speech and Writing." In *Practical Applications in Language Corpora (PALC 2003)*, edited by Barbara Lewandowska-Tomaszczyk, 165–178. Hamburg: Peter Lang.

———. 2006. *University Language: A Corpus-based Study of Spoken and Written Registers.* Amsterdam: John Benjamins.

———. 2009. "Corpus-Based and Corpus-Driven Analyses of Language Variation and Use." In *The Oxford Handbook of Linguistic Analysis*, edited by Bernd Heine and Heiko Narrog, 159–191. Oxford: Oxford University Press.

Biber, Douglas, and Federica Barbieri. 2007. "Lexical Bundles in University Spoken and Written Registers." *English for Specific Purposes* 26: 263–286.

Biber, Douglas, and Susan Conrad. 2009. *Register, Genre, and Style.* Cambridge: Cambridge University Press.

Biber, Douglas, and Edward Finegan. 1989. "Drift and the Evolution of English Style: A History of Three Genres." *Language* 65(3): 487–517.

———. 1992. "The Linguistic Evolution of Five Written and Speech-Based English Genres from the 17th to the 20th Centuries." In *History of Englishes: New Methods and Interpretations in Historical Linguistics*, edited by Matti Rissanen et al., 688–704. Berlin: Mouton de Gruyter.

———. 1997. "Diachronic Relations among Speech-Based and Written Registers in English." In *To Explain the Present: Studies in the Changing English Language in Honour of Matti Rissanen*, edited by Terttu Nevalainen and Leena Kahlas-Tarkka, 253–275. Berlin: Mouton de Gruyter.

Biber, Douglas, and Edward Finegan, eds. 1994. *Sociolinguistic Perspectives on Register.* Oxford: Oxford University Press.

Biber, Douglas, Susan Conrad, and Viviana Cortes. 2003. "Lexical Bundles in Speech and Writing: An Initial Taxonomy." In *Corpus Linguistics by the Lune: A Festschrift for Geoffrey Leech*, edited by Andrew Wilson, Paul Rayson, and Tony McEnery, 71–92. Frankfurt am Main: Peter Lang.

———. 2004. "If You Look at… Lexical Bundles in University Teaching and Textbooks." *Applied Linguistics* 25(3): 371–405.

Biber, Douglas, Sarah Conrad, and Randi Reppen. 1998. *Corpus Linguistics: Investigating Language Structure and Use.* Cambridge: Cambridge University Press.

Biber, Douglas, Stig Johansson, Geoffrey Leech, Susan Conrad, and Edward Finegan. 1999. *Longman Grammar of Spoken and Written English.* London: Longman.

Bingham, Caroline. 1974. *The Stewart Kingdom of Scotland: 1371–1603.* London: Weidenfeld and Nicolson.

Birks, Peter. 1995. "The Foundation of Legal Rationality in Scotland." In *The Civil Law Tradition in Scotland*, edited by Robin Evans-Jones, 81–99. Edinburgh: Stair Society.

Blum-Kulka, Shoshana, and Juliane House. 1989. "Cross-Cultural and Situational Variation in Requesting Behavior." In *Cross-Cultural Pragmatics: Requests and Apologies*, edited by Shoshana Blum-Kulka, Juliane House, and Gabriele Kasper, 123–154. Norwood, NJ: Ablex.

Bolinger, Dwight. 1962. "Binomials and Pitch Accent." *Lingua* 11: 34–44.

Booton, Harold W. 1987. "Burgesses and Landed Men in North-East Scotland in the Later Middle Ages: A Study in Social Interaction." Ph.D. diss., Aberdeen.

Brand, Paul A. 1992. *The Origins of the English Legal Profession.* Oxford: Oxford University Press.

Brinton, Laurel J. 2001. "Historical Discourse Analysis." In *The Handbook of Discourse Analysis*, edited by Deborah Schiffrin, Deborah Tannen, and Heidi E. Hamilton, 138–160. Oxford: Blackwell.

Brinton, Laurel J., and Elisabeth Closs Traugott. 2005. *Lexicalization in Language Change.* Cambridge: Cambridge University Press.

Britnell, Richard H. 1997. "Pragmatic Literacy in Latin Christendom." In *Pragmatic Literacy, East and West, 1200–1330*, edited by R. H. Britnell, 3–24. Woodbridge: Boydell Press.

Brown, Michael, and Steve Boardman. 2005. "Late Medieval Scotland." In *Scotland: A History*, edited by Jenny Wormald, 69–92. Oxford: Oxford University Press.

Brundage, James A. 2008. *The Medieval Origins of the Legal Profession: Canonists, Civilians, and Courts.* Chicago: University of Chicago Press.

Bugaj [Kopaczyk], Joanna. 2004a. "Middle Scots as an Emerging Standard and Why It Did Not Make It." *Scottish Language* 23: 19–34.

———. 2004b. *Middle Scots Inflectional System in the South-West of Scotland*. Frankfurt am Main: Peter Lang.

———. 2006a. "Sources of Discourse-Specific Vocabulary in Middle Scots Administrative Records: An Etymological Study of Binominals." In *Diachronic Perspectives on Domain-Specific English*, edited by Marina Dossena and Irma Taavitsainen, 109–132. Bern: Peter Lang.

———. 2006b. "Analytic of the Samyn or Synthetic Its? The Use of Neuter Possessives in Older Scots Texts." In *Types of Variation: Diachronic, Dialectal and Typological Interfaces*, edited by Terttu Nevalainen, Juhani Klemola, and Mikko Laitinen, 171–202. Amsterdam: John Benjamins.

Bugaj [Kopaczyk], Joanna, and Matylda Włodarczyk. 2006. "At 'the wylle and plesur' of 'kyng and soueraine': In Search of Motivations for Binomials as Markers of Legal Discourse." In *IFAtuation: A Life at IFA. A Festschrift for Professor Jacek Fisiak on the Occasion of his 70th Birthday*, edited by Katarzyna Dziubalska-Kołaczyk, 85–98. Poznań: Wydawnictwo Uniwersytetu im. Adama Mickiewicza.

Burke, Gerald. 1971. *Towns in the Making*. London: Arnold.

Burke, Peter. 2004. *Languages and Communities in Early Modern Europe*. Cambridge: Cambridge University Press.

Butcher, Andrew. 2004. "The Functions of Script in the Speech Community of a Late Medieval Town, c. 1300–1550." In *The Uses of Script and Print, 1300–1700*, edited by Julia Crick and Alexandra Walsham, 157–170. Cambridge: Cambridge University Press.

Butler, Christopher S. 2004. "Corpus Studies and Functional Linguistic Theories." *Functions of Language* 11(2): 147–186.

———. 2005. "Formulaic Language: An Overview with Particular Reference to the Cross-Linguistic Perspective." In *The Dynamics of Language Use*, edited by Christopher S. Butler, María de los Ángeles Gómez-González, and Susana M. Doval-Suárez, 221–242. Amsterdam: John Benjamins.

Cairns, John W. 2000. "Historical Introduction." In *A History of Private Law in Scotland*, edited by Kenneth Reid and Reinhard Zimmermann, 14–184. Oxford: Oxford University Press.

Cameron, Gordon D. L. 2005. "Scots and English Nuisance…Much the Same Thing?" *Edinburgh Law Review* 9: 98–121.

Carpenter, Sarah. 2003. "Performing Diplomacies: The 1560s Court Entertainments of Mary Queen of Scots." *Scottish Historical Review* 82(2), no. 214: 194–225.

Carswell, R. D. 1967. "The Origins of the Legal Profession in Scotland." *American Journal of Legal History* 11(1): 41–56.

Carter, Ronald, and Michael McCarthy. 2006. *Cambridge Grammar of English: A Comprehensive Guide. Spoken and Written English Grammar and Usage*. Cambridge: Cambridge University Press.

Chafe, Wallace L. 2003. "Discourse: Overview." In *International Encyclopedia of Linguistics*. Vol. 1, *AAVE–Esperanto*, edited by W. Frawley. New York: Oxford University Press.

Chafe, Wallace L., and Jane Danielewicz. 1987. "Properties of Spoken and Written Language." In *Comprehending Oral and Written Language*, edited by Rosalind Horowitz and S. Jay Samuels, 83–113. San Diego: Academic Press.

Charnock, Ross. 2006. "Clear Ambiguity." In *Legal Language and the Search for Clarity: Practice and Tools*, edited by Anne Wagner and Sophie Cacciaguidi-Fahy, 65–103. Bern: Peter Lang.

Charrow, Veda R., Jo Ann Crandall, and Robert P. Charrow. 1982. "Characteristics and Functions of Legal Language." In *Sublanguage: Studies of Language in Restricted Semantic Domains*, edited by Richard Kittredge and John Lehrberger, 175–190. Berlin: Walter de Gruyter.

Clanchy, T. M. 1979. *From Memory to Written Record: England 1066–1307.* London: E. Arnold.

Claridge, Claudia. 2008. "Historical Corpora." In *Corpus Linguistics: An International Handbook.* Vol. 1, edited by Anke Lüdeling, and Merja Kytö, 242–259. Berlin: Walter de Gruyter.

Claridge, Claudia, and Leslie Arnovick. 2010. "Pragmaticalisation and Discursisation." In *Historical Pragmatics*, edited by Andreas H. Jucker and Irma Taavitsainen, 165–192. Berlin: De Grutyer Mouton.

Clark, Peter, and Paul Slack. 1976. *English Towns in Transition: 1500–1700.* Oxford: Oxford University Press.

Collins, Ronald K. L., and David M. Skover. 1992. "Paratexts." *Stanford Law Review* 44(3): 509–552.

Conklin, Kathy, and Norbert Schmitt. 2008. "Formulaic Sequences: Are They Processed More Quickly than Nonformulaic Language by Native and Nonnative Speakers?" *Applied Linguistics* 29(1): 72–89.

Conklin, William E. 1998. *Phenomenology of Modern Legal Discourse: The Juridical Production and the Disclosure of Suffering.* Williston: Ashgate.

Conley, John M., and William M. O'Barr. 1990. *Rules versus Relationships: The Ethnography of Legal Discourse.* Chicago: University of Chicago Press.

———. 1998. *Just Words: Law, Language and Power.* Chicago: University of Chicago Press.

Connor, W. 1978. "A Nation is a Nation, is a State, is an Ethnic Group, is a . . ." *Ethnic and Racial Studies* 1: 377–400.

Conrad, Susan. 2001. "Variation among Disciplinary Texts: A Comparison of Textbooks and Journal Articles in Biology and History." In *Variation in English: Multi-Dimensional Studies*, edited by Susan Conrad and Douglas Biber, 94–107. London: Longman.

Conrad, Susan, and Douglas Biber, eds. 2001. *Variation in English: Multi-Dimensional Studies.* London: Longman.

Constable, T., and A. Constable, eds. 1898. *The compt buik of David Wedderburne, merchant of Dundee, 1587–1630.* Scottish History Society.

Cook, Guy. [1992] 2001. *The Discourse of Advertising.* 2d ed. London: Routledge.

Cooper, William E., and John R. Ross. 1975. "World order." In *Papers from the Parasession on Functionalism*, edited by R. E. Grossman, L. J. San, and T. J. Vance. Chicago: Chicago Linguistic Society.

Corbett, John. 1997. *Language and Scottish Literature.* Edinburgh: Edinburgh University Press.

———. 2003. "Language Planning and Modern Scots." In *The Edinburgh Companion to Scots*, edited by John Corbett, J. Derrick McClure, and Jane Stuart Smith, 251–272. Edinburgh: Edinburgh University Press.

Corbett, John, J. Derrick McClure, and Jane Stuart-Smith, eds. 2003. *The Edinburgh Companion to Scots.* Edinburgh: Edinburgh University Press.

Cortes, Viviana. 2002. "Lexical Bundles in Freshman Compositions." In *Using Corpora to Explore Linguistic Variation*, edited by Randi Reppen, Susan M. Fitzmaurice, and Douglas Biber, 131–146. Amsterdam: John Benjamins.

———. 2004. "Lexical Bundles in Published and Student Writing in History and Biology." *English for Specific Purposes* 23(4): 397–423.

Costa, James. 2009. "Language History as Charter Myth? Scots and the (Re)invention of Scotland." *Scottish Language* 28: 1–26.

Cotterill, Janet, ed. 2003. *Language in the Legal Process.* Basingstoke: Palgrave Macmillan.

Coulmas, F. 1994. "Formulaic Language." In *Encyclopedia of Language and Linguistics.* Vol. 3, edited by R. E. Asher, and J. M. Y. Simpson, 1292–1293. Oxford: Pergamon Press.

Cram, David. 1989. "Seventeenth-Century Punctuation Theory: Butler's Philosophical Analysis and Wilkins' Philosophical Critique." *Folia Linguistica Historica* 8(1–2): 309–349.

Crawford, P., Alison Johnson, B. J. Browse, and P. Nolan. 1999. "The Language of Mental Health Nursing Reports: Firing Paper Bullets?" *Journal of Advanced Nursing* 29(2): 331–340.

Crystal, David. 2003. *A Dictionary of Linguistics and Phonetics.* 5th ed. Oxford: Blackwell.

Crystal, David, and Derek Davy. 1969. *Investigating English Style.* London: Longmans.

Cuddon, John Anthony, and Claire Preston. [1977] 1998. *A Dictionary of Literary Terms and Literary Theory.* 4th ed. Oxford: Blackwell.

Culpeper, Jonathan, and Dawn Archer. 2008. "Requests and Directness in Early Modern English Trial Proceedings and Play Texts, 1640–1760." In *Speech Acts in the History of English*, edited by Andreas H. Jucker and Irma Taavitsainen, 45–84. Amsterdam: John Benjamins.

Culpeper, Jonathan, and Merja Kytö. 2002. "Lexical Bundles in Early Modern English: A Window into the Speech-Related Language of the Past." In *Sounds, Words, Texts, Change: Selected Papers from the Eleventh International Conference on English Historical Linguistics (11 ICEHL)*, edited by Teresa Fanego, Belén Méndez-Naya, and Elena Seoane, 45–63. Amsterdam: John Benjamins.

———. 2010. *Early Modern English Dialogues: Spoken Interaction as Writing.* Cambridge: Cambridge University Press.

Cumming, Susanna, and Tsuyoshi Ono. 1997. "Discourse and Grammar." In *Discourse Studies: A Multidisciplinary Introduction.* Vol. 1, *Discourse as Structure and Process*, edited by Teun van Dijk, 112–137. London: SAGE Publications.

Curzan, Anne. 2009. "Historical Corpus Linguistics and Evidence of Language Change." In *Corpus Linguistics: An International Handbook.* Vol. 2, edited by Anke Lüdeling and Merja Kytö, 1091–1109. Berlin: Walter de Gruyter.

Danet, Brenda. 1980. "Language in the Legal Process." *Law and Society Review* 14(3): 445–564.

———. 1984. "The Magic Flute: A Prosodic Analysis of Binomial Expressions in Legal Hebrew." *Text* 4: 143–172.

———. 1997. "Speech, Writing and Performativity: An Evolutionary View of the History of Constitutive Ritual." In *The Construction of Professional Discourse*, edited by Britt-Louise Gunnarsson, Per Linell, and Bengt Nordberg, 13–41. Harlow: Longman.

Danet, Brenda, and Bryna Bogoch. 1992. " 'Whoever alters this may God turn his face from him on the day of judgement': Curses in Anglo-Saxon Legal Documents." *Journal of American Folklore* 105: 132–165.

———. 1994. "Orality, Literacy, and Performativity in Anglo-Saxon Wills." In *Language and the Law*, edited by John Gibbons, 100–135. London: Longmans.

Dawson, Jane E. A. 2007. *Scotland Re-formed. 1488–1587.* Edinburgh: Edinburgh University Press.

Dennison, E. Patricia. 2007. "Urban Society and Economy." In *Scotland: The Making and Unmaking of the Nation c. 1100–1707*. Vol. 2, *Early Modern Scotland: c. 1500–1707*, edited by Bob Harris and Alan R. MacDonald, 145–165. Dundee: Dundee University Press.

Dennison, E. Patricia, and Michael Lynch. 2005. "Crown, Capital, and Metropolis. Edinburgh and Canongate: The Rise of a Capital and an Urban Court." *Journal of Urban History* 32(1): 22–43.

Devitt, Amy J. 1989. *Standardizing Written English: Diffusion in the Case of Scotland 1520–1659*. Cambridge: Cambridge University Press.

———. 2004. *Writing Genres*. Carbondale: Southern Illinois University Press.

Dickinson, William Croft, ed. 1937. *The Court Book of the Barony of Carnwath 1523–1542*. Edinburgh: Scottish History Society.

——— ed. 1957. *Early Records of the Burgh of Aberdeen: 1317, 1398–1407*. Edinburgh: Scottish History Society.

Dieckmann, Johann Andreas. 2004. "Scots Influence on English Law: The Guarantor's Right to Derivative Recourse (Subrogation)." *Edinburgh Law Review* 8: 329–359.

Dodds, W. E. 1927. "A Few Comparisons between English and Scots Law. II. The Law of Personal Relations." *Journal of Comparative Legislation and International Law* 9(1), 3rd series: 40–58.

Dolezalek, Gero. 2010. *Scotland under Jus commune: Census of Legal Literature in Scotland, Mainly between 1500 and 1660*. Vol. 1. Edinburgh: Stair Society.

Donaldson, Gordon. 1970. *Scottish Historical Documents*. Edinburgh: Scottish Academic Press.

Donaldson, Gordon, ed. 1952. *Protocol Book of James Young 1485–1515*. Edinburgh: Scottish Record Society.

Dossena, Marina. 2001. "Committed Wittingly, Willinglie and of Purpose: Exclusiveness and Intensification in Early Modern English Legal Texts." In *Modality in Specialized Texts: Selected Papers of the 1st CERLIS Conference*, edited by Maurizio Gotti and Marina Dossena, 113–131. Bern: Peter Lang.

———. 2003. "Scots." In *Germanic Standardizations. Past to Present*, edited by Ana Deumert and Wim Vandenbussche, 383–404. Amsterdam: John Benjamins.

———. 2005. *Scotticisms in Grammar and Vocabulary*. Edinburgh: John Donald.

Doty, Kathleen L. 2010. "Courtroom Discourse." In *Historical Pragmatics*, edited by Andreas H. Jucker and Irma Taavitsainen, 621–650. Berlin: De Gruyter Mouton.

Doty, Kathleen L., and Risto Hiltunen. 2009. "Formulaic Discourse and Speech Acts in the Witchcraft Trial Records of Salem, 1692." *Journal of Pragmatics* 41: 458–469.

Dressler, Wolfgang. 1972. *Einführung in die Textlinguistik*. Tübingen: Niemeyer.

Drout, Michael D. C. 2006. "A Meme-Based Approach to Oral Traditional Theory." *Oral Tradition* 21(2): 269–294.

DSL = Dictionary of the Scots Language. Available at: http://www.dsl.ac.uk.

Dudley-Evans, Tony, and Maggie-Jo StJohn. 1998. *Developments in ESP: A Multi-Disciplinary Approach*. Cambridge: Cambridge University Press.

Duncan, Andrew G. M. 1992. *Green's Glossary of Scottish Legal Terms*. 3d ed. Edinburgh: W. Green/Sweet & Maxwell.

Duncan, Archibald A. M. 1975. *Scotland: The Making of the Kingdom*. Edinburgh: Mercat Press.

Durkan, John. 1983. "The Early Scottish Notary." In *The Renaissance and Reformation in Scotland: Essays in Honour of Gordon Donaldson*, edited by Ian B. Cowan, and Duncan Shaw, 22–40. Edinburgh: Scottish Academic Press.

Edinburgh Records = *Extracts from the Records of the Burgh of Edinburgh A.D.1573–1589*. 1882. Edinburgh: Scottish Burgh Records Society.

Edington, Carol. 1998. "Paragons and Patriots: National Identity and the Chivalric Ideal in Late-Medieval Scotland." In *Image and Identity: The Making and Re-making of Scotland through the Ages*, edited by Dauvit Broun, R. J. Finlay, and Michael Lynch, 69–81. Edinburgh: Edinburgh University Press.

Erman, Britt, and Beatrice Warren. 2000. "The Idiom Principle and the Open Choice Principle." *Text* 20(1): 29–62.

Erskine, Caroline, Alan R. MacDonald, and Michael Penman, eds. 2007. *The Making and Unmaking of the Nation c. 1100–1707*. Vol. 5, *Major Documents*. Dundee: Dundee University Press.

Ewan, Elizabeth L. 1988. "The Community of the Burgh in the Fourteenth Century." In *The Scottish Medieval Town*, edited by Michael Lynch, Michael Spearman, and Geoffrey Stell, 228–244. Edinburgh: John Donald.

———. 1992. "Scottish Portias: Women in the Courts in Mediaeval Scottish Towns." *Journal of the Canadian Historical Association* 3(1): 27–43.

———. 2005. "'To the longer liver': Provisions for the Dissolution of the Marital Economy in Scotland, 1470–1550." In *The Marital Economy in Scandinavia and Britain 1400–1900*, edited by Maria Ågren and Amy Louise Erickson, 191–206. London: Ashgate.

Fenk-Oczlon, Gertraud. 1989. "Word Frequency and Word Order in Freezes." *Linguistics* 27(3): 517–556.

Fergusson, Sir James, ed. 1970. *The Declaration of Arbroath 1320*. Edinburgh: Edinburgh University Press.

Fernando, Chitra, and R. H. Flavell. 1981. *On Idiom: Critical Views and Perspectives*. Exeter: University of Exeter Press.

Fetzer, Anita, ed. 2007. *Context and Appropriateness*. Amsterdam: John Benjamins.

Fetzer, Anita, and Etsuko Oishi, eds. 2011. *Context in Contexts*. Amsterdam: John Benjamins.

Finegan, Edward. 1982. "Form and Function in Testament Language." In *Linguistics and the Professions: Proceedings of the Second Annual Delaware Symposium on Language Studies*, edited by Robert Di Pietro, 113–120. Norwood, NJ: Ablex.

Finlay, John. 2000. *Men of Law in Pre-Reformation Scotland*. East Linton: Tuckwell Press.

———. 2007. "The Lower Branch of the Legal Profession in Early Modern Scotland." *Edinburgh Law Review* 11: 31–61.

———. 2009. "The History of the Notary in Scotland." In *Handbuch zur Geschichte des Notariats der europäischen Traditionen*, edited by Matthias Schmoeckel and Werner Schubert, 393–428. Baden-Baden: Nomos.

Finnegan, Ruth H. 1976. *Oral Literature in Africa*. Oxford: Oxford University Press.

First Scottish Books. 2006. National Library of Scotland. Available at: http://digital.nls.uk/firstscottishbooks/index.html.

Firth, J. R. [1957] 1968. "A Synopsis of Linguistic Theory, 1930–1955." In *Selected Papers of J. R. Firth 1952–59*, edited by F. R. Palmer, 168–205. London: Longmans, Green and Co.

Fischer, Olga, and Wim van der Wurff. 2006. "Syntax." In *A History of the English Language*, edited by Richard Hogg and David Denison, 109–198. Cambridge: Cambridge University Press.

Fish, Stanley E. 1976. "Interpreting the 'Variorum.'" *Critical Inquiry* 2(3): 465–485.

Fitzmaurice, Susan. 2000. "Coalitions and the Investigation of Social Influence in Linguistic History." *European Journal of English Studies* 4(3): 265–276.

Fletcher, William H. 2003/2004. "Phrases in English." Available at: http://pie.usna.edu/. The work on PoS frames started on this website in 2003 and has continued since then. All the changes to the website are available at http://phrasesinenglish.org/changes.html.

Ford, J. D. 2007. *Law and Opinion in Scotland during the Seventeenth Century.* Oxford: Hart Publishing.

Foucault, Michel. 1972. *The Archaeology of Knowledge.* London: Tavistock.

Fox, R. 1983. "Urban Development, 1100–1700." In *An Historical Geography of Scotland*, edited by G. Whittington and Ian D. Whyte, 73–92. London: Academic Press.

Frade, Celina. 2007. "Power Dynamics and Legal English." *World Englishes* 26(1): 48–61.

Fragmenta Collecta. 1868. In *Ancient Laws and Customs of the Burghs of Scotland A.D. 1124–1424*, edited by Cosmo Innes, 160–186. Edinburgh: Scottish Burgh Records Society.

Frankot, Edda. 2010. "Maritime Law and Practice in Late Medieval Aberdeen." *The Scottish Historical Review* 89(2), No, 228: 136–152.

Frow, John. 2006. *Genre: The New Critical Idiom.* New York: Routledge.

Galdia, Marcus. 2009. *Legal Linguistics.* Frankfurt am Main: Peter Lang.

Garvin, Paul L., ed. 1970. *Method and Theory in Linguistics.* The Hague: Mouton.

Giammarresi, Salvatore. 2010. "Formulaicity and Translation: A Cross-Corpora Analysis of English Formulaic Binomials and their Italian Translations." In *Perspectives on Formulaic Discourse: Acquisition and Communication*, edited by David Wood, 257–273. London: Continuum.

Gibb, Dewar. 1992. "Preface." In *Green's Glossary of Scottish Legal Terms*, edited by Andrew G. M. Duncan. 3d ed. Edinburgh: W. Green/Sweet & Maxwell.

Gibbons, John. 1999. "Language and the Law." *Annual Review of Applied Linguistics* 19: 156–173.

———. 2003. *Forensic Linguistics: An Introduction to Language in the Justice System.* Oxford: Blackwell.

Gill, A. M., and K. Whedbee. 1997. "Rhetoric." In *Discourse Studies: A Multidisciplinary Introduction.* Vol. 1, *Discourse as Structure and Process*, edited by Teun van Dijk, 157–184. London: SAGE Publications.

Given-Wilson, Chris. 2005. "General Introduction." In *The Parliament Rolls of Medieval England*, edited by C. Given-Wilson et al. Leicester: Scholarly Digital Editions. Available at: http://www.sd-editions.com/PROME.

Glenn, H. Patrick. 2007. *Legal Traditions of the World.* 3d ed. Oxford: Oxford University Press.

Godfrey, Mark. 2002. "Arbitration and Dispute Resolution in Sixteenth Century Scotland." *Tijdschrift voor Rechtsgeschiedenis* 70: 109–135.

González-Álvarez, Dolores, and Javier Pérez-Guerra. 1998. "Texting the Written Evidence: On Register Analysis in Late Middle English and Early Modern English." *Text* 18(3): 321–348.

Goodwin, Charles, and Alessandro Duranti. 1991. "Rethinking Context: An Introduction." In *Rethinking Context: Language as an Interactive Phenomenon*, edited by Alessandro Duranti and Charles Goodwin, 1–42. Cambridge: Cambridge University Press.

Goody, Jack, ed. 1968. *Literacy in Traditional Societies.* Cambridge: Cambridge University Press.

Görlach, Manfred. 2001. "A History of Text Types: A Componential Analysis." In *Towards a History of English as a History of Genres*, edited by Hans-Jürgen Diller and Manfred Görlach, 47–88. Heidelberg: Winter.

———. 2002. *A Textual History of Scots.* Heidelberg: Winter.

———. 2004. *Text Types and the History of English.* Berlin: Mouton de Gruyter.

Gotti, Maurizio. 2001. "The Experimental Essay in Early Modern English." *European Journal of English Studies* 5(2): 221–239.

———. 2008. "Customising the Model Law on International Commercial Arbitration." In *Obscurity and Clarity in the Law: Prospects and Challenges*, edited by Anne Wagner and Sophie Cacciaguidi-Fahy, 89–108. Aldershot: Ashgate.

———. 2012. "Text and Genre." In *The Oxford Handbook of Language and Law*, edited by Lawrence M. Solan and Peter M. Tiersma. New York: Oxford University Press. Accessed at Oxford Handbooks Online.

Gouldesbrough, Peter. 1985. *Formulary of Old Scots Legal Documents.* Edinburgh: Stair Society.

Goźdź-Roszkowski, Stanisław. 2004. "Multi-Word Lexical Units in Legal Genres—The Pedagogic Perspective." In *Practical Applications in Language and Computers*, edited by Barbara Lewandowska-Tomaszczyk, 401–416. Frankfurt am Main: Peter Lang.

———. 2006a. "Frequent Phraseology in Contractual Instruments: A Corpus-Based Study." In *New Trends in Specialized Discourse Analysis*, edited by Maurizio Gotti and Davide S. Giannoni, 147–162. Bern: Peter Lang.

———. 2006b. "Recurrent Word Combinations in Judicial Argumentation. A Corpus-Based Study." In *Langue, droit, société / Language, Law, Society*, edited by D. Bartol, A. Duszak, H. Izdebski, and J.-M. Pierrel, 139–152. Nancy: Presses universitaires de Nancy.

———. 2011. *Patterns of Linguistic Variation in American Legal English: A Corpus-based Study.* Frankfurt am Main: Peter Lang.

Grabarczyk, Zenon. 1989. "Scientific Discourse against the Background of Standard Language." In *Special Language: From Humans Thinking to Thinking Machines*, edited by Christer Laurén and Marianne Nordman, 180–189. Clevedon: Multilingual Matters.

Gries, S. Th. 2006. "Introduction." In *Corpora in Cognitive Linguistics: Corpus-Based Approaches to Syntax and Lexis*, edited by S. Th. Gries and A. Stepanowitsch, 1–17. Berlin: Mouton de Gruyter.

Gustafsson, Marita. 1974. "The Phonetic Length of the Members in Present-Day English Binomials." *Neuphilologische Mitteilungen* 75: 663–677.

———. 1975. *Binomial Expressions in Present-Day English.* Turku: University of Turku.

———. 1976. "The Frequency and 'Frozenness' of Some English Binomials." *Neuphilologische Mitteilungen* 77: 623–637.

———. 1984. "The Syntactic Features of Binomial Expressions in Legal English." *Text* 4: 123–141.

Hall, Derek. 2002. *Burgess, Merchant and Priest: Burgh Life in the Scottish Medieval Town.* Edinburgh: Birlinn Ltd./Historic Scotland.

Halliday, M. A. K. 1973. *Explorations in the Functions of Language.* London: Edward Arnold.

———. 1978. *Language as a Social Semiotic: The Social Interpretation of Language and Meaning.* London: Edward Arnold.

Halliday, M. A. K., and Ruqaiya Hasan. 1976. *Cohesion in English.* London: Longman.

———. 2000. "System and Text: Making Links." *Text* 20(2): 201–210.

Halliday, M. A. K., Angus McIntosh, and Peter Strevens. 1964. *The Linguistic Sciences and Language Teaching.* London: Longmans.

Hamilton-Grierson, Phillip J. 1924. "Fencing the Court." *Scottish Historical Review* 21: 54–62.

Hart, H. L. A. 1961. *The Concept of Law.* Oxford: Clarendon.

Hasan, Ruqaiya. 1978. "Text in the Systemic-Functional Model." In *Current Trends in Textlinguistics*, edited by Wolfgang Dressler, 227–246. Berlin: Walter de Gruyter.

Hatzidaki, Ourania. 1999. "Part and Parcel: A Linguistic Analysis of Binomials and its Application to the Internal Characterisation of Corpora." Ph.D. diss., University of Birmingham.

Haugen, Einar. 1966. "Linguistics and Language Planning." In *Sociolinguistics. Proceedings of the UCLA Sociolinguistics Conference 1964*, edited by William Bright, 50–71. The Hague: Mouton.

Heffer, Chris. 2003. "'If you were standing in Marks and Spencers': Narrativisation and Comprehension in the English Summing-Up." In *Language in the Legal Process*, edited by Janet Cotterill, 228–245. Basingstoke: Palgrave Macmillan.

Helmholz, R. H. 2008. "The Canon Law." In *The Book in Britain.* Vol. 3, *1400–1557*, edited by Lotte Hellinga and J. B. Trapp, 387–398. Cambridge: Cambridge University Press.

Hickey, Raymond, ed. 2010. *Varieties of English in Writing: The Written Word as Linguistic Evidence.* Amsterdam: John Benjamins.

Hiltunen, Risto. 1990. *Chapters on Legal English: Aspects Past and Present of the Language of the Law.* Helsinki: Suomalainen Tiedakademia.

———. 2012. "The Grammar and Structure of Legal Texts." In *The Oxford Handbook of Language and Law*, edited by Lawrence M. Solan and Peter M. Tiersma. New York: Oxford University Press. Accessed at Oxford Handbooks Online.

Hinneburg, Alexander, Heikki Mannila, Samuli Kaislaniemi, Terttu Nevalainen, and Helena Raumolin-Brunberg. 2007. "How to Handle Small Samples: Bootstrap and Bayesian Methods in the Analysis of Linguistic Change." *Linguistic and Literary Computing* 22(2): 137–150.

Hockett, Charles F. 1958. *A Course in Modern Linguistics.* New York: Macmillan.

Hoey, Michael. 1991. *Patterns of Lexis in Text.* Oxford: Oxford University Press.

———. 2006. *Lexical Priming: A New Theory of Words and Language.* London: Routledge.

Hoppenbrouwers, Peter. 2006. "Such Stuff as Peoples are Made On: Ethnogenesis and the Construction of Nationhood in Medieval Europe." *Medieval History Journal* 9: 195–242.

Horobin, Simon, and Jeremy J. Smith. 2002. *An Introduction to Middle English.* Edinburgh: Edinburgh University Press.

Horsbroch, Dauvit. 1999. "Nostra vulgari lingua: Scots as a European Language 1500–1700." *Scottish Language* 18: 1–16.

Hough, Carole. 2001. "Legal and Documentary Writings." In *A Companion to Anglo-Saxon Literature*, edited by Phillip Pulsiano and Elaine Treharne, 170–187. Oxford: Blackwell.

Hubbard, Tom. 2003. "Early Scottish Internationalism through Translation: Landmark Records in the Bibliography of Scottish Literature in Translation (BOSLIT)." *Scottish Language* 22: 36–45.

Huddleston, Rodney, and Geofrey K. Pullum. 2005. *A Student's Introduction to English Grammar.* Cambridge: Cambridge University Press.

Hudson, Jean. 1998. *Perspectives on Fixedness: Applied and Theoretical.* Lund: Lund University Press.

Hutton, Christopher. 2009. *Language, Meaning and the Law.* Edinburgh: Edinburgh University Press.

Hyland, Ken. 2008a. "Academic Clusters: Text Patterning in Published and Postgraduate Writing." *International Journal of Applied Linguistics* 18(1): 41–62.

———. 2008b. "As Can Be Seen: Lexical Bundles and Disciplinary Variation." *English for Specific Purposes* 27: 4–21.

Hymes, Dell. 1974a. "Ways of Speaking." In *Explorations in the Ethnography of Speaking,* edited by Richard Bauman and Joel Sherzer, 433–452. London: Cambridge University Press.

———. 1974b. *Foundations of Sociolinguistics.* Pittsburgh: University of Pennsylvania Press.

Innes, Cosmo. 1868. "Preface." In *Ancient laws and Customs of the Burghs of Scotland.* Vol. 1, *A.D. 1124–1424,* edited by Cosmo Innes, xx–l. Edinburgh: Scottish Burgh Records Society.

Jackson, Bernard S. 1988. *Law, Fact and Narrative Coherence.* Liverpool: Deborah Charles Publications.

———. 1995. *Making Sense in Law: Linguistic, Psychological and Semiotic Perspectives.* Liverpool: Deborah Charles Publications.

Jacobs, Andreas, and Andreas H. Jucker. 1995. "The Historical Perspective in Pragmatics." In *Historical Pragmatics: Pragmatic Developments in the History of English,* edited by Andreas H. Jucker, 3–33. Amsterdam: John Benjamins.

Jakobson, Roman. 1960. "Closing Statement: Linguistics and Poetics." In *Style in Language,* edited by Thomas A. Sebeok, 350–377. New York: MIT Press and Wiley.

———. 1971. *Selected Writings.* Vol. 2, *Word and Language.* The Hague: Mouton.

Jakobson, Roman, and Morris Halle. 1964. *Podstawy języka* [Fundamentals of Language]. With a preface by Leon Zawadowski. Wrocław/Warszawa: Zakład Narodowy im. Ossolińskich.

Janigová, Slavká. 2008. *Syntax of -ing Forms in Legal English.* Berlin: Peter Lang.

Jauss, Hans Robert. 1970. *Literaturgeschichte als Provokation der Literaturwissenschaft.* Frankfurt am Main: Suhrkamp.

Johnston, Paul. 1997. "Older Scots Phonology and its Regional Variation." In *The Edinburgh History of the Scots Language,* edited by Charles Jones, 47–111. Edinburgh: Edinburgh University Press.

Jones, Charles. 2002. *The English Language in Scotland: An Introduction to Scots.* East Linton: Tuckwell Press.

Jones, Charles, ed. 1997. *The Edinburgh History of the Scots Language.* Edinburgh: Edinburgh University Press.

Jucker, Andreas H. 2005. "News Discourse: Mass Media Communication from the Seventeenth to the Twenty-First Century." In *Opening Windows on Texts and Discourses of the Past,* edited by Janne Skaffari et al., 7–21. Amsterdam: John Benjamins.

Jucker, Andreas H., and Joanna Kopaczyk. Forthcoming. "Communities of Practice as a Locus of Language Change." In *Communities of Practice in the History of English,* edited by Joanna Kopaczyk and Andreas H. Jucker. Amsterdam: John Benjamins.

Jumpertz-Schwab, Cornelia. 2000. *The Development of the Scots Lexicon and Syntax in the 16th Century under the Influence of Translations from Latin.* Frankfurt am Main: Peter Lang.

Kachru, Braj B. 2006. "'Socially-realistic linguistics': The Firthian Tradition." In *World Englishes: Critical Concepts in Linguistics.* Vol. 1, edited by Kingsley Bolton and Braj B. Kachru, 22–45. Abingdon, Oxon: Routledge.

Kelham, Charles A. 1986. "Bases of Magnatial Power in Later Fifteenth-Century Scotland." Ph.D. diss., University of Edinburgh.

Kemp, Herman C., ed. 2004. *Oral Traditions of Southeast Asia and Oceania: A Bibliography.* Jakarta: Yayasan Obor Indonesia.

Kendall, Calvin B. 1991. *The Metrical Grammar of 'Beowulf'.* Cambridge: Cambridge University Press.

Ketelaar, Eric. 2010. "Records Out and Archives In: Early Modern Cities as Creators of Records and as Communities of Archives." *Archival Science* 10(3): 201–210.

Kevelson, Roberta. 1982. "Language and Legal Speech Acts: Decisions." In *Linguistics and the Professions*, edited by Robert J. Di Pietro, 121–131. Norwood, NJ: Ablex.

King, Anne. 1997. "The Inflectional Morphology of Older Scots." In *The Edinburgh History of the Scots Language*, edited by Charles Jones, 156–181. Edinburgh: Edinburgh University Press.

Kinghorn, A. M., ed. 1970. *The Middle Scots Poets.* London: Edward Arnold.

Kohnen, Thomas. 2001. "On Defining Text Types within Historical Linguistics: The Case of Petitions/Statutes." *European Journal of English Studies* 5(2): 197–203.

———. 2010. "Religious Discourse." In *Historical Pragmatics*, edited by Andreas H. Jucker and Irma Taavitsainen, 523–547. Berlin: De Gruyter Mouton.

Kopaczyk, Joanna. 2009. "Multi-Word Units of Meaning in 16th-Century Legal Scots." In *Selected Proceedings of the 2008 Symposium on New Approaches in English Historical Lexis (HEL-LEX 2)*, edited by R. W. McConchie, Alpo Honkapohja, and Jukka Tyrkkö, 88–95. Somerville, MA: Cascadilla Proceedings Project.

———. 2011a. "Long Lexical Bundles and Standardisation in Historical Legal Texts." *Studia Anglica Posnaniensia* 47(2–3): 3–26.

———. 2011b. "Latin and Scots Versions of Scottish Medieval Burgh Laws (*Leges Quatuor Burgorum*)." *Scottish Language* 30: 1–18.

———. 2012. "Repetitive and Therefore Fixed? Lemmatic Bundles and Text-Type Standardisation in Fifteenth-Century Administrative Scots." In *English Historical Linguistics 2008. Selected Papers from the 15th ICEHL, Munich, 24–30 August 2008.* Vol. 2, *Words, Texts and Genres*, edited by Hans Sauer and Gaby Waxenberger, 189–208. Amsterdam: John Benjamins.

———. 2013. "Rethinking the Traditional Periodization of Scots." In *Selected Papers from the Forum for Research on the Languages of Scotland and Ulster, Aberdeen, July 2012*, edited by Robert McColl Millar and Janet Cruickshank.

———. Forthcoming. "Middle Scots Legal and Administrative Discourse: A Community of Practice Creates a Text Community." In *Communities of Practice in the History of English*, edited by Joanna Kopaczyk and Andreas H. Jucker. Amsterdam: John Benjamins.

Koskenniemi, Inna. 1968. *Repetitive Word-Pairs in Old and Early Middle English Prose.* Turku: Turun Yliopisto.

Krause, Wolfgang. 1922. "Die Wortstellung in den zweigliedrigen Wortverbindungen, untersucht für das Altindische, Awestische, Litauische und Altnordische." *Zeitschrift für vergleichende Sprachforschung* 50: 74–129.

Kryk-Kastovsky, Barbara. 2000. "Representations of Orality in Early Modern English Trial Records." *Journal of Historical Pragmatics* 1(2): 201–230.

———. 2002. "Can Words Behead? Perlocutions in Early Modern English Trial Records." In *Scripta Neophilologica Posnaniensia* 4, edited by Stanisław Puppel, 15–27. Poznań: Wydział Neofilologii UAM.

———. 2006a. "Historical Courtroom Discourse: Introduction." In *Historical Courtroom Discourse. Special issue of Journal of Historical Pragmatics* 7(2), edited by Barbara Kryk-Kastovsky, 163–179.

———. 2009. "Speech Acts in Early Modern English Court Trials." *Journal of Pragmatics* 41: 440–457.

———. 2010. "Power in Early Modern English Courtroom Discourse." In *Discourses in Interaction*, edited by Sanna-Kaisa Tanskanen, Marja-Liisa Helasvuo, Marjut Johansson, Johanna Karhukorpi, and Mia Raitaniemi, 153–171. Amsterdam: John Benjamins.

Kryk-Kastovsky, Barbara, ed. 2006b. *Historical Courtroom Discourse. Special issue of Journal of Historical Pragmatics* 7(2). Amsterdam: John Benjamins.

Kucera, Henry, and W. Nelson Francis. 1967. *Computational Analysis of Present-Day English.* Providence, RI: Brown University Press.

Kurzon, Dennis. 1986. *'It is hereby performed': Explorations in Legal Speech Acts.* Amsterdam: John Benjamins.

———. 1989. "Language of the Law and Legal Language." In *Special Language: From Humans Thinking to Thinking Machines*, edited by Christer Laurén and Marianne Nordman, 283–290. Clevedon: Multilingual Matters.

———. 1997. "'Legal lanugage': Varieties, Genres, Registers, Discourses." *International Journal of Applied Linguistics* 7(2): 119–139.

Kytö, Merja. 2010. "Data in Historical Pragmatics." In *Historical Pragmatics*, edited by Andreas H. Jucker and Irma Taavitsainen, 33–68. Berlin: De Gruyter Mouton.

———. 2012. "New Perspectives, Theories and Methods: Corpus Linguistics." In *English Historical Linguistics: An International Handbook*, Vol. 1., edited by Alexander T. Bergs and Laurel J. Brinton, 1059–1531. Berlin: De Gruyter Mouton.

Labov, William. 1972a. "Some Principles of Linguistic Methodology." *Language in Society* 1: 97–120.

———. 1972b. *Sociolinguistic Patterns.* Philadelphia: University of Pennsylvania Press.

Lakoff, George, and Mark Johnson. [1980] 2003. *Metaphors We Live by.* Chicago: University of Chicago Press.

Lambrecht, Knud. 1984. "Formulaicity, Frame Semantics, and Pragmatics in German Binomial Expressions." *Language* 60(4): 753–796.

Lanark Records = Extracts from the Records of the Royal Burgh of Lanark. 1893. Glasgow: printed by Carson & Nicol for the Subscribers. Scottish Burgh Records Society.

Lee, David Y. W. 2001. "Defining Core Vocabulary and Tracking its Distribution across Spoken and Written Genres: Evidence of a Gradience of Variation from the British National Corpus." *Journal of English Linguistics* 29(3): 250–278.

Lee, Ki-Suk. 1990. "The Phonological Constraints on English Binomials." *Journal of Studies in Language* 7: 177–206.

Leech, Geoffrey. 1969. *A Linguistic Guide to English Poetry.* London: Longman.

Leges = *Leges Quatuor Burgorum*, In *Ancient Laws and Customs of the Burghs of Scotland.* Vol. 1, *A.D. 1124–1424*, edited by Cosmo Innes, 3–58. 1868. Edinburgh: Scottish Burgh Records Society.

Lehmann, Christian. [1982] 1995. *Thoughts on Grammaticalization.* Munich: LINCOM.

Lehto, Anu, Alistair Baron, Maura Ratia, and Paul Rayson. 2010. "Improving the Precision of Corpus Methods." In *Early Modern English Medical Texts. Corpus description and studies*, edited by Irma Taavitsainen and Päivi Pahta, 279–289. Amsterdam: John Benjamins.

Leith, Dick. [1983] 1997. *A Social History of English.* London: Routledge.

Lewandowska-Tomaszczyk, Barbara. 2005. "Analiza języka z zastosowaniem korpusu [Analysing Language with Corpora]." In *Podstawy językoznawstwa korpusowego* [Introduction to Corpus Linguistics], edited by Barbara Lewandowska-Tomaszczyk, 133–173. Łódź: Wydawnictwo Uniwersytetu Łódzkiego.

Lindsay of Pittscottie, Robert. [1565] 1728. *The Historie and Chronicles of Scotland,* 1436–1565. EEBO.

Linguistic Atlas of Older Scots v.1.1. compiled and edited by Keith Williamson. 2008. Available at: http://www.lel.ed.ac.uk/ihd/laos1/laos1.html.

Linnel, Per, Johan Hofvendahl, and Camilla Lindholm. 2003. "Multi-Unit Questions in Institutional Interactions: Sequential Organizations and Communicative Functions." *Text* 23(4): 539–571.

Locher, Miriam A., and Jurg Strässler, eds. 2008. *Standards and Norms in the English Language.* Berlin: Mouton de Gruyter.

Lord Cooper. 1952. *The Dark Age of Scottish Legal History.* Glasgow: Jackson, Son & Co.

Lüdeling, Anke, and Merja Kytö, eds. 2008/2009. *Corpus Linguistics: An International Handbook.* Vols. 1–2. Berlin: Walter de Gruyter.

Lynch, Michael, Michael Spearman, and Geoffrey Stell, eds. 1988. *The Scottish Medieval Town.* Edinburgh: John Donald.

Lyons, John. 1977. *Semantics.* Vol. 1. Cambridge: Cambridge University Press.

———. 1981. *Language and Linguistics: An Introduction.* Cambridge: Cambridge University Press.

Macafee, Caroline. 1989. "Middle Scots Dialects—Extrapolating Backwards." In *Bryght lanternis: Essays on the Language and Literature of Medieval and Renaissance Scotland,* edited by J. D. McClure, and M. R. G. Spiller, 429–441. Aberdeen: Aberdeen University Press.

Macafee, Caroline, and A. J. Aitken. 2002. "A History of Scots to 1700." In *A Dictionary of the Older Scottish Tongue.* Vol. 12. Oxford: Oxford University Press.

MacDonald, Alan R. 2002. "Deliberative Processes in Parliament c. 1567–1639: Multicameralism and the Lords of the Articles." *Scottish Historical Review* 81(1): 23–51.

Mackie, J. D. 1923. *The Estate of the Burgesses in the Scots Parliament and its Relation to the Convention of Royal Burghs.* St Andrews: W. C. Henderson & Son.

MacQueen, Hector L. 1986. "Pleadable Brieves, Pleading and the Development of Scots Law." *Law and History Review* 4(2): 403–422.

———. 1997. "The Foundation of Law Teaching at the University of Aberdeen." In *The Civilian Tradition and Scots Law: Aberdeen Quincentenary Essays*, edited by David L. Carey Miller and Reinhard Zimmermann, 53–72. Berlin: Duncker & Humblot.

———. 2000. "Scots Law and the Road to the New Ius Commune." *Electronic Journal of Comparative Law* 4(4). Available at: http://www.ejcl.org/44/art44-1.html.

———. 2002a. "Laws and Languages: Some Historical Notes from Scotland." *Electronic Journal of Comparative Law* 6(2). Available at: http://www.ejcl.org/62/art62-2.html.

———. 2002b "Expectations of the Law in 12th and 13th Century Scotland." *Tijdschrift voor Rechtsgeschiedenis* 70(3): 279–290.

Mair, Craig. 1988. *Mercat Cross and Tolbooth.* Edinburgh: John Donald.

Makkai, Adam. 1978. "Idiomaticity as a Language Universal." In *Universals of Human Language.* Vol. 3, *Word Structure*, edited by Joseph Greenberg, 401–448. Stanford, CA: Stanford University Press.

Maley, Yon. 1994. "The Language of the Law." In *Language and the Law*, edited by John B. Gibbons, 11–50. London: Longman.

Malinowski, Bronisław. [1923] 1966. "The Problem of Meaning in Primitive Languages." In *The Meaning of Meaning*, edited by C. K. Ogden and I. A. Richards, 296–336. London: Kegan Paul.

Malkiel, Yakov. 1959. "Studies in Irreversible Binomials." *Lingua* 8: 113–160.

Mann, Alastair J. 2000. *The Scottish Book Trade 1500–1720. Print Commerce and Print Control in Early Modern Scotland.* East Linton: Tuckwell Press.

Mann, Alastair J., and Sally Mapstone, eds. 2013. *The Edinburgh History of the Book in Scotland.* Vol. 1, *Medieval to 1707.* Edinburgh: Edinburgh University Press.

Mapstone, Sally. 2007. "Older Scots Literature and the Court." In *The Edinburgh History of Scottish literature.* Vol. 1, *From Columba to the Union (until 1707)*, edited by Thomas Owen Clancy and Murray Pittock, 273–285. Edinburgh: Edinburgh University Press.

Martin, J. R. 2010. "Semantic Variation—Modelling Realisation, Instantiation and Individuation in Social Semiosis." In *New Discourse on Language: Functional Perspectives on Multimodality, Identity and Affiliation*, edited by Monika Bednarek and J. R. Martin, 1–34. London: Continuum.

Marwick, Sir James D. 1897. *Charters and Other Documents Relating to the City of Glasgow, A.D. 1175–1649. Part I.* Glasgow: Scottish Burgh Records Society.

Mathews, Jana. 2002. "Land, Lepers, and the Law in The Testament of Cresseid." In *The Letter of the Law: Legal Practice and Literary Productions in Medieval England*, edited by Emily Steiner and Candace Barrington, 40–66. Ithaca, NY: Cornell University Press.

Mattila, Heikki E. S. 2006. *Comparative Legal Linguistics*, translated by Christopher Goddard. Aldershot: Ashgate.

———. 2012. "Legal Vocabulary." In *The Oxford Handbook of Language and Law*, edited by Lawrence M. Solan and Peter M. Tiersma. New York: Oxford University Press. Accessed at Oxford Handbooks Online.

McCarthy, Michael. 1998. *Spoken Language and Applied Linguistics.* Cambridge: Cambridge University Press.

McCarthy, Michael, and Ronald Carter. 1994. *Language as Discourse.* London: Longman.

McClure, J. Derrick. 1994. "English in Scotland." In *The Cambridge History of the English Language.* Vol. 5, *English in Britain and Overseas: Origins and Development*, edited by Robert Burchfield, 23–93. Cambridge: Cambridge University Press.

———. 1995a. "Lowland Scots: An Ambivalent National Tongue." In *Scots and its Literature*, edited by J. D. McClure, 5–19. Amsterdam: John Benjamins.

———. 1995b. "Scottis, Inglis, Suddroun: Language Labels and Language Attitudes." In *Scots and its Literature*, edited by J. D. McClure, 44–56. Amsterdam: John Benjamins.

McIntosh, Angus. 1978. "The Dialectology of Medieval Scots: Some Possible Approaches to its Study." *Scottish Literary Journal Supplement* 6: 38–44.

McIntosh, Angus, M. L. Samuels, and Michael Benskin. 1986. *A Linguistic Atlas of Late Medieval English.* Vol. 1, *General Introduction, Index of Sources, Dot Maps.* Aberdeen: Aberdeen University Press.

McKenzie, Donald F. 1985. *Oral Culture, Literacy and Print in Early New Zealand: The Treaty of Waitangi.* Wellington: Victoria University Press.

McWilliam, Colin. 1975. *Scottish Townscape.* London: Collins.

Mellinkoff, David. 1963. *The Language of the Law.* Boston: Little Brown.

Meston, M. C., W. D. H. Sellar, and Lord Cooper. 1991. *The Scottish Legal Tradition.* New enlarged edition. Oxford: Saltire.

Meurman-Solin, Anneli. 1997. "Differentiation and Standardisation in Early Scots." In *The Edinburgh History of the Scots Language*, edited by Charles Jones, 3–22. Edinburgh: Edinburgh University Press.

———. 2000a. "On the Conditioning of Geographical and Social Distance in Language Variation and Change in Renaissance Scots." In *The History of English in a Social Context*, edited by Dieter Kastovsky and Arthur Mettinger, 227–255. Berlin: Mouton de Gruyter.

———. 2000b. "Change from Above or from Below? Mapping the Loci of Linguistic Change in the History of Scottish English." In *The Development of Standard English 1300–1800*, edited by Laura Wright, 155–170. Cambridge: Cambridge University Press.

———. 2001. "Genre as a Variable in Sociohistorical Linguistics." *European Journal of English Studies* 5(2): 241–256.

———. 2004a. "Data and Methods in Scottish Historical Linguistics." In *The History of English and the Dynamics of Power: Proceedings of the 8th Italian Conference on the History of the English Language*, edited by Ermano Barisone, M. L. Maggioni, and P. Tornaghi, 25–42. Alessandria: Edizioni dell'Orso.

———. 2004b. "Towards a Variationist Typology of Clausal Connectives. Methodological Considerations Based on the Corpus of Scottish Correspondence." In *Methods and Data in English Historical Dialectology*, edited by Marina Dossena and Roger Lass, 171–197. Bern: Lang.

———. 2007a. *Manual to the Corpus of Scottish Correspondence.* Available at: http://www.helsinki.fi/varieng/csc/manual/.

———. 2007b. "Relatives as Sentence-Level Connectives." In *Connectives in the History of English*, edited by Ursula Lenker and Anneli Meurman-Solin, 255–287. Amsterdam: John Benjamins.

Meurman-Solin, Anneli (comp.). 1993. *The Helsinki Corpus of Older Scots* [HCOS]. Oxford: Oxford Text Archive.

Mey, Jacob L. 1993. *Pragmatics: An Introduction.* Oxford: Blackwell.

———. 2011. "Speech Acts in Context." In *Context in Contexts*, edited by Anita Fetzer and Etsuko Oishi, 171–180. Amsterdam: John Benjamins.

Millar, Robert McColl. 2005. *Language, Nation and Power: An Introduction.* Houndmills: Palgrave.

———. 2012. "Scots." In *English Historical Linguistics: An International Handbook*, Vol. 2, edited by Alexander Bergs and Laurel J. Brinton, 1951–1960. Berlin: De Gruyter Mouton.

Milroy, James, and Lesley Milroy. 1985. "Linguistic Change, Social Network and Speaker Innovation." *Journal of Linguistics* 21: 339–384.

———. [1985] 1991. *Authority in Language: Investigating Language Prescription and Standardisation.* London: Routledge.

Milroy, Lesley. 1980. *Language and Social Networks.* Oxford: Blackwell.

———. 2000. "Social Network Analysis and Language Change: Introduction." *European Journal of English Studies* 4(3): 217–223.

Minkova, Donka. 2003. *Alliteration and Sound Change in Early English.* Cambridge: Cambridge University Press.

Moessner, Lilo. 1997. "The Syntax of Older Scots." In *The Edinburgh History of the Scots Language,* edited by Charles Jones, 112–155. Edinburgh: Edinburgh University Press.

———. 2001. "Genre, Text Type, Style, Register: A Terminological Maze?" *European Journal of English Studies* 5(2): 131–138.

Moffat, Alistair. 2005. *Before Scotland: The Story of Scotland before History.* London: Thames & Hudson.

Mollin, Sandra. 2012. "Revisiting Binomial Order in English: Ordering Constraints and Reversibility." *English Language and Linguistics* 16(1): 83–103.

Moon, Rosamund. 1994. "The Analysis of Fixed Expressions in Text." In *Advances in Written Text Analysis,* edited by Malcolm Coulthard, 117–135. London: Routledge.

———. 1998. *Fixed Expressions and Idioms in English: A Corpus-Based Approach.* London: Clarendon Press.

Moss, Ann. 2003. *Renaissance Truth and the Latin Language Turn.* Oxford: Oxford University Press.

Murison, David. 1974. "Linguistic Relationships in Medieval Scotland." In *The Scottish Tradition: Essays in Honour of Ronald Gordon Cant,* edited by G. W. S. Barrow, 71–83. Edinburgh: Scottish Academic Press.

———. 1979. "The Historical Background." In *Languages of Scotland,* edited by A. J. Aitken and Tom McArthur, 2–13. Edinburgh: Chambers.

Murray, David. 1910. *Legal Practice in Ayr and the West of Scotland in the Fifteenth and Sixteenth Centuries: A Study in Economic History.* Glasgow: James MacLehose and Sons, Publishers to the University.

Nevalainen, Terttu. 2000. "Mobility, Social Networks and Language Change in Early Modern England." *European Journal of English Studies* 4(3): 253–264.

———. 2001. "Continental Conventions in Early English Correspondence." In *Towards the History of English as a History of Genres,* edited by Hans-Jürgen Diller and Manfred Görlach, 203–224. Heidelberg: Winter.

———. 2006. *An Introduction to Early Modern English.* Edinburgh: Edinburgh University Press.

Nevalainen, Terttu, and Ingrid Tieken-Boon van Ostade. 2006. "Standardisation." In *A History of the English Language,* edited by Richard Hogg and David Denison, 271–311. Cambridge: Cambridge University Press.

Norrick, Neal R. 1988. "Binomial Meaning in Texts." *Journal of English Linguistics* 21(1): 72–87.

O'Halloran, Kieran A., and Caroline Coffin. 2004. "Checking Overinterpretation and Underinterpretation: Help from Corpora in Critical Linguistics." In *Applying English Grammar: Functional and Corpus Approaches,* edited by Caroline Coffin, Ann Hewings, and Kieran A. O'Halloran, 275–297. London: Hodder Arnold.

O'Keeffe, Anne, Michael McCarthy, and Ronald Carter. 2007. *From Corpus to Classroom: Language Use and Language Teaching.* Cambridge: Cambridge University Press.

O'Rourke, Stephen. 2004. *Glossary of Legal Terms.* 4th ed. Edinburgh: Thomson & W. Green.

Oden, Gregg C., and Lola L. Lopes. 1982. "Preference for Order in Freezes." *Linguistic Inquiry* 12(4): 673–679.

OED = Oxford English Dictionary. Available at: http://www.oed.com.

Office of the Scottish Parliamentary Counsel. 2006. *Plain Language and Legislation.* Available at: http://www.scotland.gov.uk/Publications/2006/02/17093804/0.

Ogura, Michiko. 2002. *Verbs of Motion in Medieval English.* Cambridge: DS Brewer.

Ong, Walter J. [1982] 2002. *Orality and Literacy: The Technologizing of the Word.* 2d ed. London: Routledge.

Ostler, Nicholas. 2008. "Corpora of Less Studied Languages." In *Corpus Linguistics: An International Handbook,* Vol. 1, edited by Anke Lüdeling and Merja Kytö, 457–483. Berlin: Walter de Gruyter.

Partington, A., and J. Morley. 2004. "From Frequency to Ideology: Investigating Word and Cluster/Bundle Frequency in Political Debate." In *Practical Applications in Language and Computers. PALC 2003,* edited by Barbara Lewandowska-Tomaszczyk, 179–192. Frankfurt am Main: Peter Lang.

Pawley, Andrew. 1986. "Lexicalization." In *Language and Linguistics: The Interdependence of Theory, Data, and Application,* edited by Deborah Tannen and James Alatis, 98–120. Washington, DC: Georgetown University.

Peebles Records = Extracts from the Records of the Burgh of Peebles 1652–1714, with Appendix 1367–1665. [Preface by R. Renwick]. 1910. Glasgow: Scottish Burgh Records Society.

Persson, Gunnar. 1974. *Repetition in English.* Uppsala: Acta Universitatis Uppsaliensis.

Pharr, Clyde. 1945. "A Thirteenth Century Formula of Anathema." *American Journal of Philology* 66(2): 135–150.

Piao, Scott Songlin. 2002. *Multi-lingual Corpus Tools.* [MLCT] Lancaster University. Available at: http://cw.routledge.com/textbooks/0415286239/resources/.

Pordány, László. 1986. "A Comparison of Some English and Hungarian Freezes." *Papers and Studies in Contrastive Linguistics* 21: 119–127.

Price, Glanville. 2000. "Pictish." In *Languages of Britain and Ireland,* edited by Glanville Price, 127–131. Oxford: Blackwell.

Pryde, George S. 1965. *The Burghs of Scotland: A Critical List.* London: Oxford University Press.

Pryde, George S., ed. and introduced. 1937. *Ayr Burgh Records 1534–1624.* Edinburgh: University Press.

Purves, David. 2002. *A Scots Grammar: Scots Grammar and Usage.* Edinburgh: Saltire Society.

Puttenham, George. 1589. *The arte of English poesie Contriued into three bokes...* Lib.III "Of Ornament". London: Richard Field. [Early English Books Online.]

Ramsay, Nigel. 2008. "Law." In *The Cambridge History of the Book in Britain.* Vol. 2, *1100–1400,* edited by Nigel Morgan and Rodney M. Thomson, 250–290. Cambridge: Cambridge University Press.

Raumolin-Brunberg, Helena. 1991. *The Noun Phrase in Early Sixteenth-Century English: A Study Based on Sir Thomas More's Writings.* Helsinki: Société Néophilologique.

Reeves, William Peters. 1893. *A Study in the Language of Scottish Prose before 1600.* Johns Hopkins University dissertation. Baltimore: John Murphy & Co.

Reid, Kenneth G. C., and Reinhard Zimmerman. 2000. *A History of Private Law in Scotland.* Vol. 1, *Introduction and Property.* Oxford: Oxford University Press.

Renwick, R., ed. 1910. *Ancient Laws and Customs of the Burghs of Scotland.* Vol. 2, *A.D. 1424–1707.* Edinburgh: Scottish Burgh Records Society.

RHCAHMS [Royal Commission on the Ancient and Historical Monuments of Scotland]. Available at: http://www.rcahms.gov.uk/about-us.html.

Rissanen, Matti. 1996. "Genres, Texts and Corpora in the Study of Medieval English." In *Anglistentag 1995 Greifswald,* edited by Jürgen Klein and Dirk Vanderbeke. Tübingen: Max Niemayer Verlag.

———. 1999. "Language of Law and the Development of Standard English." In *Writing in Nonstandard English,* edited by Irma Taavitsainen, Gunnel Melchers, and Päivi Pahta, 189–203. Amsterdam: John Benjamins.

———. 2000. "The World of English Corpora: From Cædmon to the Computer Age." *Journal of English Linguistics* 28(1): 7–20.

———. 2008. "Corpus Linguistics and Historical Linguistics." In *Corpus Linguistics: An International Handbook.* Vol. 1, edited by Anke Lüdeling and Merja Kytö, 53–68. Berlin: Walter de Gruyter.

Robertson, J. J. 1997. "The Canon Law Vehicle of Civilian Influence with Particular Reference to Scotland." In *The Civilian Tradition and Scots Law: Aberdeen Quincentenary Essays,* edited by David L. Carey Miller and Reinhard Zimmermann, 117–133. Berlin: Duncker & Humblot.

Robinson, Jon. 2008. *Court Politics, Culture and Literature in Scotland and England, 1500–1540.* Aldershot: Ashgate.

Robinson, Mairi, ed. 1985. *The Concise Scots Dictionary. [CSD]* Aberdeen: Aberdeen University Press.

Robinson, O. F., T. D. Fergus, and W. M. Gordon. 2000. *European Legal History: Sources and Institutions.* Oxford: Oxford University Press.

Robinson, Peter, and Elizabeth Solopova. 1993. "Guidelines for the Transcription of the Wife of Bath's Prologue." *Canterbury Tales Project Occasional Papers I*: 19–52.

Rodger, Richard, and Jennifer Newman. 1988. "Property Transfers and the Register of Sasines: Urban Development in Scotland since 1617." *Urban History* 15: 49–57.

Romaine, Suzanne. 1982. *Socio-Historical Linguistics, Its Status and Methodology.* Cambridge: Cambridge University Press.

———. 1983. "The English Language in Scotland." In *English as a World Language,* edited by R. W. Bailey and Manfred Görlach, 56–83. Ann Arbor: University of Michigan Press.

Rosch, Eleanor. 1983. "Prototype Classification and Logical Classification: The Two Systems." In *New Trends in Conceptual Representation: Challenges to Piaget's Theory?* edited by Ellin K. Scholnick, 73–86. Hillsdale, NJ: Erlbaum.

Rossini, Christine. 1998. *English as a Legal Language.* London: Kluwer.

Salmi-Tolonen, Tarja. 1994. "The Linguistic Manifestations of Primary and Secondary Functions of Law in the National and Supranational Contexts." *International Journal for the Semiotics of Law* 7(19): 13–39.

Sanderson, Margaret H. B. 2002. *A Kindly Place? Living in Sixteenth-Century Scotland.* East Linton: Tuckwell Press.\

Sandig, B., and M. Seltig. 1997. "Discourse Styles." In *Discourse Studies: A Multidisciplinary Introduction.* Vol. 1, *Discourse as Structure and Process*, edited by Teun van Dijk, 138–156. London: SAGE Publications.

Sauer, Hans. 2011. "Twin-Formulae and More in Late Middle English: *The Historye of the Patriarks*, Caxton's *Ovid*, Pecock's *Donet*." Paper presented at the 7th International Conference on Middle English, Lviv, Ukraine, August 2011.

———. 2013. "Reginald Pecock and his Vocabulary: A Preliminary Sketch." In *Historical English Word-Formation and Semantics*, edited by Jacek Fisiak and Magdalena Bator, 89–123. Frankfurt am Main: Peter Lang.

Schane, Sanford. 2006. *Language and the Law.* London: Continuum.

Schiffrin, Deborah. 1985. "Functions of and in Discourse." *Journal of Pragmatics* 10: 41–66.

Schmitt, Norbert. 2005. "Formulaic Language: Fixed and Varied." *Estudios de Lingüística Inglesa Aplicada* 6: 13–39.

Schon, Donald A. [1963] 1967. *Invention and the Evolution of Ideas.* London: Buttler & Tanner.

Scott, Michael. 1997. "PC Analysis of Key Words—and Key Key Words." *System* 25(1): 1–13.

———. 1998/2007. *WordSmith Tools v. 3 and v. 4.* Oxford: Oxford University Press.

Scott, Tom, ed. 1967. *Late Medieval Scots Poetry.* London: Heineman.

Scottish Government, The. 2009. "Audit of Current Scots Language Provision." Available at: http://www.scotland.gov.uk/Publications/2009/01/23133726/3.

Searle, John R. 1976. "Indirect Speech Acts." In *Syntax and Semantics.* Vol. 3, *Speech Acts*, edited by Peter Cole and Jerry L. Morgan, 59–82. New York: Academic Press.

Selkirk, Elisabeth. 1977. "Some Remarks on Noun Phrase Structure." In *MSSB-UC Irvine Conference on the Formal Syntax of Natural Language*, edited by A. Akmajian, P. Culicover, and T. Wasaw, 225–245. Irvine: University of California.

Sellar, W. David H. 2000. "Scots Law: Mixed from the Very Beginning? A Tale of Two Receptions." *Edinburgh Law Review* 4(1): 3–18.

———. 2007. "Legal Writing 1314–1707." In *The Edinburgh History of Scottish Literature.* Vol. 1, *From Columba to the Union (until 1707)*, edited by Thomas Owen Clancy and Murray Pittock, 238–244. Edinburgh: Edinburgh University Press.

Shapiro, James. 2005. *A Year in the Life of William Shakespeare: 1599.* London: HarperCollins.

Shrefler, Nathan. 2011. "Lexical Bundles and German Bibles." *Literary and Linguistic Computing* 26(1): 89–106.

Simon, Jocelyn. 1960. "English Idioms from the Law, Parts 1–2." *Law Quarterly Review* 76: 283, 429.

———. 1962. "English Idioms from the Law, Part 3." *Law Quarterly Review* 78: 245.

———. 1965. "English Idioms from the Law, Part 4." *Law Quarterly Review* 81: 52.

Sinclair, John. 1991. *Corpus, Concordance and Collocation.* Oxford: Oxford University Press.

———. 1994. "Trust the Text." In *Advances in Written Text Analysis*, edited by Malcolm Coulthard, 12–25. London: Routledge.

———. 2003. *Trust the Text. Language, Corpus and Discourse*, edited with Ronald Carter. London: Routledge.

———. 2004. "Corpus and Text: Basic Principles." In *Developing Linguistic Corpora: A Guide to Good Practice*, edited by Martin Wynne. Oxford: Arts and Humanities Data Service. Available at: http://users.ox.ac.uk/~martinw/dlc/.

Slusher, Jeffrey L. 1991. "Runic Wisdom in 'Njal's Saga' and Nordic Mythology: Roots of an Oral Legal Tradition in Northern Europe." *Cardozo Studies in Law and Literature* 3(1): 21–39.

Smith, Jeremy J. 2000. "Scots." In *Languages of Britain and Ireland*, edited by Glanville Price, 159–170. Oxford: Blackwell.

Smith, T. B. 1955. *The United Kingdom: The Development of its Laws and Constitutions.* Vol. 1, *Scotland. The Channel Islands.* London: Stevens & Sons Ltd.

Sokol, B. J., and Mary Sokol. 2000. *Shakespeare's Legal Language: A Dictionary.* London: Continuum.

Solan, Lawrence M., and Peter M. Tiersma (eds.) 2012. *The Oxford Handbook of Language and Law.* New York: Oxford University Press. Accessed at Oxford Handbooks Online.

SPCB Language Policy. 2011. Available at: http://www.scottish.parliament.uk/PublicInformationdocuments/Lang_policy2012.pdf.

Sperber, D., and D. Wilson. 1995. *Relevance: Communication and Cognition.* 2d ed. Oxford: Blackwell.

Steiner, Emily, and Candace Barrington, eds. 2002. *The Letter of the Law: Legal Practice and Literary Productions in Medieval England.* Ithaca, NY: Cornell University Press.

Stewart, William J. 1995. *Scottish Contemporary Judicial Dictionary of Words and Phrases.* Edinburgh: W. Green/Sweet & Maxwell.

Stirling Records. Charters and other documents relating to the royal burgh of Stirling, A.D. 1124–1705. 1884. *Glasgow: Printed for the Provost, Magistrates and Council of the Burgh of Stirling.* Burgh Records Society.

Stock, Brian. 1983. *The Implications of Literacy: Written Language and Models of Interpretation in the Eleventh and Twelfth Centuries.* Princeton, NJ: Princeton University Press.

Stringer, Keith. 2005. "The Emergence of a Nation-State, 1100–1300." In *Scotland: A History*, edited by Jenny Wormald, 38–68. Oxford: Oxford University Press.

Stubbs, Michael. 1996. *Text and Corpus Analysis: Computer-Assisted Studies of Language and Culture.* Oxford: Blackwell.

———. 2002. "Two Quantitative Methods of Studying Phraseology in English." *International Journal of Corpus Linguistics* 7(2): 215–244.

———. 2005. "Conrad in the Computer: Examples of Quantitative Stylistic Methods." *Language and Literature* 14(1): 5–24.

———. 2007. "An Example of Frequent English Phraseology: Distributions, Structures and Functions." In *Corpus Linguistics 25 Years on*, edited by Roberta Facchinetti, 89–106. Amsterdam: Rodopi.

Stubbs, Michael, and Isabel Barth. 2003. "Using Recurrent Phrases and Text-Type Discriminators: A Quantitative Method and Some Findings." *Functions of Language* 10(1): 61–104.

Studer, Patrick. 2008. *Historical Corpus Stylistics: Media, Technology and Change.* London: Continuum.

Stygall, Gail. 1991. "The 'Transmission' of Jury Instructions in an Indiana Trial." In *Textual Dynamics of the Professions: Historical and Contemporary Studies of Writing in Professional Communities*, edited by Charles Bazerman and James Paradis, 234–253. Madison: University of Wisconsin Press.

Styles, Scott, and Niall R. Whitty, comps. and eds. 2003. *Glossary: Scottish and European Union Legal Terms and Latin Phrases.* 2d ed. Edinburgh: Law Society of Scotland, LexisNexis UK.

Swales, J. 1990. *Genre Analysis: English in Academic and Research Settings.* Cambridge: Cambridge University Press.

Symms, Peter S. M. 1986. "Social Control in a Sixteenth-Century Burgh: A Study of the Burgh Court Book of Selkirk 1503–1545." Ph.D. diss., University of Edinburgh.

———. 1988. "Market Regulation in the Early 16th-Century Burgh." *Proceedings of the Society of Antiquaries of Scotland* 118: 277–287.

———. 1993. "Introduction. The Selkirk Protocol Books—their Importance in Historical Research." In *Selkirk Protocol Books 1511–1547*, edited by Teresa Maley and Walter Elliot, xi–xxiv. Edinburgh: Stair Society, Walter Mason Trust.

Taavitsainen, Irma. 2001a. "Changing Conventions of Writing: The Dynamics of Genres, Text Types, and Text Traditions." *European Journal of English Studies* 5(2): 139–150.

———. 2001b. "Middle English Recipes: Genre Characteristics, Text Type Features and Underlying Traditions of Writing." *Journal of Historical Pragmatics* 2(1): 85–113.

Taavitsainen, Irma, and Päivi Pahta, eds. 2010. *Early Modern English Medical Texts: Corpus Description and Studies.* Amsterdam: John Benjamins.

Tannen, Deborah. 1987. "Repetition in Conversation as Spontaneous Formulaicity." *Text* 7: 215–243.

Templeton, Janet M. 1973. "Scots: An Outline History." In *Lowland Scots*, edited by A. J. Aitken, 4–19. Edinburgh: Association for Scottish Literary Studies.

Teuton, Christopher B. 2010. *Deep Waters: The Textual Continuum in American Indian Literature.* Lincoln: University of Nebraska Press.

Thomson, Rodney M., and Nigel Morgan. 2008. "Language and Literacy." In *The Cambridge History of the Book in Britain.* Vol. 2, *1100–1400*, edited by Nigel Morgan and Rodney M. Thomson, 22–38. Cambridge: Cambridge University Press.

Tiersma, Peter M. 1999. *Legal Language.* Chicago: University of Chicago Press.

———. 2006. "Some Myths about Legal Language." *Law, Culture and the Humanities* 2: 29–50.

———. 2012. "A History of the Languages of Law." In *The Oxford Handbook of Language and Law*, edited by Lawrence M. Solan and Peter M. Tiersma. New York: Oxford University Press. Accessed at Oxford Handbooks Online.

Tognini-Bonelli, Elena. 2001. *Corpus Linguistics at Work.* Amsterdam: John Benjamins.

Tomlin, R. S., L. Forrest, M. M. Pu, and M. H. Kim. 1997. "Discourse Semantics." In *Discourse Studies: A Multidisciplinary Introduction.* Vol. 1, *Discourse as Structure and Process*, edited by Teun van Dijk, 63–111. London: SAGE Publications.

Tracy-Ventura, Nicole, Douglas Biber, and Viviana Cortes. 2007. "Lexical Bundles in Spanish Speech and Writing." In *Working with Spanish Corpora*, edited by G. Parodi, 217–231. London: Continuum.

Trosborg, Anna. 1991. "An Analysis of Legal Speech Acts in English Contract Law." *Hermes* 6: 1–25.

———. 1995. "Statutes and Contracts: An Analysis of Legal Speech Acts in the English Language of the Law." *Journal of Pragmatics* 23: 31–53.

———. 1997a. *Rhetorical Strategies in Legal Language: Discourse Analysis of Statutes and Contracts.* Tübingen: Narr.

———. 1997b. "Text Typology: Register, Genre and Text Type." In *Text Typology and Translation*, edited by Anna Trosborg, 3–23. Amsterdam: John Benjamins.

Trudgill, Peter. 2003. *A Glossary of Sociolinguistics*. Edinburgh: Edinburgh University Press.

Tyrkkö, Jukka, Raymond Hickey, and Ville Marttila. 2010. "Exploring Early Modern English Medical Texts." In *Early Modern English Medical Texts: Corpus Description and Studies*, edited by Irma Taavitsainen and Päivi Pahta, 219–277. Amsterdam: John Benjamins.

Ure, Jean. 1971. "Lexical Density and Register Differentiation." In *Applications of Linguistics: Selected Papers of the Second International Congress of Applied Linguistics, Cambridge 1969*, edited by G. E. Perren and J. L. M. Trim, 443–452. Cambridge: Cambridge University Press.

van Dijk, Teun A. 1997. "The Study of Discourse." In *Discourse Studies: A Multidisciplinary Introduction*. Vol. 1, *Discourse as Structure and Process*, edited by Teun van Dijk, 1–34. London: SAGE Publications.

Virtanen, Tuija. 2009. "Corpora and Discourse Analysis." In *Corpus Linguistics: An International Handbook*, Vol. 2, edited by Anke Lüdeling and Merja Kytö, 1043–1070. Berlin: Walter de Gruyter.

Waldron, Ronald. 2001. "Doublets in the Translation Technique of John Trevisa." In *Lexis and Texts in Early English: Studies Presented to Jane Roberts*, edited by Christian J. Kay and Louise M. Sylvester, 269–292. Amsterdam: Rodopi.

Walker, David M. 1990. *A Legal History of Scotland*. Vol. 2, *The Later Middle Ages*. Edinburgh: W. Green.

———. 1995. *A Legal History of Scotland*. Vol. 3, *The Sixteenth Century*. Edinburgh: T&T Clark.

———. 2001. *The Scottish Legal System: An Introduction to the Study of Scots Law*. 8th ed. Edinburgh: W. Green/Sweet & Maxwell.

Wang, Shih-Ping. 2005. "Corpus-Based Approaches and Discourse Analysis in Relation to Reduplication and Repetition." *Journal of Pragmatics* 37: 505–540.

Watson, Alan. 1987. "The Evolution of Law: Continued." *Law and History Review* 5(2): 537–570.

Weinert, R. 1995. "The Role of Formulaic Language in Second Language Acquisition: A Review." *Applied Linguistics* 12: 365–382.

Wenger, Etienne. 1998. *Communities of Practice: Learning, Meaning and Identity*. New York: Cambridge University Press.

Widdowson, H. G. 2004. *Text, Context, Pretext: Critical Issues in Discourse Analysis*. Oxford: Blackwell.

Williams, Christopher. 2005. *Tradition and Change in Legal English*. Bern: Peter Lang.

———. 2007. "Crossovers in Legal Cultures in Westminster and Edinburgh: Some Recent Changes in the Language of the Law." *ESP across Cultures* 4: 101–118.

———. 2011. "Legal English and Plain Language: An Update." *ESP across Cultures* 8: 139–151.

Williams, Joshua. 1876. *The seisin of the freehold; being twelve lectures delivered in Gray's Inn Hall in the months of January and February, 1876*. London: H. Sweet.

Williamson, Keith. 1982. "Lowland Scots in Education: An Historical Survey. Part 1." *Scottish Language* 1: 54–77.

———. 2000. "Changing Spaces: Linguistic Relationships and the Dialect Continuum." In *Placing Middle English in Context*, edited by Irma Taavitsainen et al., 141–179. Berlin: Mouton de Gruyter.

———. 2002a. "The Dialectology of 'English' North of the Humber, c. 1380–1500." In *Sounds, Words, Texts and Change*, edited by Teresa Fanego et al., 253–286. Amsterdam: John Benjamins.

———. 2002b. "Notarial Protocol Books as a Source for a Linguistic Atlas of Older Scots." Paper presented at 4th International Conference on Medieval English, Vienna, July 2002.

Williamson, Keith, comp. and ed. 2008. *Edinburgh Corpus of Older Scots.* [ECOS] Edinburgh: University of Edinburgh.

Witczak-Plisiecka, Iwona. 2007. *Language, Law and Speech Acts: Pragmatic Meaning in English Legal Texts.* Łódź: Wyższa Szkoła Studiów Międzynarodowych.

Włodarczyk, Matylda. 2007a. *Pragmatic Aspects of Reported Speech.* Frankfurt am Main: Peter Lang.

———. 2007b. "Two, Three or Four of a Kind—Binomials in Selected Early Modern English Texts or, Applying Pragmatics to the Institutional History." In *Current Trends in Pragmatics*, edited by Piotr Cap and Joanna Nijakowska, 304–322. Newcastle: Cambridge Scholars Publishing.

Wood, Johanna L. 2009. "Structures and Expectations: A Systematic Analysis of Margaret Paston's Formulaic and Expressive Language." *Journal of Historical Pragmatics* 10(2): 187–214.

Wormald, Jenny. 1981. *Court, Kirk and Community: Scotland 1470–1625.* Edinburgh: Edinburgh University Press.

Wray, Alison. 2002. *Formulaic Language and the Lexicon.* Cambridge: Cambridge University Press.

Wray, Alison, and Michael R. Perkins. 2000. "The Functions of Formulaic Language: An Integrated Model." *Language & Communication* 20: 1–28.

Wright, Saundra K., Jennifer Hay, and Tessa Bent. 2005. "Ladies First? Phonology, Frequency, and the Naming Conspiracy." *Linguistics* 43(3): 531–561.

Xiao, Richard. 2008. "Well-known and Influential Corpora." In *Corpus Linguistics: An International Handbook,* Vol. 1, edited by Anke Lüdeling and Merja Kytö, 383–457. Berlin: Walter de Gruyter.

Youmans, Gilbert. 1990. "Measuring Lexical Style and Competence: The Type-Token Vocabulary Curve." *Style* 24(4): 584. Academic Search Complete, EBSCO host.

Zwicky, Arnold M., and Ann D. Zwicky. 1982. "Register as a Dimension of Linguistic Variation." In *Sublanguage*, edited by Richard Kittredge and John Lehrberger, 213–218. Berlin: Walter de Gruyter.

INDEX OF SCOTS LANGUAGE TERMS

Entries are listed as they appear in the EdHeW corpus after spelling normalization

SUBJECT INDEX